The Seven Perennial Sins
and Their Offspring

The Seven Perennial Sins
and Their Offspring

by Ken Bazyn

Continuum

NEW YORK · LONDON

To my parents, Bill and Dorothea,
who tried to teach me right from wrong.

2003

The Continuum International Publishing Group Inc
370 Lexington Avenue, New York, NY 10017

The Continuum International Publishing Group Ltd
The Tower Building, 11 York Road, London SE1 7NX

Printed in the United States of America

Library of Congress Cataloging-in-Publication Data

Bazyn, Ken.
The seven perennial sins and their offspring / Ken Bazyn.
p. cm.
Includes bibliographical references and index.
ISBN 0-8264-1437-0
1. Deadly sins. I. Title.

BV4626 .B39 2002
241'.3—dc21
2002009386

Contents

Introduction

Some years ago I sorted through my various articles and sermons to see if I might turn them into a book. One common theme that emerged was the seven cardinal sins and variations on them. Since then I have preached on these issues at the Chelsea United Methodist Church in Chelsea, Iowa, and St. Paul's Episcopal Church in nearby Grinnell. (My thanks to the members for enduring first drafts of a number of these chapters.) I have continued to do research, expanding and polishing my original observations into more formal essays, which I hope will appeal to a broader Christian audience.

With the widespread adoption of the Revised Common Lectionary in recent years, there is less topical preaching in Protestant and Catholic circles. Still, one must cover the basics in one form or another. In the thirteenth century, Richard of Wetheringsett identified these essential themes: the creeds, the Lord's Prayer, God's gifts, the virtues, the vices, the sacraments, the Ten Commandments and two evangelical precepts, works of mercy, the rewards of the just and pains of the wicked, the errors of the people, and things to be avoided and things to be done.[1] That the seven cardinal sins were an important feature of medieval preaching can be seen by the way the Saram *Prymer* lists them alongside the Paternoster, Ave, Credo, and Decalogue.[2] Archbishop Peckham, in the *Constitutions,* directed parish priests to instruct the people four times a year in such areas as the seven cardinal sins.[3] Like the Ten Commandments, they form a fine catechetical device for teaching basic responsibility in ethics.

Although the seven cardinal sins are not listed, as such, in Scripture, they originate from ancient wisdom as the desert fathers discerned.[4] Anglican H. V. S. Eck referred to them as "root-sins": "Why, it might be asked, does such a sin as murder find no place in a list of so-called deadly sins? The answer is that murder is not a root-sin; murder is, in fact, a symptom of some sin which underlies the commission of murder; murder springs sometimes from the capital sin of envy, sometimes from that of anger, sometimes from that of avarice, sometimes from all three. Men, unless they are maniacs, do not murder other men for the sake of murdering them, but because they are impelled to it by some root-sin which is the real disease of which their souls are sick."[5] Thus, meditating on these seven sins can be one lifelong form of self-purification.

I have decided *not* to follow the standard Gregorian sequence (as it was modified by later writers): pride, anger, envy, sloth, avarice, gluttony, and lust. I have done this for several reasons. First, I don't think (as some writers do) that one sin in this sequence inevitably leads, like an interlocking block, into the next; this too-neat formula falls flat if examined closely (e.g., how do the slothful suddenly become avaricious?). Nor do I see a descending hierarchy in which the first five so-called "spiritual" sins are worse than the last two "carnal" ones. What possible empirical evidence could one give to substantiate this? All seven are disruptive and heinous; indeed I find them simultaneously prevalent in every era, although they sometimes parade as healthy reactions to the excesses or deficiencies of the preceding generation. We repeat them over and over partly because, as the Argentine poet and short-story writer Jorge Luis Borges puts it, "our minds are porous with forgetfulness."[6]

These seven "root" or "perennial" sins shape much of human behavior and the evils traceable to them can be multiplied almost indefinitely. To highlight this idea, I've added one feature to this genre, a subsin following each of the seven main ones—e.g., fault-finding after pride, hedonism after lust, violence after anger—to reinforce how all-embracing and useful the original seven designations are. This is meant to start the reader thinking of his or her own subcategories. An exception to my pattern is the chapter on fasting (coming after gluttony), which accents a positive good, in order to demonstrate that one could just as easily focus on virtues instead of vices. My approach multiplies foibles as does that medieval devotional for anchoresses, *Ancrene Wisse*, which compares the cardinal sins to assorted animals: lion as pride, bear as sloth, fox as covetousness, and so on. Each animal, in turn, begets its own young. Thus the poisonous snake of envy breeds ingratitude, suspicion, regret at another's good, sowing of hostility, and plenty more.[6a] I decided, too, that the seven sins could use an introduction and conclusion, so I begin with chapters on sin and guilt and end with those on Satan and love.

I should add a word or two about my use of stories and quotations. Ethicist Alasdair MacIntyre observes, "In all those cultures, Greek, medieval or Renaissance, where moral thinking and action are structured according to some version of the scheme that I have called classical, the chief means of moral education is the telling of stories."[7] Stories flesh out abstract principles and imprint them on our memories. They provide us with a reservoir of images and metaphors to help us cope with life's complexities and contradictions.[8] One of the most popular texts for teaching Buddhism, *The Dhammapada,* is thought to consist of memory verses known as "gathas," which summed up entire sermons.[9] Isn't Jesus himself particularly remembered because of his parables and aphorisms, plus those great symbolic acts such as his baptism, healings, cleansing of the temple, Last Supper, and resurrection? Dramatization can lead to pathos, where we are affected on an emotional as well as intellectual level. "A verse may finde him, who a sermon flies, / And turn delight into a sacrifice," as that parson/poet George Herbert surmised.[10]

Literature has a pleasing indirectness that catches us unawares. In Emily Dickinson's opinion:

> Tell all the Truth but tell it slant—
> Success in Circuit lies
> Too bright for our infirm Delight
> The Truth's superb surprise
> As Lightning to the Children eased
> With explanation kind
> The Truth must dazzle gradually
> Or every man be blind—[11]

All of us are dominated by illusions that we will abandon only after intense struggle. As a consequence, Kierkegaard adopted a strategy whereby "one who is under an illusion must be approached from behind" since "by direct attack" the author "only strengthens a person in the illusion and also infuriates him." Above all, tact and gentleness were called for.[12] Jesus' parables are masterpieces of understatement as he borrows images from everyday life—a banquet, a wedding, sowing seed, shepherding a flock—and turns these simple events into profound metaphors for our relationship with God. He teases us into self-awareness, just as a bowler hooks his ball towards the center pin, hoping for a strike. So Hamlet, with a company of actors, plots to perform a play and so bring the king of Denmark's guilt to the fore.[13]

A peculiar pleasure of mine has been to retrieve anecdotes from medieval literature (e.g., Dante, Langland, Chaucer, Spenser), a spiritual reservoir largely neglected outside Catholic and Anglican circles. Too, whenever possible, I have referred to the original sources themselves in order to let you carefully scrutinize my conclusions and carry out your own independent study. (Wasn't the extensive use of primary materials one of Eusebius's most notable contributions?[14]) Often even a short excerpt will bring out an author's trademark ideas and themes.[15]

Literature also enables us to view the world through eyes very different from our own, states critic C. S. Lewis, and hence serves to broaden our perspective. "Those of us who have been true readers all our life seldom fully realise the enormous extension of our being which we owe to authors. We realise it best when we talk with an unliterary friend. He may be full of goodness and good sense but he inhabits a tiny world." Then Lewis nearly shouts, "My own eyes are not enough for me, I will see through those of others."[16] At times I, too, have felt that "shock of recognition," which Melville spoke of concerning Hawthorne,[17] as I have uncovered souls I genuinely admire, and whom I imagine to be somewhat like myself. Yes, felicitous language wrapped around stupendous truths, for me, approaches epiphany—the more condensed and explosive, the better. By means of proverbs, *Homo sapiens* has organized and compressed experience into striking maxims that can inform and illumine others.[18] Such sayings may begin as serendipitous discoveries, random reflections, or stray jottings, but are soon distilled into epigrams.[19] My hope is that the ones I've included in this book may turn out to be what Persian moralist Sa'di calls "pearls of curative admonition."[20]

While in our day autobiography and self-revelation are often thought to be the "truest" forms of expression, historically Christian thinkers have doubted this. With sin so pervasive and the devil so subtle, we may be telling and arranging our personal narratives, inadvertently or consciously, in a manner that deceives others as well as ourselves. Ambrose Bierce in *The Devil's Dictionary* once defined "diary" as "a daily record of that part of one's life, which he can relate to himself without blushing."[21] Memoirs, at their best, are but experiments in candor.

Petrarch, on the other hand, wrote to Cardinal Giovanni Colonna di San Vito on September 25, 1342, "If anyone asks why I so abound with quotations and seem to dwell on them so lovingly, I can merely reply that. . . . Nothing moves me so much as the quoted maxims of great men. I like to rise above myself, to test my mind to see if it contains anything solid or lofty. . . . And there is no better way of doing this . . . than by comparing one's mind with those it would most like to resemble."[22] Montaigne's essays, too, arose from collections of classical quotations taken from his reading (e.g., particularly Seneca and Plutarch[23]), which he applied to himself and his times, then gradually expanded into short moral discourses.[24] These sayings, he felt, helped him to focus and to expand on what was in his own mind;[25] thus, he compared himself to a bee gathering nectar from a profusion of flowers in order to concoct its own peculiar brand of honey.[26] Quotations, said Petrarch, enabled him "to find if my mind has been lying to me about itself"[27]—a worry that modern confess-all enthusiasts disregard to their peril. "Last night I dreamed I saw / God, and was talking to God;" cautioned Spanish poet Antonio Machado, "and I dreamed that God was listening . . . / And then I dreamed I was dreaming."[28] I believe that the combination of self-revelation, theology, and prayer, so evident in Augustine's *Confessions,* is closer to Christian reality and I have feebly incorporated some of those elements into my own chapters.

History, too, illustrates and provides a context or framework for our faith. When we think we have discovered some startling new truth, should we look more closely, we find our path strewn with the footprints of forebears. Even Emerson, that prototypical American so enamored with concepts of insight and self-reliance, acknowledged, "The student of history is like a man going into a warehouse to buy cloths or carpets. He fancies he has a new article. If he go to the factory, he shall find that his new stuff still repeats the scrolls and rosettes which are found on the interior walls of the pyramids of Thebes."[29]

Far too many Protestants believe that they can magically leapfrog from our modern era directly back into the first-century church, as though the intervening centuries of theological discussion and institutional growth meant little. Yet *The Book of Common Prayer,* perhaps the most beautiful prayer book in Protestantism, depends heavily on translations and adaptions of such medieval predecessors as the Gelasian, Gregorian, and Leonine sacramentaries.[30] This Protestant nearsightedness betrays a weak understanding of cultural continuity and is far too dismissive of the ongoing work of the Holy Spirit. Great ideas, even those arising from "inspired teachers," do not blossom overnight, as Tractarian John Henry Newman notes in *An Essay on the Development of Christian Doctrine.*[31] Often concepts first emerge in a rudimentary form, then are debated, distorted, retarded, or absorbed by counterideas, going through all manner of vicissitudes before reaching a certain level of maturity, or are sometimes "shattered" by "some original fault within."[32] A people ignorant of history are too prone to the latest passing fad.

I also strongly believe that no branch of, or period in, Christianity embodies all truth,[33] so have drawn exemplars from Eastern Orthodox, Roman Catholic, and Protestant sources in varied settings from across the centuries. In this vein I'd like to refer to "The Story of the Antichrist" which nineteenth-century Russian philosopher Vladimir Solovyov attached to the end of his last work, *The Three Conversations,* where the figure of the antichrist desires to seduce those who oppose him by offering olive branches to the three main branches of Christianity. To the Catholics he proposed "spiritual authority" for the common good centered in Rome as the basis for all moral order and discipline; for the Orthodox he planned to establish a world museum of Christian artifacts dedicated to "sacred tradition," whether it be prayers, hymns, icons, ancient rites, or symbols; for the Protestants he would pursue funding for a world institute of free inquiry into the Scriptures, so that all viewpoints might be explored, along with other ancillary subjects. Though, in the end, the antichrist's ploy doesn't work, Solovyov's point is well-taken.[34]

Even when we are on the right track, that fifteenth-century master of paradox Nicholas of Cusa warns, "The intellect, which is not truth, never comprehends truth so precisely but that it could always be comprehended with infinitely more precision. The intellect is related to truth as a polygon to a circle. The inscribed polygon grows more like a circle the more angles it has. Yet even though the multiplication of its angles were infinite, nothing will make the polygon equal the circle."[35]

Glimmerings of God's light shine in unexpected places. John once reported to Jesus, "'Teacher, we saw someone casting out demons in your name, and we tried to stop him, because he was not following us.' But Jesus said, 'Do not stop him; for no one who does a deed of power in my name will be able soon afterward to speak evil of me. Whoever is not against us is for us'" (Mark 9:38–40). Fourteenth-century Europeans were astounded to hear, from Marco Polo's travels, of Christian communities (usually Nestorian) scattered along the Old Silk Road as far as the great Chinese ports of the Pacific, and to learn of a sizable Christian kingdom in what is now Inner Mongolia.[36]

We are members not only of some particular church but of a universal church, consisting of the church militant (which Vatican II prefers to call "the pilgrim church"[37]) and the church victorious.[38] That's why I so enjoy the liturgy of All Saints' Day, when we hear a roll call of greater and lesser figures who have gone before us, remembering those who have died in the faith, some of whom we knew personally. "O Almighty God, who has knit together thine elect in one communion and fellowship in the mystical body of thy Son Christ our Lord," begins the collect in *The Book of Common Prayer*, "grant us grace so to follow thy blessed saints in all virtuous and godly living."[39] Apparently All Saints' began in practices in the Eastern church in honor of martyrs; then, after 609, it was expanded in the West, when Boniface IV dedicated the Pantheon to Mary and all martyrs. Later, under Gregory III, the day came to encompass all saints.[40] Since Protestants understand a "saint" to be any true believer, the separate Roman Catholic festivals of All Saints' and All Souls' (All the Faithful Departed) became conflated.[41] That unbroken unity between those now living and those now dead was depicted by Byzantine mystic Symeon the New Theologian as a golden chain: "The saints in each generation, joined to those who have gone before, and filled like them with light, become a golden chain, in which each saint is a separate link, united to the next by faith, works, and love." So, "the holy Trinity, pervading everyone from first to last, from head to foot, binds them all together."[42]

The papacy, grown to be the world's most powerful religious office, magnificently illustrates the high and low points of the church; thus, Catholicism has been blessed with such godly, foresighted figures as Gregory the Great and John XXIII and cursed with absolute scoundrels like Sergius III and Alexander VI.[43] By being specific throughout the book, I not only want to paint our dilemma in bright, vivid colors, but to point to lives worth emulating and advice worth following, which can move us closer to the kingdom. Even my favorites (e.g., Augustine and Luther) are illumined under both a favorable lamp for their worthy insights and under a harsh bulb for their gross distortions. Theologian Alister McGrath uses an old mariner's term for such accumulated wisdom: a "routier" (also "rutter") refers to a detailed log, or journal, kept by the pilot of a certain route in order that it could be safely retraced. Perhaps he sailed so many days at such-and-such a bearing. Important landmarks might be recorded as well how deep were the channels; good harbors, dangerous shoals, or sources of food highlighted. The information a rutter contained was priceless; so, in a competitive, seagoing age, some logs were written in code or contained falsified data in order to render them useless if they fell into the wrong hands.[44] In my most self-aggrandizing dreams, I would like to believe that the ensuing chapters are transparent rutters for the navigation of the soul.

I have also followed early church father Justin Martyr's lead, in that "whatever has been spoken aright by anyone belongs to us Christians,"[45] and thus have brought out findings from a broad spectrum of such disciplines as sociology, economics, philosophy, psychology, and biology, which I believe blend in with and help fill out my perspective. Calvin, in his *Institutes,* commends astronomers and medical doctors for their great learning: "Indeed, men who have either quaffed or even tasted the liberal arts penetrate with their aid far more deeply into the secrets of the divine wisdom."[46] Sin is inextricably entwined with anthropology, so disciplines seeking to explain human behavior are especially critical to my research. Others may argue with some conclusions, as well they should, since even our most elementary understanding of human nature is in need of constant revision, but I believe much will remain that is worthwhile and merits attention. I have tried to refrain from getting on my high horse to attack certain pet peeves or to become too embroiled in ephemeral controversies—a malady endemic among preachers and essayists in this genre. I have tried, too, to avoid triteness. "Why, I would ask, is most religious verse so bad; and why does so little religious verse reach the highest levels of poetry?" wrote T. S. Eliot. "Largely, I think, because of a pious insincerity. . . . People who write devotional verse are usually writing as they want to feel, rather than as they do feel."[47] Pietistic formulas simply won't do. Please select for yourself, among these historical tales and the literature I've quoted, lessons that you feel are helpful and valid; then appropriate them in your own ongoing struggle with temptation.

Writing itself is a frustrating affair. Even when you do have something of consequence to say (a rarity!), the tools available—vocabulary and grammar—never seem precise enough to convey the exact nuance or tone. More often do my expressions turn into entangled loops of confusion or meandering streams of misunderstanding. One longs for a language that has a one-to-one correspondence between idea and morpheme, or where one could qualify and bracket each noun with "not this . . . but that," or, in an act of extreme self-indulgence, place a running commentary alongside the newly minted text. "Words strain, / Crack and sometimes break, under the burden," complained T. S. Eliot in "Burnt Norton," "Under the tension, slip, slide, perish, / Decay with imprecision, will not stay in place."[48] If only one had a talent for coining neologisms like Shakespeare, whose "combinations of words," Eliot believed, "offer perpetual novelty" and "enlarge the meaning of the individual words joined."[49] Indeed, how far removed from today's call for a lucid style without artifice is Shakespeare's sheer delight in pyrotechnics.[50] Or if only I had a crystal ball, as Puritan Robert Traill allows, to discern which controversies I'll generate, and to correct misunderstandings ahead of time by altering ambiguous terms.[51] Or lacking a bardic voice, like some Zen master I could give you the perfect *koan* to bring about instantaneous *satori*.[52]

Finally, as Augustine says, "We, who preach and write books, . . . write while we are still making progress. We learn something new every day. We dictate books at the same time as we are searching for answers. We speak in sermons while we still knock at God's door for understanding. I urge you all, on my behalf and in my own case, that you should not take any previous book or preaching of mine as Holy Scripture."[53] I welcome your input.

CHAPTER 1

Everyman's Dilemma

M an is the Only Animal that blushes. Or needs to," said humorist Mark Twain.[1] The Puritan's *New-England Primer* started children learning the alphabet with this entry: "In *Adam's* fall, / We sinned all."[2]

A major theme in Scripture is sin and our need for redemption. It is especially evident in the lectionary readings during Lent. And rightly so, since that forty-day preparation for the Christian Passover calls for renunciation, prayer, and compassion. It begins on Ash Wednesday, where we are reminded that from dust we came and to dust we return, and ends in the heartrending spectacle of the crucifixion, where the forces of evil triumph, if only for a season. In the early church, this was a time for self-scrutiny, when candidates readied themselves for the public confession of their faith through the rite of baptism.

Genesis points to the origin of the world's dilemma in a deceptively simple story. God placed the first couple in a garden paradise and made one clear stipulation: You shall not eat of the fruit of the tree of the knowledge of good and evil or you shall die (Gen. 2:16–17). That's like telling a child he can play everywhere in the yard except the flower beds. If you look out a few minutes later, where do you suppose he'll be? During the Sung dynasty poet Su Tung-p'o wrote from exile, "I am forbidden to visit the Western Lake. / There is no place else I want to go."[3] There's a certain perverseness in our nature. "Out of the crooked timber of humanity," declared philosopher Immanuel Kant, "no straight thing was ever made."[4] Perhaps that's why English dramatist Ben Jonson took as his emblem the broken compass, meaning that the circle can never be fully complete, so cognizant was he of his own imperfections.[5]

In his *Confessions,* Augustine recites an episode from his teens, when he and some companions decided to steal a neighbor's pears. The crime itself seems insignificant, but what it told Augustine about himself was quite disturbing. He wasn't poor or hungry, nor did the pears look particularly appetizing. He admitted that there were better ones in his own garden. Too, he doubted whether he would have carried out the theft alone, but egged on by others crying, "Let's go! Let's do it!" he joined in. And what do you suppose happened to that eagerly desired fruit after it had been shaken from the tree? The boys took a few bites and threw the rest to the hogs.

On one level it sounds like some hilarious adventure of Tom Sawyer, but Augustine saw that it had deeper implications. "Perhaps it was the thrill of acting against Your law," he writes, "the delight a prisoner might have in making some small gesture of liberty—getting a deceptive sense of omnipotence from doing something forbidden without immediate punishment." He goes on to berate himself, "Could you find pleasure only in what was forbidden, and only because it was forbidden?"[6] One needs to but compare the two great "autobiographies" in ancient Western literature, namely Marcus Aurelius's *Meditations* and Augustine's *Confessions*. The former almost never exposes his weaknesses, lest he fall short of the heroic mold, while the latter defies prominent canons of classicism to bear witness to human fallibility.[7] "The Christian estimate of human evil is so serious," theologian Reinhold Niebuhr concluded, "precisely because it places evil at the very center of human personality: in the will."[8]

What is forbidden takes a more extreme form in Joseph Conrad's novella *Heart of Darkness,* where Mr. Kurtz penetrates into Africa as an apostle of civilization, seeking to uplift the savages, carve out empires, and bring the light of civilization to the furthest reaches of the known world, but instead falls under the spell of the wilderness, which whispers back to him dark secrets until he is capable of all manner of evil—e.g., killing in order to obtain ivory and afterward hanging the heads outside his hut as decoration. "I think it had whispered to him things about himself which he did not know," one character concluded. "It echoed loudly within him because he was hollow at the core."[9]

Hans Christian Andersen in "The Snow Queen," relates his own myth of the fall; here a mirror invented by a demon has the perverse property of diminishing the good and magnifying the bad. Thus, "the most beautiful landscapes reflected in it looked like boiled spinach, and the best people became hideous, or else they were upside down and had no bodies." One freckle might appear to take up the entire nose and mouth. The demon's pupils were anxious to carry the mirror up to heaven to mock the angels, but it slipped out of their hands and splintered into millions of pieces. Ever since, tiny bits have become lodged in people's eyes, distorting everything they looked at and occasionally, horribly, falling into people's hearts, turning them gradually into lumps of ice.[10]

But let's go back to the story of Genesis and look at a few specifics. The serpent inquires of Eve, "Did God say, 'You shall not eat of *any* tree of the garden'?" Eve replies that there is only one problematic tree, but God won't even let us touch that. Eve, isn't there a little exaggeration here? But too late. The serpent is pressing home the advantage: "You won't die, for God knows when you eat the fruit your eyes will be opened and you'll be like God, knowing good and evil" (Gen. 3:1–5, author's paraphrase).

But sin, instead of bringing Adam and Eve together, isolates them and turns them against each other. Then starts the age-old blame game, which I'm surprised that Parker Brothers or Merv Griffin Productions hasn't turned into a handsome profit. Adam says, "It wasn't my fault. I simply took the fruit from the woman you gave me." And Eve responds, "The serpent tricked me." Is our reaction to guilt much different? I know if the boss wonders why I'm running late, I'm likely to shout, "The damned typesetter is screwing up again!" Or, "If you only knew how many projects I have to do this week." "When was the last time you gave me work too close to a deadline?" "Oh, give me a break; nobody's perfect." Rather than coming up with another hackneyed excuse, however, I should acknowledge my faults and cry out like poet George Herbert: "O that I could a sinne once see! / . . . Sinne is flat opposite to th' Almighty."[11] As the prophet Isaiah confesses, upon having a vision of God's holiness, "Woe is me! . . . for I am a man of unclean lips, and I live among a people of unclean lips; . . . my eyes have seen the King, the Lord of hosts!" (Isa. 6:5). This is what comparative religion scholar Rudolf Otto has called experiencing *mysterium tremendum et fascinans,* when one recognizes the "wholly other's" absolute goodness.[12]

The medieval miracle plays tried to flesh out dramatically some of these archetypal stories. Let me quote a few passages from the York *Fall of Man:*

> Satan: In a worm's likeness will I wend,
>   And fand to feign a loud leasing.
>   Eve! Eve!
> Eve: Who is there?
> Satan: I, a friend;
>   And for thy good is the coming
>   I hither sought.
>   Of all the fruit that ye see hang
>   In Paradise, why eat ye nought?

And a little later:

> Satan: Yea, why trowest thou not me?
>   I would by no kins ways
>   Tell nought but truth to thee.

> Eve: Then will I to thy teaching trust,
>   And fang this fruit unto our food.

Here she eats the fruit, an apple.

> Satan: Bite on boldly, be not abashed,
>   And bear Adam to amend his mood
>   And eke his bliss.

Satan departs.

> Eve: Adam, have here of fruit full good.[13]

Thus the lid of Pandora's box was opened and all manner of evils and plagues loosed upon our planet. Masaccio's powerful fresco "The Expulsion" depicts Adam covering his face due to shame and grief, while an anguished Eve moans under the pain.[14] In *Perelandra,* on the other hand, C. S. Lewis hypothesizes of other worlds where Adam and Eve didn't sin and are in paradise still.

"*O felix culpa*" announces the ancient hymn sung at the lighting of the paschal candle during Easter Vigil: "O happy fault, O necessary sin of Adam, / which gained for us so great a Redeemer."[15] Paul completes the story in Romans 5 by demonstrating how a second Adam's life of obedience has overturned the first one's fall. It's as though history were an O. Henry short story rolling merrily along, until suddenly one unusual twist changes everything. Now the whole tale must be reevaluated in the light of that decisive event.

In verse 14, Paul uses the Greek word *typos,* meaning a pattern or impression, such as a seal leaves in wax, and then draws a loose comparison between the original type (Adam) and the impression or antitype (Christ). One's disobedience brought sin, the other's obedience brought righteousness; one death, the other life; one condemnation, the other justification. (Incidentally, the same theme of obedience is found in the temptation story in Matthew 4, where Jesus rebukes the devil, quoting each time from the Book of Deuteronomy, making clear how important knowing and applying Scripture is to overcoming evil. But as if life weren't complicated enough, the devil, too, can twist Scripture to his own advantage; so there's no truly safe haven.)

What is sin? Luther, drawing on a distinction from the scholastics, said humanity is *incurvatus in se* (curved upon itself) at its deepest levels.[16] That is, our priorities are warped. We put our own interests above anyone else's; we judge our neighbors too harshly and ourselves too lightly. What are some of the earliest words children learn? "Me! Mine!" And if I can borrow a few lines from A. A. Milne:

"What about a story?" asked Christopher Robin.

"*What* about a story?" I said.

"Could you very sweetly tell Winnie-the-Pooh one?"

"I suppose I could," I said. "What sort of stories does he like?"

"About himself. Because he's *that* sort of Bear."[17]

Aren't we all *that* sort of bear? When the Athenians celebrated their victory over the invading Persian king Xerxes, each officer took a ballot from the altar and inscribed upon it the names of those who had rendered the highest service. And wouldn't you know it? Everyone put his own name first and that of the Athenian leader Themistocles second.[18]

There is, furthermore, an irrational element in sin. We are not even masters of our own house, declares Freud, but must frequently rely on mere scraps of information about our unconscious motivation.[19] We are east of Eden, where Cain can slay an intimate rival, namely, his own brother. The plea of "temporary insanity" won't explain away evil, for the simple reason that Cain (and countless others since) has grown inordinately upset and flown off the handle, but that doesn't constitute insanity.[20]

Sin begins "like a thread of a spider's web," Rabbi Akiba is reported to have said, "but in the end it becomes like a ship's cable."[21] G. K. Chesterton's priest-detective Father Brown admonishes a daring thief who has just stolen three enormous diamonds known as the "flying stars": "I want you to give them back, Flambeau, and I want you to give up this life. There is still youth and honour and humour in you; don't fancy they will last in that trade. . . . Your downward steps have begun. You used to boast of doing nothing mean, but you are doing something mean tonight. You are leaving suspicion on an honest boy with a good deal against him already; you are separating him from the woman he loves and who loves him. But you will do meaner things than that before you die."[22]

The Christian realizes, according to Swiss spiritual writer Adrienne von Speyr, "that he is quite capable of greater sins, even though seldom guilty of them. . . . Even when he has not committed any definite sins, he is conscious of a general negligence which shows plainly that he is always capable of and, in some sense, ready for, sin, and that it is perhaps only a special protection, a special grace, a lack of opportunity that has kept him from it."[23] One thinks of Leonardo da Vinci's masterpiece, "Last Supper," in which the disciples are stunned by Jesus' announcement that one of them would betray him, so they appeal one after another, "Surely not I, Lord?" (Matt. 26: 22). The variety of dramatic gestures and the deep psychological realism make Leonardo's painting stand out from his predecessors.'[24] It reminds us, too, that a measure of self-doubt before God is always healthy.

Right perception is not enough. "You may believe that smoking is bad for your health," remarked Albert Einstein, "and nevertheless be a heavy smoker. And this holds for all the evil impulses that poison life. I do not need to emphasize my respect and appreciation for every possible effort in the direction of truth and knowledge. But I do not believe that the lack of moral and aesthetic values can be counterbalanced by purely intellectual effort."[25] Though the surgeon general may convince us intellectually that smoking is harmful, it's much more difficult to kick the habit. The sinner, for me, resembles thirteenth-century Korean poet Yi Cho-nyŏn's description of "An ignorant bird / [who] Repeats and repeats its song."[26]

We don't even do what's obviously good for us. "Oh, tell me," derides Dostoyevsky's underground man, "who was it first announced, who was it first proclaimed, that man only does nasty things because he does not know his own interests; and that if he were enlightened, if his eyes were opened to his real normal interests, man would at once cease to do nasty things, would at once become good and noble because, being enlightened and understanding his real advantage, he would see his own advantage in the good and nothing else, . . . through necessity, he would begin doing good? Oh, the babe! Oh, the pure, innocent child!"[27]

Sin misshapes our outlook as Eve found out after the serpent's beguiling speech. In verse 6, we suddenly read, "the woman saw that the tree was good for food, and that it was a delight to the eyes, and that the tree was to be desired to make one wise" (Gen. 3:6). Created in the likeness of God, we've been given radical freedom. In Hans Christian Andersen's tale, Kay, after a speck falls from the demon's mirror into both his eye and heart, starts calling Gerda ugly because she cries, takes notice of a worm in a rose, mimics, and makes fun of other people's peculiarities and failings.[28] It's as if Adam and Eve were to coauthor a best-seller on how it was a promotion to be thrown out of paradise and that the fall was really a step upwards in our evolution.

Take the old Basuto prayer: "O Lord, we are such liars that even if the tail of a fish was sticking out of our mouth, we would swear we had not eaten it."[29] Or we are like the suspect rounded up by the St. Louis police department for breaking a window in the Supreme Poultry Company and allegedly stealing a duck. To any and all questions he muttered, "I don't know a thing about it." But this was soon contradicted by a loud quack from inside his shirt.

Which of us can't identify with this W. B. Yeats poem?

> Things said or done long years ago
> Or things I did not do or say
> But thought that I might say or do,
> Weigh me down, and not a day
> But something is recalled,
> My conscience or my vanity appalled.[30]

As the psalmist puts it, "For I know my transgressions, / and my sin is ever before me" (Ps. 51: 3). "There is no man so good," insists the French essayist Montaigne, "that if he placed all his actions and thoughts under the scrutiny of the laws, he would not deserve hanging ten times in his life."[31]

Even during worship we're liable to sinful thoughts. Samuel Johnson's biographer, James Boswell, in his journal for Sunday, November 28, 1762, recounts: "I went to St. James's Church and heard service and a good sermon on 'By what means shall a young man learn to order his ways,' in which the advantages of early piety were well displayed. What a curious, inconsistent thing is the mind of man! In the midst of divine service I was laying plans for having women, and yet I had the most sincere feelings of religion."[32] John Donne, dean of St. Paul's in London from 1621–31, mentions how his mind wandered even during times of private prayer (a problem of which many of us are acutely aware): "I throw my selfe downe in my Chamber, and I call in, and invite God, and his Angels thither, and when they are there, I neglect God and his Angels, for the noise of a Flie, for the ratling of a Coach, for the whining of a doore; I talke on, in the same posture of praying; Eyes lifted up; knees bowed downe; as though I prayed to God; and, if God, or his Angels should aske me, when I thought last of God in that prayer, I cannot tell: Sometimes I finde that I had forgot what I was about, but when I began to forget, I cannot tell."[33]

The Christian, Luther observed in his Wittenberg lectures on Romans during 1515–16, is *simul iustus et peccator,* "at the same time a righteous person and a sinner."[34] By acknowledging our frailties, we come to rely on Christ's merits, not our own. Luther compared our lot to that of a sick man who believes his physician's assurances that he will recover. "Can one say that this sick man is healthy?" asks Luther. "No; but he is at the same time both sick and healthy. He is actually sick, but he is healthy by virtue of the sure prediction of the physician whom he believes. For the physician reckons him already healthy because he is certain that he can cure him, indeed, because he has begun to cure him and does not reckon him his sickness as death."[35]

Grace liberates us from the vicious circle of unrelieved guilt, so that peace, forgiveness, and hope can reign. After confession the psalmist says, "Fill me with joy and gladness; let the bones which thou hast broken rejoice" (Ps. 51:8 RSV). The rabbis divided repentance into two distinct acts: *charatah,* or regret for the past, and *teshubhah,* or a return to God. "I know no superficial, halfway, and perfunctory repentance," Montaigne affirms. "It must affect me in every part before I will call it so, and must grip me by the vitals and afflict them as deeply and as completely as God sees into me."[36] Thus Eustace Scrubb, in C. S. Lewis's *The Voyage of the "Dawn Treader,"* needs to have his skin (and scales) painfully removed by the lion Aslan, in order to signal how total his reorientation was.[37] For to mechanically confess one's sins and again commit the same misdeed would prove the confessor's insincerity. The true test of repentance, then, was to put someone in the same identical situation to see if this time he refrained from transgression.[38]

Insincerity is apparent in this scene from Shakespeare's *Hamlet,* where King Claudius would seek relief in prayer from the guilt of his brother's death:

> But, O, what form of prayer
> Can serve my turn? 'Forgive me my foul murder'?
> That cannot be, since I am still possessed
> Of those effects for which I did the murder,
> My crown, mine own ambition, and my queen.

He considers that litmus test question: "May one be pardoned and retain th' offense?" Still, anxious to kneel, he exhorts his weak will: "Bow, stubborn knees, and, heart with strings of steel, / Be soft as sinews of the newborn babe." Shortly afterward, however, Claudius rises up convinced—"My words fly up, my thoughts remain below. / Words without thoughts never to heaven go."[39]

Yet as Christians we should never write off any sinner as beyond the pale. Commenting on Luke 15, where the prodigal son announced, "I shall arise and go to my father and say to him, 'Father, I have sinned against heaven and against thee,'" Augustine, perhaps the most influential of all Christian thinkers, wrote (according to a gloss by Bonaventure): "Whatever need drives a sinner to penitence, neither the number of his sins nor the scandal of his life nor the depth to which he has fallen will exclude him from forgiveness if only there be a complete change of his will; but God receives into the ample bosom of his love his prodigal sons who turn back to him."[40] When we see the father's tender embrace, both hands resting on the ragged garments of his kneeling son's shoulders, in Rembrandt's painting "The Return of the Prodigal Son," we recognize that God is merciful and true homecoming is possible.[41] Having been left among the artist's belongings at his death in 1669 and later completed by a pupil, the painting represents the last rendition of a scene Rembrandt had wrestled with several times previously.[42] Produced in his characteristic "chiaroscuro" style, where light emerges from darkness, the bright spots, in particular, are charged with emotional intensity.

Who needs this forgiveness? I'm afraid we all do. As long as a room remains in darkness, according to nineteenth-century Russian monk, Theophan the Recluse, we don't apprehend the surrounding dirt and dust, but bring in a powerful light (that is, stand before the Lord in your heart), and you do become aware of your failings.[43] Hemingway, in one of his short stories, mentions a joke circulating in Madrid. It seems that a remorseful father placed a personal ad in the newspaper *El*

Liberal, which read: "PACO MEET ME AT HOTEL MONTANA NOON TUESDAY ALL IS FORGIVEN PAPA." However when the father, who was unversed in the power of the media, arrived at the appointed hour, a squadron of the Guardia Civil had to be called out. Why? Paco, short for Francisco, was such a popular Spanish name that some eight hundred young men had answered the ad.[44]

Perhaps this Lent we can strive to overcome one of our own besetting sins, remembering that even piety can get in the way of goodness. In a Flannery O'Connor short story, two teenage girls jokingly call each other "Temple One" and "Temple Two." These nicknames are traceable to Sister Perpetua's instructions on what to do if accosted by a young man in "an ungentlemanly manner . . . in the back of an automobile." Loudly announce, "Stop sir! I am a Temple of the Holy Ghost!"[45]

Let us meditate along with John Donne:

> Wilt thou forgive that sinne where I begunne,
>   Which is my sin, though it were done before?
> Wilt thou forgive those sinnes through which I runne,
>   And doe them still: though still I doe deplore?
>   When thou hast done, thou hast not done,
>   For, I have more.
>
> Wilt though forgive that sinne by which I wonne
>   Others to sinne? and, made my sinne their doore?
> Wilt thou forgive that sinne which I did shunne
>   A yeare or two: but wallowed in, a score?
>   When thou hast done, thou hast not done,
>   For, I have more.
>
> I have a sinne of fear, that when I have spunne
>   My last thred, I shall perish on the shore;
> Sweare by thy selfe; that at my death thy Sunne
>   Shall shine as it shines now, and heretofore;
>   And, having done that, Thou hast done,
>   I have no more.[46]

CHAPTER 2

Guilt Unraveled

Guilt matters. Guilt must always matter.
Unless guilt matters the whole world is
Meaningless.[1]

uilt matters because guilt affects us every waking hour. A child feels guilty if a
parent dies; a single woman feels guilty for not being married; a sick person
feels guilty for being a burden to others. A professor who has unread journals sitting on his shelves, a doctor who bills an uncured patient,[2] a parent who raises un-
ruly children, a family man who loses his job, a rich person who makes money
without really trying, and any person who fails to help needy friends—all feel the
weight of an inner accusing voice.

Guilt plagues our very existence. But why do we feel guilty? What intensifies or
alleviates our anxiety? How can we distinguish between true and false guilt? "The
most important task of the pastoral counselor, perhaps of any counselor," writes
Edward Stein, "is to help the counselee shift his concern from guilt feelings to
what he genuinely *is* guilty of and to help the person explore and find ways of
making value decisions about his life and acting on these."[3]

Swiss psychiatrist Paul Tournier makes this trenchant comment: "There is no
life without conflict; no conflict without guilt."[4] Priorities, goals, and personal relationships entail decision making—and decisions mean guilt. "We know of two
origins of the sense of guilt," states Freud, "one arising from fear of an authority,
and the other, later on, arising from fear of the superego."[5] A child experiences
conflict every time he's scolded. The parents' reproach arouses fear; the child re-

frains from misbehavior lest they no longer love him. Soon this fear is internalized and his own superego distinguishes between right and wrong.

This is the Freudian model of guilt. According to Jung, our conflicts can be traced to an unwillingness to accept the "shadow" side of our personalities. We deny our unconscious tendencies and so walk around like half men. According to Martin Buber, we suffer guilt whenever we manipulate another human being and we violate the "I-Thou" relationship. Thus, Tournier remarks, "Guilt towards oneself is the psychological language of C. G. Jung; guilt towards others is the existential language of Martin Buber; guilt towards God is the religious language of the Bible."[6]

We feel regret, notes William James,[7] who approvingly quotes Medea's speech in Ovid, *"Video meliora proboque, deteriora sequor"* ("I see the better and approve it, but I follow the worse").[8] This feeling would be meaningless if we did not have free will. We say, "I'm sorry I hurt you," "I feel guilty for not going to work," or "It was my fault you fell." Guilt and responsibility are inseparable. "I'm not guilty, it's a misunderstanding," writes German novelist Franz Kafka. "And if it comes to that, how can any man be called guilty? We are all simply men here, one as much as the other." Then he concludes, "[Yes,] that's how all guilty men talk."[9]

For our protests only condemn us as the apostle Paul discovered. In Romans, chapter 7, several times he tries to beg off by saying that an outside principle, a "law" or "sin" is overruling his goodness. Evil is not really a part of who he is. But finally, courageously, he acknowledges his guilt and confesses, "I myself, with my mind, serve the law of God but, with my flesh, the law of sin" (Rom. 7:25 NAB). Choice is a human prerogative, and as Augustine puts it, "The fact is that we do many things which we would most certainly not do if we did not choose to do them."[10]

Pascal, in particular, is adamant about our duality. "It is dangerous to make man see too clearly his equality with the brutes without showing him his greatness. It is also dangerous to make him see his greatness too clearly, apart from his vileness. . . . But it is very advantageous to show him both."[11] Our divided nature is chillingly framed in *The Strange Case of Dr. Jekyll and Mr. Hyde* by Robert Louis Stevenson. The central character, Dr. Jekyll, discovers a drug that will allow him to change both his nature and appearance at will. He can be the kind, good, and respectable Dr. Jekyll as well as the vicious, depraved, and deformed Mr. Hyde. His good side, however, is slowly given over to the evil, which "lay caged in his flesh, where he heard it mutter and felt it struggle to be born; and at every hour of weakness, in the confidence of slumber, prevailed against him and deposed him out of life."[12]

This inscrutability of human behavior has driven poets to such extremes as paeans to angels or dirges for devils, when a more plausible middle explanation may exist. "That man whom you saw so adventurous yesterday," Montaigne postulates, "do not think it strange to find him just as cowardly today: either anger, or necessity, or company, or wine, or the sound of a trumpet, had put his heart in his belly. His was a courage formed not by reason, but by one of these circumstances; it is no wonder if he has now been made different by other, contrary circumstances."[13] Sometimes those two souls at war within one chest reflect a shift in mood, a differing set of variables, or may yet make sense in some still-to-be-determined symmetry.

Guilt binds us to our pasts. Our memory banks are put on perpetual recall. Modern existentialists, in particular, have captured this haunting quality of guilt. In Camus's *The Fall*, Clamence, a successful Parisian lawyer, did nothing to prevent a stranger's suicide. Later, he comments, "I realized, calmly as you resign yourself to an idea the truth of which you have long known, that the cry which had sounded over the Seine behind me years before had never ceased . . . to travel throughout the world, across the limitless expanse of the ocean, and that it had waited for me there until the day I had encountered it. I realized likewise that it would continue to await me on seas and rivers, everywhere, in short, where lies the bitter water of my baptism."[14]

Clamence's guilt excites what philosopher Paul Ricoeur calls a "shut in" feeling of futility. St. Paul himself remembers feeling "shut up" under the law (Gal. 3:23 KJV). In Greek mythology, the Danaids personify this paradox of repetitive action that leads nowhere, when, due to the murder of their husbands, each is condemned to collect water in a leaky vessel forever in Hades. "The guilty conscience," notes Ricoeur, "is shut in first of all because it is an isolated conscience that breaks the communion of sinners." The whole weight of evil is placed upon its shoulders. "The guilty conscience is shut in even more secretly by an obscure acquiescence in its evil," becoming its own worst tormentor, continues Ricoeur. "It is in this sense that the guilty conscience is a slave and not only conscious of enslavement; it is the conscience without 'promise.'"[15]

One thinks of Rev. Dimmesdale in Hawthorne's *The Scarlet Letter*. He is an empathic, rising young star in the Puritan community, whom we soon discover was the secret lover of Hester Prynne, who has been condemned to wear the scarlet *A* for her adultery. Hester is unwilling to name her daughter's father and Dimmesdale is unwilling to acknowledge his guilt in public. Instead he preaches against sin in symbolic terms, reminding his listeners of their own frailty. His health deteriorates from sleeplessness, nightmares, and malaise. One night, when all are asleep, he goes into the square and places himself in the pillory, where Hester had been forced to stand in shame for three long hours. Guilt, as Hawthorne portrays it, makes numerous twistings and turnings, becoming lost in convoluted detours until it's formally admitted and dealt with. Hester, by contrast, accepts her punishment and sets up business in needlework; by her later acts of kindness and mercy, the townspeople gradually come to see her in a new light.

Occasionally sin seems to overwhelm us. Hester once saw herself in a convex mirror, which, owing to its optical properties, represented the *A* "in exaggerated and gigantic proportions, so as to be greatly the most prominent feature of her appearance. In truth, she seemed absolutely hidden behind it."[16] After aiding her husband to become the king of Scotland by murdering Duncan, Lady Macbeth compulsively washes her hands and, while sleepwalking, cries, "Out, damned spot! Out, I say!"[17] But the blood simply will not go away. Restless and unable to quell her clanging conscience, she commits suicide. Her husband had inquired of the physician, "Canst thou not minister to a mind diseased, / Pluck from the memory a rooted sorrow, / Raze out the written troubles of the brain, / And with some sweet oblivious antidote / Cleanse the stuffed bosom of that perilous stuff / Which weighs upon the heart?"[18]

Freud's research uncovers guilt even further back. Childhood betrayals, traumatic disturbances in psychological growth, and taboos arising from overly prudish parents wreak havoc for generations. We have inherited "irrational anxieties" from our parents, contends historian G. Rattray Taylor, and no matter how hard we try, we pass along others equally destructive to our children. It is in this sense that we are, as novelist Blasco Ibáñez once said, ruled by the dead.[19] When Jung invented the term "psychological complex," he didn't exonerate us, he merely told us that we are not as free as we had thought.[20]

How often we react poorly to situations due to learned behavior patterns. My father was a perfectionist. His 240-acre Iowa farm always seemed the best mowed, least weedy, and most intensely cultivated land for miles around. One reason I decided against a career in agriculture was that it just looked like too much work. However, as Freud predicted, my father's superego is still with us. I'm still too likely to measure my time in terms of "productivity." I'm too willing to berate my wife, friends, and fellow employees for "inefficiency." I cringe before authority figures whose dogmatism sends shivers down my spine. Clinical evidence has amply demonstrated that children who clash with their parents are prone to quite destructive fantasies.[21] So I am not at all surprised that psychologists believe guilt is especially pronounced in children whose parents treated them with a combination of firm discipline and warm affection.[22]

The threads of responsibility are sometimes so interwoven that untangling them is practically impossible. Let me cite a personal example. One hot July afternoon my brother and I were hitting golf balls in the orchard. Suddenly my brother started his backswing. The next thing I knew, a seven iron was wedged above my left eye. After we ran home, everyone pounced on my brother: "Why don't you look around before swinging?" However, it wasn't long before my shrewd parents started asking me, "Why were you standing so close to him anyway?" No doubt we were both partly to blame.

On the question of temptation and free will, Luther, quoting a story from *Vitae Patrum,* preached that we cannot prevent the birds from flying over our heads, but we can prevent them from building nests in our hair.[23] Here he follows Augustine's teaching on *morose delectation,* locating sin in lingering over pleasure: "To be sure, one cannot deny that it is a sin when the mind takes pleasure in just thinking about unlawful acts, not indeed deciding to do them but just holding them, so to say, and fondly turning them over in its hands, when they should have been thrown away the moment they touched the consciousness. Still, it is much less of a sin than it would be if it were decided to complete it with action."[24]

When we are accused, rationalizations spring instantly to mind. We become self-righteous ("at least I'm better than the rest of the swine"), when what we actually crave is acceptance, not judgment. "Every piece of advice conceals a veiled criticism," states Tournier, "unless it has been asked for."[25] This is the essence of paternalism. "Even the good ladies of the parish," he continues, "who bring parcels to help out, unwittingly arouse by their attitude, words and gestures, innumerable feelings of guilt. . . . They have a queer way of saying, 'You mustn't eat it all at once; your mother is very poor; you must make it last a long time.' Or they say to the mother: 'We thought it would be more useful to bring a few old clothes for the children rather than toys.'"[26]

The events of life, too, either add to or subtract from our feeling of guilt. As long as life is rolling smoothly along and we neither fail too much nor succeed too often, we seldom turn inward. Our conscience is lenient and the ego enjoys the "good life." As an Oriental proverb says, "Kiss the feet of Buddha when you are sick; when you are well you may forget to burn incense."[27] "Most people, when in prosperity," Benedict de Spinoza declares, "are so overbrimming with wisdom (however inexperienced they may be), that they take every offer of advice as a personal insult, whereas in adversity they know not where to turn, but beg and pray for counsel from every passerby."[28]

The moment misfortune falls our soul-searching begins in earnest. The little rewards we bestowed upon ourselves—chocolates or an extra half hour in bed—are abruptly withheld. Our conscience imposes a stricter, penitential lifestyle. We ask, "Why did this happen to me?" And like some character out of Kafka we brood, desperately seeking a cause. Perhaps we've fallen in with the wrong kind of companions; perhaps some secret sin is retarding moral progress; perhaps we've become lax in our personal affairs. This kind of introspection lowers our self-esteem. At this point we should honestly ask ourselves, as psychologist John McKenzie advises: Does our feeling of guilt refer to a situation that can realistically account for its intensity?[29]

"True" guilt, says Christianity, is universal. In an extended discourse in the early chapters of Romans, Paul finds that the Jews who have the law (e.g., the Ten Commandments), do not keep it, while the Gentiles, who have conscience as an inner sense of right and wrong, do not live up to the light they have, hence Paul sees all human beings as falling short of the glory of God (Rom. 1:18–3:23). We seek to evade responsibility like Cain by limiting our sense of responsibility: "Am I my brother's keeper?" (Gen. 4:9 NAB). As the Tom Lehrer song puts it, "Once the rockets are up, who cares where they come down? That's not my department, says Wernher von Braun."[30] Tournier tells of a medical colleague who took a similar approach to life. "'I am only a technician,'" he announced, "'and in order to do my work well I have to deal exclusively with what relates to my specialty. There are colleagues and clergy who can deal with the individual, the whole organism, psychology and the spiritual life. Each man to his trade.' At that moment the gynecologist was called to the telephone. He was dumbfounded on putting down the receiver. 'There,' he told my friend, 'the other day I examined a woman sent to me by her doctor to establish whether she was pregnant. She was not. I told her so. She left. Now her doctor rings up to tell me that she committed suicide on returning home.'"[31]

Pregnant or not, did it really matter? A human being was calling for help, and no one paid heed. Opposite to Cain's sentiment is John Donne's call for involvement, "Never send to know for whom the bell tolls; it tolls for thee."[32] "When at midnight I hear a bell toll from this steeple, must not I say to myself, what have I done at any time for the instructing or rectifying of that man's conscience, who lieth there now ready to deliver up his own account to Almighty God? If he be not able to make a good account, he and I are in danger, because I have not enabled him; and though he be for himself able, that delivers me not if I have been no instrument for the doing of it."[33] Then, in one of Donne's most famous lines, "No man is an island, entire of itself; every man is a piece of the continent, a part of the main."[34]

Freud saw another sign of guilt in human forgetfulness. Lapses in memory are sometimes caused by obstructions that show we are at war with ourselves. We seem to be conscientious, yet keep on forgetting names, places, appointments, tasks. "If anyone forgets an otherwise familiar proper name and has difficulty in retaining it in his memory—even with an effort," concludes Freud, "it is not hard to guess that he has something against the owner of the name and does not like to think of him."[35] It's even been suggested that our memories are reliable enough that they alone will provide sufficient evidence either to condemn, or possibly excuse, us on the day of judgment.

Perhaps this view of "true" guilt sits well with us, but what on earth is "false" guilt? I have chosen a career in writing rather than social action or evangelism. I feel guilty. In pragmatic America, writers and thinkers have a difficult time justifying their existence. Unless one is engaged, say, in advocacy journalism around a single burning issue or in copywriting for a Madison Avenue advertiser, one has few "results" to show for his endeavors. Finally, to paper over my guilty conscience, I give to foreign missions and world hunger organizations. Yet this is false guilt—inherent to my occupation. My guilt is unrealistic, exaggerated, and infantile. In a similar way, the survivor of a catastrophe feels guilty that he has escaped unscathed. A child feels guilty for dressing differently than his classmates. A Christian feels guilty for having fun on Sundays. Parents feel guilty for giving birth to malformed children. In such cases, the guilt far outweighs any recognizable "transgression."

In religious circles, false guilt can take the form of taboos. "This is unclean, do not touch; this is forbidden, stay away." Taboos bring down the awful wrath of God. For instance, some fundamentalists prohibit smoking, drinking, dancing, and going to the movies. A number of liberals impose equally stringent restrictions around aggression, bibliolatry, and assumed piety. The taboos have some value, but taken as our whole duty toward God they are shortsighted. They merely salve our consciences. Our lists of "do's" and "don'ts" invite self-satisfaction. "The sense of one sin," notes Charles-Henri Nodet, "has become a protection for not recognizing some other sin, which is usually a more serious and humiliating one."[36] Peter, in Acts of the Apostles, relates how a vision from God caused him to reevaluate his lifelong fear of associating with the "unclean" and so opened wide the door of opportunity to the Gentiles (Acts 11:1–18). The overscrupulous, in effect, reduce the possibilities of God from a mighty torrent to a tiny tributary, much like those Persian kings who bound themselves to drink only from the river Choaspes and so foolishly dried up all other waters on the face of the earth.[37]

Since childhood we have all custom-tailored an entire wardrobe of strategies and masks to handle social situations, some more effective than others. But problems can arise if we take our public persona too seriously and let it substitute for our true self. In a feat of rare honesty, George Orwell relates how in his role as a British police officer he once shot an elephant in Burma. He thought the act unwarranted by the degree of potential danger, yet nevertheless felt compelled to do so in order to save face before the crowd and not be laughed at. Later he remonstrates with himself, "A sahib has got to act like a sahib; he has got to appear resolute, to know his own mind and do definite things." Then, in one of those chilling Orwellian turns of phrase, he tells how the sahib "wears a mask, and his face grows to fit it."[38] Observations such as this, based on personal experience, led Orwell to write scathingly of the corrosive effects of imperialism on both the oppressor and the oppressed. Shame, to be sure, hinges more on other people's opinions than on any sense of intrinsic right or wrong. One recalls Paul's telling indictment in Romans 14—whatever does not proceed from personal conviction is sin (v. 23 REB).

"Shared staging problems; concern for the way things appear; warranted and unwarranted feelings of shame; ambivalence about oneself and one's audience," sociologist Erving Goffmann saw as "the arts of impression management," a universal phenomenon.[39] Reading people rather cynically, Pascal trumpeted that "human life is nothing but a perpetual illusion; there is nothing but mutual deception and flattery. No one talks about us in our presence as he would in our absence. Human relations are only based on this mutual deception; and few friendships would survive if everyone knew what his friend said about him behind his back, even though he spoke sincerely and dispassionately. Man is therefore, nothing but disguise, falsehood and hypocrisy."[40] Milan Kundera, in a fictional piece, recounts how the secret police did in one of the leaders of the 1968 liberalization movement in Czechoslovakia by simply taping the fellow's private conversations, full of their usual put-downs and hyperbole, then ran them as weekly radio broadcasts.[41] Each of us, like any professional actor, Goffman reckons, needs a backstage where we can feel free to let down our hair, say things off the record, and just relax, without worrying about every jot and tittle of our behavior.[42]

So we can handle guilt as sinners always have—with defense mechanisms like repression, projection, compensation, self-justification, and so on. Or we can perform penance, do good deeds, and practice self-abasement. Surely masochism will wake God from his slumber. Yet, according to Edward Stein, this only pulls us deeper into the mire. "When love is not experienced as *gift*, i.e., when one is never loved *in spite of* one's wrong, a tremendous ambivalence develops, a secret repressed hate and a fearful, abject and dependent 'love.' This is the 'goodness' that secretly always wants to be something else."[43] Or we can react as Christians always have—with self-examination, repentance, confession, request for forgiveness and restitution. As John Donne advises, sleep with clean hands either clean all day by integrity or washed clean at night by repentance.

Commenting on the character of Alexander the Great, the second-century Greek historian Arrian writes: "Most people, if they know they have done wrong, foolishly suppose they can conceal their error by defending it, and finding a justification for it; but in my belief there is only one medicine for an evil deed, and that is for the guilty man to admit his guilt and show that he is sorry for it. Such an admission will make the consequences easier for the victim to bear, and the guilty man himself, by plainly showing his distress at former transgressions, will find good grounds of hope for avoiding similar transgressions in the future."[44] "Confession of our faults," Publilius Syrus maintained, "is the next thing to innocence."[45]

Christ realized our dilemma. According to McKenzie, "He saw sin in all its violence; he felt how it alienated from God; he experienced his own condemnation of it." The key to the atonement, the secret of grace lies in Christ's own attitude. His solution may, in the end, be our only hope: "I cannot repent for another, although I can" identify with "all the pangs of hell that a loved one of mine ought to feel and must feel before forgiveness can be a reality."[46] "Unless I suffer," Christ tells his mother Mary in a chanted sermon by the Byzantine poet Romanos, "Adam will not be healed."[47]

George Forell, professor of Protestant theology at the University of Iowa, spoke of Christianity in terms of three concentric circles. The larger outside circle stood for those who accepted Christianity as a cultural phenomenon (e.g., they were raised in a Christian nation, observed holidays like Christmas and Easter). Next, was a second smaller circle consisting of people who agreed with the historic doctrines of Christianity (e.g., the Trinity, Jesus as the Son of God) and perhaps even attended church. Then, in the bull's eye, were the true Christians (e.g., those who had a vital union with the resurrected savior and sought to carry out his work). Forell traced this paradigm back to Danish philosopher Søren Kierkegaard, who in *Concluding Unscientific Postscript,* derided the broad-minded cultural Christians of his day.

Thus a naive wife complained, "Dear husband of mine, how can you get such notions into your head? How can you doubt that you are Christian? Are you not a Dane, and does not the geography say that the Lutheran form of the Christian religion is the ruling religion in Denmark? For you are surely not a Jew, nor are you a Mohammedan; what then can you be if not a Christian? It is a thousand years since paganism was driven out of Denmark, so I know you are not a pagan. Do you not perform your duties at the office like a conscientious civil servant; are you not a good citizen of a Christian nation, a Lutheran Christian state? So then of course you must be a Christian."[48] But, for Kierkegaard, Christianity is not merely an objective description of historical events (as important as that is); even less is it some accident of birth. Rather, it involves one's entire being, and turns out to be nothing short of a relationship with the living God.

"Self-surrender," according to psychologist/philosopher William James, one of the first to scientifically analyze conscious and unconscious states, "has been and always must be regarded as the vital turning-point of the religious life."[49] When

Christian reaches the cross in Bunyan's *The Pilgrim's Progress* (which Coleridge called the *"summa theologiae evangelicae"*[50]) he gives three leaps for joy and sings:

Thus far did I come loaden with my sin,
Nor could aught ease the grief that I was in,
Till I came hither. What a place is this!
Must here be the beginning of my bliss?
Must here the burden fall from off my back?
Must here the strings that bound it to me, crack?
Blessed Cross! Blessed Sepulchre! Blessed rather be
The man that there was put to shame for me.[51]

"You came into the world to save sinners," the eighteenth-century Russian monk Tychon of Zadonsk prays, "therefore you came to save me. . . . [F]or my sake gave yourself up to dishonor, insult, mockery, infamy; to be spat upon, condemned, scourged, wounded, crucified, put to death. . . . You, my Lord and sovereign, have suffered in my place. . . . How shall I repay your generosity, O my lover?"[52]

Blaise Pascal, a genius by anyone's definition, is credited with, among other things, devising the first calculating machine and founding the modern theory of probability. On November 23, 1654, he had an extraordinary religious experience, which he wrote down and sewed inside the lining of his jacket. It reads in part:

From about half past ten in the evening until half past midnight.
Fire
"God of Abraham, God of Isaac, God of Jacob," not of philosophers
    and scholars.
Certainty, certainty, heartfelt, joy, peace.
God of Jesus Christ.[53]

Such dramatic turnarounds may be a special grace sent by God. However, one should never underestimate the gospel's power to change people's lives. To be saved, insists Kafka in one of his meditations, we need a celestial chariot. "Hold fast!" he whispers, "then you too will see the unchangeable, dark distance, out of which nothing can come except one day the chariot; it rolls up, gets bigger and bigger, fills the whole world at the moment it reaches you—and you sink into it like a child sinking into the upholstery of a carriage that drives through storm and night."[54] "Forgiveness," Dag Hammarskjöld, secretary-general of the U.N. from 1953 to 1961, asserts, "is the answer to the child's dream of a miracle by which what is broken is made whole again, what is soiled is again made clean."[55]

What can elicit repentance? A helping hand extended during a particularly rough period, a word of exhortation during some trial or temptation, an attentive ear offered in a time of confusion. It can also be the persistent witness of a gentle, earnest spouse; the memory of a devoted parent; an ordinary worship service that turns into an unusual season of soul-searching. The readings can shake us utterly as poet Samuel Coleridge contends: "In the Bible there is more that *finds* me than I have experienced in all other books put together; . . . the words of the Bible find me at greater depths of my being."[56] The music can wring our hearts as Augustine testifies, "How greatly did I weep during hymns and canticles, keenly affected by the voices of your sweet-singing church! Those voices flowed into my ears, and your truth was distilled into my heart, and from that truth holy emotions overflowed, and the tears ran down, and amid those tears all was well with me."[57] Or it may suddenly dawn on us that those whom we most admire are, in fact, Christians. In Tolstoy's *Anna Karenin*, Levin decides that "the best people he knew were all believers: the old prince, Lvov, whom he liked so much, his brother Koznyshev, and all the women. His wife had a childlike faith just like his as a small boy, and . . . all the working-people whose lives inspired him with the greatest respect, believed."[58] Ah, the mediums for God's intervention are *ad infinitum*.

Second-century Christian apologist Justin Martyr drew this much-idealized portrait of the results of genuine conversion: "Those who formerly delighted in fornication now embrace chastity alone; those who formerly made use of magical arts have dedicated themselves to the good and unbegotten God; we who once valued above everything else the gaining of wealth and possessions now bring what we have into a common stock, and share with everyone in need; we who hated and destroyed one another, and would not share the same hearth with people of a different tribe on account of their different customs, now since the coming of Christ, live familiarly with them, and pray for our enemies, and try to persuade those who unjustly hate us to live according to the good advice of Christ."[59]

So then let us petition the Almighty like Ambrose in "Carmen Aurorae":

> Jesu, look on our frailty,
> And by your gaze correct us.
> If you look on, our faults shall fall away,
> And guilt dissolve in tears.[60]

CHAPTER 3

Pride: The Way up Is Down

What an extraordinary contrast between the imagery of Isaiah 14 and Philippians 2. The king of Babylon had desired power, glory, and prestige. He had made a swath of subdued nations across the Fertile Crescent. In his ambition he had said, "I will ascend to heaven; I will raise my throne above the stars of God; . . . I will make myself like the Most High" (Isa. 14:13–14). But in trying to rise too high, he became the cause of his own undoing. "How you are fallen from heaven, O Day Star, son of Dawn! How you are cut down to the ground, you who laid the nations low!" (Isa. 14:12).

Paul paints a quite different portrait of Christ and his intentions. Here we see Jesus, the creator and ruler of the universe, who, "though he was in the form of God, did not regard equality with God as something to be exploited, but emptied himself, taking the form of a slave, being born in human likeness" (Phil. 2:6–7). Jesus, willing to be born a human being, became obedient even to death on a cross. The result of such humility? God has given "him the name that is above every name, so that at the name of Jesus every knee should bend" (Phil. 2:9–10). "Down, down, says Christ," according to Luther, "you will find me in the poor; you are rising too high if you do not look for me there."[1]

How different is God's perspective from ours. We live in a society that puts great stress on wealth, power, social status, physical beauty, and intelligence.[2] But humility? When was the last time you saw a TV ad in which a politician announced, "My hardworking staff have researched bills I really don't understand. I've won a few legislative battles, but have lost or compromised on far more. I would like to help little people, but frankly, not that many turn out to vote. I've done what I could, but my opponent, too, has many admirable traits and he or she would make a fine choice as well." You'll hear a campaign speech like that when all hell converts. Yet in the topsy-turvy world of the kingdom of God, Jesus insists, "All who exalt themselves will be humbled, and all who humble themselves will be exalted" (Matt. 23:12), for paradoxically the way up is down.

Whatever is high and lofty, according to numerous Old Testament passages, is on its way to a comeuppance. "For the Lord of hosts has a day against all that is proud and lofty," announces Isaiah, "against all that is lifted up and high; against all the cedars of Lebanon . . . against all the oaks of Bashan; against all the high mountains" (Isa. 2:12–14). Indeed one of the major symbols of arrogance in Genesis is that ancient skyscraper, the Tower of Babel (Gen. 11:1–9), whose builders God reduced to linguistic confusion. In the middle ages, European cities vied with each other to build higher and more elaborate Gothic cathedrals, while more recently, New York built its Empire State Building and World Trade Center, and its Midwestern rival, Chicago, raised up the Sears Tower.

Satan in Milton's *Paradise Lost* displays an arrogance similar to the king of Babylon's:

> Farewel happy Fields
> Where Joy for ever dwells: Hail horrours, hail
> Infernal world, and thou profoundest Hell
> Receive thy new Possessor: One who brings
> A mind not to be chang'd by Place or Time.
> The mind is its own place, and in it self
> Can make a Heav'n of Hell, a Hell of Heav'n. . . .
> Here at least
> We shall be free; . . .
> Here we may reign secure, and in my choyce
> To reign is worth ambition though in Hell:
> Better to reign in Hell, than serve in Heav'n.[3]

Pride has many faces. For Milton's Satan it meant control, a desire to rule rather than to serve. Such vaunting ambition is not easy to hide. In 2 Kings, chapter 8, Hazael, a servant of King Ben-hadad of Aram, comes to the prophet Elisha. Soon the prophet begins to weep because he sees the evil that Hazael will wreak on the people of Israel—setting their fortresses on fire, slaughtering their young men, ripping open their pregnant women, and dashing their little ones to pieces. To which Hazael indignantly replies, "What is your servant, who is a mere dog, that he should do this great thing?" (2 Kings 8:12). But Elisha had divined his character correctly; perhaps he saw that Hazael was ambitious, and all the rest followed as a matter of course. Indeed, after leaving Elisha, Hazael returned to the ill Ben-hadad, smothered him, and thus became king.[4] Nietzsche crystallized this kind of ambition into the concept of a "superman," who surmounts herd-instinct and such debilitating restraints as religion and democracy to act "beyond good and evil" to form a new basis for culture.[5]

Pride can also mean an overestimation of oneself. Sa'di, the thirteenth-century Persian mystic, once generalized, "Everyone thinks himself perfect in intellect and his child in beauty."[6] We all nurture secret fantasies like Thurber's character Walter Mitty, who imagines himself a celebrated hero in an astonishing series of vignettes—gutsy pilot willing to fly into near-hurricane weather, master surgeon battling "obstreosis of the ductal tract" on a millionaire banker, the world's crack pistol shot, and a brandy-swigging soldier anxious to take out an ammunition dump against extreme odds.[7] Think of that story of the fly sitting on the axle of a chariot, who upon looking back remarked, "What a dust I do raise!"[8] Medieval artists and poets sought to cause people to consider their limitations by using a stock set of symbols to depict arrogance. Pride could be seen, they believed, in a lion proclaiming itself king of beasts, or an eagle soaring above all other birds in the heavens, or a peacock gaudily opening up its fan of shimmering feathers, or a svelte woman adoring her body in a mirror.[9] But pride is subtle, too, and not that easy to spot, as the Roman orator Cicero observes, "Those who write books about despising fame write their own names on the title page."[10]

We see pride in the Yanomanö tribe, the so-called "fierce people" of Venezuela and Brazil. An anthropologist describes their behavior: "The rules of the 'game' are to permit the man to display his ferocity (chasing women and children), even to the point of letting him discharge an arrow or two wildly into the roof. The general panic he creates strokes his ego, and the concern that the men show for him," which often consists of "very delicate, flattering entreaties to disarm," reinforces "the feeling that *here is a man to be feared and respected.*"[11] (I wonder if there are any similar rituals in masculine society in America?)

The proud often surround themselves with flatterers. To commemorate Alexander the Great's achievements, Dinocrates, an architect, proposed carving Mount Athos (six thousand feet high) into a figure of Alexander, holding a fortified city in one hand and a bowl to catch mountain streams in the other. The project, however, was never carried out.[12] (Isn't there a place out West called Mount Rushmore?) Louis XIV of France, according to one close observer, "liked nobody to be in any way superior to him. Thus he chose his ministers, not for their knowledge, but for their ignorance; not for their capacity, but for their want of it. He liked to form them, as he said; liked to teach them. . . . Naturally fond of trifles, he unceasingly occupied himself with the most petty details of his troops, his household, his mansions; would even instruct his cooks, who received like novices, lessons they had known by heart for years. This vanity, this unmeasured and unreasonable love of admiration, was his ruin."[13]

And what of those grandiloquent titles people covet, even if only for their ceremonial value? In Swift's famous satire, Gulliver meets a certain "GOLBASTO MOMAREM EVLAME GURDILO SHEFIN MULLY ULLY GUE, most mighty Emperor of Lilliput, delight and terror of the universe, whose dominions extend five thousand *blustrugs* (about twelve miles in circumference) to the extremities of the globe; monarch of all monarchs, taller than the sons of men; whose feet press down to the centre, and whose head strikes against the sun; at whose nod the princes of the earth shake their knees; pleasant as the spring, comfortable as the summer, fruitful as autumn, dreadful as winter."[14] This hyperbole is made doubly ludicrous when you learn that the Lilliputians in Gulliver's imaginary journey stand approximately six inches high!

But it's not just rulers who overinflate themselves, as sociologists Theodore Caplow and Reece McGee discovered in a study of colleges done in the 1950s. One of their most striking findings was that of the department chairs surveyed, 51 percent rated their own department as one of the top five in the country. This phenomenon came to be called "the Aggrandizement Effect," for those who belong to a group tend to give higher marks to their own members than any outsiders whom they're competing against.[15] "The best joke of all," Erasmus claims in *Praise of Folly*, is when scholars or writers of the same ilk "praise each other in an exchange of letters, verses, and eulogies, one ignorant fool glorifying another. A votes B an Alcaeus, so B votes A a Callimachus, or B thinks A superior to Cicero, so A says B is more learned than Plato. And sometimes they look for an opponent, to add to their reputation as his rivals."[16] Such exchanges are designed more to stroke people's egos than to goad one another into substantive contributions.

Jesus describes some of this in-group self-congratulation: "They [the scribes and Pharisees] love to have the place of honor at banquets and the best seats in the synagogues, and to be greeted with respect in the marketplaces, and to have people call them rabbi" (Matt. 23:6–7). In much the same vein, medieval mystic Jan van Ruysbroeck warned, "But beware of hypocrites, and of those who think themselves to be something, when in truth they are nothing. They are like bagpipes blown up with wind, which when pressed upon give out anything but a pleasant sound. So these hypocrites, who have persuaded themselves that they are saints, if they be but a trifle pressed upon, forthwith burst out into complaints; for they cannot bear and will not abide to be rebuked or taught."[17] Psychologists tell us a proud person frequently has difficulty functioning interpersonally, belittles rather than listens to others, and is blind to personal faults.[18]

Pride also manifests itself in favoritism and factions. James talks about congregations that pay too much attention to the rich and powerful, neglecting the poor. The "usher" rushes over to one who is finely dressed, saying, "Have a seat up front, please," but to the shabbily clothed, "Why don't you stand in the back?" (James 2:2–4). Some of Paul's churches are rife with divisions. One party declares, "I belong to Apollos," while another shouts, "No, I belong to Cephas," or, in the meanest retort of all, "I'm Christ's" (1 Cor. 1:12). Think of how new denominations often constitute themselves, "We're the church of the true gospel." Then a breakaway faction comes along and asserts, "We're the church of the truer gospel."

Paul speaks of those super-apostles (e.g., 2 Cor. 11:5) who were leading his spiritual children astray. I know I've run into those who claimed to be sinless or have had special visions from God. An early church father described one such pretender, Simon Magus: "He was very active in Alexandria, Egypt . . . and after gaining great skill in magic and becoming elated, he wished to be regarded as a certain Highest Power, above even the God who made the universe. Sometimes he intimates that he is Christ by calling himself the Standing One. He used this title to indicate that he would always 'stand,' since there was no cause of corruption which would make his body fail."[19] There's also Paracelsus, that strange sixteenth-century amalgam of science and pseudoscience, religion and irreligion, who bombastically announced, "I have been chosen by God to extinguish and blot out all the phantasies of elaborate and false works, of delusive and presumptuous words, be they the words of Aristotle, Galen, Avicenna, Mesva, or the dogmas of any among their followers. My theory, proceeding as it does from the light of nature, can never, through its consistency, pass away or be changed: but in the fifty-eighth year after its millennium and a half, it will then begin to flourish."[20] Or one thinks of those demagogues in history who have been utterly convinced of their own opinions; Adolf Hitler, for instance, once said, "I follow my course with the precision and security of a sleepwalker."[21]

To these I would reply with the apostle Paul: "So if you think you are standing, watch out that you do not fall" (1 Cor. 10:12). A more apt metaphor for such hubris can be found in Pieter Bruegel the Elder's satirical painting "The Blind Leading the Blind," where six men (some with vacant eye sockets) stagger forward together in a sort of human chain, but soon all will be tumbling unavoidably into a ravine, seeing as their leader has already lost his footing.[22]

In the nineteenth-century novel *The Way of All Flesh,* Samuel Butler describes a junior curate, who in his youthful exuberance felt that he was among the few "ready to give up *all* for Christ." It is an impetuousness that a number of us have probably been guilty of at one time or another. "I cannot call the visible Church Christian till its fruits are Christian," he writes. "I cordially agree with the teaching of the Church of England in most respects, but she says one thing and does another, and until excommunication—yes, and wholesale excommunication—be resorted to, I cannot call her a Christian institution. I should begin with our Rector, and if I found it necessary to follow him up by excommunicating the Bishop, I should not flinch even from this."[23]

The Book of James states, on the contrary, "God opposes the proud, but gives grace to the humble" (4:6). How do we recognize God's resistance? The seventeenth-century Puritan poet Michael Wigglesworth records his struggle against various forms of pride in these terms: "He crosseth my contrivances, and blasteth my indeavours, and disappointeth my hopes and expectations, and feeds me with the Torment of emptiness, with vexation and rebuke where I hoped to have met with comfort, so that my soul is overwhelmed with trouble," even admitting, "how little kindly melting is there for this my iniquity."[24] Yet here one should be careful, for such frustrations are also common to those who have faithfully followed the revealed will of God, as the Book of Job makes clear.

But not all that we today lump under the term *pride* is bad. It is important to have a healthy sense of self-respect, to like ourselves, and to derive a degree of satisfaction from our own accomplishments. "A desire realized," says Proverbs, "is sweet to the soul" (13:19). It's furthermore incumbent upon us to do more with our talents, to be zealous in good works, and to present all our undertakings as an offering to the Lord. Low self-esteem and an inferiority complex can be impediments to God's will.

I'm thinking of Laura in Tennessee Williams's *The Glass Menagerie*. She is nervous when in public, gets sick easily, and even drops out of business school after throwing up during a typing test. You see, Laura is crippled and has exaggerated its significance. In a conversation with an old high school classmate, she says, "'Yes, it was so hard for me, getting upstairs. I had that brace on my leg—it clumped so loud!' Jim: 'I never heard any clumping.' Laura: 'To me it sounded like—thunder!'"[25] In such cases psychologists are apt to suggest a variety of exercises to help bolster the deflated ego, which may have been damaged by early childhood experiences or simply suffer from asking too much of itself. More realistic role models may be found or a graduated series of tasks be given till the person becomes more sure of his abilities.[26] Rest assured that in God's sight, as it's been said, no one is a failure who lightens a burden for someone else.

But now let's flip over the coin, so instead of railing against the vice of pride, let's extol the virtue of humility. (And I'm not talking about the mock humility of Uriah Heep in Dickens's *David Copperfield*, who keeps calling himself "'umble,'" all the while plotting to become Mr. Wickfield's partner and to marry his daughter.)[27] Gaze out on a summer sky at Hubble's expanding universe. On an exceptionally clear night the human eye can detect maybe thirty-five hundred to four thousand stars of the sixth magnitude or brighter.[28] We are one planet in one solar system in one galaxy estimated to contain over a hundred billion stars and measure perhaps eighty thousand light-years across. The Milky Way floats in a cluster of galaxies which are, in turn, part of a supercluster maybe seventy-five million light-years in diameter.[29] When the nineteenth-century African-American evangelist Sojourner Truth perceived that God pervaded the universe, "that there was no place where God was not," she exclaimed, "Oh, God, I did not know you were so big."[30] "Humility like darkness," writes Thoreau, "reveals the heavenly lights,"[31] for by perceiving how small we are, we can better appreciate the grandeur outside us.

All of us are talented in some areas and not in others. The master French essayist Montaigne confesses, "Adroitness and agility I have never had. . . . Of music, either vocal, for which my voice is very inept, or instrumental, they never succeeded in teaching me anything. At dancing, tennis, wrestling, I have never been able to acquire any but very slight and ordinary ability; at swimming, fencing, vaulting, and jumping, none at all. My hands are so clumsy that I cannot even write so I can read it; so that I would rather do over what I have scribbled than give myself the trouble of unscrambling it. . . . I cannot close a letter the right way, nor could I ever cut a pen, or carve a table worth a rap, or saddle a horse."[32]

Even though I may be able to string a few quotations together and call them a sermon, my mechanical ability is below average. So, if your car doesn't start, my prayers might not be half as helpful as someone else's internal combustion know-how. But thankfully, we're members of the body of Christ, which is equipped with hands, feet, eyes, and ears, so we can depend on others to help fill in the gaps.

Isaac Newton, perhaps the leading physicist of all time, credited with discovering the law of universal gravitation, the composition of light, as well as differential calculus, declared, "I do not know what I may appear to the world; but to myself I seem to have been only like a boy, playing on the sea-shore, and diverting myself, in now and then finding a smoother pebble or a prettier shell than ordinary, whilst the great ocean of truth lay all undiscovered before me."[33]

Yes, every good thing comes from above (James 1:17). Our heredity, where and how we were raised, and just plain good timing or luck play a large part in anything we'll ever do with our lives. As the teacher says in Ecclesiastes, "The race is not to the swift, nor the battle to the strong, nor bread to the wise, nor riches to the intelligent, nor favor to the skillful; but time and chance happen to them all" (Eccles. 9:11). We're here today because of a long line of faithful witnesses stretching back from Abraham through the apostles to our parents, a minister, or a close friend. If someone hadn't been there at a critical time in our life, where would we be now?

At certain times, too, we may have been granted special protection; in the words of T. S. Eliot: "Who is the third who walks always beside you? / When I count, there are only you and I together / But when I look ahead up the white road / There is always another one walking beside you." In his notes Eliot says that these lines were inspired by Shackleton's account of his expedition to Antarctica—when the party of explorers, under the most extreme conditions, repeatedly felt that there was *one more member* than could actually be counted.[34] "I have no doubt that Providence guided us," Shackleton wrote concerning the grueling thirty-six-hour trek through South Georgia. "It seemed to me often that we were four, not three."[35] Concerning those who have strayed from the path, humility will freely acknowledge, "There, but for the grace of God, go I." In similar circumstances, perhaps I, too, would have succumbed.

The Anglican divine Jeremy Taylor points out how silly our vaunted sentiments are: "Our *strength* is inferior to that of many beasts. . . . Our *beauty* is in colour inferior to many flowers. . . . *He that is proud of riches* . . . how much inferior is he to a gold mine! . . . He that is *proud of birth* . . . boasts of his ancestors . . . doth confess that . . . he is degenerated."[36] In short we tend to make much ado about trifles.

One liturgical rite that highlights humility is foot washing. Referred to by Ambrose in the fourth century, it later became part of the Maundy Thursday service during Holy Week[37] and has undergone a surprising resurgence across denominational lines since around 1955.[38] It is a visual emblem of our call to be servants. By stooping down to wash off dusty, smelly feet, we are reminded of our Lord's incarnation, how he emptied himself on our behalf. "The highest goodness," notes Chinese philosopher Lao Tzŭ, "is like water, for water is excellent in benefiting all things and it does not strive. It occupies the lowest place, which men abhor."[39]

In Mahayana Buddhism there is the ideal of the "bodhisattva," who, having reached the brink of nirvana, voluntarily renounces that prize in order to return to the world and bring enlightenment to others. Thus, through innumerable selfless lives, many are helped to overcome ignorance, error, and suffering, entering nirvana partly by drawing on others' accumulated merits.[40] Bodhisattvas, says the monastic text *Mahavastu*, "do not hesitate to render all kinds of service."[41] The most famous example is a female figure, Avaloketasvara, known as the "Goddess of Mercy." How can the infinite God reach down to his sinful, finite creatures? In Kierkegaard's parable of the incarnation, where the king loves a humble maiden, God through his very nature is "moved by love," since he is "eternally resolved to reveal himself."[42]

One of the most exuberant celebrators of the incarnation is the thirteenth-century Franciscan Jacopone da Todi. He addresses the Virgin Mary, "You carry God within you, God and man. / . . . O Lady, I am struck mute." Later in that same poem, he calls out like some circus barker, "Come one and all, come running! / Come see Eternal Life in swaddling clothes!"[43] At times he refers to the Christ child in the manner of a doting parent, using such terms as "Bambolino" and "Jesulino."[44] "Sense and nobleness it seems to me," he reasoned in one of his lauds, "to go mad for the fair Messiah."[45] Elsewhere he wonders who would be mad enough to become an ant to save "an undeserving, ungrateful army of ants?" Yet Christ came to earth, abased himself, and suffered on our behalf.[46] Striking a similar note, Angelus Silesius, in one of his epigrams, says if our hearts could become a crib, God would once again become an infant on earth.[47]

There's a magical fish in George MacDonald's fantasy "The Golden Key," which epitomizes the meaning of sacrifice: "It was a curious creature, made like a fish, but covered, instead of scales, with feathers of all colours, sparkling like those of a humming-bird. It had fins, not wings, and swam through the air as a fish does through the water. Its head was like the head of a small owl." We first meet the "air-fish" using its beak to tear apart the branches of a tree that had tried to enclose the heroine. After freeing Tangle, it leads her to the house of a beautiful woman, where it promptly jumps into a pot of boiling water, then lies quietly inside.

The lady cooks the kindly fish, to Tangle's consternation, and gives it to her to eat. "In Fairyland," the woman explained, "the ambition of the animals is to be eaten by the people; for that is their highest end in that condition. But they are not therefore destroyed. Out of that pot comes something more than the dead fish." After eating it Tangle realizes that she now could hear and understand the speech of animals, and that the fish itself was transformed into a "lovely little creature in human shape, with large white wings," known as an "aëranth," which, later on, would again rescue Tangle from a tight spot.[48] "When a man says, I am low and worthless," MacDonald declares in one of his essays, "then the gate of the kingdom begins to open to him, for there enter the true, and this man has begun to know the truth concerning himself."[49]

To facilitate our humility we may choose an office degrading in the eyes of the world. One option in Eastern Orthodoxy is the "holy fool," who by renouncing position and possessions took the doctrine of *kenosis* or "self-emptying" (based on Phil. 2:5–11) to extremes, feigning madness, while at times being a prophet.[50] Thus, after the Russian tsar Ivan the Terrible had massacred thousands in the city of Novgorod and was heading toward Pskov, tradition has it that he was greeted by Nicholas the fool with harsh words and a piece of raw meat. Offended, Ivan complained, "I am a Christian, and I therefore eat no meat in Lent." To which the fool remonstrated, "Yet you drink Christian blood?" Because of this confrontation, no great slaughter came to Pskov and many lives were saved.[51] The *salos* (in Greek) or *iurodivyi* (in Russian)[52] dared to tell the truth "without any controlment" concerning "the very highest himself"[53] because life itself was not dear to him. How similar to clashes between the prophet Nathan and King David and the fool and Lear in Shakespeare's play.

In his book *Extremes,* Dutch cardiologist A. J. Dunning provides a vivid example of humility. In 1812 a three-year-old boy in the village of Coupvray was playing in his father's workshop. As children sometimes do when unsupervised, he picked up either an awl or a knife and somehow poked himself in the eye. Since that summer France's best physicians were accompanying Napoleon on his military campaign against Russia, herbs and home remedies were tried. Perhaps because of an infection or a weak response from his immune system, the other eye, too, became blind.

In those days the blind received no special assistance and often ended up as beggars. The boy's father and the local pastor tried to teach him to read by constructing letters out of hobnails hammered onto pieces of wood. His progress was slow. Fortunately, though, the Royal Institute for Blind Youth, which had been founded before the revolution, was now reorganized, up and running. At the age of ten, the boy was enrolled, became a fine student, especially in science and music, and even went on to serve as a church organist at Saint Nicholas-des-Champs, one of the largest churches in Paris.[54] But his most remarkable achievement came at the age of fifteen, when he devised a dot-dash reading system that was punched into cardboard, adapting one currently used by Captain Charles Barbier to send messages to soldiers at night.

The basic unit consisted of a "cell" of six raised dots (three high and two wide). From the sixty-three possible arrangements, he worked out an alphabet, punctuation marks, numbers, and later, a system of writing music.[55] Possibly the idea came to him from the game of dominoes, which was then quite popular. His approach was never officially accepted during his lifetime, but since has become the universal alphabet for millions of blind people around the globe. Now, a person who learns by this method can comprehend 60 to 120 words a minute, "translating" two to three thousand dots into meaningful sentences, relying merely on the tip of the index finger, which neurologists have determined is sensitive enough to detect dots a mere two millimeters apart.

His revolutionary method, it has been said, could never have been invented by a person with two good eyes, since they would never have had the intuition. He died at the age of forty-three from tuberculosis, due to his years of poverty and malnutrition. He told the former director of the institute that he was grateful to God for his blindness, because it had given him an opportunity to help others with the same plight. On the hundredth anniversary of his death, Helen Keller, who was both blind and deaf, yet had led a life of remarkable service, thanked him for bestowing a gift of such inexhaustible fertility and joy. His name, as you probably guessed by now, was Louis Braille.[56]

> O happy ones and holy!
> Lord, give us grace that we
> like them, the meek and lowly,
> on high may dwell with thee.[57]

CHAPTER 4

The Faultfinder

Let me come with these donkeys, Lord, into your land,
These beasts who bow their heads so gently, and stand
With their small feet joined together in a fashion
Utterly gentle, asking your compassion.

—Francis Jammes[1]

D o not judge others, so that God will not judge you" (Matt. 7:1 TEV), Jesus once advised. But why did he say it and what does it mean? We quickly think of the awesome ignorance of man. As Paul remarked, our knowledge is fragmentary and our prophecy is imperfect (1 Cor. 13:9). We can't read people's hearts, and even the outward behavior we do see may be deceptive. A Nigerian Christian once put it this way: "There may be a hundred things you know about a person, and all of them may be bad. But there may be just one thing you don't know. And if you did know it, your opinion might be completely changed."[2]

Take the time a metropolitan newspaper ran pictures of the new U.S. senators taking the oath of office. Afterward the newspaper received a caustic letter complaining that "the senator from Hawaii doesn't know his right hand from his left." The writer was correct in one sense—the senator had taken the oath of office with his left hand. But, you see, Dan Inouye had enlisted in the army after Pearl Harbor; serving in Italy, he received the Bronze Star, the Distinguished Service Cross, and also the Purple Heart. He took the oath of office with his left hand because his right arm was lost fighting for his country.[3]

Saki wrote a short story called "Dusk"; it contains two surprise twists. Shortly after the story begins, a young man sits down on a park bench near the main character, Norman Gortsby. The young man blurts out a sad tale of being lost in a strange city and having no money. But the shrewd Gortsby notices one crucial detail that can determine if the story is really true. So he asks the young man to show him the soap he had supposedly purchased earlier that afternoon. The young man feels around in his pockets, can't find any, and so moves on down the sidewalk. As Gortsby starts to leave, he spies on the ground, much to his chagrin, a cake of soap. He then goes in search of the young man, apologizes for his rash judgment, and gives him a loan. Surprised, the young man thanks him, then departs. However, as Gortsby returns to his park bench, he finds an elderly gentleman looking high and low for—wouldn't you know it—his missing soap.[4]

These two stories clearly illustrate the inadequacy of human judgment. We decide on the basis of what we see, but in doing so we err. Think of the hoaxes and optical illusions made possible by our fallibility. Have you ever thought that a piece of white paper looked decidedly pink when placed against a green background? Stared long enough at two curving lines of a drawing until you couldn't decide whether the inside edge was a face or the outside was the silhouette of a vase? Mistaken a bright object as larger than a dull one, though upon closer inspection, each proved to be identical in size?[5]

These are errors based on afterimages, perceptual ambiguity, and depth-and-distance misjudgments. Some are innocent enough, but others have more lasting consequences. In the past 185 years, polar expeditions were launched to look for "Crocker Land" reported by Robert Peary, "Barnard Mountains" observed by John Ross, "President's Land" mentioned by Charles Francis Hall—only to conclude that they had actually been mirages caused by the peculiar atmospheric conditions in the Arctic.[6]

Architects and artists have taken advantage of this knowledge for special effects. Because of a phenomenon known as "irradiation," columns viewed against a white sky seem to have a narrower diameter than those viewed against a dark background.[7] Lines that converge on a vanishing point suggest depth-of-field; distance is created by colors that grow paler and bluer as details are lost and outlines grow less precise.[8] One of the high points of visual illusion is the baroque painter Gaulli's decoration of the Jesuit church in Rome. When you look up, it's as though the vault of the church has opened and you're gazing straight into the glories of heaven.[9] Nature, also, camouflages and confuses through stripes, dots, and assorted mottlings. Just think of those wily chameleons. Magicians have played on our shortcomings to perform incredible feats of sleight-of-hand.

Descartes, based on his experiments with the eye of an ox, drew the first accurate description of the image that appears on the retina: it's upside down. Perhaps then it is no accident that he is also the first modern philosopher of doubt. For if vision, which had seemed so simple and matter-of-fact, turned out to be this bizarre, how could one ever hope to make sense of the larger mysteries all around us?[10] Yet just this willingness to disregard common sense and received tradition can also lead to dramatic breakthroughs. It was believed for centuries that the earth was the stable center of the universe. However, in the fifteenth century, Christian philosopher Nicholas of Cusa wrote, "For us it is clear that the earth really moves, though it does not appear to us to do so, because we do not apprehend motion except by a certain comparison with something fixed. Thus if a man in a boat, in the middle of a stream, did not know that the water was flowing and did not see the bank, how would he apprehend that the boat was moving?"[11] With the development of more precise measuring instruments science was able to make ever more accurate comparisons.

Even experts can be deceived. One of the most notorious twentieth-century instances is the obscure Dutch painter Hans van Meegeren. His fake paintings, modeled after the seventeenth-century master Vermeer, fooled art dealers, collectors, and museums. In fact the scheme only came to light after World War II, when he was arrested for being a Nazi collaborator. To prove his innocence, he told how he had sold a fake Vermeer to Herman Goring for $256,000. After admitting to additional forgeries, he demonstrated his proficiency by painting "Jesus in the Temple" in the style of Vermeer, right there in jail.[12]

The American public, which has always had its fair share of charlatans and con artists, was riveted in 1869 by the "Cardiff Giant." George Hull, a tobacco farmer and cigar maker in Binghamton, New York, had been especially incensed by a sermon he heard on Genesis 6:4, "There were giants in the earth in those days" (KJV). So he bought a five-ton gypsum block, hired two sculptors to carve the statue, simulating pores of skin by poking holes with large darning needles, and poured a gallon of sulfuric acid over the exterior to give it a dingy, aged appearance. Then he had the three-thousand-pound monstrosity transported and buried at the farm of his cousin, William Newell. The following year, Newell complained that his well was running dry; as the workmen were digging, they stumbled upon what appeared to be the fossilized remains of a man over ten feet tall. In two days Newell had a tent set up and was handing out tickets and charging admission. Scholars and celebrities flocked in—many declaring it to be authentic—until evidence accumulated by journalists and paleontologists forced a confession from Hull; but not before thousands were fooled. (If you're interested in seeing the "Cardiff Giant," it's still on display in the Farmers' Museum in Cooperstown, New York.)[13]

The apostle Paul, too, once felt he had been duped. He had looked at Jesus according to the flesh, from a worldly point of view (2 Cor. 5:16). Perhaps, like others, he thought, "Well, isn't this the carpenter's son?" "We know his mother and father." "Nazareth? That's not exactly known for its piety." "He never studied under the great rabbis." "No, I can't seem to find him in the 'Who's Who' in Palestine." "Wasn't he the one that had a bunch of fishermen around him?" "Oh, he was bad news, a troublemaker—why do you think Pilate had him crucified?" Paul even felt it his religious duty to harass the early church (Phil. 3:5–6), till one day on the road to Damascus he heard a voice asking, "Saul, Saul, why do you persecute me?" (Acts 9:4). The scales fell from his eyes, he became a new creation, and his life was never quite the same.

While illusions and hoaxes may be humorous, errors in judging others are more serious, for at times we are willfully ignorant. In Richard Sheridan's play *The Critic,* Sir Fretful cries out, "The NEWS-PAPERS!—Sir, they are the most villainous—licentious—abominable—infernal—Not that I ever read them—No—I make it a rule never to look into a newspaper."[14] I ask: Is it honest to condemn something we don't even peruse? Or sometimes we get a bee in our bonnet and start rudely shaking our finger. "We cannot see anything until we are possessed with the idea of it," Thoreau decided, "and then we can hardly see anything else."[15] Overreaction is especially pronounced in those who have recently changed allegiances and now see their past life as one humongous mistake; as Donne says, "the heresies that men leave are hated most."[16] These "heresies" can range from smoking cigarettes to eating meat, from religious "enthusiasm" to liturgies entirely in Latin. Instead one might have expected a bit more tolerance from those who once had similar leanings.

Or we extrapolate based on our own limited knowledge. Elizabeth Bennett, the spirited, intelligent heroine of Jane Austen's best-known novel, represents "prejudice" for disliking Fitzwilliam Darcy, whom she thinks to be too proud. Inclined to believe the worst, she swallows a false report from charming Mr. Wickham, who before long runs off with her fifteen-year-old sister. Remarkably, Darcy feels responsible and pays off Wickham's debts so he may properly marry Lydia. Gradually Elizabeth changes her views, until she and her sister Jane conclude: "Poor Wickham; there is such an expression of goodness in his countenance! such an openness and gentleness in his manner," yet Darcy is the one who is truly good and Wickham has only "the appearance of it."[17] That is the kind of experience we all go through in growing up, eventually learning to wait for further evidence before forming an opinion of others.

We are given to stereotypes: "If he is poor, he is a bad manager. If he is rich, he is dishonest. If he needs credit, he can't get it. If he is prosperous, everyone wants to do him a favor. If he's in politics, it's for the pie. If he is out of politics, you can't place him, and he's no good for his country. If he doesn't give to charity, he's stingy. If he does, it's for show. If he is actively religious, he is a hypocrite. If he takes no interest in religion, he's a hardened sinner. If he shows affection, he's a soft specimen. If he seems to care for no one, he's cold-blooded. If he dies young, there was a great future ahead of him. If he lives to an old age, he has missed his calling."[18]

Surely we can all find a few of our pet phrases here. Carried to extremes, however, they become a breeding ground for bigotry. "You only need to ask: / Is this or that man a threat to us? Then / Is he a Jew," mocks Bertolt Brecht.[19] Since the church and synagogue parted ways over Jesus' messianic claims, anti-Semitism has been a recurring nightmare. Let me cite three flagrant instances. John Chrysostom, the great fourth-century orator, gave a series of addresses against a "Judaizing" sect known as the Anomoeans, using highly inflammatory language:[20] "The synagogue is not only a whorehouse and a theater; it is also a den of thieves and a haunt of wild animals. . . . No better disposed than pigs or goats, [the Jews] live by the rule of debauchery and inordinate gluttony."[21] In July 1555, Paul IV issued the notorious bull *Cum Nimis Absurdum,* in which he required the Jews to live in a separate quarter of Rome, subsequently known as a ghetto ("We sanction . . . that all Jews should live in one and the same location"),[22] and also put into practice the 1234 decree of the Council of Arles that they wear distinctive attire and badges.[23] In 1523 Martin Luther made an overture to the Jews, "That Jesus Christ Was Born a Jew," which, for the most part, was shunned; however, by 1543 he railed that the Jews should be deported to Palestine,[24] and barring that, their synagogues should be set on fire, their homes broken down and destroyed, and "all their cash and valuables of silver and gold ought to be taken from them."[25] Anti-Semitism is a sad, bitter legacy that the church must ever fight tooth and nail. Otherwise that threat of mass extermination (or expulsion) already present in the Book of Esther will continue to haunt the world's imagination.[26]

When we label and pigeonhole others, we remove them from the reaches of Christian charity. Interreligious disputes have been known to get rather nasty. The founder of Methodism, John Wesley, once complained: "To say, 'This man is an Arminian,'[27] has the same effect on many hearers, as to say, 'This is a mad dog.' It puts them into a fright at once: They run away from him with all speed and diligence; and will hardly stop, unless it be to throw a stone at the dreadful and mischievous animal. . . . And it is not easy to remove the prejudice which others have imbibed, who know no more of it, than that it is 'something *very* bad,' if not '*all* that is bad!'"[28] Or eighteenth-century English writer Daniel Defoe claimed that a hundred thousand fellows were ready to fight to the death against popery, without knowing whether popery was a man or a horse.[29]

The *New-England Primer* includes a drawing of "The Pope, or Man of Sin," who is "worthy thy utmost hatred." Lines radiate out from various parts of the body to identify his manifold abominations: "Thou shalt find in his head, heresy,

. . . in his heart, malice, murder, and treachery, . . . in his knees, false worship and idolatry, in his feet, swiftness to shed blood, . . . in his loins, the worst of lusts."[30] And such a cartoon was to be taken dead seriously! Yet, that someone is in a different camp or that we hear someone is in a different camp is no reason to treat him with contempt, for Christians are allowed to have honest differences among themselves.

Too, we sometimes prejudge cases like this misguided juror: "I tell you, sir, I always make up my own mind. I am a plain man, and a reasoning man, and I am not influenced by anything the lawyers say, nor by what the witnesses say—no, nor by what the judge says. I just look at the man in the dock, and I say, If he hasn't done anything, why is he there? And I bring them all in guilty."[31] Or we jump to conclusions like that passerby who noticed a man hoeing his garden—while sitting on a chair. The passerby laughed to himself at such a classic case of laziness. A few moments later, glancing back, he noticed a pair of crutches lying on the ground beside the old man's chair. What originally looked ridiculous now seemed heroic.[32]

Jesus called into question a number of the simplistic cause-and-effect explanations prevalent in his day—e.g., diseases are due to sin, catastrophes are a judgment by God. "As he walked along, he saw a man blind from birth," says John's Gospel. "His disciples asked him, 'Rabbi, who sinned, this man or his parents, that he was born blind?' Jesus responded, 'Neither this man nor his parents sinned; he was born blind so that God's works might be revealed in him'" (John 9:1–3), then proceeded to heal the man. Another time Jesus was told about an incident where Pilate had ordered some Galileans killed, egregiously mingling their blood along with their sacrifices. "Do you think that because these Galileans suffered in this way they were worse sinners than all other Galileans?" he demanded. "No," he replied, then reiterated the point by citing a well-known accident: "Or those eighteen who were killed when the tower of Siloam fell on them—do you think that they were worse offenders than all the others living in Jerusalem? No" (Luke 13:1–5). Apparently the terrible bubonic plague in the fourteenth-century began in Asia, then moved slowly westward. The king of Tartary was so incensed by the immense destruction of his people that he began a journey with his nobles to the pope in Avignon in order to become a Christian, but twenty days into his journey, he heard that pestilence had struck the Christians, too, and so turned back to his homeland.[33]

No simple one-to-one correspondence exists between sin and suffering, though some persist in their folk beliefs. Edmund Gosse writes of his father, a widely admired British naturalist and a leader in the Plymouth Brethren in the nineteenth century: "He retained the singular superstition, amazing in a man of scientific knowledge and long human experience, that all pains and ailments were directly sent by the Lord in chastisement for some definite fault, and not in relation to any physical cause. . . . I recollect that my stepmother and I exchanged impressions of astonishment at my father's action when Mrs. Goodyer, who was one of the 'saints' and the wife of a young journeyman cobbler, broke her leg. My father, puzzled for an instant as to the meaning of this accident, since Mrs. Goodyer was the gentlest and most inoffensive of our church members, decided that it must be because she had made an idol of her husband, and he reduced the poor thing to tears by standing at her bed-side and imploring the Holy Spirit to bring this sin home to her conscience."[34] While we may want to believe that some underlying power in the universe precisely metes out rewards and punishments, life just isn't that straightforward.

Even our finest minds are products of their time and prone to mistakes, which may be so taken for granted that they go unquestioned during one's entire life. "A future psychiatry may well ransack our novels and letters," suggests anthropologist Ruth Benedict, to illumine that "type of abnormality" peculiar to our age. It's not only how we mistreat outcasts and those on the margins that will condemn us, but whom we put in positions of power. "In every society," she insists, "it is among this very group of the culturally encouraged and fortified that some of the most extreme types of human behavior are fostered."[35] Surely then one of the strongest arguments against censorship is that we squelch opinions later eras may come to regard as correct while the views reigning today are dismissed as absurd, even harmful. Indeed history teaches us, John Stuart Mill notes, that time and again the church has condemned as heresy "neglected truths, bursting the bonds which kept them down."[36]

We must instead learn to empathize with our neighbors, or the "thous" Christ died for become "its" we can't cope with. Not all start out with the same genetic and environmental advantages. "When a neurotic who has a pathological horror of cats forces himself to pick up a cat for some good reason," C. S. Lewis explains, "it is quite possible that in God's eyes he has shown more courage than a healthy man may have shown in winning the V. C.[37] When a man who has been perverted from his youth and taught that cruelty is the right thing, does some tiny little kindness, or refrains from some cruelty he might have committed, and thereby, perhaps, risks being sneered at by his companions, he may, in God's eyes, be doing more than you or I would do if we gave up life itself for a friend."[38]

We have such an unfortunate tendency to want exact carbon copies of our likes and dislikes, weaknesses and strengths. Sometimes I think the person we would most admire is our own clone. "If a man does not keep pace with his companions," says Thoreau, "perhaps it is because he hears a different drummer. Let him step to the music which he hears, however measured or far away."[39] It's not so important how people mature, or whether they do things exactly the way we've learned to do them; that they're moving in the right direction at their own pace may simply be enough.

Sometimes, too, our criticism is simply sour grapes. Like the fox in Aesop's fable, we see a delectable cluster of grapes hanging high overhead where we can't reach them, and console ourselves by saying, "Ah, they weren't ripe anyway."[40] Or we carp about petty things. "It is as if one were to become irritated and indignant with Socrates," states Renaissance philosopher Pico della Mirandola, "because, while discoursing on virtue, his sandals were untied, or his toga was disarranged, or his fingernails were improperly pared."[41]

Jesus doesn't seem to be worried about that occasional error, of which we're all guilty, but admonishes us not to continuously cut down our neighbors. We could retranslate the verse, "Do not *keep on* judging others." In other words, don't be a faultfinder. Jesus forbids the censorious temper eager to locate flaws in others, suspicious of motives, and ready to see in controversy hints of heresy. He knows that such a mind-set blinds us, since the faultfinder leaves no room for mercy. It's been said that "to look upon the world with the eyes of a judge is to see it in the flames of judgment." Which of us can't concur with Robert Burton, "In some men's censures, I am afraid I have overshot my self."[42]

Several verses later, Jesus brings up a powerful antidote: "You hypocrite, first take the log out of your own eye, and then you will see clearly to take the speck out of your neighbor's eye" (Matt. 7:5). It is just this kind of honest self-appraisal that helps overcome prejudice. "Knowledge of oneself," Harvard researcher Gordon Allport observes, "tends to be associated with tolerance for others. People who are self-aware, self-critical, are not given to the ponderous habit of passing blame to others for what is their own responsibility. They know their own capabilities and shortcomings."[43] To overcome the self-praise that can stunt artistic growth, Leonardo da Vinci recommended, "I say that when you paint you should have a flat mirror and often look at your work as reflected in it, when you will see it reversed, and it will appear to you like some other painter's work, so you will be better able to judge of its faults than in any other way."[44]

The eighteenth-century Jewish ethicist Moses Hayyim Luzzatto urged his readers to look deeply at their own behavior. "To 'scrutinize,'" he explains, "means to investigate one's conduct as a whole, and to note whether it contains anything which may be considered a transgression of the divine commandments." If so, "whatsoever is of that nature must be utterly eradicated." Luzzato also calls for "attending to one's works," by which he means, "to investigate even the good actions themselves, in order to find out whether they contain any questionable admixture, or any element of evil." Just as a good clothier closely examines each strip "to determine its quality and strength," so he who "wishes to be spiritually pure" needs to evaluate all of his actions "to find out their true nature."[45]

As poet Robert Burns prayed, "Oh wad some Power, the giftie gie us, / To see oursels as ithers see us!"[46] But who will deliver such a deflating blow? Essayist Francis Bacon suggests that the gentlest and most effective critic is probably a friend (or perhaps a spouse?). "Heraclitus saith well in one of his enigmas, *Dry light is ever the best.* And certain it is that the light that a man receiveth by counsel from another is drier and purer than that which cometh from his own understanding and judgment, which is ever infused and drenched in his affections and customs. . . . For there is no such flatterer as is a man's self, and there is no such remedy against flattery of a man's self as the liberty of a friend. . . . The calling of a man's self to a strict account is a medicine, sometime too piercing and corrosive. . . . But the best receipt (best, I say, to work, and best to take) is the admonition of a friend."[47]

But isn't that what Christian fellowship among concerned brothers and sisters should be like? Recognizing the deep emotional need for companionship, twelfth-century Cistercian abbot Aelred of Rievaulx (being much indebted to Cicero's "On Friendship"), called for close "spiritual friendships" among the celibate monks to aid in pursuit of holiness: "It is no mean consolation in this life to have someone with whom you can be united by an intimate attachment and the embrace of very holy love," Aelred discerned, "by whose spiritual kisses as by medicinal ointments you may sweat out of yourself the weariness of agitating cares. Someone who will weep with you in anxiety, rejoice with you in prosperity; seek with you in doubts," as "the sweetness of the Holy Spirit flowing between you," enables the two to become spiritually one.[48] In certain circles a mentor, or confidante, to whom one can entrust one's deepest feelings plays a similar role; he or she, in turn, acts like a sort of mirror to enable the confessor to correct himself. In the ancient Celtic church such a person was called an *anamchara* or "soul-friend."[49]

Jesus isn't advocating a skeptical lifestyle in which we withhold all judgment. There are numerous calls for the use of reason in the Gospels. We must be able to distinguish the voice of the shepherd from that of a stranger (John 10:1–18). Paul urged the Thessalonians to "test everything; hold fast to what is good; abstain from every form of evil" (1 Thess. 5:21–22) and told the Ephesians to "speak the truth in love" (Eph. 4:15 NEB). However, Jesus tries to make sure our decisions aren't based on superficial evidence, aren't due to prejudice and misleading stereotypes, and aren't the result of a nitpicky attitude that would rather criticize the speck in others' behavior than remove the log in our own. I've found one of the best tests to determine whether I have strong feelings (or perhaps prejudice?) is to see whether I define an issue only in black-and-white terms, or if I can perceive a sliding scale of various shades of gray. If only we could walk a mile in the other fellow's shoes, our entire outlook might be transformed. The faultfinder underestimates the good in others. Thus, "the pleasure of criticizing," as French essayist La Bruyère says, "deprives us of the pleasure of being keenly touched by great beauties."[50]

Beauty, though, is not the term that immediately springs to mind with reference to the Victorian tale of Joseph Merrick, otherwise known as "the elephant man." A severe sufferer from what has become known as multiple neurofibromatosis (or von Recklinghausen's disease), he made his living as a sideshow freak. One day Frederick Treves, a surgeon at London Hospital, encountered what he called "the most disgusting specimen of humanity" he had ever seen: "The most striking feature about Merrick was the enormous and misshapened head. . . . The face was no more capable of expression than a block of gnarled wood." The right hand, "large and clumsy," seemed more like "a fin or paddle." From his back hung "sacklike masses of flesh covered by . . . loathesome cauliflower skin," from his chest hung a similar protuberance which looked like "a dewlap suspended from the neck of a lizard." Merrick also had developed hip disease when a boy and "could only walk with a stick." As if the mere sight of him weren't nauseating enough, there arose from the fungous skin growths "a very sickening stench which was hard to tolerate."[51]

Amazed at the progression of the disease, Treves brought Merrick in for an exam and even published a paper about him. Two years later, when "the elephant man" was abandoned by a show in Belgium, he made his way back to the Liverpool Street train station. There, after showing the police Treves's card, Merrick was picked up by the good doctor and placed in an isolation ward in the hospital attic. After sufficient funds had been raised, the patient was moved downstairs and made a permanent resident.

Merrick's life is a classic instance of the problem of judging by appearances. "I can imagine no state so horrible and unbearable," Montaigne opined, "as to have my soul alive and afflicted, without means to express itself."[52] Treves, all along, had thought "the elephant man" an imbecile from birth, since his speech and gestures were so difficult to fathom. Over time, however, it dawned on those who came in contact with Merrick that he was intelligent, sensitive, and even a bit of a romantic. During an earlier stay in a hospital, he had learned to read and, on his own, had studied newspapers and knew large portions of Scripture and *The Book of Common Prayer*. Merrick's religious side deepened as he was instructed by the hospital chaplain, then was confirmed privately by the Bishop of Bedford; he was able to take part in chapel services by standing in the vestry.[53] Indeed one legacy of his spiritual life, still on display at the hospital medical college museum, is a model he constructed of a cathedral, using colored paper and cardboard, based on two churches he could see from his window.[54]

Treves's views had evolved from considering Merrick as a curiosity to a scientific sample, from a fellow human being to someone to be looked up to. Though Merrick's body was deformed in the extreme, ugly by almost any standard, the personality that shone through was gentle and kind despite years of abuse. "As a specimen of humanity," Treves reckoned, "Merrick was ignoble and repulsive; but the spirit of Merrick, if it could be seen in the form of the living, would assume the figure of an upstanding and heroic man, smooth browed and clean of limb, and with eyes that flashed undaunted courage."[55] Finally, after becoming something of a celebrity for several years, "the elephant man" died.

Who would have ever guessed that such a monstrosity could become a child of God and a witness to his glory? Jesus had warned that harlots and tax collectors would enter into the kingdom of God before the chief priests and elders (Matt. 21:23, 31) and made plain that "many who are first will be last, and the last will be first" (Matt. 19:30). In "Revelation," a Flannery O'Connor short story, the "respectable, hard-working, church-going" Ruby Turpin noticed a purple light in the sky near sunset, then had an apocalyptic vision: "She saw the streak as a vast swinging bridge extending upward from the earth through a field of living fire. Upon it a vast horde of souls were rumbling toward heaven." But those proceeding upward were far different from what she had supposed. "There were whole companies of white-trash, clean for the first time in their lives, and bands of black niggers in white robes, and battalions of freaks and lunatics shouting and clapping and leaping like frogs." Bringing up the rear were decent folk, like herself, who "always had a little of everything and the God-given wit to use it right." Yet she realized from "their shocked and altered faces that even their virtues were being burned away."[56]

Faultfinders, take note! Someday, too, our illusions and ruses will undergo a sustained jolt. So, remembering our own sinfulness, let us pray for God's guidance in the manner of the Southwell Litany: "Give us true knowledge of our brethren in their differences from us and in their likenesses to us, that we may deal with their real selves, . . . but patiently considering their varied lives and thoughts and circumstances; and in all our relations to them, from false judgments of our own, from misplaced trust and distrust, from misplaced giving and refusing, from misplaced praise and rebuke, Save us and help us, we humbly beseech Thee, O Lord."[57]

Envy, the Secret Sin

Cain envied his brother Abel, so one day in the field, he rose up and slew him. The youngest son of Jacob was his favorite—that, as well as Joseph's grandiose dreams, made his brothers jealous, and before long he was sold into slavery to Egypt. Saul grew annoyed at the increasing popularity of young David, especially the song of the women, "Saul has killed his thousands, and David his ten thousands" (1 Sam. 18:7), so several times, in a melancholy mood, he sought to spear him. Pilate perceived that the temple leaders were handing Jesus over for execution partly because he was their upstart rival; he was attracting far too many followers (Matt. 27:18). All these stories concern envy, which has been called the "secret sin," since behind the scenes it seeks to mar, deface, and destroy, whether it be property, a reputation, or occasionally, another's life.

The Middle English allegorical poem *Piers the Ploughman* graphically personifies envy: "With his shriveled cheeks, and scowling horribly, he looked like a leek that has been lying too long in the sun. His body was all blistered with wrath, and he went about biting his lips and twisting his fingers, always scheming some vengeance by word or deed, and looking for a chance to carry it out. His tongue was like an adder's: every word he spoke was backbiting and detraction. He made his living by slander and bearing false witness; and in whatever company he showed his face, he displayed his manners by flinging dirt at everyone." He owned up, "I swear I would far rather see Bert, my neighbor, get into trouble, than win half a ton of Essex Cheese tomorrow."[1]

Though the details of Genesis are sketchy, it's generally believed that envy was the sin of Cain. The first hint of tragedy comes when we hear, "And the Lord had regard for Abel and his offering, but for Cain and his offering he had no regard" (Gen. 4:4–5). But why? One line of interpretation stresses the offering itself. Earlier the text says that Abel brought the *firstborn* of his flock, while Cain simply carried "an offering of the fruit of the ground." Later legends elaborated on this discrepancy, asserting that Abel had sacrificed his finest lambs, while Cain just threw a few flax seeds on the altar.[2] In one medieval miracle play, for instance, Cain scowls, "Here I tithe this unthende sheaf: / Let God take it or else leave."[3] Another view is that the two brothers were prompted by altogether different motives. Accordingly, Abel sought to humbly please his creator, while Cain trudged along, albeit grudgingly. A third position is that God preferred the blood of animals over vegetable offerings. (Leviticus, however, indicates that both types were acceptable.)

What caused the first murder? Cain saw Abel's sacrifice consumed and his rejected, then directed his anger not at himself but at his brother. Psychologists have gone on to speculate that there was an imbalance in family affection—Adam and Eve loved Abel but were ill at ease with Cain. In *East of Eden* John Steinbeck writes, "From his first memory Cal [Cain] had craved warmth and affection. . . . [F]rom the very first people were won instantly to Aron [Abel] by his beauty and his simplicity."[4] But Genesis itself is silent on such questions.

Envy, or jealousy, is prominent, too, in that most enduring of fairy tales, *Cinderella*. Being the daughter of her father's first marriage, Cinderella is mistreated by her stepmother, who flagrantly prefers her two natural daughters. At the bottom of the pecking order, Cinderella is asked to do the most demeaning tasks around the house, such as washing the dishes or cleaning the floor. Her sisters, too, order her about. But Cinderella, having a gentle disposition, tries to make the best of her lot. Upon finishing her work, she would sit down near the fireplace among the ashes, hence she becomes known as the "cinder-girl."[5]

Then one day the prince decides to put on a lavish ball, inviting people from far and near. Cinderella's sisters spend hours putting on their makeup, doing their hair, and deciding on what clothes to wear, but will not permit Cinderella to accompany them. Then, in the midst of her tears, her fairy godmother appears, who with a wave of her magic wand turns a pumpkin into a coach, a rat into a coachman, mice into horses, lizards into footmen. Off Cinderella goes, making a big splash at the ball, yet remembering to hurry home before midnight, when everything returns to normal. The next evening a similar chain of events occurs, but this time she loses her glass slipper. After much searching, the prince finds the one and only true fit, and asks Cinderella to be his bride. She happily accepts. Her sisters beg for forgiveness; that very day she brings them to the palace and soon marries them off to lords. Ah, if only we all had magic wands.

I'd like to look more closely at this phenomenon of envy, which Augustine calls "sorrow over other men's good fortune and joy over other men's misfortune."[6] What causes envy and how do we tell its symptoms? Aristotle noticed that envy was particularly intense among equals, who felt that they should be able to compete on even ground. Perhaps that's why we've already encountered two tales of sibling rivalry, namely between Cain and Abel and Cinderella and her sisters. He also saw envy as especially prevalent among those who are ambitious.[7] "If one who is forced to walk on foot envies a great man for keeping a coach and six," wrote Mandeville in *The Fable of the Bees*, "it will never be with that violence or give him that disturbance which it may to a man who keeps a coach himself, but can only afford to drive with four horses."[8] Thus, the B+ student is jealous of the one who receives straight As, the pretty girl of the one who is beautiful,[9] the first string player of the captain of the squad. Competition may be healthy, but when we start inventing stories, tripping up rivals, mobilizing popular opinion to our side, we've stepped over the line into envy and hurt. As the laurel, that traditional emblem for victory, exclaims in Achilles Paraschos's poem, "Ignoble envy poisons every one of my leaves."[10]

The English essayist Francis Bacon thought that we envy those who receive a sudden windfall or get a dramatic promotion more than those who move up the ladder slowly and steadily and seem, thereby, more deserving of reward.[11] Old aristocratic wealth tends to look down its nose at the *nouveau riche*. The youngest vice president soon discovers opposition among the old guard, who are actively or passively subverting his efforts. And how quickly a neighbor's eyes turn green at the news of an inheritance. Notice how the laborers in Jesus' parable begrudge the landowner his generosity when he decides to pay them all the same wage, whether they worked a full or a partial day (Matt. 20:15).

The envier, too, sees himself as somehow inferior. In one of Shakespeare's most powerful sonnets, he complains (as we all do on occasion):

> When, in disgrace with Fortune and men's eyes,
> I all alone beweep my outcast state,
> And trouble deaf Heaven with my bootless cries,
> And look upon myself and curse my fate,
> Wishing me like to one more rich in hope,
> Featured like him, like him with friends possessed,
> Desiring this man's art, and that man's scope,
> With what I most enjoy contented least.[12]

We sigh, if only I had as much natural talent as so-and-so, or if I could do my work as accurately and efficiently as my officemate. If only I had a more effervescent, winning personality, or maybe just a smoother complexion?

It's easy to see why envy has been called the "secret sin." People have been known to boast of greed, lust, or pride, but how can one boast of feeling inferior?

Instead envy relies on stealth and treachery to achieve its ends. It conjures up for me the picture of a witch who secretly sticks pins in the image of the one she wants to injure, exactly how and where she wants the damage done. It was the envious person who, according to folklore, had the "evil eye," and could cast a hateful look that withered crops, animals, and people. For instance, among the Navaho or the Dobu Islanders, a frequent complaint is that one man's field flourishes and another's fails due to sorcery.[13] This appeal to the supernatural to explain one's misfortunes occurs in the romantic adventures of Don Quixote, who, when his noble intentions don't come to fruition, ejaculates, "Some envious enchanter has prevented it." Thus, in a well-known episode, he blames Friston for turning "those giants into windmills, to cheat me of the glory of conquering them."[14]

The gossip columnist also signifies an envious age.[15] Readers want to be titillated by the private lives of the rich and famous, thinking thus to knock them off their pedestals. Psychohistorians routinely "debunk" great figures of the past, not in the name of a "warts and all" realism, but like leeches who seize upon minor character flaws in order to sully or destroy a reputation. "In their censures," notes Mandeville, "they are captious as well as severe, make mountains of mole-hills, and will not pardon the least shadow of a fault, but exaggerate the most trifling omission into a capital blunder."[16]

An infamous example of a political smear, published after its target died (because it would have been too dangerous to attack him while he was alive), is the "Secret History" written by Procopius, an assistant to the Byzantine general Belisarius. Its tone is entirely different from his public account of the wars engaged in by the Emperor Justinian from A.D. 527 to 553. Now Procopius abandons objectivity; the descriptions are scurrilous, at times based on hearsay; his calumny seems to know no bounds. Thus, his portrait of the young Theodora as a prostitute (who later became coruler) borders on the pornographic. And elsewhere in the narrative, he makes the case that the emperor is the "Prince of Demons" posing as a human being, who, along with his fellow fiend Theodora, is intent upon destruction of the human race.[17]

Rivalry in academia can be intense, with colleagues destroyed by slander, innuendo, and half-truths. "Schollers are men of peace, they beare no arms," proclaimed Thomas Browne, "but their tongues are sharper than Actius his razor, their pens carry farther, and give a lowder report than thunder; I had rather stand the shock of a Basilisco, than the fury of a mercilesse Pen."[18] Predictably, the Book of James (3:1) affirms that teachers are held to a stricter standard, then (vv. 4–8) compares the tongue to a spark that can set forests ablaze; to a rudder able to steer a large ship; to poison that may contaminate the whole body; to a ferocious animal no one seems able to tame. Anyone who bridles his tongue, and makes no mistakes, may rightly be called "perfect" (v. 2). I'm afraid my own immaturity is quite evident when, in the heat of argument, I exaggerate, overdramatize, and even bolster my case with fictitious sources. "I submit that the world would be much happier, if men were as fully able to keep silence as they are to speak," Spinoza reasoned, for "experience abundantly shows that men can govern anything more easily than their tongues."[19]

Victims can be quite innocent of the malicious charges laid against them. As an elderly preacher once put it, "You could be a beautiful white dove floating in the heavens, and someone would still shoot you down for a crow." "We pervert even the good points," Latin poet Horace warns, "and are anxious to smudge a clean bowl."[20] In one "Rambler" essay, Samuel Johnson claimed that much "of the misery which the defamation of blameless actions, or the obstruction of honest endeavours brings upon the world, is inflicted by men that propose no advantage to themselves, but the satisfaction of poisoning the banquet which they cannot taste, and blasting the harvest which they have no right to reap."[21]

Subtle distinctions are lost on the envious. Sa'di, the Persian moralist, tells the story of a fox who was seen to be fleeing. When asked what was up, he replied, "I have heard that camels are being forced into service." The bystanders laughed that anyone would mistake him for a camel. The fox's rejoinder? "Hush. If the envious malevolently say that I am a camel and I am caught, who will care to release me or investigate my case?" Even those who are upright, Sa'di concedes, may fall prey to the calumny of competitors or enemies lying in ambush.[22]

Too, the envious are so pained by another's happiness that they would rather suffer harm themselves than see another go rewarded. In one medieval legend, St. Martin meets both an envious and a covetous man. Being a miracle worker, he offers to grant the request of either, with the only proviso that his companion would receive twice as much. The offer turns into a game of who can keep quiet the longest. At last, unable to contain himself, the covetous bursts out, "Yea you or nay you, I must have the double of your share, for all your cunning and caution. Ask, or I will beat you more grievously than ever yet was beaten donkey at Pont." The envious obliges by asking the saint to blind him in one eye, in order that his companion be blinded in both.[23]

Envy sometimes is confused with emulation, which represents a healthy striving after excellence. Paul exhorts the Corinthians, "Be imitators of me, as I am of Christ" (1 Cor. 11:1). "Saints" in popular parlance are heroes who have distinguished themselves by showing unusual charisms of God's grace. They are models of holiness, exemplars who help us see how to "love our neighbor as ourselves" through concrete acts, and so inspire us to greater deeds of holiness. Biographies with a moral have been quite influential throughout church history. Athanasius's

Life of Antony helped spur the desert monastic movement, while Jonathan Edwards's publication of the diaries of David Brainerd has sent forth countless missionaries. *The Golden Legend,* consisting of stories about the saints and written by Jacobus de Voragine, was one of the most popular books of the late middle ages, while Butler's *Lives of the Saints,* originally published in 1759, has since become a staple in the homes of many devout Catholics. Emulation, the moral philosopher Adam Smith believed, served to enhance introspection, improve one's capacity for taking on the role of another, and led to a more critical evaluation of one's own failings.[24] On feast days throughout the liturgical year, one can reflect on lessons from these meritorious lives, and even more so, if one is able to separate the real human being from the legendary accretions.

Personal renewal can spring not merely from reading inspiring biographies but from looking upon wondrous visual images. John of Damascus, during the eighth-century iconoclastic controversy, penned, "What more conspicuous proof do we need that images are the books of the illiterate, the never silent heralds of the honor due the saints, teaching without use of words those who gaze upon them, and sanctifying the sense of sight? Suppose I have few books, or little leisure for reading, but walk into the spiritual hospital—that is to say, a church—with my soul choking from the prickles of thorny thoughts, and thus afflicted I see before me the brilliance of the icon. I am refreshed as if in a verdant meadow, and thus my soul is led to glorify God. I marvel at the martyr's endurance, at the crown he won, and inflamed with burning zeal I fall down to worship God through his martyr, and so receive salvation."[25] God speaks through the eye as well as the ear. Thus poet W. B. Yeats prayed, "O sages standing in God's holy fire / As in the gold mosaic of a wall, / Come from the holy fire, perne in a gyre, / And be the singing-masters of my soul, / Consume my heart away; sick with desire / And fastened to a dying animal / It knows not what it is; and gather me / Into the artifice of eternity."[26]

How can we overcome envy? One way is to heed Paul's admonition in Romans 12:15: "Rejoice with those who rejoice, weep with those who weep." We then put into practice what the fifth-century monk John Cassian called *contraria contrariis sanantur* or "contraries are cured by their contraries."[27] We supplant envy with pity, showing active concern for others. A stranger, walking past a group of children, was surprised to see them all crying. "Why, what's the matter?" he inquired. They replied, "We all have a pain in Billy's stomach." That's empathy! Doesn't the third verse of the hymn "Blessed Be the Tie that Binds" say, "We share our mutual woes, Our mutual burdens bear; And often for each other flows the sympathizing tear"?[28]

Still, if we're honest with ourselves, who won't admit to a tinge of happiness if a fellow employee's productivity falls below our own? if a classmate doesn't get the part she dreamed about and practiced so hard for? or a brother or sister turns out to be not quite the success we are? In the world according to Dante, the punishment must fit the crime, so in *Purgatorio* the envious have their eyes closed with threads of iron wire, much in the way the trainers of hawks used to pull waxed silk through the eyelids of their birds so as to blind and tame them. To Dante this seemed particularly appropriate for those who, during their lives, could not bear to look on the joy of others.[29]

Our pity only goes so far. As the French aphorist La Rochefoucauld explains, "We all have strength enough to endure the troubles of others."[30] James Boswell once posed this question to eighteenth-century English literary titan Samuel Johnson: "'But suppose, now, Sir, that one of your intimate friends were apprehended for an offence for which he might be hanged.' Johnson: 'I should do what I could to bail him, and give him any other assistance; but if he were once fairly hanged, I should not suffer.' Boswell: 'Would you eat your dinner that day, Sir?' Johnson: 'Yes, Sir; and eat it as if he were eating it with me. Why, there's Baretti, who is to be tried for his life tomorrow, friends have risen up for him on every side; yet if he should be hanged, none of them will eat a slice of plum-pudding the less. Sir, that sympathetick feeling goes a very little way in depressing the mind.'"[31]

We can combat envy and callousness by simply being ourselves. Scrutinize the gifts and values you have to see how you can make a unique contribution to your family, workplace, or community. Envy is due to comparisons that put us in an unfavorable light. But in other areas, possibly, we can excel. Maybe your rival is unbeatable in the one-hundred-yard dash, but you have a pretty fair chance against him in the high jump. Or maybe she's a whiz at stenography, but your proofreading skills are superior. Maybe the couple across the street does have a larger house or a motorboat, but their family life is in shambles. Don't be myopic; broaden your vision and things may not appear so bleak. As the old hymn reminds us, "Count your many blessings—name them one by one, And it will surprise you what the Lord hath done."[32]

Shakespeare pulls himself out of depression in that same sonnet by recalling that he is loved, and that is a far more precious gift than a little more talent:[33]

> Desiring this man's art, and that man's scope,
> With what I most enjoy contented least;
> Yet in these thoughts myself almost despising,
> Haply I think on thee, and then my state,
> Like to the lark at break of day arising
> From sullen earth, sings hymns at heaven's gate;
>   For thy sweet love rememb'red such wealth brings,
>   That then I scorn to change my state with kings.[34]

The powerful mood swings in Shakespeare's sonnet are reminiscent of those in the Psalms. One minute the petitioner is fretting about the way the wicked flourish; then he looks around and they are no more. Their "success" had proved fleeting in the moving wheel of fortune. Or mired in self-pity, overwhelmed by guilt, all at once the psalmist remembers God's faithfulness and feels a fresh wave of forgiveness.

Peter Shaffer's play *Amadeus* is a study of the intense rivalry between those eighteenth-century composers Salieri and Mozart. While critics have rightly questioned its historical accuracy, I'd like to consider it for a moment as a morality play. The gifted Salieri, court composer to Emperor Joseph II of Austria, has dedicated his musical talents to God. In the first act, at the age of sixteen, he prays to God in a kind of bargain, "*Signore,* let me be a composer! Grant me sufficient fame to enjoy it. In return, I will live with virtue. I will strive to better the lot of my fellows. And I will honor You with much music all the days of my life."[35]

Then along comes that child prodigy—the brash, immature, pleasure-loving Wolfgang Amadeus Mozart, whose compositions make Salieri's look like those of an amateur. How could God be so cruel, he reasons, to let such beauty flow from an unconsecrated, unworthy vessel? Eventually Salieri sinks deeper and deeper into despair as Mozart's compositions eclipse his own. He resorts to a number of stratagems to attack Mozart's ego—discouraging prospective students, sabotaging his performances, and even threatening his very life. Salieri's downfall is the prototype of what envy can do to anyone who thinks God should run the universe his way or else.

How far this is from the way Moses or Paul handled competition. The Israelites murmured continuously against Moses' leadership in the wilderness, yet he was able to keep a surprisingly even temper. After seventy elders had been set apart to assist him, it was reported that back in camp Eldad and Medad were also prophesying. Joshua urged Moses to stop them. But he magnanimously replied, "Are you jealous for my sake? Would that all the Lord's people were prophets, and that the Lord would put his spirit on them" (Num. 11:29). When it was pointed out to Paul that others were also proclaiming the gospel, and sometimes for base reasons, he responded, "What does it matter? Just this, that Christ is proclaimed in every way, whether out of false motives or true; and in that I rejoice" (Phil. 1:18).[36] The Dutch humanist scholar Erasmus, after disputing Luther's views on free will, graciously offered, "Although I am an old man, it will not shame or anger me to learn from a young man, if he teaches me more evident doctrines with evangelical gentleness."[37] It is an axiom evangelist Henry Drummond thought: "Whenever you attempt a good work you will find other men doing the same kind of work, and probably doing it better. Envy them not."[38]

Yes, the spirit-filled Christian has an altogether different mind-set. "The glory of Christian love," the blind nineteenth-century Scottish preacher George Matheson declares, "is its refusal of monopoly. The spiritual artist—the man who paints Christ in his soul—wants no solitary niche in the temple of fame. He would not like to hear anyone say, 'He is the first of his profession; there is not one that can hold a candle to him.' He would be very sad to be distinguished in his profession of Christ, marked out as a solitary figure. The gladdest moment to him will always be the moment when the cry is heard, 'Thy brother is coming up the ladder also; thy brother will share the inheritance with thee.'"[39]

In the films *Jean de Florette* and *Manon of the Springs* (which were later turned into novels), Marcel Pagnol portrays an uncle and a nephew who are deeply resentful of a newcomer who inherits lucrative property nearby. Their new neighbor, an exuberant hunchback, is determined to make good, so he reads up on and tries new scientific methods of farming, including breeding rabbits who eat Asian squash. But all his labors come to nought because of the lack of rain, and because, unknown to him, Cesar and Ugolin Soubeyran have covetously plugged up a little-known spring on his land. Jean dies tragically, dynamiting for a new well, and his neighbors obtain the estate.

Some years later, a blind woman scolds Cesar for not answering a letter, which, it turns out, he never received, probably because his military company was on the move in Africa. But from what she says, he concludes that the hunchback he had connived against was actually his own son by the one true love of his life. Horrified by what he had done and truly repentant, he confesses to the priest, and decides to make peace with Manon, the hunchback's daughter, who until then he had treated as a rival; so before he dies, he passes on to her son (his great-grandson) the family fortune. The drama closes with a startling letter, which reads in part: ". . . your father was my son, my Soubeyran, that I missed all my life, and whom I let die little by little, because I did not know who he was. I had only to tell him about the spring, and he would still be playing his mouth organ, and all of you would have come to live in our family house. Instead of that, a lingering death. Nobody knows it, but all the same I am ashamed before everybody, even the trees. . . .

"I always kept away from him. I did not know his voice, nor his face. I never saw his eyes close up, which were perhaps like my mother's. I only saw his hump and his distress, all the harm I did to him. Now you understand why I long to die. . . . I have no fear of him. On the contrary, he knows he is a Soubeyran; he is not a hunchback anymore because of my fault; he has understood that it is all because of a stupidity, and I am sure that instead of attacking me, he will defend me."[40] As Pagnol's parable clearly demonstrates, those who envy hurt themselves most.

Let us return again to Abel. He is not meant to be viewed as a competitor who has been more successful in currying God's favor, but should be seen for what he truly is, and always has been, namely our brother. Are you tempted by envy? Listen again to Genesis: "The Lord said to Cain, 'Why are you angry, and why has your countenance fallen? If you do well, will you not be accepted? And if you do not do well, sin is lurking at the door; its desire is for you, but you must master it" (Gen. 4:6–7).

CHAPTER 6

The Overzealous Egalitarian, or Leveler

One of the reasons why many of us like to watch or play sports is that here at least the world seems somewhat fair. Each game has an agreed-upon set of rules along with stated eligibility requirements. Contestants who have practiced long and hard and played well in earlier, preliminary contests are still in the running. There is a narrowly defined way to score, and, unless you can put that ball through the hoop or into the hole or across the net, the rest simply doesn't count. Events can be precisely timed; they take place in public arenas, where both spectators and the media can observe and scrutinize the play-by-play. Statisticians are able to compare your performance with that of your fellows as well as to legendary predecessors in the sport. Taking bets either for or against yourself is strictly forbidden. Referees help to curb excesses by handing out penalties for infractions. Still, that's not to say some won't bend the rules to their own advantage or play rather loosely with the gray areas. Yet, on a given day, we may feel comfortable saying that *the* best (or *one* of the best) players or teams won, although, even then, enough unresolved questions may remain to make for a heated argument.

The overzealous egalitarian, or leveler, however, works from a different set of assumptions. He wants strict equality in all segments of life (politically, socially, economically), lest elites mushroom and become entrenched. Drawing distinctions of any sort only serves to separate us from our neighbors. After all, why should one person make decisions for the group when we can all come to our own conclusions, thank you, and then head off in a hundred different directions? He is strong on *vox populi*, letting the little guy have a say, but weak on authority structures to carry out items on the agenda. Grades? Tests? Couldn't we just take classes pass-fail, preferably the former? The sport he is most fond of is the "Caucus-race" from

Lewis Carroll's *Alice's Adventures in Wonderland.* In it the Dodo "marked out a race-course, in a sort of circle ('the exact shape doesn't matter,' it said), and then all the party were placed along the course, here and there. There was no 'One, two, three, and away!', but they began running when they liked, and left off when they liked, so that it was not easy to know when the race was over." After about a half hour of this running hither and thither, however, the Dodo suddenly called a halt. When the competitors crowded around breathlessly asking, "But who has won?" it replied, "*Everybody* has won, and *all* must have prizes."[1]

But such a position is unrealistic, untenable. So, I say, beware of utopias. All of us are endowed by our creator with differing and unequal gifts, temperaments, or advantages. We can't possibly choose our sex, race, family, or place of birth, and learn early to "make do" with what we're given. So it's foolish to think that all can begin at the same starting line and far-fetched to believe that the rules of the competition are fair at every stage of our journey. Seventeenth-century English philosopher John Locke promulgated the view that at birth all minds are blank slates and all children are equally and infinitely teachable: "Let us then suppose the mind to be . . . white paper, void of all characters, without any ideas."[2] Or again, "I imagine the minds of children as easily turned, this or that way as water itself."[3] However, this just doesn't square with human experience. "I have seen, in the Hospital of Foundlings," wrote former president John Adams, "fifty babies in one room;—all under four days old; all in cradles alike; all nursed and attended alike; all dressed alike; all equally neat. . . . I never saw a greater variety, or more striking inequalities, in the streets of Paris or London. Some had every sign of grief, sorrow, and despair; others had joy and gayety in their faces. Some were sinking in the arms of death; others looked as if they might live to fourscore. Some were as ugly and others as beautiful, as children or adults ever are; these were stupid; those sensible. These were all born to equal rights, but to very different fortunes; to very different success and influence in life."[4]

Nor can one create harmonious, self-sustaining economic units, as nineteenth-century French social thinker Charles Fourier believed, simply by eliminating scarcity.[5] Life doesn't consist of an abundance of goods nor is affluence alone likely to create a paradise. "Equality," warned that astute French observer of human affairs Alexis de Tocqueville, "begets in man the desire of judging of everything for himself; it gives him in all things a taste for the tangible and the real, a contempt for tradition and for forms."[6] So, it's not surprising that in eighteenth- and nineteenth-century America a host of communities arose seeking to embody new experiments in human relations—Ephrata in Pennsylvania, Oneida in upstate New York, New Harmony in Indiana, Brook Farm in Massachusetts, Amana in Iowa. But most died out rather quickly, having underestimated how age-old vices could defeat new-fangled dreams.[7] Occasionally, though, one caught glimpses of how society might be reshaped.

Communism preached a classless society: "From each according to his ability, to each according to his needs," Karl Marx wrote.[8] But the upheavals necessary for full social equality meant millions of peasants were arrested, deported, or starved during the early 1930s when the the the Soviet Union used draconian methods to enforce collectivization of farms.[9] Also, millions more died in China from 1958 to 1961, when Mao's attempt to surpass Britain's agricultural and industrial output in one great economic leap forward ended in such a pitiful harvest that famine became rampant.[10] (This sort of social disruption has been underestimated as far back as Thomas More's *Utopia*, when he said that a son who wasn't naturally gifted in his father's trade could be transferred to, and adopted by, another family, and once there, would somehow come to feel at home with the new arrangement.[11]) A last, and most significant, rule in communism, according to Orwell's satire *Animal Farm*, was: "All Animals Are Equal, But Some Animals Are More Equal Than Others."[12] Historically, instead of the much-touted "dictatorship of the proletariat," power actually flowed from an old line of hereditary monarchs to new megalomaniacs, whose intolerance frequently led to imprisonment or reeducation of their opponents. It may be all right to dream of better worlds, but not on such a grandiose scale, not through state compulsion, and not, for heaven's sake, by demanding instantaneous change.

We need a more "realistic" understanding of human nature, theologian Reinhold Niebuhr wrote, one that maintains a constant tension between our potential for good and our proclivity for evil. Created in the image of God, we are capable of astonishing achievements, yet at the same time, we're fallen and fallible, equally capable of the most savage depravities. In the influential "Federalist Papers" penned between 1787–88 to encourage ratification of the American constitution, Publius declares, "As there is a degree of depravity in mankind which requires a certain degree of circumspection and distrust, so there are other qualities in human nature which justify a certain portion of esteem and confidence."[13] Philosophies which don't take this duality into account only end up compounding our problems, rather than pointing to long-term solutions. Of recent history, political scientist Glenn Tinder concedes, "those who hunger and thirst after perfect justice have almost always become, in action if not in principle, enemies of liberty." There was a premonition of this political nightmare in Dostoyevsky's *The Brothers Karamazov* when Ivan, driven to the edge of madness, concluded that a just society had to be created here and now, even if that entailed universal enslavement by the Grand Inquisitor.[14]

Niebuhr's influential masterpiece, *The Nature and Destiny of Man*, describes those conflicts in our nature (e.g., pride and sensuality) as well as in history (e.g., *finis* and *telos*), demonstrating that all social institutions are wracked with ambiguity. While we should encourage the best in ourselves and others, it's also imperative that governments have a system of checks and balances to keep power from being consolidated in one individual or institution, since even the best-intentioned person or group inevitably falls short of expectations. "Power tends to corrupt," Lord Acton wrote Mandrell Creighton, "and absolute power corrupts absolutely."[15] Niebuhr preferred to see history in terms of "irony,"[16] where a state's laws and actions may actually bring about the opposite of what was intended—whether due to unforeseen consequences, individuals more intent upon finding loopholes than had been thought possible, expectations of human nature that were just too high, or other factors. Thus the temperance movement, seeking to eliminate the prevailing form of substance abuse, pushed to pass a constitutional amendment in 1919 that prohibited the sale, manufacture, and transportation of alcoholic beverages. Enforcement, however, proved elusive as the law was widely disregarded. Indeed bootlegging spread, as gangsters attempted to control trade by means of graft and violence, before the amendment was finally repealed in 1933. These years, too, can be construed as a failed "utopian" experiment.

Change on a smaller scale, however, is frequently called for. The church, by forming a collective institution that could stand up to the state, has been instrumental in creating a private space or buffer for voluntary associations.[17] The decentralizing of power in the West in the form of political parties, labor unions, special-interest groups, and charitable organizations means that personal liberty has been "expanded," enabling ordinary citizens to organize and make a difference in society at large. The Soviet Union, during its time of enforced collectivization, discovered that when a peasant was granted a small private plot to grow his own crops and allotted a cow or two, both overall productivity and morale went up significantly.[18] Give people a little room, a few incentives, and a chance to perform, and you might be pleasantly surprised by the outcome.

That blueprint behind most monasteries and religious orders, *The Rule of Benedict*, written in the sixth century, owes its wide appeal to Benedict's acute understanding of human nature. Improving on earlier models, Benedict avoids the extremes of too much solitude, overly rigorous asceticism, and focusing exclusively on intellectual development or back-breaking labor. Instead there's a balance in the monk's schedule, a rhythm, which allows time for introspection and corporate worship, work as well as study. One estimate of a typical Benedictine day runs: 6½ hours for manual labor, 4½ hours for reading and meditation, 3½ hours for religious office, 1 hour for eating, and 8½ hours of sleep.[19] This loose, skeletal structure has been adapted to a thousand different locales. "Historians have vied in praising" Benedict's "genius and clear-sightedness," wrote de Montalembert; "they have supposed that he intended to regenerate Europe, to stop the dissolution of society, to prepare the reconstitution of political order, to re-establish public education, and to preserve literature and the arts. . . . I firmly believe that he never dreamt of regenerating anything but his own soul and those of his brethren, the monks."[20]

Egalitarianism, too, helps to explain the rise of Christian perfectionism in nineteenth- and twentieth-century America, with its belief that one could be judged free of "intentional" sin. Sometimes this came in the form of a second decision after conversion known as complete consecration, as in the Keswick conferences held in England. In the holiness-Pentecostal movement, perfectionism became synonymous with the infilling of the Holy Spirit, manifested in such gifts as speaking in tongues. I have my doubts, though, that sanctification is a once-and-for-all event instead of a lifelong arduous struggle, where some days we make progress and other days we relapse.[21] Perfectionism, I believe, puts one closer to the camp of heretics than to true believers. In 1312 the Council of Vienne, in *Ad nostrum,* condemned the free spirits, some of whom were German beguines and beghards, who allegedly taught that one can become so pure "that he is rendered completely sinless and need progress no further in grace"; need no longer be required to fast or pray since his passions are totally under control; nor need be "subject to human obedience, nor obligated to fulfill the commandments and precepts of the church." To cement this, they appealed to 2 Corinthians 3:17, "where the Spirit of the Lord is, there is freedom."[22]

Augustine, on the other hand, viewed baptism as the start of a lifelong process of convalescence rather than a once-and-for-all clean slate. He had learned the hard way how deeply ingrained were his previous habits and became convinced that he would always remain infected by sin, ultimately problematic. In *Confessions,* he prays, "But you, O Lord my God, hear me, look upon me and see me; have mercy and heal me, you in whose sight I have become a riddle to myself."[23] In Tolstoy's *Anna Karenin,* the prosperous landowner Konstantine Levin undergoes a gradual spiritual awakening. He has been especially struck by a peasant's explanation of why a certain man was good—because he lived for his soul and he remembered God.[24] Levin resolves to live on a higher ethical plane yet soon becomes disillusioned by his own failings. The novel, however, ends on a note of realism: "I shall still lose my temper with Ivan the coachman, I shall still embark on useless discussions and express my opinions inopportunely; there will still be the same wall between the sanctuary of my inmost soul and other people, even my wife; I shall probably go on scolding her in my anxiety and repenting of it afterwards."[25] While God does not fashion new personalities out of thin air, he does remold our desires and redirect our aims.

A healthy skepticism of perfectionism was needed in the 1830s when John

Humphrey Noyes founded what would eventually become the Oneida community. Converted by evangelicals, he attended Yale Divinity School, receiving a license to preach from the Congregational Church. Soon afterward, however, he started espousing a doctrine of sinless perfection and lost his license in 1834. By 1846 he was calling for "complex marriages," which freed people from the restraints of sexual exclusiveness. Eyebrows were raised, Noyes was indicted on charges of adultery, and the whole community had to relocate.[26] "When it comes to virtuous appearances," political scientist Glenn Tinder writes, "our ability to deceive ourselves—and our willingness to be deceived—should not be underestimated."[27] The prophet Jeremiah put it even more bluntly, "The heart is deceitful above any other thing, desperately sick; who can fathom it?" (Jer. 17:9 REV).

One has but to observe the evasiveness in Napoleon's memoirs. At first he seems to blame his decisive defeat at Waterloo on his subordinates—Grouchy's failure to come up with Blucher on June 18; then he takes the tack that it was actually an indecisive battle, which could have been undone by further campaigning; finally, he appears to have persuaded himself that he had actually won, ending his memoirs on a note of sympathy for the people of London "when they learnt of the catastrophe which had befallen their army." Such twisted reasoning is only possible because the supreme commander can't admit to his own faulty judgment.[28]

Because of our inordinate capacity for self-deception, I adhere to what theologian Paul Tillich referred to as the "Protestant principle," wherein we need to reform even the reformers, who, though they started out in a good direction, then wandered off from the path themselves;[29] as that old Latin adage has it, *Ecclesia Reformata semper reformanda* ("The church of the Reformation continually stands in need of reformation.").[30] However, laying stress on sinfulness goes contrary to certain currents in contemporary culture, such as the human potential movement, possibility thinking, and the behaviorist's stress on positive reinforcement (rather than negative prohibitions), all of which seek to bolster our self-esteem rather than to cast doubts on our perfectibility.

The church has even been known to represent itself as a utopian community, often by painting opponents blacker than they should be or by exaggerating its own internal harmony. In reality church history is riddled with counterfeits, fraudulent claims, even faked miracles. One prominent example was the annual "descent of the holy fire" at the Church of the Holy Sepulcher in Jerusalem; for centuries local church officials made it appear as though fire came down from heaven to light the lamps on the altar during the Holy Saturday ceremony of Easter Vigil. Its precise timing always aroused suspicion, and was a major reason why Moslem caliph al-Hakim ordered the church destroyed in A.D. 1009; still, it was later rebuilt and the tradition revived.[31] Or there's the so-called "Donation of

Constantine," a document fabricated sometime around the eighth century, which purported to be a decree from the fourth-century Emperor Constantine granting Rome authority over the other principal sees in early Christianity. It was frequently used as a weapon against Eastern Orthodoxy until it was exposed as a forgery by the Renaissance scholar Lorenzo Valla around A.D. 1440.[32] Furthermore, the trade in healing potions, relics, good-luck saint's charms, and other questionable practices should always give one pause.

Erasmus, the Renaissance humanist who published an early critical text of the Greek New Testament, made fun of the "sea of superstition" surrounding the medieval cult of the saints. For instance, a person seeing a painting of St. Christopher is sure he won't die that day; another who addresses a statue of St. Barbara in the prescribed manner is convinced he'll return unhurt from battle. Erasmus goes on to list districts where saints will, respectively, relieve toothaches, aid women in childbirth, help in the recovery of stolen objects, care for shipwreck survivors, and so on. "The ordinary life of Christians everywhere abounds in these varieties of silliness," moans Erasmus, rewriting a passage from Virgil:

> Had I a hundred tongues, a hundred mouths,
> A voice of iron, I could not count the types
> Of fool, nor yet enumerate the names
> Of every kind of folly.[33]

Pious fictions, however, only increase skepticism among outsiders and needlessly divide the body of Christ. The modern Pentecostal movement with its exaggerated claims of "signs and wonders" has been an especially nefarious culprit. When the "spirit of religion" is joined to "the love of wonder," cautioned Scottish philosopher David Hume, watch out! "A religionist may be an enthusiast, and imagine he sees what has no reality: he may know his narrative to be false, and yet persevere in it, with the best intentions in the world, for the sake of promoting so holy a cause."[34] But to propagate what we know, or suspect, to be a lie doesn't honor the Lord but defames him. When Jesus' own life was on the line, he told the vacillating Pilate, "For this I was born, and for this I came into the world, to testify to the truth" (John 18:37).

If a person or group believes they have all the truth and the right to implement it, then that is "utopian" concludes Niebuhr.[35] The modern Polish poet Wislawa Szymborska characterizes utopia as an "Island where all becomes clear. / . . . If any doubts arise, the wind dispels them instantly. / . . . Unshakable Confidence towers over the valley. / Its peak offers an excellent view of the Essence of Things."[36] Papal infallibility, even when qualified by "ands," "ifs," and "buts," has seen a number of reversals, inconsistencies, and not a few outright contradictions.[37] So when you come into the sanctuary, my advice is, don't leave your reason in the vestibule. Didn't Jesus himself warn that "many will say to me, 'Lord, Lord, did we not prophesy in your name, and cast out demons in your name, and do many deeds of power in your name?'" Then at the great assize he will reply, "I never knew you; go away from me, you evildoers" (Matt. 7:22–23).

If pride is the temptation of the overachiever, then envy is the temptation of the underachiever (and egalitarian). It is what Dorothy Sayers calls the vice of the "have-not."[38] Madame de Staël refers to "that strongest of all antipathies, the antipathy of a second-rate mind to a first-rate one,"[39] whereby the modestly talented attack those who have achieved a degree of recognition or start redefining the parameters of success till their small niche is considered a major arena. Maybe you've written a few bluegrass numbers, but that doesn't put you in the same league as Beethoven or Bach. Or you've painted a few successful self-portraits and now refer to yourself as a Rembrandt? (Or to cite Erasmus, you've traced three arcs with a compass and imagine yourself a Euclid?[40]) By casting aspersions on any distinction between high- and low-brow culture, we, in effect, encourage mediocrity. "If we cannot make music," social critic Henry Fairlie writes, "we will simply make a noise and persuade others that it is music. If we can do nothing at all, why! we will strum a guitar all day, and call it self-expression. As long as no talent is required, no apprenticeship to a skill, everyone can do it and we are all magically made equal."[41] Envy posits that the standards are biased, the judges are about to give the prizes to their friends, and there is, after all, no real difference between levels of skill.

For the most part, the person who envies isn't into bettering himself; he just wants the competition to swallow a reducing pill. As an old proverb says, "The envious man thinks that if his neighbor breaks a leg, he will be able to walk better himself."[42] This venomous outlook is common in literary portraits. In Spenser's parade of sins in *The Faerie Queene,* Envie rides "upon a ravenous wolfe, and still did chaw / Between his cankred teeth a venemous tode, / That all the poison ran about his chaw." He wears a variously colored woolen garment full of eyes and has a "hatefull Snake" curled secretly in his bosom. He grudges "all good workes and vertuous deeds." "He does backebite, and spightfull poison spues / From leprous mouth on all, that ever writt."[43] "As vultures are attracted to ill-smelling places and fly past meadow after meadow and pleasant, fragrant regions," early church father Basil of Caesarea writes, "as flies pass by healthy flesh and swarm eagerly to a wound, so the envious avert their gaze from the brightness in life and the loftiness of good actions and fix their attention upon rottenness." Thus, "envious persons are skilled in making what is praiseworthy seem despicable by means of unflattering distortions. . . . The courageous man they call reckless; . . . the clever man, cunning," often labeling people exactly the opposite of what they really are.[44]

The egalitarian's notion of God and the universe stems more from man-made constructs than God's own book of nature. As technocrats we admire optimum efficiency—every part has a specific purpose and must fit just so—our model being a well-oiled engine. But is that how God works? In nature we see miscarriages, still-births, deformities, sudden accidents, slow and painful deaths, in short, much extravagance and waste. That's certainly not how economist Adam Smith would run his pin factories. Essayist Annie Dillard once compared God to the manager of the Southern Railroad, who in trying to determine how many engines should be on the steep grade between Lynchburg and Danville, Virginia, goes to the expense of building nine thousand gleaming locomotives, sending them all out on the run at once. The result? "Although there are engineers at the throttles, no one is manning the switches. The engines crash, collide, derail, jump, jam, burn. . . . At the end of the massacre you have three engines, which is what the run could support in the first place. . . . You go to your board of directors and show them what you've done. And what are they going to say? You know what they're going to say. . . . It's a hell of a way to run a railroad." Then Dillard poignantly asks, "Is it a better way to run a universe?"[45] I'm afraid that God puts up with an incredible amount of trial and error and fantastically slow learning curves on the part of his creatures.

That we don't live in a perfect world doesn't mean that we should espouse uniformity or resort to totalitarian methods. Rather we need to learn how to be content whatever state we're in, as Paul explains, whether we abound or whether we are abased (Phil. 4:11–12). "A Knight whose heart is set upon the way," says Confucius, "but who is ashamed of wearing shabby clothes and eating coarse food, is not worth calling into counsel."[46] How then should we respond to the egalitarian criticism of maldistribution? "Whoever speaks ill of you or does you ill," advises *Ancrene Wisse,* the medieval devotional for anchoresses, "take note and understand that he is your file, such as metal workers have, and files away all your rust and roughness of sin; for he devours himself, alas, as he does the file, but he makes your soul smooth and bright."[47] We should strive with all our might to rectify social injustice, but not at the cost of personal freedom.

Instead of a utopia, the Christian model is the "communion of the saints." Paul visualizes the church as a living body (e.g., 1 Cor. 12:12–27), whose parts are all interdependent and animated by Christ the head. But social organizations of any kind must set boundaries, maintain structural stability and flexibility, as well as create their own environments. The early Christians, says historian Wayne Meeks, borrowed patterns from the surrounding culture (e.g., households, voluntary associations, synagogues, schools) to organize their loose structures. Church gatherings centered around the rituals of baptism and communion and commemorating Christ's death, resurrection, and imminent return. Internal ties were strongly forged; there was an openness to new members. In fact one of Paul's favorite metaphors for the church was that of a family, in which new spiritual brothers and sisters supplemented, or supplanted, earlier ties of kinship.[48] Henceforth, the old social fault lines determined by gender, nationality, or social status would no longer be valid (cf. Gal. 3:28).

Orthodox thinker Timothy Ware refers to this body of Christ as "a continued pentecost." Church life "does not mean the ironing out of human variety, nor the imposition of a rigid and uniform pattern upon all alike," he declares, "but the exact opposite. The saints, so far from displaying a drab monotony, have developed the most vivid and distinctive personalities."[49] In the age to come, Pseudo-Macarius declared in one of his homilies, "Peter is Peter, Paul is Paul, Philip is Philip. Each one retains his own nature and personal identity, but they are all filled with the Spirit."[50] Here unity is held in tension with diversity. Each member is viewed as an indispensable link in a chain. Still, as roles become more differentiated, some inevitably being accorded higher status than others, bickering and jealousy proliferate.[51] Other distortions appear. The church of Rome has been criticized for excessive centralization, too much worldly power and pomp, and an overly high demand for conformity—thus purchasing unity at the price of diversity,[52] while Protestants who splinter off into smaller and smaller denominations over minor issues are guilty of the opposite tendency. There is, also, the recurring problem of churches that come to resemble clubs, where one's lifestyle and values are reinforced rather than challenged, so that Christ's prophetic voice is stifled.[53]

Over time congregations become what Robert Bellah and his fellow sociologists call "communities of memory," as stories are told and retold about members' acts of devotion, kindness, and heroism, or where past mistakes are acknowledged.[54] Sharing these experiences helps individuals alleviate feelings of isolation and anonymity. "In history," Glenn Tinder reminds us, "very few are remembered; in Christ none are forgotten."[55] Medieval Christians lived within walking distance of the church, awoke to its bells, followed its calendar, took animals there to be blessed;[56] so, too, many today find a sense of meaning and a call to service from being part of a community of faith.

A type of spirituality, says Peruvian theologian Gustavo Gutiérrez, begins when one individual receives a deep insight into discipleship, then attracts others to that way of life, offering it back as a gift to the church.[57] Thus, we can speak, for instance, of the Franciscan/Dominican/Ignatian/Carmelite[58] or Lutheran/Reformed/Anabaptist or *hesychast/skete* traditions. "The great spiritualities in the life of the church continue to exist," Gutiérrez writes, "because they keep sending their followers back to the sources."[59] In our own day, we have witnessed the rise of such unusual ministries as Mother Teresa's Missionaries of Charity, which pro-

vide food, clothing, shelter, and medical care for the poorest of the poor; Roger
Shutz's *Taizé,* which fosters a bond of Christian unity by a life of common prayer;
Jean Vanier's *L'Arche,* which lends dignity to those who are mentally and physically disabled by recognizing their spiritual gifts;[60] Millard Fuller's Habitat for
Humanity International, which via "sweat equity" and no-interest loans helps the
working poor to own their own homes.[61] These four groups have had a world-
wide impact, but there are many others, far too numerous to mention. By forming new organizations, communities, and orders, the church stays in the forefront
of ministering to each era's needs, reinvigorates itself, and extends a single individual's vision for generations.

A stirring modern experiment in corporate life was the Preachers' Seminary at
Finkenwald, Germany, described in Dietrich Bonhoeffer's *Life Together.* There was
structured daily prayer, singing, meditation, mutual care and support, confession
one to another, and a common theological training. Renouncing clerical privilege
freed the "brethren" to accept emergency calls from churches.[62] Forms of service
consisted, for instance, of helping others, listening, bearing one another's burdens,
and holding one's tongue.

Bonhoeffer spoke out strongly against those who had fallen so in love with an
ideal that they couldn't cope with wounded reality. Of these "utopians" he wrote:
"Innumerable times a whole Christian community has broken down because it
had sprung from wishful dreaming . . . rapturous experiences and lofty moods that
come over us like a dream." He continues, "God is not a God of the emotions, but
the God of truth. Only that fellowship which faces such disillusionment with all its
unhappy and ugly aspects, begins to be what it should be in God's sight, begins to
grasp in faith the promise that is given to it. The sooner this shock of disillusionment comes to an individual and to a community, the better for both. A community which cannot bear and cannot survive such a crisis, which insists upon
keeping its illusion when it should be shattered, permanently loses in that moment
the promise of Christian community. Sooner or later it will collapse."[63] Bonhoeffer echoes Luther's view that "the church is an inn and an infirmary for the sick
and for convalescents."[64] Only when we renounce utopianism and follow in the
footsteps of the broken Messiah, can we, the crushed, truly be made whole again.
In the end, it is not the self-proclaimed ideologue but the wounded healer who
likely ministers best. As Niebuhr, ever the realist, prayed, "God grant me— / The
serenity to accept the things I cannot change, / The courage to change the things I
can, / And the wisdom to distinguish the one from the other."[65]

An Antidote to Anger

Mary and Martha—still squabbling after all these years? Does sibling rivalry never cease? (Luke 10:38–42). "Mother, why doesn't Mary help me? I always end up doing the dishes, while she's jabbering with her friends. Can't you get her to do her fair share of the work? I'm sick and tired of all this cooking and house-cleaning." Somehow I feel this isn't the first time Martha uttered such a complaint. Yet this small domestic scene from first-century Palestine still resonates with us because we, too, experience conflict, become irritated, and lash out at others. How can we reduce the number of such incidents, make conflict more constructive, and so better understand ourselves and those around us? In other words, how should a Christian handle anger?

We know how potent rage is from both personal experience and literature. That early Greek masterpiece, *The Iliad,* begins, "Sing, O Muse, of the wrath of Achilles." The greatest Achaean warrior is sulking in his tent because his commander Agamemnon has taken away his female captive. Because of personal animosity, the whole tide of the Trojan war seems to be turning.[1] In the Pentateuch, Moses, that chosen deliverer of the Hebrew people from the oppressive hand of Pharaoh and performer of signs and wonders, could not enter into the Promised Land, partly due to his uncontrolled anger at the Israelites' murmuring in the wilderness at Meribath-Kadesh (Num. 20:10–12).

Herman Melville describes a certain Captain Ahab, who was obsessed with hunting down a white whale: "Moby Dick had reaped away Ahab's leg, as a mower a blade of grass in the field. No turbaned Turk, no hired Venetian or Malay, could have smote him with more seeming malice. . . . Ever since that almost fatal encounter . . . the White Whale swam before him as the monomaniac incarnation of all those malicious agencies which some deep men feel eating in them till they are left living on with half a heart and half a lung."[2] Despite the valiant efforts of the first mate to prevent disaster, the entire crew of the *Pequod* was lost, save one.

Then there's that ancient Colchis sorceress Medea. Jason and the Argnonauts were able to retrieve the golden fleece because she provided the ointment that protected them from the bulls of Hephaestus; also, her spell had put to sleep the dragon guarding it. Upon returning home, Jason and Medea had two sons together. One day, however, the king of Corinth proposed that Jason wed his daughter. He accepted. In her wrath, Medea designed a poisoned dress which consumed the bride's flesh, then murdered her own children in the temple of Hera.[3]

When my wife and I were living in an apartment in Manhattan, a boy moved in with the girl next door; he was even helping an elderly woman we knew put in a new floor. Yet a conversation I had with him one afternoon left me quite unsettled. There was a deep-seated rage in his heart, and I even advised Barbara to be careful around him. Several months later we were awakened early one morning when federal agents had surrounded the building and one was loudly knocking on our neighbor's door, demanding, "Open up, Eddie, with your hands up!" Apparently the day before he had taken part in a bank robbery and was about to flee the country.

The Stoic philosopher Seneca graphically enumerates the consequences of uncontrolled rage: "Some through too much passion have burst their veins . . . and sickly people have fallen back into illnesses. . . . Many have continued in the frenzy of anger, and have never recovered the reason that had been unseated. . . . These all call down death upon their children, poverty upon themselves, destruction upon their house. . . . They become enemies to their closest friends and have to be shunned by those most dear. . . . In anger men have stabbed the bodies that they loved and have lain in the arms of those whom they have slain."[4]

Anger often starts out as a minor irritation. Sei Shōnagon, a lady-in-waiting to Empress Sadako in tenth-century Japan, was an inveterate list-keeper; in fact, there are 164 lists in her "pillow book." An acute observer of day-to-day details, she ventured an opinion about everything. In one chapter entitled "Hateful Things," she mentions: "One is in a hurry to leave, but one's visitor keeps chattering away. . . . One is just about to be told some interesting piece of news when a baby starts crying. . . . One has gone to bed and is about to doze off when a mosquito appears, announcing himself in a reedy voice. . . . Very hateful is a mouse that scurries all over the place. . . . I detest anyone who sneezes. . . . I cannot stand people who leave without closing the panel behind them." And on and on.[5]

There seems to be a certain progression in anger. The cartoon example is, of course, the husband who gets chewed out at the office by his boss, who goes home and shouts at his wife, who before long is scolding the child, who steps outside and kicks the dog.[6] Gossip, too, ratchets up the tension. "I fed them with such a hash of spiteful gossip," Anger recalls in *Piers the Ploughman*, "that the two of them would sometimes burst out 'Liar!' together, and slap each other across the face. . . . If they'd both had knives, they'd have slaughtered each other!"[7]

Some adopt the ploy of smoldering silence (one that I've been known to use a few times myself). Robert Louis Stevenson describes a room in Edinburgh where, as legend had it, two unmarried sisters had lived together. One day, after a terrible falling out, "a chalk line" was "drawn upon the floor" in order to separate them into "two domains; it bisected the doorway and the fireplace." Never again was there a word, "black or white," uttered between the two. "So, for years, they co-existed in a hateful silence."[8] This form of anger builds high, invincible walls.

William Blake's poem "A Poison Tree" offers a profound anatomy of anger:

> I was angry with my friend;
> I told my wrath, my wrath did end.
> I was angry with my foe;
> I told it not—my wrath did grow.
>
> And I watered it in fears,
> Night and morning with my tears,
> And I sunned it with my smiles,
> And with soft deceitful wiles.
>
> And it grew both day and night,
> Till it bore an apple bright.
> And my foe beheld it shine,
> And he knew that it was mine,
>
> And into my garden stole
> When the night had veiled the pole.
> In the morning glad I see
> My foe outstretched beneath the tree.[9]

There are two extremes when it comes to anger, either suppressing it or expressing it, either burying it deep inside or letting it all out. Neither extreme is healthy.[10] Both Judaism and Christianity teach that nothing is wrong with strong emotion (as some forms of Buddhism and Stoicism claim), but that it must be handled with care. So Paul writes to the Ephesians: "Be angry but do not sin; do not let the sun go down on your anger, and do not make room for the devil" (Eph. 4:26–7). In that earlier incident from Luke, Jesus doesn't seem particularly disturbed by Martha's outburst; instead he urges her to seek the higher path.

The fourth-century Christian apologist Lactantius wrote a treatise "The Wrath of God," in which he attacked Epicureans (and, to a lesser extent, Stoics) who believed that God was emotionless. "Activity and anxiety, anger and kindness are not in harmony" with divinity, Epicurus had argued.[11] Lactantius insisted, however, that a righteous God does reward good and punish evil. He is not some tranquil, philosophical *summum bonum,* but an active agent in history, who grows perturbed by sin, becomes upset by injustice, and is ever anxious to realize his goals.[12] While the incarnation shows the lengths to which his love will go, the resurrection proclaims that his purposes won't be thwarted.

Anger, says Aristotle, is like a dog who "barks if there is but a knock at the door, before looking to see if it is a friend."[13] It's been said that if a person could actually see himself when he becomes angry—with swollen veins, eyes popping out, and distorted facial features—next time he might think twice about flying off the handle.[14] On such occasions, Plutarch thought it would be useful if a companion handed over a mirror.[15] The Latin poet Horace described anger as "a brief madness."[16] In truth, we do somewhat resemble those archaic representations of the Furies—with their fiery eyes, serpents entangled in their hair, and bearing torches and whips with which to torture their victims.[17]

When angry, our first response should be restraint. Count to ten (or recite the letters of the alphabet like Caesar Augustus[18]), walk around the block, listen to soothing music like Seneca,[19] or let off steam in a nonconfrontational manner. A few have even suggested that we go into our room and scream.[20] Sometimes we just need to recognize that we're tired and are having a bad day. I've found that a good night's sleep can do wonders in helping put things in perspective.

Lincoln's secretary of war, Edwin Stanton, was known for his short fuse. "Once, when he complained to Lincoln about a certain general," as the story goes, "Lincoln told him to write the man a letter. 'Tell him off,' Lincoln advised. Stanton, bolstered by the president's support, promptly wrote a scathing letter in which he tore the man to shreds. He showed the letter to the president. 'Good,' said Lincoln, 'first rate. You certainly gave it to him.' As Stanton started to leave, Lincoln asked, 'What are you going to do with it now?' 'Mail it, of course,' said Stanton. 'Nonsense,' snorted the President. 'You don't want to send that letter. Put it in the stove! That's what I do when I have written a letter while I am angry. You had a good time writing that letter. Now write another."[21] In the same manner, Gandhi, that great modern exponent of nonviolence, recommended that his grandson keep an "anger journal" to pour his frustrations into until he figured out a more constructive response.[22]

Or we can deflect anger with humor. Socrates, that Athenian gadfly, who loved to call into question his fellow citizens' beliefs, once received a box on the ear for his rudeness. His response? It's a fine state of affairs, he said, when a man going for a walk, can't tell whether he needs to wear a helmet or not.[23] In the fundamentalist-modernist controversy surrounding the Scopes trial in the 1920s, one North Carolina clergyman remarked, "Take a jackass, a hog and a skunk and tie them together and you have a scientific evolutionist or a Modernist." H. L. Mencken, a leader in the countercharge, called fundamentalist ministers "shamans," "one-horse Popes," and "amateur Messiahs," whose "childish theology" was "cunningly rolled in sugar and rammed down unsuspecting throats."[24] The world can always use a new Voltaire, who by subjecting the characters in *Candide* to all manner of outrages and abuses made it painfully obvious how shallow was Leibniz's philosophy that "this is the best of all possible worlds."

But humor can also be too cutting, too aggressive, as when you wish someone were dead. A fierce attack was made on writer Edmond de Goncourt in *Figaro* by Maurice Talmeyr, who ended the piece by calling for the formation of a funeral committee. It was this same Talmeyr, de Goncourt suspected, who, earlier in *La Plume,* had expressed sorrow whenever a hearse passed him on the street, not to see the fiction writer Alphonse Daudet inside.[25] But Talmeyr, so adept at insults, may here have stepped over the line into vitriolic abuse. The Christian, it seems to me, would be better served by following the recommendation of Erasmus in his preface to *Praise of Folly*: "I have not only refrained from naming anyone but have also moderated my style so that the sensible reader will easily understand that my intention was to give pleasure, not pain."[26]

Next, one must decide if one's anger's justified. Couldn't I just buy a new tie if food was spilled on this one? If one child likes to do task X, and the other likes to do task Y, couldn't we just swap their duties? Even the teenage Anne Frank could write in her diary concerning Mr. Dussel: "For one fleeting moment I thought, 'Him and his lies. I'll smack his ugly mug so hard he'll go bouncing off the wall!' But the next moment I thought, 'Calm down, he's not worth getting so upset about!'"[27] Then a few weeks later, she writes at the bottom of another entry: "P.S. Will the reader please take into consideration that this story was written before the writer's fury had cooled?"[28]

Perhaps our petty irritations need to be handled in a similar manner. If they aren't, we run the risk of becoming known for our touchiness. Kenkō, a fourteenth-century Japanese essayist, mentions the story of Ryōgaku, a Buddhist priest who had a reputation for a bad temper. Since a large nettle tree stood next to the monastery, people began calling him "Nettle Tree High Priest." "'That name is outrageous,'" he said, and cut down the tree. The stump still being left, people referred to him as the Stump High Priest. More furious than ever, Ryōgaku had the stump dug up and thrown away, but this left a big ditch." So what did people do but tag him "Ditch High Priest"?[29] Our nicknames are hard to break if our behav ior never changes. Bacon (echoing Virgil) pleads with us not to be like the bees, whose signature is the sting they leave behind.[30]

Prolonged conflict often takes place between two people of different temperaments. One wants to get things done early; the other likes to wait till the last minute. One is eager to socialize; the other thinks polite conversation is a cross to bear. One likes to think things through and make long lists of pluses and minuses; the other just says, "Let's do it!" The extrovert misunderstands the introvert, the intuitive the rational, as Carl Jung methodically delineates in his landmark study *Psychological Types*. This is typical of marriage, where opposites attract. I know it came as a bit of a revelation in my own starry-eyed newlywed days. Yet part of this daily "having it out" shows how much each spouse wants to invest in the marriage to make it work as they tentatively move toward a future both have helped to shape.[31] In such an intimate relationship, the deepest wounds are likely to be inflicted, as each side knows the other's soft underbelly and lunges straight for it in an unguarded moment.

We need to talk things out frankly, tactfully, and in private, as Jesus recommends in Matthew 18:15: "If another member of the church sins against you, go and point out the fault when the two of you are alone. If the member listens to you, you have regained that one." By confronting the one who injured us, we may learn what bothers him and how we helped to provoke the incident, and we might conceivably hear an apology. If possible, (and I have trouble with this!) avoid hyperbole and name-calling. Achilles didn't help his cause when he referred to his commander Agamemnon as "a drunkard, with eyes like a bitch and heart like a fawn! You never arm yourself with your men for battle, you never go out on a raid with the fighting men," et cetera.[32] How much better to heed that ancient Hebrew proverb, "A soft answer turns away wrath, but a harsh word stirs up anger" (Prov. 15:1).

Don't avoid conflict or your anger will fester into a lifelong grudge as William Blake made plain in his poem, "A Poison Tree." Yet we must learn to lower our rhetoric or it will surely escalate from words to blows, harangues to violence, as we see our society plagued with cases of spouse-battering and child abuse. Terrorists blow up innocent victims in a foreign embassy or an airplane, believing in their twisted minds that these acts make strong political statements when, in effect, they are cowardly deeds done by those unable or unwilling to confront their opponents face-to-face. If we don't take appropriate steps, we'll end up like that imaginary world Gulliver stumbled into during his travels, where people were actually declaring war over which end of an egg should be broken first—the big or the small.[33]

Such tactics, however, are about as effective as what psychologist G. Stanley

Hall, in the first modern scientific study of anger in 1899, could have labeled the "Stupid Inanimate Object." "Our returns abound," writes Hall, "in cases of pens angrily broken because they would not write, brushes and pencils thrown that did not work well, buttonholes and clothes torn, mirrors smashed, slates broken, paper crushed, toys destroyed, knives, shoes, books thrown." When inanimate objects don't behave as they ought to, we try to show them who's boss. More likely, though, if we kick the vending machine that swallowed our money, we end up with a bruised toe.[34]

Instead of hurling objects or annihilating innocent civilians, it would be better to hear the other side out, always taking their self-esteem into account. It may even be acceptable to let them show disgust, snarl, and make menacing motions, yet not to follow through on their threats. A painting by Velázquez depicts the surrender of the Dutch to the Spanish after the battle of Breda in 1625. The Spanish commander puts his hand on the shoulder of the Dutch commander, who is offering him the keys to the city. Via this gesture, Spinola graciously acknowledges the dignity of his opponent, in effect, saying, on a different day perhaps I would be in your place.[35]

Also, we just can't let ourselves get worked up over each and every slight. "A man must swallow a toad every morning," the French aphorist Chamfort allows, "if he wishes to be sure of finding nothing still more disgusting before the day is over."[36] It's pointless to become overwrought, Stoic philosopher Marcus Aurelius insisted, since people "will go on doing the same things no less even if you burst yourself with anger."[37] Sinners are not demons, but everyday people like you and me, perhaps temporarily blinded by some *idée fixe,* yet God may still open their eyes.[38]

The church of late antiquity had a stern rite of reconciliation for those who had committed severe offenses. According to Greenacre and Haselock, the penitents were to prostrate themselves *cum lacrymis* (with tears) on the pavement of the church while the bishop put ashes on their foreheads. They were then clothed with sackcloth and asked to prostrate themselves once more while the entire assembly recited the seven penitential psalms and accompanying litanies. After preaching on Adam's expulsion from paradise, the bishop ejected the penitents from the church. As they knelt outside, he exhorted them "not to despair of the Lord's mercy but to devote themselves to fasting, to prayers, to pilgrimages, to almsgiving and to other good works, so that the Lord may lead them to the worthy fruit of true repentance."[39] Then the church doors were solemnly closed.

Perhaps the most famous use of this rite was when Ambrose, the bishop of Milan, confronted Emperor Theodosius for retaliating with excessive force against a riot in Salonica. Apparently a mob of chariot race fanciers had murdered and mutilated several of his military officers, including the commander, after one of the crowd's favorite drivers had been arrested and imprisoned on charges of homosexual rape. Enraged, Theodosius secretly ordered retaliation. During a subsequent chariot race, the new garrison closed the gates of the hippodrome and for several hours indiscriminately butchered seven thousand spectators. By the time Theodosius had simmered down enough to rescind his order, it was too late. So Ambrose wrote a letter to Theodosius, refusing him Holy Communion until he had done public penance. "You are a man," he wrote, "and temptation has come to you: conquer it. . . . Sin is only taken away by tears and penitence." Thus during the last months of A.D. 390, the empire witnessed the extraordinary spectacle of the ever-victorious, sacred eternal Augustus, lord of the world putting aside his royal garments in order to weep and moan like an ordinary penitent at the cathedral before being finally restored at Christmas. It was a great victory for human decency, made possible by a fearless church leader and a genuinely contrite church member.[40]

If the world seems so out of whack that we are tempted toward violence, we should remember that God is still on the throne. "Beloved," announced the apostle Paul, "never avenge yourselves, but leave room for the wrath of God; for it is written 'Vengeance is mine, I will repay, says the Lord'" (Rom. 12:19). Evil may triumph for a season, but there is a coming day of reckoning. Meanwhile, we should forgive, considering all that God has done for us. And I mean genuine forgiveness, not the kind that secretly harbors hurt. "I have the most kindly temperament," allowed nineteenth-century German poet Heinrich Heine. "My wants are modest—a hut, a thatched roof, but a good bed, good food, milk and butter, all very fresh; flowers at my window, a few beautiful trees at my door. And if the good Lord wants to make me quite happy he will give me the pleasure of seeing some six or seven of my enemies strung up on them. With all my heart I shall forgive them, before their death, all the evil they have committed against me while I was alive. Yes, one should always forgive one's enemies—but not until they are hanged."[41]

"Nothing keeps so well as a decoction of spleen,"[42] English essayist William Hazlitt once observed. There's a certain tit-for-tat mentality in the back of our minds, which my grandfather used to characterize as "When someone's down, stomp on him." Sufi poet Sa'di relates how smoldering rage can wait for just the appropriate moment to wreak revenge. A soldier, abusing his authority, hit a dervish on the head with a stone (which the dervish kept). Later, when circumstances changed and the king had the soldier imprisoned in a well, the dervish dropped that same stone on the man's head. The soldier yelled up, "Who art thou, and why hast thou hit my head with this stone?" To which the dervish replied, "I am the same person whom thou hast struck on the head with this stone on such and such a day." The soldier wondered, "Where hast thou been all this time?" "I was afraid of thy dignity," the dervish called back, "but now when I beheld thee in the well I made use of the opportunity."[43] As Christians, though, it would be much better if we were reciting the *Agnus Dei,* just as the wrathful are in Dante's purgatory: "Lamb of God, who takes away the sins of the world, have mercy on us."[44]

Walter Raleigh, who had seen many an injustice in the courtroom, longed for a future, impartial assize in his poem "The Passionate Mans Pilgrimage":

> From thence to heavens Bribeles hall
> Where no corrupted voyces brall,
> No Conscience molten into gold,
> Nor forg'd accusers bought and sold,
> No cause deferd, nor vaine spent Journey,
> For there Christ is the Kings Atturney:
> Who pleades for all without degrees,
> And he hath Angells, but no fees.[45]

We can declare as Luther did at the Diet of Worms in 1521, "Here I stand, I cannot do otherwise";[46] or defend the law like Thomas More, even if the king himself is making a mockery of it; or be an agitator against social evil like William Wilberforce in his campaign against slavery in nineteenth-century England; or be willing to offer up our own life like that fourth-century monk Telemachus, who rushed into the arena to separate the gladiators, only to be stoned to death by the enraged spectators. (Yet it was his martyrdom, according to legend, that led Emperor Honorius to abolish the combats.)

Or we can simply assert the truth, like that courageous Soviet dissident Aleksandr Solzhenitsyn, whose unremitting exposé of the system of labor camps and prisons in the gulag archipelago from 1918 to 1956, based on his own experiences and the "reports, memoirs, and letters by 227 witnesses," unveiled the horrid excesses of atheistic communism to a shocked, disbelieving world. "In this book," he wrote, "there are no fictitious persons, nor fictitious events. People and places are named with their own names."[47]

But far, far more likely our anger is like Martha's frustration, "Lord, do you not care that my sister has left me to do all the work by myself?" (Luke 10:40). Then, according to Thomas à Kempis, we need a dollop of humility: "Be not angry that you cannot make others as you wish them to be, since you cannot make yourself as you wish to be."[48] Or we could use a tincture of patience, as eighteenth-century poet William Cowper calls for in "Mutual Forbearance":

> The kindest and the happiest pair
> Will find occasion to forbear;
> And something, ev'ry day they live,
> To pity, and, perhaps, forgive.[49]

In his short story "God Sees the Truth but Waits," Tolstoy tells of a man who was wrongly convicted of robbing and killing a merchant. He was flogged then sent to Siberia. There he made boots, read the lessons, and sang in the prison church, gradually becoming known for his meekness and fairness. Twenty-six years later, a new convict was brought into camp; from certain remarks he makes, it dawned on Aksyonof that here might be the fellow who actually committed the murder. One night Aksyonof noticed dirt being pushed out of the barracks; he recognized his enemy. The next day, when the guards uncovered the tunnel and sought to find who dug it, Aksyonof, after weighing the matter carefully, decided not to rat on Semyonitch. Yet this act of pity so affected the other convict that he secretly came and admitted that he was the man who had murdered the merchant and put the bloody knife in Aksyonof's belongings, and was now begging for his forgiveness. Together they wept. At last Aksyonof announced, "God will forgive you! . . . Maybe I am a hundred times worse than you."[50]

I say, let Jesus be our primer, who, although he was wrongly executed, while on the cross prayed, "Father, forgive them; for they do not know what they are doing" (Luke 23:34). If only we could heed that admonition from Thomas Browne: "Let not the Sun . . . go down upon thy wrath, but write thy wrongs in Ashes. Draw the Curtain of night upon injuries, shut them up in the Tower of Oblivion and let them be as though they had not been."[51] Dag Hammarskjöld, who had seen much international strife and conflict in his years as secretary-general of the U.N., came to believe that "forgiveness breaks the chain of causality because he who 'forgives' you—out of love—takes upon himself the consequences of what *you* have done."[52]

In sixteenth-century England, when lord chancellor Thomas More refused to subscribe to the Act of Supremacy making King Henry VIII head of the Church of England, More was sentenced to death for treason. Yet, in his son-in-law's account, More, that "angelical wit" and man of "clear, unspotted conscience," told the court which had condemned him, "I verily trust, and shall therefore right heartily pray, that though your lordships have now here in earth been judges to my condemnation, we may yet hereafter in heaven merrily all meet together, to our everlasting salvation."[53] We are simply awestruck by More's generosity of spirit—to anticipate a future reunion with those now arrayed against him.

Since an essay can reveal more about its author than one would like, then I confess I, too, have much to learn in the school of Christ on anger. Here's a prayer I would like to make my own from the Christian author /activist who fought so hard against apartheid in South Africa, Alan Paton: "Take all hate from my heart,

O God, and teach me how to take it from the hearts of others. Open my eyes and show me what things in our society make it easy for hatred to flourish and hard for us to conquer it. Then help me to try to change these things. And so open my eyes and my ears that I may this coming day be able to do some work of peace for Thee."[54] Amen.

CHAPTER 8

Violence Begets More Violence

We live in a violent world. Men beat their wives (or girlfriends), women abuse children, children torment fellow classmates. Employees assault their bosses. We hear of far too many instances of kidnapping, rape, and murder. Terrorists release poisonous gas in subways or plant bombs in high-rise towers. Authoritarian regimes torture dissidents. Police brutalize suspects they've arrested. Furthermore, it seems to be an axiom that access to weapons only multiplies the damage incurred. And all these are but small-scale spectacles compared to the mayhem unleashed in war, when whole villages are burned down and ethnic groups are rounded up and put in internment camps—as the fatalities and suffering among both combatants and civilians go right off the charts. That thirteenth-century Mongol conqueror, Genghis Khan, who ruled one of the largest land empires in world history, is alleged to have said, "Man's highest joy is in victory: to conquer one's enemies, to pursue them, to deprive them of their possessions, to make their beloved weep, to ride on their horses, and to embrace their wives and daughters."[1]

Yet, for Christians, can violence ever be justified? While it's true that theologians have formulated narrow theories of just war that allow one nation to rise up against another for specified reasons to pursue limited objectives, while adhering to strict guidelines on how campaigns should be waged, they have yet to agree on a common rationale that allows one individual to inflict injury against another except in self-defense. Indeed when a follower of Jesus, eager to defend him from unlawful arrest, cut off the ear of the high priest's slave, Jesus rebuked the man with that powerful maxim, "all who take the sword will perish by the sword" (Matt. 26:52).

It's the old story—violence begets more violence. Today we see the results in such political "hot spots" as Northern Ireland, the Balkans, Israel, and the Indian/Pakistani border, where decades of ethnic and religious violence have bred cultures of almost unremitting vendettas. Incendiaries on either side, indoctrinated in their own version of the past, react to each fresh atrocity with a rapid counter-reprisal. In these locations world organizations like the United Nations vigorously seek to halt the spread of nuclear weapons, lest one accidental or premeditated strike engulf the whole world in chaos. The same dysfunctional pattern can be seen in cases of domestic violence, frequently perpetrated by parents who themselves were abused as children.

What causes ordinary short-term anger, often arising from a specific incident or insult, to spiral out of control into reckless violence? Sometimes a certain personality type is too thin-skinned, too easily provoked. One clear-cut example is the Renaissance goldsmith and sculptor, Benvenuto Cellini. His autobiography is filled with contention. By the age of sixteen, he was banished from Florence for taking part in a brawl. A few years later he committed murder to avenge his brother's death. Always the braggart, always the daredevil, even his artistic skills seemed a sublimated form of combat. Life to him was either a battle or a banquet, and either could serve the purposes of advancement.[2] Once while demonstrating his marksmanship defending the Castel Sant' Angelo, he fired a shot that split a Spanish soldier in two. Flabbergasted, Pope Clement VII sent for him to explain what had happened, then absolved Cellini of all homicides, past and future, committed in the service of the church.[3] Invariably the hero of all his tales, whether it was as the most outrageous prankster at a party or the greatest escape artist from prison, he had a hard time giving credit or praise to others. His sharp tongue could end friendships instantly. A jealous lover, he caused rivals to feel the sting of his distemper. And, as might be expected of one who constantly dwells on personal slights and injuries, Cellini perceived plots against himself at almost every turn.

In addition to personality types prone to violence, there are those who imagine war to be a way to achieve personal glory. In *The Book of the Courtier,* that arbiter of Renaissance aristocratic mores, Castiglione, remarks, "I hold that the principal and true profession of the Courtier must be that of arms; which I wish him to exercise with vigor; and let him be known among the others as bold, energetic, and faithful to whomever he serves. . . . [The more our Courtier excels in this art, the more will he merit praise."[4] This is the portrait of a resourceful warrior capable of doing in an opponent from numerous angles. Such were the humanist ideals found at the court of the Duke of Urbino, typical of masculine sentiments throughout the ages.

Yet battle often is not glamorous, as those early twentieth-century idealists who fought in that "war to end all wars," soon found out. Some were so horrified at the prospect of hurting another that they weren't able to shoot. Others fell victim to confusion in the ranks, so-called "friendly fire." A number had to return home with debilitating psychological traumas. On the battlefield, courage often proved not to be as critical as technological superiority or topographical advantage. Soldiering could mean days of drudgery, marching from one nondescript location to another or scrambling about in endless trenches.

Wilfred Owen, who was a company commander in the Artists' Rifles, captured the inglorious moments in these lines:

> Rain, guttering down in waterfalls of slime
> Kept slush waist-high, and rising hour by hour. . . .
> Gas! Gas! Quick, boys!—An ecstasy of fumbling,
> Fitting the clumsy helmets just in time. . . .
> And saw a sad land, weak with sweats of dearth,
> Gray, cratered like the moon with hollow woe. . . .
> Across its beard, that horror of harsh wire,
> There moved thin caterpillars, slowly uncoiled. . . .
> The shrill, demented choirs of wailing shells. . . .
> Foreheads of men have bled where no wounds were. . . .
> What passing-bells for these who die as cattle?
> —Only the monstrous anger of the guns.[5]

As is often the case, political leaders determined the outcome, since the military campaigns themselves were indecisive, but the peace treaty of Versailles proved so harshly punitive, it's often been cited as a cause for World War II.

There are also those revolutionaries who can rationalize even the most sadistic attacks against the state. British statesman Edmund Burke strongly opposed their views in his *Reflections on the Revolution in France*. Although an ardent supporter of the grievances of the American colonies against George III and a defender of the Glorious Revolution of 1688, which granted Parliament authority over the king, he nevertheless felt the French had gone too far. He complained that they "despise experience" and "will blow up, at one grand explosion, all examples of antiquity, all precedents, charters, and acts of parliament,"[6] as if history could begin again at year 1. By destroying the good, the bad, and the indifferent, they failed to perceive how crucial were those great social institutions that had been formed incrementally over centuries by means of trial and error, continuous give-and-take. If such institutions falter, Burke strongly advocated reform, but he thought sweeping innovation a risky business since far too many lives were at stake.[7]

Such revolutionaries were passionate about such abstract principles as "liberty, equality, and fraternity," yet not concerned enough about the concrete, everyday problems of individuals. These ideologues, Burke believed, loved mankind dearly but could not abide men.[8] They didn't recognize that human passions were the driving forces of society and, as such, couldn't be rooted out simply by changing leaders or by setting up another form of government.[9] In many ways history has proven Burke's analysis correct. The French Revolution did fall prey to an unquenchable guillotine, mob rule, and a reign of terror in which Robespierre triumphed over the moderate forces of the Girondists, followed later by that romantic hero Napoleon, whose conquest of Europe reshaped the political contours of the modern world. It took France decades to recover from its own excesses.

I know perhaps the scariest levels of intolerance I've ever encountered were when I attended the University of Iowa during the Vietnam War era. The campus radicals were so insistent that they knew what was right, that they saw little point in holding roundtable discussions in order to hear differing viewpoints, but would seize the podium and shout down opponents. Students who didn't agree couldn't even be allowed to peaceably attend class. The radicals were so fixated on America's involvement in what they considered to be an atrocity that everything else paled in significance. To vent their spleen, they would break into downtown stores and loot local merchants. The temporary building where rhetoric classes were being held was burned down. As the spring weather warmed up, clashes with police escalated. Eventually the administration had no choice but to close the school early.

A revolutionary fervor exists also among the paramilitary groups of our own day, who have swallowed conspiracy theories whole. Often drawn from those who are hurting, insecure, or marginalized by society, impotent before staggering economic and social complexities, the members form small, intense bands seemingly bent on finding a scapegoat for their personal quandaries. Meeting in secret, they fulminate against outsiders in harsh apocalyptic "us and them" terms, disassociating themselves from the worldview of their contemporaries.[10] It's not surprising, therefore, that such a subculture breeds a Timothy McVeigh, who can blow up the federal building in Oklahoma City, killing 168 people (including 19 children in a second-floor day-care center), and injuring approximately 600 others in one of the worst acts of domestic terrorism in U.S. history.[11] Through a tortured, bizarre logic, he had perhaps convinced himself that innocent office workers were somehow paying the price for the FBI's mishandling of Waco, where more than eighty Branch Davidians and cult leader David Koresh had set fire to themselves and their compound rather than be taken alive by federal agents.[12]

Such acts of terrorism make about as much sense as the haphazard revenge of the Nazis during World War II. "If a telephone wire was cut or a railway line displaced," notes historian Mark Arnold-Forster, "the Germans would simply arrest the first 100 people they could find as hostages. They were prepared to kill them. . . . German reprisals were ruthless, swift, and did not even pretend to punish the guilty. Anyone would do. . . . In France they burnt the entire population of Oradour-sur-Glane in the village church as punishment for an act of sabotage which had been committed somewhere else. . . . There is strong evidence that the people of Oradour-sur-Glane were burnt by mistake. The Germans had intended to massacre the inhabitants of another village with a similar name. But they lost their way."[13] The landscape of unbridled hate is littered with countless futile tragedies.

Yet sometimes the so-called good citizens of the community take the law into their own hands and commit lynchings and burnings. In Walter Van Tilburg Clark's novel *The Ox-Bow Incident,* an excited youth passes on a rumor that a popular rancher has been murdered and his cattle stolen. Eventually an angry mob of townspeople decide they can't wait for the sheriff for fear that the desperadoes will get away, so they form a makeshift posse. Riding long and hard, they discover three strangers and a herd of steers near an oxbow in the river. The strangers claim that they had paid for their cattle that morning and don't know anything about a murder. Despite their repeated pleas of innocence, the mob casts a guilty verdict, except for five who vote that they be turned over to the courts. The strangers are summarily hung. Then, as the vigilantes return to town, they meet the sheriff and the rancher whom they believed had been killed. It turns out that the strangers had been telling the truth all along and the men they had lynched had nothing to do with the rustling.[14]

Crowds, as such, are more irrational and more easily exploited than individuals. "Because the participants in a crowd are all on one level," observes Kingsley Davis, "because their attention is focused on one thing, because their inhibited impulses find ready release in spontaneous action, the crowd is highly suggestible. The participants react to one another's gestures, postures and cries in an almost automatic animal-like way, with a swiftness that precludes thoughtful interpretation or rational foresight."[15] Elias Canetti calls an event that sets off the crowd a "discharge," then points to their fascination with noise and brightness, the sound of breaking glass, and setting fires.[16] Scarcely able to "distinguish between the subjective and objective," the crowd, says sociologist Gustav Le Bon, "accepts as real the images evoked in its mind, though they most often have only a very distant relation with observed fact,"[17] hence the mob's willingness to take rumor for reality. Lacking restraint, the crowd brooks neither moderation nor delay.[18]

Violence insists on taking a short cut to "justice." Devil may care, it never knows for sure how the other side will react, yet pursues its agenda with frightful abandon. German romantic Heinrich von Kleist tells the story of a horse trader, Michael Kohlhaas, who the world "would have had every reason to bless . . . if he had not carried one virtue to excess. But his sense of justice turned him into a brigand and a murderer."[19] His horses had been mistreated by an aristocrat; when his attempts at satisfaction were rebuffed, he took the law into his own hands, quickly attracting around him a band of riffraff and opportunists who terrorized the countryside, wronging others hundreds of times more than he had been wronged.

Yet by committing violence, we ourselves are changed, as the line between good and evil blurs, and we start to resemble our enemy. "The end cannot justify the means," states Aldous Huxley, "for the simple and obvious reason that the means employed determine the nature of the ends produced."[20] If our enemy tortures captives and we do, too, how are we much different? If he resorts to chemical and biological weapons, and so do we, perhaps our victory will be hollow, for our hands, too, have been stained.

The church has not always heeded this lesson. "The theologian may indulge the pleasing task of describing Religion as she descended from Heaven, arrayed in her native purity," Edward Gibbon wryly comments. "A more melancholy duty is is imposed on the historian. He must discover the inevitable mixture of error and corruption, which she contracted in a long residence upon earth, among a weak and degenerate race of beings."[21] Some portions of the past even the ardent apologist cannot gloss over.

Think of the fundamental ambiguity of holy war. The dubious initiative of Pope Urban II in 1095, which became known as the crusades, affected millions of people over several hundred years. Military orders like the knights of the Templars and Hospitallers were founded; indulgences were granted to those who fought, while those who died in the recovery of the Holy Land were considered martyrs. "Fly then to arms," inveighed Bernard of Clairvaux at the start of the second crusade, "let a holy rage animate you in the fight, and let the Christian world resound with these words of the prophet, 'Cursed he be who does not stain his sword with blood!'"[22] When the first crusade climaxed with the fall of Jerusalem in 1099, the soldiers, in a terrible orgy, massacred men, women, and children, even burning alive the nonpartisan Jewish community who had gathered for refuge in the main synagogue. Eyewitness Fulcher of Chartres spoke of nearly ten thousand who had been beheaded in the Temple of Solomon, adding, "If you had been there your feet would have been stained to the ankles in the blood of the slain."[23] William of Tyre wrote, "Everywhere lay fragments of human bodies. . . . [T]he spectacle of the headless bodies and mutilated limbs strewn in all directions roused horror in all who looked upon them."[24] The brutality of the Christian troops so incensed Muslims that relations between the two faiths were strained for generations. Then, in a revealing act of hypocrisy, Pope Innocent III treated the fourth crusade's sacking and looting of Constantinople, thus decimating his Orthodox rival, as a way to unite Christendom. The crusaders appear as if straight out of Spenser's portrait of Wrath: "And in his hand a burning brond he hath, / The which he brandisheth about his hed; / His eyes did hurle forth sparkles fiery red, / And stared sterne on all, that him beheld. / . . . His ruffin raiment all was staind with blood."[25]

The word *crusade* itself seems a misnomer, almost a parody, when we recall that the etymology is linked to the cross, and thus Jesus' own death in agony. In one of George Orwell's best-known essays, "Politics and the English Language," he speaks of those euphemisms governments resort to for papering over their crimes. "Defenceless villages are bombarded from the air, the inhabitants driven out into the countryside, the cattle machine-gunned, the huts set on fire with incendiary bullets: this is called *pacification*. Millions of peasants are robbed of their farms and sent trudging along the roads with no more than they can carry: this is called *transfer of population* or *rectification of frontiers*. People are imprisoned for years without trial, or shot in the back of the neck or sent to die of scurvy in Arctic lumber camps: this is called *elimination of unreliable elements*."[26] Disingenuous language exposes the author's insincerity. "When there is a gap between one's real and one's declared aims," Orwell pointed out, "one turns as it were instinctively to long words and exhausted idioms, like a cuttlefish squirting out ink."[27] In religious circles, we see such fundamental terms as *evangelism* or *conversion* redefined and uprooted from their original context in order to promote a particular political or social agenda. Occasionally groups, too, attempt to maintain their identity by publishing a misleading catalogue of "errors of one's opponents"; then, having indoctrinated their adherents, a seedbed is established, which extremists can cultivate for the purposes of recrimination and retaliation.[28]

Heretics have been punished by what Dante called the unholy alliance of sword and crook.[29] Think of the Spanish Inquisition, which Thomas Aquinas had helped sanction by arguing that heretics deserved not only excommunication but death for corrupting the soul,[30] or the St. Bartholomew's Day massacre on August 23, 1572, in which thousands of Protestants were treacherously murdered by the French government; afterward, the bells of St. Peter's pealed out, medals were struck, and Pope Gregory XIII summoned the eminent painter Vasari from Florence to celebrate the triumph in a series of frescoes.[31] Luther, too, felt, "Heretics are not to be disputed with, but to be condemned unheard."[32]

How could sincere Christians consent to the tortures so amply documented in *Foxe's Book of Martyrs*? Theodore Beza, Calvin's successor in Geneva, summed up much previous thinking when he declared religious freedom "a most diabolical dogma, because it means that everyone should be left to go to hell in his own way."[33] This traditional gloss, however, has been strongly questioned. Harvard psychologist William James considered such violent acts reflected instead, "that inborn hatred" of the "alien," "eccentric," and nonconformist; he concluded that "piety is the mask, the inner force is tribal instinct."[34] Evangelization, of course; persuasion, yes; but one should not resort to brute force. Samuel Butler has immortalized the flawed reasoning in his well-known couplet: "He that complies against his Will, / Is of his own opinion still."[35] How far from the parable where Jesus admonishes us not to separate the wheat from the tares until the end of the age, lest we inadvertently pull up the genuine article with the counterfeit (Matt. 13:24–30). Two men may outwardly appear the same, wrote Sufi mystic, Rumi, but one is a friend and the other is a foe, "for naught is what it seems of all things 'neath the sun."[36] In "One Foot in Eden," Scottish poet Edwin Muir imagines, "Nothing now can separate / The corn and tares compactly grown. / . . . Evil and good stand thick around / In the fields of charity and sin."[37] Absolute purity, it seems, must await celestial discernment.

When confronted with aggression, animals respond in one of several ways. They may puff themselves up to scare off an opponent; make threatening gestures; cede some territory, but not all; or adopt a submissive posture to inhibit further aggression. I'm not saying that we should acquiesce before violence as helpless victims, but we have fruitful alternatives. According to Indian lore, a dangerous cobra was ordered by a swami to stop biting worshipers on the way to the temple. Eventually, as people's fears subsided, the snake became something of a plaything that was tossed about and taken advantage of, even by the village children. When the swami saw the serpent again, he was shocked at its appearance and saddened by its story. He reminded the wounded creature that though it was not allowed to bite, it could certainly still hiss.[38]

Contrary to Machiavelli's dictum that skill in making war is the most important attribute to look for in a prince,[39] I say with Jesus, "Blessed are the peacemakers" (Matt. 5:9). We should encourage any who are gifted at the art of diplomacy. Able negotiators and mediators listen to each side's complaints, propose feasible solutions, then return time and again for additional input to fine-tune the settlement. By such means, long-lasting compromises can be reached and untold suffering prevented. People have been known to get worked up about rather minuscule points, which the Chinese call "three in the morning." What is meant by "three in the morning" you may ask? "In Sung there was a keeper of monkeys. Bad times came and he was obliged to tell them that they must reduce their ration of nuts. 'It will be three in the morning and four in the evening.' The monkeys were furious. 'Very well then,' he said, 'you shall have four in the morning and three in the evening.' The monkeys accepted with delight."[40] The issues between warring factions may not be so pronounced as they first appear; other times standoffs cannot be so easily resolved.

Another option for Christians is the one taken by Martin Luther King Jr., who through his civil rights campaigns became a master of nonviolent civil disobedience. Instead of meeting opponents kick for kick, beating for beating, firebombing for firebombing, he sought to arouse the conscience of the nation through protest rallies, economic boycotts, voters' rights marches, and peaceful sit-ins and demonstrations, deliberately choosing as the focus of a sustained effort Birmingham, Alabama, a city then considered the most flagrant segregationist stronghold in America, notorious for its police brutality and the myriad unsolved crimes against blacks on its books.[41] If the Southern Christian Leadership Conference could make steps toward racial equality there, what northern or southern city would not be the next to fall? In King's "Letter from Birmingham Jail," he recommends that the "one who breaks an unjust law must do so openly, lovingly. . . . [A]n individual who breaks a law that conscience tells him is unjust, and who willingly accepts the penalty of imprisonment in order to arouse the conscience of the community over its injustice, is in reality expressing the highest respect for law."[42] It goes without saying that American society is more integrated, more multiracial today because of the legacy of King and his associates' hard-fought, nonviolent battles.

The Book of Proverbs declares, "One who is slow to anger is better than the mighty, and one whose temper is controlled, than one who captures a city" (16:32). The great Roman commander Sertorius once gave a demonstration to his troops about the meaning of patience and perseverance. He brought in two horses, one strong and young, the other feeble and lean. He asked one of his most powerful soldiers to pull the hair off the tail of the feeble horse. Yet try as he might, grasping hard and pulling with both hands, nothing happened. Sertorious also asked one of his puniest soldiers to pull the hair off the tail of the larger horse, but doing so one hair at a time. It took a while, but this he was able to accomplish. "You see, fellow soldiers," Sertorious announced afterward, "that perseverance is more prevailing than violence, and that many things which cannot be overcome when they are together, yield themselves up when taken little by little. Assiduity and persistence are irresistible, and in time overthrow and destroy the greatest powers whatever. Time being the favorable friend and assistant of those who use their judgment to await his occasions, and the destructive enemy of those who are unreasonably urging and pressing forward."[43]

Change, for the most part, is gradual. "All government, indeed every human benefit and enjoyment, every virtue and every prudent act," Edmund Burke sets forth, "is founded on compromise and barter."[44] It's unrealistic to storm the Bastille today and think that tomorrow inequities will magically vanish. Instead, we should cultivate the virtue of patience, leaving the future in God's hands. And if we do violence to those around us, we usurp God's and society's roles as arbiter and judge. For peace isn't the absence of conflict; it simply means carrying the battle forward on a higher, more persevering level. As poet Paul Valéry advises:

> Patience, patience,
> Patience in the blue sky! . . .
> The glad surprise will come; . . .
> When we shall fall on our knees.[45]

Jean-Pierre de Caussade, an eighteenth-century Jesuit priest, gave a spiritual thrust to the doctrine of providence. He thought that all things in life come from the benevolent hand of God and he urged "abandonment." "Every moment we live through," he declared, "is like an ambassador who declares the will of God, and our hearts always utter their acceptance."[46] Not some passive resignation to "whatever will be, will be," this is an active cooperation in God's will as it is revealed in the people we meet and the circumstances that come our way. We should embrace all that we meet, de Caussade advocates, like bread to nourish us, soap to cleanse us, fire to purify us, and a chisel to shape us.[47] "Somebody placed the shuttle in your hand," Dag Hammarskjöld counsels, "somebody who had already arranged the threads."[48]

Scripture uses the metaphor of a farmer to depict our work in the Lord—sowing, watering, then patiently waiting for the harvest. Like Augustine, who penned *The City of God* partly to rebut those who felt the fall of the imperial city meant the end of God's purposes on earth, we should not grow weary or give up, though it appears that the world is going to hell in a handbasket. "If you see an eclipse," Muslim thinker Muhammed Abduh remarked, "let it remind you of God, and wait for the reappearance of the light."[49] Now what we see are haphazard pieces of a jigsaw puzzle, but in God's good time, we may yet come to perceive the overarching whole.

Meanwhile we should persevere in the manner suggested by Lincoln in his second inaugural address: "With malice toward none; with charity for all; with firmness in the right, as God gives us to see the right, let us strive on to finish the work we are in; to bind up the nation's wounds; to care for him who shall have borne the battle, and for his widow, and his orphan—to do all which may achieve and cherish a just, and a lasting peace, among ourselves, and all nations."[50] I say, carry on in this noble struggle.

CHAPTER 9

Avarice, the Gleaming Deception

Gold! Gold! Gold! Gold!
Bright and yellow, hard and cold,
Molten, graven, hammer'd, and roll'd;
Heavy to get, and light to hold;
Hoarded, barter'd, bought, and sold,
Stolen, borrow'd, squander'd, doled;
Spurn'd by the young, but hugg'd by the old
To the very verge of the churchyard mould;
Price of many a crime untold.[1]

This is the moral Thomas Hood drew in his long poem, "Miss Kilmansegg and her Precious Leg," a sad tale of the power of avarice or greed. "For the love of money," Paul wrote Timothy, echoing Hellenistic philosophers, "is a root of all kinds of evil" (1 Tim. 6:10). We think of such misers as Dickens's Ebenezer Scrooge, the surviving partner in a London lending firm, who is convinced that Christmas is a plot concocted by the working class to pick the pockets of their employers. He begrudges giving a paid holiday to his clerk, Bob Cratchit, and when his nephew invites him to a Christmas feast, he calls the holiday "humbug." To those who come collecting alms for the poor, he exclaims, "Are there no prisons? . . . And the Union workhouses? . . . Are they still in operation?"[2] Dickens describes him as "a squeezing, wrenching, grasping, scraping, clutching, covetous old sinner! Hard and sharp as flint, from which no steel had ever struck out generous fire, secret, and self-contained, and solitary as an oyster."[3]

An equally tightfisted fellow is the father in Balzac's *Eugénie Grandet*. Even though he's extremely wealthy, he puts his household on a short leash. No fires in the fireplace before November 1 or after March 31, no matter how cold it gets; accordingly, the women resort to carrying around a small brazier to take off the chill during April and October. He doles out each one's quota of candles just as he does daily rations of bread and other provisions.[4] And although his brother commits suicide due to impending bankruptcy, instead of lifting a finger to help, Monsieur Grandet casts off the now penniless nephew to the New World to fend for himself. Maybe "you can't take it with you," but with misers of this sort, you're not likely to lay hold of much of it either, at least while they're alive.

At the opposite end of the spectrum is the spendthrift, who obscenely disposes of his money like Jay Gatsby in F. Scott Fitzgerald's novel. Gatsby was known for the lavish parties given at his Long Island home built in imitation of the Hôtel de Ville in Normandy; there he had a marble swimming pool and a forty-acre estate of lawns and gardens.[5] Spendthrifts crave attention, resorting to such extravagant gestures as building a humongous mansion, marrying a glamorous spouse, dining on gourmet food, and vacationing in exotic locales. Economist Thorstein Veblen skewered this lifestyle in early twentieth-century America, coining the term "conspicuous consumption." Business tycoons looted Old World arts and crafts (e.g., paintings, tapestries, china, furniture) to decorate their lodgings, partly to make it appear that the conniving manipulators had turned into discriminating connoisseurs of culture. Or they indulged in such outlandish stunts as giving a party for their dog and presenting it with a diamond collar, or wrapping their cigarettes with hundred-dollar bills to inhale the wealth.[6]

In ancient Rome, the novelist Petronius, too, satirized extravagance with his description of "Trimalchio's dinner." While the guests were gorging themselves, the host sat gaudily dressed in gold armlets and ivory circlets. The first dish brought in had his own name prominently inscribed alongside the exact weight in silver. A later tray was arranged around the twelve signs of the zodiac—with beef steak near Taurus the bull; an African fig near Leo the lion; a balance containing a tart on one pan and a cake in the other near Libra; a lobster near Scorpio; and so on. Then Trimalchio's servants brought in a stuffed boar, which a carver proceeded to cut open; out flew a flock of thrushes, which fowlers stationed around the room caught with limed reeds. The wine was that Roman favorite, old Falernian, aged one hundred years! And, of course, to clean his teeth, Trimalchio pulled out his silver toothpick.[7]

Greed, like a yawning mouth, is never quite satisfied. In a Tolstoy fable, there's a country of nomads where a man is allowed to own as much land as he can walk around in a single day for the price of a thousand rubles, provided that he returns to the starting point before sunfall. So, shelling out his money, Pakhom paces off the distance he had envisioned for his first turn; then, upon making his quota for the second side, he notices a well-watered hollow he simply *must* include. Finally, starting to tire, he goes only two miles on his third leg, when, as the sun begins to sink, he makes a run for it lest he lose everything. Huffing and puffing back just in time, he collapses at the chief Bashkir's feet, dead, probably from a heart attack. The answer to the fable's question "How much land does a man need?" is rather straightforward—enough to bury him in.[8] It's not an uncommon lot for those consumed with acquisitiveness; workaholics still succumb.

Gulliver, in Swift's best-known satire, describes imperialism's acquisitiveness in these words: "For instance, a crew of pirates are driven by a storm they know not whither; at length a boy discovers land from the topmast; they go on shore to rob and plunder; they see an harmless people, are entertained with kindness, they give the country a new name, they take formal possession of it for their king, they set up a rotten plank or a stone for a memorial, they murder two or three dozen of the natives, bring away a couple more by force for a sample, re-turn home." Afterward, more ships are sent and "the natives driven out or de-stroyed, their princes tortured to discover their gold; a free licence given to all acts of inhumanity and lust." And wouldn't you know it? "This execrable crew of butchers employed in so pious an expedition, is a *modern colony* sent to convert and civilize an idolatrous and barbarous people."[9] At the high tide of Western imperialism in the 1930s, it was estimated that perhaps 80–85 percent of the land surface of the globe had been a colony of a European power, with those few holdouts being parts of Arabia, Persia, Afghanistan, Mongolia, Tibet, China, Siam, and Japan.[10]

At some point one must ask this indelicate question, "How were your riches ob-tained?" The Greek philosopher Plato ventured, "To be at once exceedingly wealthy and good is impossible."[11] In *The Devil's Dictionary*, Ambrose Bierce defines "hand" as "a singular instrument worn at the end of a human arm and commonly thrust into somebody's pocket."[12] In our day we've witnessed the savings-and-loan debacle, where investors who hoped to cash in on interest rates several points above going market value ended up being swindled by overly optimistic and overextended institu-tions. Or there's the spectacle of insider trading on the stock exchange with the pros-ecution and sentencing of such notorious figures as Michael Milken and Ivan Boesky, who could pocket hundreds of thousands of dollars from a single transaction. Even that great eighteenth-century exponent of the free market, Adam Smith, admitted, "People of the same trade seldom meet together, even for merriment and diversion, but the conversation ends in a conspiracy against the public, or in some contrivance to raise prices."[13] When it comes to finances, either old laws must be more closely adhered to or new laws must be written to handle the ingenuity of evil.

Yet just as wealth isn't necessarily due to sweat and hard work, neither is poverty inevitably the result of laziness or bad habits; sometimes it stems from oppression. Butte, Montana had one of the largest copper mines in the world; for years more than one third of all the copper ore extracted in the United States came from there. By rights it should be one of the wealthiest places in the West, but early on, the owners, who lived in New York and Washington, decided to take as much money as possible out of the region and keep the wages low. In fact it wasn't until the New Deal that the city even had a sewer system, paved streets, playgrounds, and parks.[14] In much the same fashion, "poor, backward" pockets exist all over the globe, where "development" by multinational corporations means that local people receive back only a small portion of the wealth they helped create.

"Don't ask how your bread is buttered," the world says, "it may make you sick if you do. Better to remain ignorant than to be called an alarmist or fanatic." While one may not personally deplete a significant portion of the world's fossil fuels or be engaged in sweatshop labor practices or dump pollutants into neighboring streams, we are all passive participants in a web of ambivalence. "I do not believe that most women in Paris or New York would give very much for a fox as it looks when it is put down on the counter of an Arctic store," French explorer Gontran de Poncins supposed, "—grimy, yellowy white, covered with frozen blood."[15] But the fur trade (and much else) flourishes because the seamier aspects are papered over, tidied up. Certainly merchants will put their best face forward. Modern fast-food restaurants contribute to consolidation in agriculture and the rise of the factory farm; the obesity of the public due to unbalanced, high-fat, high-starch diets; as well as the economic straits of the less well-educated since the industry pays low salaries and mediocre benefits.[16] Indeed if much of world commerce were placed under a powerful microscope, patterns and networks of unsavory elements would instantaneously be revealed.

Yet, as long as one rubs shoulders with the public, compromises are inevitable. "The virtue assigned to the affairs of the world," according to Montaigne, "is a virtue with many bends, angles, and elbows, so as to join and to adapt itself to human weakness; mixed and artificial, not straight, clean, constant, or purely innocent. . . . He who walks in the crowd must step aside, keep his elbows in, step back or advance, even leave the straight way, according to what he encounters. He must live not so much according to himself as according to others, not according to what he proposes to himself but according to what others propose to him."[17] Our hands will most likely get dirty, and we will be pushed in directions we're uncomfortable with; but we need not lose our integrity.

The abuses and insensitivity of modern industrialists led a series of popes, beginning in the late nineteenth century, to issue landmark social encyclicals covering everything from inhumane working conditions to a just wage, child labor practices to the right to strike, formation of workmen's associations to employer-employee relations. Leo XIII's *Rerum Novarum* from 1891 reads, "Every man has by nature the right to possess property as his own. . . . It is neither justice nor humanity so to grind men down with excessive labor as to stupefy their minds and wear out their bodies. . . . Work which is suitable for a strong man cannot reasonably be required from a woman or a child. . . . Remuneration must be enough to support the wage-earner in reasonable and frugal comfort."[18]

Yet some will always lust after what glitters. If the Roman historian Suetonius be believed, Emperor Caligula developed such a passion for the feel of gold that he would spill his coins on the floor, then walk on them in his bare feet before lying down on them to roll over and over.[19] Gems and precious metals, because of their rarity and aesthetic value rather than any real practical use, have caused mass stampedes throughout history. The conquistadors, enamored of tales of "El Dorado," sought a kingdom near the source of the Amazon, whose capital buildings, furniture, clothing, even weapons, were covered with gold. It was rumored that once a year the king, after being rubbed with oil, was dusted with gold powder.[20] "The sight of gold," seventeenth-century essayist Robert Burton held, "will make a man run to the antipodes, or tarry at home and turn parasite, lie, flatter, prostitute himself, swear and bear false witness; he will venture his body, kill a king, murder his father, and damn his soul to come."[21]

Cortez and his men fell under the spell of that yellow metal. As they approached the Aztec capital, Montezuma sent envoys to the expedition bearing objects of gold. "When they were given these presents," it was reported, "the Spaniards burst into smiles; their eyes shone with pleasure. . . . They picked up the gold and fingered it like monkeys. . . . The truth is that they longed and lusted for gold. Their bodies swelled with greed, and their hunger was ravenous. . . . They snatched at the golden ensigns, waved them from side to side and examined every inch of them."[22] In this case gold was to be had, though later much of it apparently was lost at sea. It's more common, though, for gold diggers to slink back home months or years afterward—empty-handed, exhausted, and a trifle wiser.

Greed is a powerful, all-consuming master, as Jesus proclaims, "You cannot serve both God and money" (Matt. 6:24 TEV). In one of the few violent acts of his life, he took a whip and drove the moneychangers who were selling sacrificial birds and animals out of the temple, declaring, "'My house shall be called a house of prayer'; but you are making it a den of robbers" (Matt. 21:13). In El Greco's painting of the scene, an indignant Jesus arcs his arm back in a motion like a farmer scything grass, a forceful purplish-red amid a sea of lemon-lime.[23] Martin Luther, too, stood up to the abuses of the medieval church where, for a time, it was actually decreed that one could offer money to free a loved one from the pangs of purgatory. The indulgence sellers promised, "As soon as the coin in the coffer rings, / The soul from purgatory springs."[24] I'm afraid this isn't the first time, nor will it be the last, that the institutional church has conferred spiritual benefits on those who have helped alleviate its temporal difficulties. However, misuse of money imperils the soul. "They who are of the opinion that money will do everything," the Marquess of Halifax wrote, "may very well be suspected to do everything for money."[25]

"You shall take no bribe, for a bribe blinds the officials, and subverts the cause of those who are in the right," the Book of Exodus proscribes (23:8). Impartial judges are a bulwark against corruption, since the poor and those who have no defender (e.g., widows and orphans) are particularly susceptible to miscarriages of justice. In the *Inferno* Dante reserves some of his coarsest, most grotesque language for the fifth pouch of the eighth circle, in which sinners who committed graft—a charge leveled against Dante himself—are submerged in boiling pitch.[26] Perhaps there is no more succinct definition of bribery, says law professor John Noonan Jr., than Dante's description of the city of Lucca (XXI: 42), "where No becomes Yes for money."[27] Balak, the king of Moab, hoped to stop the Israelite advance into the Promised Land by paying the prophet Balaam to curse them, but to his chagrin, Balaam blessed them instead (Num. 22–24).

Still, some will always be up for sale; just their price will be in question. Recall how Judas betrayed Jesus for a mere thirty pieces of silver (Matt. 26:15). Joseph Addison concludes his essay, "How to settle arguments": "There is another way of Reasoning which seldom fails. . . . I mean convincing a Man by ready Mony, or, as it is ordinarily called, Bribing a Man to an Opinion. This Method has often proved successful, when all the others have been made use of to no purpose. . . . Gold is a wonderful Clearer of the Understanding: It dissipates every Doubt and Scruple in an Instant: Accomodates it self to the meanest Capacities; Silences the Loud and Clamorous, and brings over the most Obstinate and Inflexible."[28] So if logic and appeals to self-interest fall short, look for the unscrupulous to turn to this magic bullet.

Money, though, has many legitimate uses, bringing opportunities in, and access to, education, travel, the arts, medicine, and on and on. Perhaps that's why its dramatic renunciation created several of Christianity's most powerful movements. In the third century, a twenty-year-old Egyptian walked into a church, and upon hearing the story of the rich young ruler and (somewhat later) Jesus' call not to worry about the morrow, gave away all that he had, retreating farther and farther into the desert. Eventually—thanks to an especially admiring biography by Bishop Athanasius—Antony emerged as the leading role model for the early monastic movement.[29]

Similarly, at about the age of twenty-seven, the son of a wealthy Italian textile merchant, during the feast of St. Matthias in 1208, hearing a sermon on the story of Jesus sending out the twelve, abandoned all that remained of his possessions in order to devote the rest of his life to preaching and caring for the poor and sick.[30] After attracting a number of followers, he composed a short rule and, when the pope's approval came, formed a new order. Since then, Francis of Assisi has become one of the most revered figures in church history. In his last testament, he said that his followers "gave *whatever they had* to the poor and were content with one tunic, patched inside and out, with a cord and short trousers."[31] When he revised his rule, he stipulated: "Let the brothers not make anything their own, neither house, nor place, nor anything at all. As pilgrims and strangers in this world, serving the Lord in poverty and humility."[32]

Perhaps our life should be known, says Thoreau, by what we can live without. "Simplify, simplify" was his motto. Boil life down to its essentials, and don't waste time on the incidentals.[33] "The truly wise man," the philosopher Epicurus believed, "is the one who can be happy with a little."[34] But how can we do that when modern industrial capitalism has set before us an almost endless variety of choices, which advertisers and marketers do their best to convince us we cannot live without? What we need is a reliable gauge to measure the value of our money. "The farmer," Emerson explained, "is covetous of his dollar, and with reason. It is no waif to him. He knows how many strokes of labor it represents. His bones ache with the days' work that earned it. He knows how much land it represents—how much rain, frost and sunshine. He knows that, in the dollar, he gives you so much discretion and patience, so much hoeing and threshing. Try to lift his dollar; you must lift all that weight."[35]

Also, we mustn't forget that simple budget lesson Mr. Micawber gave David Copperfield: "Annual income twenty pounds, annual expenditure nineteen nineteen six, result happiness. Annual income twenty pounds, annual expenditure twenty pounds ought and six, result misery."[36] In our easy-credit culture, the arithmetic is not always that cut-and-dried, but the principle is still valid. Too, don't wish away your troubles. In Aristophanes' play *Clouds*, Socrates, like a Freudian analyst, puts his friend Strepsiades on the couch, asking him to freely associate in order to identify his malady, although it seems pretty clearcut—his finances. So . Strepsiades starts talking about, of all things, the moon. "If I hired a Thessalian witch," he fantasizes, "pulled the moon down, / Shut it up in a round helmet box like a mirror, / And kept it there." Socrates interrupts, "What good would that do you?" To which Strepsiades replies, "Because bills fall due at new moon."[37] He feels that if the moon doesn't wax and wane, neither will his monthly bills come due. What a novel way of handling one's economic difficulties.

"If a man owns land, the land owns him," Emerson warned. "Now let him leave home, if he dare."[38] By almost any statistical measure, a middle-class American, although he or she may not feel that way, is among the world's wealthiest 10–20 percent, since billions have little more than a roof over their heads, sleep in crowded, leaky rooms, and aren't even sure where tomorrow's bread is coming from. Wealth binds us; its extraneous details demand maintenance. It also may blind us. "I used to think, when I was a child," wrote Dom Helder Camara, the Brazilian archbishop who devoted his life to seeking justice for the poor, "that Christ might have been exaggerating when he warned about the dangers of wealth. Today I know better. I know how very hard it is to be rich and still keep the milk of human kindness. Money has a dangerous way of putting scales on one's eyes, a dangerous way of freezing people's hands, eyes, lips, and hearts."[39] One thinks of the Goncourt brothers' journal entry for May 4, 1868, which mentions how "M. Marcellus, the Christian grandee, took communion at his château only with consecrated wafers stamped with his coat of arms."[40]

Having grown up as a pragmatic, hardheaded Midwesterner who counts his change before leaving the cash register, I'm forced to admit that when it comes to finances, there's a bit of extravagance, even wild abandon, in the Gospels. For instance there's the woman who poured expensive ointment on Jesus' head. When the disciples complained that the money could have been better spent, Jesus praised her by saying that she was preparing him for burial and her deed would be recounted wherever the gospel was proclaimed (Matt. 26:6–13). Or in the parable where the master returns to reckon with his stewards; the two who had taken their talents and added more are praised, but from the one who was overly cautious, who buried his lone talent for fear of losing it, even what he had was taken away (Matt. 25:14–30). So, like good entrepreneurs, we should be willing to take a few chances with our lives.

In Victor Hugo's *Les Misérables,* Jean Valjean, recently released from prison and down on his luck, was directed by a kindly passerby to the house of Bishop Bienvenu. Welcoming Valjean, feeding him, and giving him a place to sleep, the bishop announced, "This is not my house; it is Christ's. It does not ask any guest his name but whether he has an affliction. You are suffering; you are hungry and thirsty; you are welcome. . . .[Y]our name is my brother."[41]

Valjean, not being used to a real bed to sleep in, awoke, and couldn't take his mind off the silver place settings he had seen earlier that evening. He departed rather early the next morning and without the appropriate adieus. It wasn't long, though, before the police found him, recognized the silver, and brought him back to the bishop's house.

Seeing Valjean coming, the bishop exclaimed, "Ah, there you are! I'm glad to see you. But I gave you the candlesticks, too, which are silver like the rest and would bring you two hundred francs. Why didn't you take them along with your cutlery?"[42] The bewildered Valjean accepts the candlesticks, and the gendarmes release their suspect. Yet by that simple act of kindness, the bishop had consecrated the former convict's life, and as the rest of the novel unfolds, Jean Valjean goes on to give many others a second chance.[43]

All that we have, as Bienvenu knew, is on loan. Admit God, and the concept of private ownership and legal possession grow rather murky. An ancient Irish poem concerning the fort of Rathangan in county Kildare lists its former owners, the kings of the Ui Berraidi of Leccach. For a while it was Bruidge's, Cathal's, Aed's, Ailill's, Conaing's, Cuiline's, and Mael-Duin's. The fort still stands, but all the kings are asleep in the ground.[44] You want to ask, "Whose fort is it now?"

Or there's Isak Dinesen's short story "Babette's Feast," about a French chef who, escaping political persecution, is taken in by two devout Norwegian spinsters who oversee a small church that meets regularly in their house. They have no idea of Babette's background until one day, having won the lottery, she spends all she has to make one lavish banquet that is a kind of "thank you" for the way she has been received and accepted by her hosts and the other church members. Importing odd and unusual dishes from abroad, she cooks the most memorable meal ever seen in those parts, preparing it for people who were largely unable to discriminate between the flavors or even appreciate her culinary arts.

Yet somehow during that meal old grievances that had festered for years were transcended. One man finally admitted to another that he had once cheated him on a timber deal, and was forgiven. Two women who had slandered each other forty years before and thus ruined a marriage and an inheritance, tonight overcame their differences and reminisced of their youth, when they had hand in hand filled the roads around Berlevaag with singing. It was as though the past, which can linger over a small town like a dense fog, had temporarily been lifted. The church members, too, remembered their founder's saying: "The only things which we may take with us from our life on earth are those which we have given away!"[45]

In Oscar Wilde's "The Happy Prince," a magnificent statue, moved by the plight of those it sees, asks a swallow to take a ruby from its sword hilt to help a seamstress's sick son; a sapphire from one of its eyes to aid a cold, starving playwright; the sapphire from its other eye to give to a matchstick girl who has just lost her matches; and assorted pieces of its gold leaf covering to help the poor. Found now in such a shabby state, the statue is no longer considered beautiful, so town officials take it down and melt it in a furnace, leaving only its lead heart. But God had seen all that took place. "Bring me the two most precious things in the city," he tells one of his angels, who proceeds to retrieve the lead heart and the dead bird. "You have rightly chosen," he pronounced, "for in my garden of Paradise this little bird shall sing for evermore, and in my city of gold the Happy Prince shall praise me."[46]

According to Thomas More, there are two kinds of misers. "What about those who pile up money, not because they want to do anything with the heap, but so they can sit and look at it? Is that true pleasure they experience?" he asks. "Or what of those with the opposite vice, the men who hide away money they will never use and perhaps never ever see again? In their anxiety to hold onto their money, they actually lose it."[47] I'd like to ask you, are you more likely to be a miser or a spend-thrift?

In the days of the Roman empire pagan observers were struck by the way the church cared for its own and those in need. Customs varied from place to place, but according to Tertullian, each month members made a voluntary donation to a fund he likened to a "treasure chest." This money could then be distributed to "support and bury poor people, to supply the wants of boys and girls destitute of means and parents, and of old persons confined now to the house; such, too, as have suffered shipwreck; and if there happens to be any in the mines, or banished to the islands, or shut up in the prisons." The recipients, became, in effect, the pensioners of their confession. Bewildered onlookers could only utter, "See, . . . how they love one another,"[48] for Christians felt under a mandate to help the disadvantaged.[49] "Whenever we have an opportunity," Paul egged on the Galatians, "let us work for the good of all, and especially for those of the family of faith" (Gal. 6:10).

Augustine counted greed a keen eagerness in the heart for earthly things.[50] "Every species of property is preyed on by its own enemies," Emerson said, "as iron by rust; timber by rot; cloth by moths; provisions by mold, putridity, or vermin; money by thieves; an orchard by insects; a planted field by weeds."[51] Are your riches subject to dust, mildew, or termites? Can vandals break in and deface what you own? The early church father Jerome, in one of his letters, held up for an example Marcella, a Christian widow who he said preferred "to store her money in the stomachs of the needy rather than hide it in a purse."[52] May we follow her lead, lavishing our life and possessions on the Lord.

CHAPTER 10

The Workaholic

One of my favorite Charlie Chaplin movies is *Modern Times,* which pokes fun at the modern assembly line. The film begins with a scene of sheep being led into a pen for slaughter, then shifts to people streaming out of a subway toward a factory. According to historian Lewis Mumford, "The clock, not the steam engine, is the key machine of the modern industrial age."[1] (As Gulliver pulls out his pocket watch in Swift's satire, explaining how he consults it for nearly every action he takes, the Lilliputians start to wonder whether it might be "the god that he worships."[2]) Thus in the film we see the plant president anxious to invest in a new feeding machine, so that the traditional lunch hour can be reduced to but a few minutes. While the worker stands in front of the contraption, soup is poured between his lips, corn on the cob is twirled between his teeth, and cubes of meat are placed on his tongue. However, the machine quickly goes haywire; in fact, after dining, Charlie should really take a shower and change those splattered clothes.

Later in the film, falling behind at his particular task of tightening bolts, he is sucked onto the conveyor belt, where he disappears down a yawning duct at the end of the line. Then we see Emerson's maxim—"Machinery is aggressive. The weaver becomes a web, the machinist a machine"[3]—come literally true, for Charlie begins going round and round among huge gears. Eventually he cracks under the strain of his job's repetitiveness and, before long, starts ballet dancing around the factory floor, squirting everyone in the face with his oil can and twisting any protuberance he finds with his wrench, including the buttons on a woman's blouse.[4]

This is the workplace gone bonkers. But how does a Christian develop a healthy attitude towards labor, so one doesn't turn into a workaholic? Economist E. F. Schumacher believed that work should (1) give people a chance to use and develop their faculties; (2) enable them to overcome ego-centeredness by joining with others in a common task; and (3) bring forth goods and services needed for a becoming existence.[5] Work, in and of itself, is not a curse, for even in the Garden of Eden God has Adam till the soil, tend the plants, and name the animals (Gen. 2:15–19). Indeed a human being can be relatively happy, theologian Thomas Aquinas believed, simply because he is endowed with reason and has hands to make things.[6] *The Rule of St. Benedict*, the single most influential document in Western monasticism, advises, "Idleness is the enemy of the soul. Therefore, the brothers should have specified periods for manual labor as well as for prayerful reading."[7] By breaking the day up into small but regular segments of work, study, and prayer, the monks were less likely to become bored or exhausted. Augustine defined the boundaries: "No man has a right to lead such a life of contemplation as to forget in his own ease the service due to his neighbor; nor has any man a right to be so immersed in active life as to neglect the contemplation of God."[8]

What kinds of labor are to be blessed? All sorts. God has created a bountiful, diverse world. Quoting Ecclesiastes 3:11: "He hath made every *thing* beautiful in his time" (emphasis in KJV), Rabbi Zutra bar Tobiah remarks, "The Holy One made every trade seem beautiful in the eyes of him who plies it."[9] Wasn't Jesus himself a carpenter (Mark 6:3)? Paul supported his missionary journeys by leather-working and making tents (Acts 18:3). Indeed the second-century pagan philosopher Celsus complained of uneducated Christian manual laborers ("wool-workers, cobblers, laundry-workers") who thought to teach others how to live.[10] Just listen to the invigorating cacophony of occupations in Carl Sandburg's "Chicago":

> Hog Butcher for the World,
> Tool Maker, Stacker of Wheat,
> Player with Railroads and the Nation's Freight Handler;
> Stormy, husky, brawling
> City of the Big Shoulders: . . . .
> Bareheaded,
> Shoveling,
> Wrecking,
> Planning,
> Building, breaking, rebuilding,
> Under the smoke, dust all over his mouth, laughing with white teeth.[11]

Rabbi Judah went so far as to say, "He who does not teach his son a craft is as though he taught him to be a brigand."[12]

In the world of commerce, there are manifold temptations, any number of underhanded approaches. So honesty should be foremost, as it's incumbent upon both the owner and the employee not to shortchange others. As that ancient Hebrew adage says, "Accuracy of scales and balances is the Lord's concern; all the weights in the bag are his business" (Prov. 16:11 REV). The fourteenth-century allegory *Piers the Ploughman* cites several illustrations of ill-gotten gain. Covetousness confesses that he learned to use false weights when selling wares as an apprentice to Sim-at-the-Stile; went to school with the drapers, where he was taught how to stretch ten to eleven yards of cloth so that it could be sold as thirteen; and put his wife into business brewing beer, where she mixed a little good ale with a lot of small beer, hence became known as "Rose the Racketeer."[13] In Dante's *Inferno,* we meet a certain "Master Adam," whom we soon discover to be a counterfeiter. At the instigation of Conti Guidi of Romena, he illegally minted florins consisting of twenty-one carats of gold (and three of alloy), instead of the twenty-four required by law. With the lily stamped on one side and the image of John the Baptist on the other, this gold piece had become a standard throughout Christendom; consequently, the Florentines demanded Master Adam be burned alive in 1281.[14]

A better pattern for believers is the eighteenth-century Quaker John Woolman. "It had been my general practice to buy and sell things really useful," he writes. "Things that served chiefly to please the vain mind in people I was not easy to trade in, seldom did it, and whenever I did I found it weakened me as a Christian." Here is the real McCoy, that businessman who genuinely wants to help his customers. "It is the custom where I lived," he continues, "to sell chiefly on credit, and poor people often get in debt, and when payment is expected, not having wherewith to pay, their creditors often sue for it at law. Having often observed occurrences of this kind, I found it good for me to advise poor people to take such goods as were most useful and not costly."[15] Quality, dependability, and a fair price are all important. One should make or sell goods that are meant to last, which will adequately perform their required functions and bring aesthetic pleasure to their users. "It would be the height of folly to make material so it should wear out quickly," inveighed economist E. F. Schumacher, "and the height of barbarity to make anything ugly, shabby or mean."[16]

Not only should we avoid shortchanging others, neither should we become too caught up in our own insecurity. Retirement plans encourage us to think that no nest egg is ever large enough. The philosophy of insurance companies seems to be, "If you have an anxiety, we have a policy." Of course, one should certainly both plan ahead and set aside something in case of emergencies, but such measures can be carried to extremes. "Riches and abundance come hypocritically clad in sheep's clothing," Søren Kierkegaard noticed, "pretending to be security against anxiety"; instead "they become then the object of anxiety" and "secure a man against anxieties just about as well as the wolf which is put to tending the sheep secures them . . . against the wolf."[17] Instead of a relatively carefree existence, the affluent simply spend more time protecting their assets, worrying about the return from investments, and fending off appeals for charity. Such anxieties are what Cyprian, the third-century bishop of Carthage, referred to as "gilded torments."[18]

"The world is too much with us, late and soon," bemoaned nineteenth-century poet William Wordsworth. "Getting and spending, we lay waste our powers."[19] In Lewis Carroll's *Through the Looking-Glass,* Alice meets a knight in tin armor, who keeps falling off his horse. Partly he is so weighted down with useless equipment and paraphernalia that he is unable to keep his seat. He has both a beehive and a mousetrap tied to his saddle. "You see," he explains to Alice, "it's as well to be provided for *everything.* That's the reason the horse has all those anklets around his feet." Mystified, Alice asks, "But what are they for?" He matter-of-factly replies, "To guard against the bites of sharks."[20] I don't know about you, but when I look around our house, I see far too many possessions protecting *me* from sharkbite— things that might come in handy some day, objects to have around just in case.

In our materialistic culture, it's difficult to separate what's required from what's luxury. Paul wrote Timothy, "If we have food and clothing [and shelter?], we shall be content with that" (1 Tim. 6:8 NAB).[21] To combat covetousness among the monks, Benedict, in his rule, stipulated that "the abbot is to provide all things necessary: that is, cowl, tunic, sandals, shoes, belt, knife, stylus, needle, handkerchief and writing tablets."[22] Economist John Maynard Keynes claims that our needs fall into two classes: those "which are absolute in the sense that we feel them whatever the situation of our fellow human beings may be, and those which are relative in the sense that we feel them only if their satisfaction lifts us above, makes us feel superior to, our fellows."[23]

Social conventions may encourage unnecessary extravagance, say, in funeral rites, as Jessica Mitford has so amply documented in *The American Way of Death.* Already in the fifth century B.C., Chinese philosopher Mo Tzu was castigating elaborate funerals. "Even when an ordinary and undistinguished person dies, the expenses of the funeral are such as to reduce the family almost to beggary; and when a ruler dies, by the time enough gold and jade, pearls and precious stones have been found to lay by the body, wrappings of fine stuffs to bind round it, chariots and horses to bury with it in the tomb, and the necessary quantity of tripods and drums under their coverings and awnings, of jars and bowls on tables and stands, of halberds, swords, feather-work screens and banners, objects in ivory and in leather, have been made . . . the treasuries of the state are completely exhausted."[24]

With each rise in our standard of living, expectations shoot up, as household objects and brand names increasingly come to define social status. It could be argued, for instance, that indoor plumbing was one of the great technological breakthroughs of the twentieth century, but now we hardly give it a second thought. Following World War II, such household appliances as the refrigerator, stove, and vacuum cleaner became commonplace.[25] The radio, telephone, and television have made mass communication and mass entertainment possible. The automobile, which rolled off Henry Ford's assembly line, has affected our nation perhaps more than any other single modern invention. But do we buy the most recent innovation because we think it will significantly improve our quality of life, or do we rather want to keep up with the Joneses, and so end up on some self-perpetuating treadmill? "The modes of dress and furniture are continually changing," economist Adam Smith perceived, "and that fashion appearing ridiculous today which was admired five years ago, we are experimentally convinced that it owed its vogue chiefly or entirely to custom and fashion."[26]

Commercialization has even invaded the church year. Ever since the mid-1820s, American merchants have sought to redefine Christmas in ways that would boost sales. For centuries Christmas meant feasting and celebration, but the custom of giving gifts usually took place separately, say, at New Year's or Epiphany. Clement Moore's poem "Visit from St. Nicholas," published in 1823, with its now familiar portrait of Santa Claus bearing gifts on his reindeer-led sleigh, became such a cultural icon that it was instrumental in merging the two holidays. Not long afterward, gifts started edging out the newborn king. In a late nineteenth-century diary, to go "a-Christmasing" becomes virtually synonymous with going downtown to shop, where some, at least, felt crushed by all those shoppers, appalled by the garish displays of tinsel and glitter, and only dispiritedly sought to fill the laundry list of items children had asked Santa for.[27] The old custom of making items by hand, especially for the occasion, had been replaced by giving mass-produced goods, which should they be returned, could be exchanged for anything else in the store.[28]

The new form that Christmas would take was already apparent in 1832: "*Christmas-eve,* in the city of New-York, exhibits a spectacle," one observer wrote. "Whole rows of confectionary stores and toy shops, fancifully, and often splendidly, decorated with festoons of bright silk drapery, interspersed with flowers and evergreens, are brilliantly illuminated with gas-lights, arranged in every shape and figure that fancy can devise. During the evening, until midnight, these places were crowded with visitors of both sexes and all ages; some selecting toys and fruits for holyday presents; others merely lounging from shop to shop to enjoy the varied scene. But the most interesting, and, in our estimation, the most delightful sight of all, is the happy and animated countenances of children."[29] Ever since, Christmas has been sentimentalized even further and more eroded by the forces of mammon.

But let's turn back the clock six hundred years and juxtapose an altogether different scene, this one from the life of Francis of Assisi. He was eager to make the birthday of our Lord, that "feast of feasts," accessible to the poor and embrace all living creatures. So he set up a Nativity crèche, "to see as much as is possible with my own bodily eyes," he wrote, "the discomfort of his infant needs, how he *lay in a manger,* and how, with an ox and an ass standing by, he rested on hay." Participants, bearing candles and torches, lit up the night sky; the brothers broke out in joyous caroling. Then Francis preached "about the birth of the poor King" in the town of Bethlehem, which, for effect, he pronounced in the manner of a bleating sheep. Biographer Thomas of Celano declared, "There simplicity is given a place of honor, / poverty is exalted, / humility is commended, / and out of Greccio is made a new Bethlehem."[30] I'll let you decide which is closer to the spirit of Jesus—Fifth Avenue store windows overflowing with a cornucopia of gifts in every price range or a handful of farm animals lowing near a makeshift manger?

On the first Sunday in Advent 1943, Dietrich Bonhoeffer wrote to his parents from the Tegel Prison concerning a painting he had been thinking about. It was the "Birth of Christ" by the sixteenth-century German Albrecht Altdorfer, which depicts the holy family huddling together "amidst the ruins of a dilapidated house." Bonhoeffer wonders whether "Christmas can, and should, be celebrated in this way, too."[31] Ten years earlier, in a sermon on the Magnificat, he had asked, "Who among us will celebrate Christmas right?" then continued, "those who stand by the lowly and let God alone be exalted, those who see in the child in the manger the glory of God."[32]

Workaholics, on the other hand, tend to justify their labor by the added income it generates; Gregory the Great, however, felt that greed led to "restlessness" and "hardness of heart."[33] It does seem that there is a callousness as one moves up the economic ladder. "Wherever riches have increased," John Wesley wrote, "the essence of religion has decreased in the same proportion. Therefore I do not see how it is possible, in the nature of things, for any revival of true religion to continue long. For religion must necessarily produce both industry and frugality, and these cannot but produce riches. But as riches increase so will pride, anger, and love of the world in all its branches."[34] The Greek church father, John Chrysostom heaped scorn on the selfish rich. In a homily on 1 Corinthians, he denounced those who added expensive clothes to their wardrobe while in the streets were some nearly naked, shivering from the cold, and barely able to stand up—yet also created in God's image.[35] A few years after Francis of Assisi's death, we see the strange spectacle of his followers calling upon celebrated artists and architects to construct two magnificent churches, an upper and lower basilica, dedicated to Lady Poverty's troubadour—despite the fact that Francis had earlier disapproved of a sumptuous structure built near St. Mary of the Angels and had ordered it demolished.[36]

Greed may also take the form of what economists call "bubbles" or "manias," when the value of a commodity skyrockets for awhile, then abruptly comes down. One of the most curious is the tulip mania that seized Holland in the 1630s. This flower, recently imported from Turkey, almost overnight became a status symbol. New varieties improved upon color, petal size, or shape. By 1636 Amsterdam, Rotterdam, and a host of other cities had futures markets in, if you can believe it, tulips. The bulbs became so valuable that a more precise measure, known as a "perit" (less than a grain), was added to the scale to insure the accuracy of the transaction. One bulb of the flamed and striped type, *Semper Augustus,* weighing two hundred perits, could sell for fifty-five hundred florins. Investors, as is common during bubbles, were certain that tulip prices would rise forever, yet one day the bottom dropped out. Thousands lost their savings, and the entire Dutch economy reeled from the effects.[37] To be sure, money can be had during eras of speculation, but you have to possess a crystal ball to know when to jump in and when to bail out.

Instead of looking for easy money, we should come to see work as a natural part of the rhythm of life, though not its raison d'être. Sociologist Lewis Coser coined the term "greedy institutions" to describe those corporations, administrations, or arrangements that usurp the loyalty of those who serve them, so that employees are effectively cut off from outside contacts and deep commitments to other persons or organizations.[38] The same can be said of churches who encourage members to participate in a smorgasbord of activities nearly every night of the week—whether "Christian" baseball leagues, "Christian" scout troops, "Christian" aerobics, "Christian" cooking classes, or the more traditional small group Bible studies, youth groups, and so on. This simply means that we now have the opportunity to experience burnout at church as well as at the office.

A strong case should be made for forms of leisure where we can pursue hobbies, do volunteer work, share more time with the family, or learn new skills. Catholic essayist G. K. Chesterton once expressed a whimsical desire for nothing more than "a colored pencil long enough" for him "to draw on the ceiling" while lying in bed.[39] As the old Shaker hymn says, "'Tis the gift to be simple, 'tis the gift to be free."[40] It's in moments of solitude that intimacy between couples can grow, an artist's creativity bloom. Incubation allows the strands of our ideas to coalesce. German chemist Friedrich Kekulé, contemplating the structure of the benzene molecule in 1865, had a daydream in which atoms took the shape of a snake seizing its own tail; this was just the clue he needed to arrive at his model of a ring of six carbon atoms, each attached to one of hydrogen—a discovery that would prove pivotal in the rise of organic chemistry.[41] Exercises of contemplation, "looked upon by those who stay at home as a form of the Higher Laziness," discerns spiritual writer Evelyn Underhill, "are in reality the last and most arduous labors which the human spirit is called to perform. They are the only known methods by which we come into conscious possession of all our powers."[42]

On other occasions, "doing nothing" is just what the soul needs to repair its frayed nerves. "How vainly men themselves amaze / To win the palm, the oak, or bays;" Andrew Marvell pointed out in his poem "The Garden," "While all flowers and all trees do close / To weave the garlands of repose."[43] When the church fathers referred to *otium sanctum,* or "holy leisure," they were describing that sense of balance where one could be both active and at peace; while working, one could enjoy everyday beauties and common pleasures.[43a] One of my favorite activities is to take walks in the country, where I become lost in nature reveries. Then, in Wordworth's words, a field of wildflowers, when "recollected in tranquillity,"[44] can "flash upon that inward eye," until one "dances with the daffodils."[45] For we live in what theologian William Temple calls a "sacramental universe," where any (and all) elements can be vehicles for revelation, vehicles for grace.[46] So Thomas Browne sighs, if only we "knew better how to joyne and read these mysticall letters" and thus "suck Divinity from the flowers."[47]

The workaholic is too wrapped up in his possessions or chasing after a raise, a promotion, some further recognition. He subscribes to political theorist Thomas Hobbes's view that "life is a race with no other good but to be foremost."[48] The German novelist Thomas Mann, too, at times, seems to be in this camp. In his novella *Death in Venice,* the partially autobiographical hero, Gustave Aschenbach, has a soul "bent on fame," invigorated by, as well as crushed by, the "burden of his genius." One observer said of him at the age of thirty-five: "'You see, Aschenbach has always lived like this'—here the speaker closed the fingers of his left hand to a fist—'never like this'—and he let his open hand hang relaxed from the back of his chair." Writing was a difficult, dreary business for Aschenbach, who strained for hours after insight, then rewrote and polished so often that his creations resembled layers of an archaeological dig. His favorite motto, of course, was "Hold fast!" The narrator remarks, "Gustave Aschenbach was the poet-spokesman of all those who labor at the edge of exhaustion; of the overburdened, of those who are already worn out but still hold themselves upright."[49] Driven by some kind of inner compulsion, these types spend such enormous energy on their work that they often neglect everyday life and relationships. But whenever writers measure their productivity by the ream, or retailers by how many competitors they've driven out of the market, something is terribly out of whack. These have succumbed to that maxim Max Weber unearthed in his study of capitalism: "One does not work to live; one lives to work."[50]

A figure who did develop a healthy rhythm in his daily walk with God is the seventeenth-century Carmelite lay brother, Lawrence of the Resurrection. For years he served as a cook and a sandal maker at a monastery in Paris. He wasn't noticeably brilliant or gifted; nevertheless, he cultivated what he called "the practice of the presence of God."[51] Referring to himself as "a piece of stone," he asked God "to carve out" "his perfect image" in his soul,[52] praying submissively, "My God, I am all yours; Lord, fashion me according to your heart."[53] He advised others to keep their "eyes fixed on God in everything" they said, did, or undertook.[54] Even though he began with a strong aversion to kitchen duty, he gradually became proficient at his assigned responsibilities and was able to lift up the most menial task to the love of God.[55] Simplicity and directness are at the core of his spirituality, which he likens to a continuous conversation with the indwelling deity.[56] German epigrammatist Angelus Silesius once ejaculated, "How accessible God is! The peasant maid he taught / As much as he did you the art of kissing God."[57]

We honor God by heartfelt dedication, no matter how paltry our service may appear to others. In the medieval tale "Our Lady's Tumbler," an illiterate entered a monastery, but it became apparent that he exhibited none of the skills necessary to help maintain it. Being unable to read or sing, he felt left out, too, during the chanting of the hours. Then one day in the crypt, he decided to leap and jump and walk on his hands, as he had in his former life, not for the delight of adoring crowds but to please a statue of the Virgin Mary. He turned somersaults and performed all manner of vaults day after day with abandon. Once the abbot learned of this odd form of devotion, instead of being offended, he consecrated the tumbler's acrobatics as a gift to the monastery, urging him, if possible, to expand his repertoire.[58]

Or consider the spontaneous nature of ancient Celtic piety, where God and nature seem to blend so harmoniously together. Even centuries afterward, noted folklorist Alexander Carmichael could discern its influence in the prayers, songs, and blessings he gathered in the Outer Hebrides, off the coast of Scotland, to put into his famed *Carmina Gadelica*. Here's a milking croon:

Bless, O God, my little cow,
Bless, O God, my desire;
Bless Thou my partnership
And the milking of my hands, O God.

Bless, O God, each teat,
Bless, O God, each finger;
Bless Thou each drop
That goes into my pitcher.[59]

And here's a reaping blessing:

> God, bless Thou Thyself my reaping,
> Each ridge, and plain, and field,
> Each sickle curved, shapely, hard,
> Each ear and handful in the sheaf,
>> Each ear and handful in the sheaf. . . .
>
> Encompass each goat, sheep and lamb,
> Each cow and horse, and store,
> Surround Thou the flocks and herds,
> And tend them to a kindly fold,
>> Tend them to a kindly fold.[60]

We can all learn to pray in such a straightforward manner during our work week, though maybe not so rhythmically or poetically.

Finally, let us remember God's unmerited favor. "Every good gift and every perfect gift is from above," insists the Book of James (1:17 KJV). Every day in every way, our lives are enriched by manifold kindnesses we've never earned. "Can the most complacent reactionary," asks historian James Harvey Robinson, "flatter himself that he invented the art of writing or the printing press, or discovered his religious, economic, and moral convictions, or any of the devices which supply him with meat and raiment or any of the sources of such pleasures as he may derive from literature or the fine arts? In short," Robinson concludes, "civilization is little else than getting something for nothing."[61] And concerning the vast cosmos around us, G. K. Chesterton once wisecracked, "There is no way in which a man can earn a star or deserve a sunset."[62]

Grace was a dominant theme for Augustine, who believed, "God also helps those who do not help themselves in order that they may help themselves."[63] For it is in our weakness that we truly come to rely on God, when we become as helpless as the baby Jesus in Mary's arms. C. S. Lewis puts it this way: "We are mirrors, whose brightness, if we are bright, is wholly derived from the sun that shines upon us. . . . Grace substitutes a full, childlike and delighted acceptance of our Need, a joy in total dependence. We become 'jolly beggars.'"[64] All that we are, all that we have, all that we'll ever become is due to the Lord. The Old Testament practices of tithing and offering up the first fruits makes clear that we are not our own, as God requires, "All that first opens the womb is mine" (Exod. 34:19). Grace says to the workaholic: Scrutinize that list of achievements. Was something left behind in your striving: family? friends? values? Can your fame or possessions compensate for what's been lost? "We need not envy certain people their great wealth," counsels French essayist La Bruyère, "they acquired it at a heavy cost, which would not suit us; they staked their rest, their health, their honor and their conscience to acquire it; the price is too high, and there is nothing to be gained by such a bargain."[65] Instead let us, like the lilies of the field and birds of the air, unobtrusively enter into the kingdom as "jolly beggars" (Matt. 6:25–34).

CHAPTER 11

Lust: From Attraction to Commitment

S ociety," said novelist John Galsworthy, "is built on marriage—marriage and its consequences."[1] One of contemporary America's most cherished values is the freedom of sexual expression. The guarantee of "life, liberty, and the pursuit of happiness," interpreted under a variety of right-to-privacy laws, has increasingly come to mean that consenting adults can have sex with whomever and however they like. Legal sanctions against adultery have, for the most part, been removed. No-fault divorce, which began in California in 1970, is now common in all fifty states.

We encourage unchaperoned dating and let teenagers have access to cars, which, in effect, serve as portable bedrooms. Advertisers use sexy young saleswomen to sell everything from coffee to cigarettes. Condoms are available to any walk-in customer at local pharmacies; erotic films and magazines are ubiquitous (and pornographic web sites are among the most popular on the Internet); on college campuses, coed dorms are the norm. We have let lust run rampant in the land with too few safeguards for fidelity.

Sexual freedom does have its good side. Most experts agree that now there is "greater frankness, greater tolerance, greater willingness to experiment."[2] The "fallen" woman, so common in nineteenth-century literature, is no longer a social outcast. The Victorian repressions that shocked psychoanalysts seem to be on the decline. Sex education starts in the early grades in our public schools. Family planning is becoming commonplace. Advances in medicine have provided effective treatment for a number of forms of sexually transmitted diseases. Women are increasingly being heard on issues like rape, abortion, and harassment in the workplace.

But I'm afraid that this has all come at a heavy cost in terms of social stability. Unless trends change, a high proportion of the marriages performed today will end in divorce. And recent findings indicate that divorce hits hardest at young children, who will often have added adjustment problems, and at women, who will earn significantly less income during their careers than men.[3] Teenage pregnancies, which result in a small child at home, are likely to disrupt the mother's education and lessen her chances for advancement. Too, the children of divorce report increased fears of abandonment.[4] Our exorbitant rates of rape and incest have left in their wake hurt, humiliation, and bitterness—choking off future relationships.[5] Contemporary society, so sharply focused on the happiness of the parent, sadly neglects the best interests of the child.[6] Alarm bells should be ringing in our churches and legislatures over real family values, but instead, we watch liberals and conservatives bicker over issues like homosexuality and abortion, which affect only a small segment of our population, while ignoring more fundamental difficulties.

Christianity teaches that the body is good and that sex can be beautiful within a committed marriage. As the psalmist says, we are "fearfully and wonderfully made" (Ps. 139:14). "Your body is a temple of the Holy Spirit," proclaimed the apostle Paul, "therefore glorify God in your body" (1 Cor. 6:19–20). Through the body one learns to express his personality and form his self-image. However, if we're honest with ourselves, we'll more than likely agree with the seventeenth-century epigrammatist Angelus Silesius, "My closest friend, my body, is also my worst foe."[7] Francis of Assisi captured the mixed feelings we all have about this network of skin, muscles, nerves, and bones by calling his body "Brother Ass." "*Ass* is exquisitely right," comments C. S. Lewis, "because no one in his senses can either revere or hate a donkey. It is a useful, sturdy, lazy, obstinate, patient, lovable and infuriating beast; deserving now the stick and now a carrot; both pathetically and absurdly beautiful. So the body."[8]

However, Christians have not always promulgated such healthy views. The early church was especially prone to glorifying asceticism and subduing the body. It was said of Antony, the model desert monk, that he never changed his clothes or washed his feet, and that he blushed whenever he ate or exercised any bodily function.[9] Origen castrated himself in a futile attempt to achieve victory over the flesh, only to discover that amputation does not eliminate sexual desire. Jerome, having fled from the temptations of society, could find no relief from his fevered imagination. "How often when I was established in the desert," he wrote Eustochium, "I imagined myself back in the pleasures of Rome. . . . I wore rough sackcloth. . . . I neglected my skin which looked like an Ethiopian's. . . . I had sentenced myself to this prison with scorpions and wild beasts as my only friends. But I was often surrounded by dancing girls. . . . My flesh was almost dead but passionate fires were alight within me."[10]

Augustine felt fallen humanity so prey to irrational lusts that he established a pyramid of values that is nearly the reverse of what we now consider normal. At its apex was permanent virginity; next, celibacy—after previous sexual experience;

then sex within marriage—solely for giving birth; and at the lowest tier, sex within marriage—out of love or simply for pleasure (merely a venial sin).[11] The repercussions of this view can be seen in that medieval best-seller, *The Misery of the Human Condition,* written by Cardinal Segni in 1195: "Everyone knows that intercourse, even between married persons, is never performed without the itch of the flesh, the heat of passion, and the stench of lust. Whence the seed conceived is fouled, smirched, corrupted, and the soul infused into it inherits the guilt of sin, the stain of evil-doing, that primeval taint."[12] Only with Luther and the Reformation did this pyramid begin to crumble.[13]

Protestants have come to believe that intercourse was intended both for pleasure and companionship, and if God wills, procreation.[14] Thus Milton can write, "Lonelines is the first thing which Gods eye nam'd not good."[15] Individual males and females often have a sense of incompleteness, as can be seen in Heine's allegory of the trees, where a northern fir, laden with snow and ice, set on a bare, cold height, dreams of a far-off palm, sad and lonely on her cliff of scorching rock.[16] Physical attraction is celebrated in the Song of Songs, which rhapsodizes: "my breasts were like towers" (8:10); "my beloved put his hand to the latch, and my heart was thrilled within me" (5:4 RSV); "your rounded thighs are like jewels" (7:1), "your kisses like the best wine" (7:9). The dialogue between lovers consists of such elements as flirtation, lovesickness, fear of loss, sensuous longing, and fulfillment.[17] The beloved is depicted in an astonishing assortment of images: flowers (e.g., rose, lily), trees (e.g., cedar, palm), animals (e.g., dove, sheep, gazelle), colors (e.g., ivory, alabaster), structures (e.g., tower, wall).[18]

Anglican priest John Donne wittily expounds the joys of conjugal bliss in his poem, "To his Mistress Going to Bed":

> Off with that girdle, like heaven's zone glistering,
> But a far fairer world encompassing.
> Unpin that spangled breastplate which you wear,
> That th' eyes of busy fools may be stopped there. . . .
>
> License my roving hands, and let them go
> Before, behind, between, above, below.
> O my America, my new found land . . . .
>
> Full nakedness, all joys are due to thee.

Then he closes in a teasing mood: "To teach thee, I am naked first, why then / What needst thou have more covering than a man."[19] Nudity both exposes and entices a more transparent relationship, whereby two solitary beings become a more effectual whole. Foreplay and intercourse can kindle mutual affection.

In the modern era, however, I believe we've tilted too far in the direction of pleasure at the expense of commitment, following romantic notions that stray far from Christian morality. It should be remembered that for centuries parents arranged their children's marriages, feeling that two young people not overly antagonistic could forge a successful alliance. Now you hear even churchgoers speak of "love at first sight," "irresistible passion," and "fated lovers." Today our ideal mate is not truly a matter of our own choosing, but bears the imprint of Hollywood producers, Madison Avenue advertisers, Miss America pageants, as well as our own unconscious psychological needs. Despite claims to the contrary, most marriages still take place between people of the same religion, race, class, and educational background. "You may dream of a rich, handsome, and gallant corporate executive who will swoop down to woo you," says Max Lerner, "but you actually marry the boy down the street, whose mother knows your mother and who gives you his high-school . . . pin to wear. Only the very attractive and successful have anything like a large range of choice."[20]

Or we wistfully sigh that "the grass is always greener over the *next* ridge," knowing in our heart of hearts that the next hill is probably not much different from the one we're on now, and what has really captured our fancy is the yearning for something new. We "expect irresistible love to produce some revelation" either regarding ourselves or about life at large,[21] and are disappointed to return to everyday cares and frustrations—how are we going to pay the rent? who will feed the baby? which of us should clean the toilet? Perhaps we long for a spontaneous, passionate encounter, and end up instead having intercourse without appropriate safeguards, and afterward, feel a sense of emptiness and loss. That monogamy is not romance's ultimate goal can be seen by rule thirty-one of the twelfth-century manual, *The Art of Courtly Love*, penned by the chaplain to the Countess Marie of Champagne, "Nothing forbids one woman being loved by two men or one man by two women."[22]

A case of immoderate expectations and of later disillusionment is Emma Bovary in Flaubert's novel. An avid reader of romances, she can't seem to reconcile herself to the tedium of life as the wife of a country doctor. Flaubert writes, "She longed for lives of adventure, for masked balls, for shameless pleasures that were bound, she thought, to initiate her to ecstasies she had not yet experienced."[23] But she was enmeshed in the humdrum of day-to-day existence. "Charles's conversation was commonplace as a street pavement. . . . He had never had the curiosity, he said, while he lived at Rouen, to go to the theatre to see the actors from Paris. He could neither swim, nor fence, nor shoot, and one day he could not explain some term of horsemanship to her that she had come across in a novel." Shouldn't "a man," she thought, "know everything, excel in manifold activities, initiate you into the energies of passion, the refinements of life, all mysteries?" Charles, it seemed to her, "taught nothing, knew nothing, wished nothing."[24] When he did try to invent a machine that would help improve a boy's club foot, it was a fiasco. Out of disgust and boredom, Emma had begun the first of two unfortunate affairs. The second, she ended, with debts mounting, by taking arsenic. Therapist Margaret Oldham speaks of that fruitless search for the one person who will stop us from feeling alone, when so much of the difficulty lies in our own immaturity.[25]

Another sad tale of romantic infatuation is that of Adele Hugo, the younger daughter of the French writer Victor Hugo. While her family was in exile, she had an affair with a soldier named Albert Pinson. He grew disenchanted with Adele and was only too happy when his regiment was ordered to Nova Scotia. Undaunted, Adele wrote in her diary: "This incredible thing—that a young girl shall walk over the sea, from the Old into the New World, to join her lover—this I shall accomplish."[26]

However, when she arrived in Halifax, Lieutenant Pinson shunned her, made love to other women, and ignored her notes. Gradually she became obsessed—haunting alleyways, spying on his mistresses, and disregarding her health. Following him to Barbados, eventually she was taken in by a kindly black woman, who wrote to Victor Hugo, "Sorrow has broken Adele's body and soul. The body may heal, but the soul is probably lost." Adele was returned to France and placed in a special clinic—where she gardened, played the piano, and wrote her diary in a secret code—for the next forty years.[27] Declarations of love, promises of fidelity can only be as sure as their guarantor. "My woman says there's nobody she'd rather marry / than me, not even Jupiter himself if he asked her," heralded the Latin poet Catullus, who grew increasingly disillusioned at his relationship with the bright and beautiful Clodia.[28] "She says, but what a woman says to a hungry lover / you might as well scribble in wind and swift water."[29]

Romantic love attaches too much importance to physical appearance. In a light-hearted Spanish ballad, a bewitching young woman enters church, yet what a ruckus she creates! A member of the choir loses his place during the creed, and the acolytes, instead of "Amen, Amen," chant *"Amor, Amor."*[30] "To be in love," satirist H. L. Mencken remarked, "is merely to be in a state of perceptual anesthesia—to mistake an ordinary young man for a Greek god or an ordinary young woman for a goddess."[31] Thus we resort to cosmetics to cover over nature's flaws, claim "clothes make the man," and depend on plastic surgery to salvage even the ugly. But what has beauty to do with genuine love? Is Miss America the happiest woman in the land? She's far more likely to attract ambitious males looking for a status symbol than that affable guy with a heart of gold.

Shakespeare makes fun of the far-fetched metaphors and similes sentimentalists like to crank out:

My mistress' eyes are nothing like the sun;
Coral is far more red than her lips' red;
If snow be white, why then her breasts are dun; . . .
I have seen roses damasked, red and white,
But no such roses see I in her cheeks, . . .
I love to hear her speak, yet well I know
That music hath a far more pleasing sound.

He ends, "And yet, by heaven, I think my love as rare / As any she belied with false compare."[32]

Romanticism reveals its pagan undercurrent in those well-known stories of Romeo and Juliet or Tristram and Iseult, when one lover ends up committing suicide to be with the other. Each had decided, in effect, that God could not comfort their tragic loss or foolishly believed that God had ordained one, and only one, possible mate for all eternity and any other would be second-rate. It's then we see how far removed the world of romance is from Christian love.

As Christians we need to move from attraction to commitment, what psychologist William James calls the "fiat." Then we throw all our weight on one possibility rather than another. We say, "Let *this* be reality for me."[33] Before I looked for one who would please me, now I try to please the one I have chosen. Then that mystery occurs, the two "become one flesh" and, as Jesus makes known, "what God has joined together, let no one separate" (Matt. 19:6). The ring, given during the marriage ceremony as a pledge of fidelity, symbolizes our solid and unbroken love. Couples then, of course, desire intimacy and exclusion. "I am my beloved's, and his desire is for me," cries out the female in the Song of Solomon (7:10).[34] The opposite of love, psychologist Rollo May suggests, is not hate—but apathy.[35] We make no promises, we only want to test the waters. Should things not work out, we can always call the whole thing off. Indeed less stable relationships like cohabitation (or even stepfamilies) are more likely to breed violence and abuse.[36]

Even the strongest of bonds, though, can be stretched to the breaking point by one partner's infidelity. A typical chain of events can be seen in Englishman Samuel Pepys's diary. His wife, on September 27, 1667, hires Deb Willet to be her lady-in-waiting. About a year later, she discovers her husband and Deb in a passionate embrace. Unsure how much his wife had actually seen, he admits to nothing. He writes on November 9: "Up, and I did by a little note which I flung to Deb, advise her that I did continue to deny that ever I kissed her, and so she might govern herself. The truth [is] that I did adventure upon God's pardoning me this lie." The story follows a familiar formula—clandestine encounters are smoothed over by elaborate fabrications; defiance alternates with tears of repentance; relations in bed are sometimes hot, sometimes cold; there are reproaches, threats, smoldering suspicions; fantasies linger on, which are difficult to suppress. At last Deb is sent away, and despite vows to the contrary, Samuel continues to see her. By January 31, though, he writes: "And thus ended this month, with many different days of sadness and mirth, from differences between me and my wife, from her remembrance of my late unkindness to her with Willet."[37] The marriage had managed to survive a particularly rocky period, but both sides were left wounded.

As creatures of the flesh, none of us is immune from lust. Our battle begins in earnest during puberty and doesn't die till the grave. Peter Abelard, perhaps the outstanding philosopher in twelfth-century Europe, admired for his use of the dialectical method, fell victim. In "The Story of His Misfortunes," he confesses, "I began to think myself the only philosopher in the world, with nothing to fear from anyone, and so I yielded to the lusts of the flesh."[38] When he fell in love with a young pupil, he talked her uncle into letting him live with the family—ostensibly to free Abelard from household chores, in order for him to save money, and of course, to allow ample occasion to educate the niece.

But Abelard's experience proves the old truism that impure relationships are first consummated in the mind. "I find myself following the nape of a neck—for the pleasure of looking at it—" diarist Edmond de Goncourt blurted out, "as other men follow a pair of legs."[39] Eastern church father Basil of Caesarea, taking Jesus' admonition against lust seriously (Matt. 5:27–28), conceded, "I have never known a woman, yet I am not a virgin."[40] If only we could keep a lid on roving eyes and flee from situations that compromise integrity, as Joseph did from Potiphar's wife (Gen. 39). Instead Abelard plots to be alone with Heloise: "Her studies allowed us to withdraw in private, as love desired, and then with our books open before us, more words of love than of our reading passed between us, and more kissing than teaching. My hands strayed oftener to her bosom than to the pages."[41] When the uncle does find out, he breaks up the arrangement. Soon Heloise realizes she's pregnant, so Abelard has her sent to his sister's house. After she gives birth, he agrees to a secret marriage (since philosophers, as true "lovers of wisdom," were supposed to be above carnal desires). But the story leaks out; Heloise is mistreated by her uncle for denying it; and once again Abelard has her removed secretly, this time to a convent. The uncle, enraged by this apparent breach of their earlier agreement, hires thugs to castrate Abelard. So for the rest of their lives, these starcrossed lovers reside in separate monasteries.

The tragedy of Abelard and Heloise's entanglement may partially be due to their own defective theory of morality. They thought motive (or intention) to be the sole arbiter of right and wrong, and almost disregarded both the act and its consequences. In the words of Abelard, "God considers not the action, but the spirit of the action. It is the intention, not the deed wherein the merit or praise of the doer consists."[42] Thus, in Abelard's view, should you do something noble or just desire to—you are equally to be commended: "Whether you actually give alms to a needy person, or charity makes you ready to give, makes no difference to the merit of the deed. The will may be there when the opportunity is not."[43] Nonetheless, to me it does matter if the poor actually receive alms or merely a bouquet of good wishes. Should a doctor who prescribed the wrong medicine simply be let off the hook if he meant well? No way! Good intentions can fall short of their goal through any number of obstacles—ignorance, carelessness, lack of foresight, irresolution, and so on. Yet to some extent we are accountable for the kind of person we've become, shaped by a lifetime of previous intentions.[44] Under Levitical law even unintentional sins required sacrifices (and the sprinkling of blood) before full atonement was possible (Lev. 4:2 ff).

I believe Abelard and Heloise placed too much weight on the conscience. "When we do not violate our conscience," Abelard held, "we have little fear of God holding us guilty of a fault."[45] Oh—and what about a Rousseau, who in a certain mood could boast, "My passions are extremely strong, and while I am under their sway nothing can equal my impetuosity. I am amenable to no restraint, respect, fear, or decorum. I am cynical, bold, violent, and daring. No shame can stop me, no fear of danger alarm me. Except for the one object in my mind the universe for me is non-existent."[46] Such a conscience, held in check like some well-groomed dog, will not interfere with ego's gratification. "When the compass, the square, and the ruler are off," Montaigne deduced, "all the proportions drawn from them, all the buildings erected by their measure, are also necessarily imperfect and defective."[47] Scripture warns of deceitful souls, "whose consciences" have been "seared with a hot iron," who are no longer capable of distinguishing between right and wrong (1 Tim. 4:2). Of itself, conscience cannot be the pivot of our decision making, for without God's help it has difficulty finding its true north. If Abelard and Heloise's morality had encompassed both the intention and the act, I wonder, would they have been spared a few heartaches?

Instead of surreptitious rendezvous and elaborate machinations, why not consider the advantages of simple wedded life? The fifteenth-century French woman of letters, Christine de Pisan, calls marriage "a sweet state," admitting she has "a good and wise husband," who liked to confide, "God brought you to me, / Sweet lover, and I think he raised me / To be of use to you." His gentleness and way of saying he's all hers much inflamed her reciprocal passion.[48] About that same period, Italian Francesco Barbaro rejoices: "For what is sweeter than to have a modest wife, a companion in prosperity and adversity, a helpmate and friend to whom you may confide your most intimate reflections, to whom you commit your common children, in whose sweet conversation you lay down all cares and anxieties, whom you so love that in her welfare you esteem a very part of your own life to be included?"[49]

God, said Martin Luther, has a unique way of bestowing grace upon his people. He disguises himself as our neighbor and then moves us to love that neighbor. Then through that neighbor, we come to see our own prejudices and flaws. In marriage, too, God disguises himself as a husband or wife, then moves us to love our spouse and so set forth on a new life together, which becomes a kind of school for character.[50]

Adjustments, both major and minor, are continuously called for in any relationship. You can't step into the same river twice, Presocratic philosopher Heraclitus supposed (at least in Plato's rendering), for all is in flux and nothing remains the same.[51] Sometimes the tide is spring, sometimes neap, as events ebb and flow. "When the bleak days come," advises Jeremiah Gotthelf, "when flaws appear in one or the other of you, do not think of your ill luck, of your unhappiness. Think of God rather, who has long since known all these flaws and who has brought you together precisely because of them, so that you may help each other to correct your flaws. This is the purpose and the task of your coming together."[52] It is then good to recall one's wedding vows, as the sixteenth-century Sarum Manual puts it: "I, N., take the[e], N., to my weddyd wyfe [husbande] to haue and to holde (from this day forward), for better for wurs, for rycher for porer, in syckenes and in helthe tyll deth us departe."[53] When Thomas Cranmer incorporated this wording into *The Book of Common Prayer,* the entire English-speaking world was affected.[54]

As the Persian mystic Rumi describes: "Hearts shudder before Love as though threatened by death; / For Love brings death to that dark despot, the self."[55] No one likes to die, he wants rather to retain the special pleasures, annoying habits, nervous mannerisms, and self-centered behavior he has built up since childhood. No force in heaven or on earth can change this behavior more completely than committed love. And only then, by stages, do we relinquish our private domain in order to achieve a deeper intimacy. We struggle, feel put upon, scream every inch of the way, but the dividends multiply over a lifetime. Studies make it clear that a spouse's gentle prodding helps to eradicate bad habits, and so contributes to the overall health and longevity of the mate.[56] I know my own eating habits have improved considerably over twenty-seven years of wedded life.

There's a scene in *Fiddler on the Roof,* when Tevye, the Jewish dairyman, asks his wife Golde, "But do you love me?" She goes on to enumerate how for twenty-five years she's washed his clothes, cooked the meals, cleaned the house, and milked the cow. When he persists, she adds that she's lived with him, fought with him, starved with him. "Twenty-five years my bed is his. / If that's not love, what is?" (Incidentally, she then does admit she "loves" him, which is what he wanted all along.) I find her definition, couched as it is in images of staying power, a quite compelling one.[57]

Frequently in marriage, God throws in that extra bonus, the blessing of children. The birth of Levin and Kitty's first child in Tolstoy's *Anna Karenin* was a means to Levin's spiritual renewal. Tolsoy writes: "Like the small uncertain flame of a night-light—a human being who had not existed a moment ago but who, with the same rights and importance to itself as the rest of humanity, would live and create others in its own image." Overwhelmed at the sudden appearance of this mysterious being, Levin asks, "But the baby? Whence, wherefore had it come, and who was it? He could not understand at all, nor accustom himself to the idea. It seemed to him too much, a superabundance, to which he was unable to get used for a long time."[58] Even today, when we're conversant with many of the details in reproduction and can trace various strands of DNA, we are no less bewildered and enchanted by each new face.

So the body is good. Sex can be beautiful within a committed marriage. Romantic love, however, places too high a premium on physical beauty and questing after the new. Finally, there comes a time for commitment, when we must learn to live with each other's flaws. All that's left is what ethicist Henry Fairlie calls "gazing." We cannot hope to understand a painting or a symphony or a poem unless we give it our undivided attention. We return in a variety of moods to discover hidden treasures. Sometimes one aspect speaks to us, sometimes another. Nuances are revealed that we had previously overlooked. On other occasions, nothing seems to happen; perhaps we've come for the wrong reason or don't have a proper sense of anticipation. We want to learn, but don't know how best to listen. It takes months, even years, perhaps a lifetime, to recognize and value that painting or symphony or poem on its own terms, not the ones we had tried so hard to impose upon it. The same is true for love.[59]

On the seventh level of the *Purgatorio,* Dante encounters real flames, where the lustful are doing penance. They are singing the hymn *Summae Deus clementiae* from the regular matins for Saturday, then reciting to themselves models of chastity, such as the Virgin Mary or faithful husbands and wives they have personally known. It is still a potent prayer and may help us come to terms with our own lust.

> And set our hearts from error free,
> More fully to rejoice in Thee. . . .

> Gird thou our loins, each passion quell,
> And every harmful lust expel.[60]

CHAPTER 12

The Hedonist or Aesthete

Psalm 1 draws a sharp contrast between the righteous who flourish like a long-lived tree, giving shade and fruit for years, while the wicked resemble chaff, which is swiftly blown away. Bildad the Shuhite says of those "who forget God," that "their confidence is gossamer, a spider's house their trust" (Job 8:13–14). Jesus proclaims that one who heeded his words was like a wise man who had built his house upon a rock. But one who did not take his words to heart was like a foolish man who had constructed on sand; when the rain fell and the floods came, great was his fall (Matt. 7:24–28). Second Peter 2 describes those who indulge in fleshly desires as being bold, willful revelers who despise authority, yet have no stable anchor to their lives. Elaborating on such comparisons, I'm anxious to show how the hedonist, or aesthete, lives on a physical, superficial level, while the one who puts his trust in God rests on a sure and solid foundation.

Late seventeenth- and early eighteenth-century Japanese culture was known for its portraits of *ukiyo* or "the floating world." The age esteemed above all else—the passing moment. In that segment of society portrayed, primarily the red-light district of what is now Tokyo, men and women thought nothing of having affairs. Relationships were as fickle as the human heart. The Chinese poet Li Shang-yin explains, "In this floating world there are many meetings and partings."[1] Art bordered on the risqué, taking the form of easy-to-reproduce woodblock prints. In literature the leading characters were frequently courtesans or Kabuki actors. People were judged more by their appearance than their moral stature—a physical blemish could be more detrimental to advancement than a deep character flaw. The disciplined life was not highly prized; why put extensive effort into learning a skill which might never pay off? Later historians, seeking for greatness, were more likely to find artifacts of mediocrity. To give you some idea of the level of aspiration, suffice it to say that these woodblock prints influenced nineteenth-century French artist Toulouse-Lautrec to dash off posters of can-can girls in Paris's Moulin Rouge. For me, the floating world appears like a shiny mobile hanging above a baby's crib. While there's a certain amount of charm, a pleasant, tinkling sound, one discerns little substance behind the form.

To give you more of a flavor for the era, I'd like to quote from one of its most famous books, Ihara Saikaku's *Five Women Who Loved Love*: "The sea and fields were still, as the setting sun vied with the resplendent red garments of our ladies for favor in the eyes of all. In the company of ladies dressed in such brilliant colors, the wisteria and yellow rose went unnoticed by the throng of other picnickers who had come to see the flowers but now peered instead into our party's curtained enclosure and were charmed by the sight of pretty maids inside. Forgetting the hour for departure, forgetting everything, these picnickers opened up casks of wine and proclaimed drunkenness man's greatest delight. Thus, with the enticing sight of the ladies as an appetizer for the afternoon's revels, they enjoyed themselves to their hearts' content."[2] Such was a typical scene in the Genroku period.

In Asai Ryōi's tales, *ukiyo* was defined as "living only for the moment, turning our full attention to the pleasures of the moon, sun, the cherry blossoms and the maple leaves, singing songs, drinking wine, and diverting ourselves just in floating, floating, caring not a whit for the pauperism staring us in the face, refusing to be disheartened, like a gourd floating along with the river current."[3] Because of their short-lived beauty, fall maple leaves and spring cherry blossoms came to symbolize the pursuit of pleasure before it vanished. In the woodcuts one sees banqueting, picnics, expeditions to hot springs, flower-viewing excursions, boating parties—a seemingly endless string of delightful enchantments.[4] Of course, luxurious clothes and a daub of extravagance helped lift the occasion above the ordinary. Still, beneath the apparent exuberance lay an underlying melancholy at the sad impermanence of earthly things, fired, as Buddha believed, by the endless cycle of desire.[5] The mores resemble those in John Suckling's poem "The Constant Lover": "Out upon it, I have loved / Three whole days together! / And am like to love three more, / If it hold fair weather."[6]

In the West this philosophy of hedonism, which sets pleasure as life's highest goal, is usually associated with the Greek philosopher Aristippus, who lived in the fifth century B.C. According to Diogenes Laërtius's account, Aristippus did not go out of his way to seek pleasure, but enjoyed whatever lay close at hand.[7] He counted pleasures of the body to be more important than those of the mind, perhaps because they could be felt more intensely.[8] It's not too surprising then that he was accused of living with concubines, at least one of whom claimed to have given birth to his child.[9] True to his precepts, he savored each simple pleasure as it came, and didn't worry overmuch about the aftereffects.[10]

"Eat, drink and be merry, for tomorrow we die" was, and still is, a popular taunt by hedonists (cf. 1 Cor. 15:32). The libertine Don Juan, who had scores of lovers, in Byron's poem mocks: "Let us have wine and woman, mirth and laughter, / Sermons and soda-water the day after."[11] Today's practitioners might, instead, exclaim, "Party on!" Life is viewed as a kind of carousel, and we gaily ride our painted horses round and round. If boredom sets in, we simply up the ante. In revolver roulette, first you put one bullet into the chambers of the six-shooter, then the next time two, and so on. If you can stand up after seven beers, why not try eight?

Hedonism is rooted in a naturalism that denies both God and the transcendent. The soul is not immortal; there is no day of judgment, just one pleasing sensation after another. In his pioneering work on America's sexual behavior, Alfred Kinsey labels sex as a "normal biologic function, acceptable in whatever form it is manifested,"[12] as if the entire range of social and psychological constraints established over centuries to help rein it in were no longer necessary. The problem with hedonism, as I see it, is that pleasure should be a by-product of a good life not its goal. Short-term highs can end up to be long-term downers. And we may, albeit inadvertently, harm those around us as well as ourselves. In the second circle of Dante's "lex talionis" *Inferno,* there is a raging tempest. Why? Because those who sowed the winds of lust are now reaping an eternal whirlwind: "Hither and thither, upward and downward it drives them."[13]

One of the finest critiques of hedonism is Aldous Huxley's futuristic fantasy *Brave New World.* It is a society where drugs help to maintain an equilibrium of mild euphoria. "Soma" is the universal tranquilizer and apparently has few or no side effects. One dose increases worker efficiency, another decreases tension, and so on. At a staff meeting, the Controller asks, "Has any of you been compelled to live through a long time-interval between the consciousness of a desire and its fulfillment?"[14] as though delayed gratification were the worst possible evil. Humanity is arranged into a caste system with "Alphas" on top and "Epsilons" on the bottom, all especially bred and conditioned for their particular function in society.

Sex is free and indiscriminate since "every one belongs to every one else."[15] Gone are a host of outmoded ideas such as "loyalty," "familial solidarity," or "morality" since they tend to obstruct one's pursuit of pleasure. Art, religion, literature, and love have long been banished.[16] The "feelies," a popular form of entertainment, are three-dimensional movies where the audience can actually experience the sensations of the actors on screen.[17] Little time is allowed for leisure since then one might actually start to think for oneself and question prevailing assumptions.[18] Death is sentimentalized so that one never sees its ugliness, terror, or pain.[19] And the crosses all have their tops lopped off, leaving simply letter *T*s, in honor of society's hero, Henry Ford, who invented the Model T.[20] It's a place where as nineteenth-century essayist Thomas De Quincey once remarked concerning a tincture of opium: "Happiness might now be bought for a penny, . . . portable ecstasies might be had corked up in a pint bottle: and peace of mind could be sent . . . by the mail coach."[21] Yet it's also a starkly superficial world, which Huxley ridicules by introducing a "savage," who, representing older, more traditional values, throws a glaring light on how stunted and warped society has become.

Christianity, however, believes that suffering does have value and that any attempt to completely remove or deaden it diminishes our humanity. The problem of evil is one of the universe's deep mysteries and has long puzzled our greatest minds, yet surely one piece in this jigsaw is that pain can serve as a warning signal to the body. Leprosy, one of the most feared diseases in history, was thought to spread indiscriminately like a fungus, first causing ulcers on the hands and feet, often progressing to infection and loss of limbs. However, Dr. Paul Brand, working with patients in twentieth-century India, determined that leprosy only numbed the extremities of the body; tissue damage occurred because lepers were not aware of their predicament. Lepers might put their hands in a fire or allow rats to bite off toes simply because their reaction system had been switched off. What the lepers needed, Brand concluded, was "the gift of pain," for pain would shout to them, "Stop, watch what you're doing," just as the heat from a fire tells a child not to move too close in.[22] (This is not meant to be a case against anesthesias, such as chloroform, which if used responsibly can be significant boons. Church officials who argue against alleviating pain in childbirth will often cite Gen. 3:16, claiming that interference of any kind is "unnatural."[23] However, if God only wanted events to run their natural course, why did Jesus spend so much time healing in the Gospels?)

We have come to realize, too, that pain is, to some extent, subjective, dependent on past experience and future expectations. Nobel Prize winner, Ivan Pavlov, illustrated this in his experiments with dogs. Whenever he brought an electrical current into contact with their paws, the dogs usually growled and barked ferociously. However, when he started giving them tasty treats after the shock, their anger turned to delight. Soon they would start wagging their tails, rushing toward the table, even if the current was increased, so sure were they of upcoming morsels.[24]

Suffering can also build character. "We *require* at all times a certain quantity of care or sorrow or want," philosopher Arthur Schopenhauer remarked, "as a ship requires ballast, in order to keep on a straight course."[25] Eleanor Roosevelt was convinced that Franklin's long bout with polio was the key to shaping his strength and depth, though at first it nearly destroyed his rising political star. She writes, "I never heard him mention golf from the day he was taken ill until the end of his life. That game epitomized to him the ability to be out of doors and to enjoy the use of his body." However, "he soon discovered that the way to lighten all burdens is to take them cheerfully" and was able to regain "his joy in living, his hearty laughter, his ability to be happy over little things." The victory was so remarkable that when he later told the nation, "The only thing we have to fear is fear itself," they knew he truly believed it.[26] Too, Helen Keller, who became deaf and blind at the age of two due to a fever, related, "I thank God for my handicaps, for through them I have found myself, my work, and my God."[27]

Suffering can bring out empathy as well. German theologian Dietrich Bonhoeffer, who was executed for taking part in a plot on Hitler's life, reasoned that "only the suffering God can help."[28] In this he shows his indebtedness to Luther's concept of *theologia crucis*,[29] wherein God's self-revelation is manifest in weakness and scandal. In Bonhoeffer's famous work, *The Cost of Discipleship*, he makes a distinction between "cheap" and "costly" grace, seeing the Sermon on the Mount as the blueprint for true discipleship. God, as revealed in Christ, is so powerless he can redeem humanity only by suffering for it. So, too, the church should follow in his footsteps and serve all who are hurting. For suffering sensitizes us to the frailties and needs of others, allowing us to comfort them afterward with that heartening affirmation, "I have been there too." Bonhoeffer had a particular distaste for all philosophies of ethereal individualism that separated us from involvement in God's world; when he spoke of the earth, he might add, in which the cross of Jesus Christ is planted.

Thus suffering can be a wake-up call, mold character, and sensitize us to the needs of others. Its opposite is the floating world, where one's goal is to be carefree as a gourd floating downstream, or, as we in the West might put it, "A rolling stone gathers no moss." The postponing of tough decisions is symptomatic of our humanity. Augustine admitted that in his youth he had prayed halfheartedly: "'Give me chastity and continence, but not yet!' For I feared that you would hear me quickly, and that quickly you would heal me of that disease of lust, which I wished to have satisfied rather than extinguished."[30] How similar is libertine Don Juan's flippant comment in Mozart's opera, whenever his servant complains that some day he must pay for his misdeeds: "Time enough for that."[31] Augustine tries to fend off God by stalling, "'Right away. Yes, right away.' 'Let me be for a little while.' But 'right away—right away' was never right now, and 'Let me be for a little while' stretched out for a long time."[32] Finally he recognized how far in bondage he really was: "The enemy had control of my will, and out of it he fashioned a chain and fettered me with it. For in truth lust is made out of a perverse will, and when lust is served, it becomes habit, and when habit is not resisted, it becomes necessity."[33]

As Augustine discerned (and modern sociology affirms), there is a certain measure of rebelliousness in improper behavior. Centuries before, Job had spoken of "those who rebel against the light" (Job 24:13). "Doing wrong is like sport to a fool" (Prov. 10:23) says an ancient Hebrew proverb. In historian John Burnham's study of such "bad habits" as excessive drinking, smoking, taking drugs, gambling, and sexual impropriety, he sees the pattern of rebelliousness exacerbated by the rise of large American corporations such as brewers, tobacco companies, casinos, or pornographers, who, intent on maximizing profits regardless of how their product affects the consumer, develop trade names and trade symbols that they aggressively promote via slick coming-of-age models, all the while disseminating misinformation to shield their companies from possible lawsuits. The rebel's devil-may-care attitude can fly in the face of family upbringing and social convention, deny responsibility by claiming one's actions don't injure anyone (despite overwhelming evidence to the contrary), and even seek to shift the blame to the victim. Rape? Wasn't that scantily clad woman in a pool hall after hours simply asking for it?[34]

But decisions do have consequences and you may be the one who has to pay. "He who lives looking for pleasures only, his senses uncontrolled, immoderate in his food, idle, and weak," says the Buddhist *Dhammapada,* "Māra (the tempter) will certainly overthrow him, as the wind throws down a weak tree."[35] In his book *Extremes,* Dutch cardiologist A. J. Dunning offers a sobering list of famous writers whose unconventional behavior ultimately ruined their health. Thus Baudelaire, after a life of womanizing and taking opium, died of syphilis at the age of forty-six. Poet Heinrich Heine, who spent too much time in Paris flophouses, died from syphilitic spinal deterioration. German philosopher Friedrich Nietzsche suffered from delusions of grandeur that, too, could be traced to syphilis. Romantic writer Alfred de Musset, according to Dunning, "had valves so leaky that at each heartbeat, his head bobbed in time with his pulse." French cardiologists still speak of *signe de Musset* to describe syphilis of the aortic valves. Finally, Dunning cites medical historian William Osler's opinion that those who serve the gods of Bacchus (wine and revelry) and Venus (love) do not reach the age of sixty.[36] All these made important, noteworthy contributions, but also underwent years of mental and physical anguish, becoming ever more embittered, and died premature deaths, due to lifestyles that acted as slow forms of poison. Even now syphilis and other forms of venereal disease, particularly if left untreated or discovered late, can cause severe damage.

If we're simply drifting through life, the current may keep us afloat for a time, but once it lets go, who knows where we'll end up? So we need to take charge of our lives, form a personal code of ethics, and not cave in to peer pressure or outside norms. Sociologist David Riesman calls for an autonomous individuality, "the nerve of failure"—when we "defend an independent view of the self and of what life holds"; muster the courage to "accept the possibility of defeat, of failure, without being morally crushed"; and can stand as a "lonely thinker," who is "unimpressed by the judgments passed on his views, his personality, his system of values by the dominant authorities of his day."[37] Then we will not be so easily buffeted by prevailing winds. In the days when England wavered back and forth between Catholicism and Protestantism, some flexibility was called for just to survive, but Dr. Perne of Peterhouse, who altered his religious allegiances with each new sovereign—four times in twelve years—became a byword for moral weakness. Wits jested, "A Papist a Protestant a Papist a Protestant but still Andrew Perne," while others translated the Latin verb *perno, pernare* as "I turn, I rat, I change often."[38]

At the other end of the spectrum from the floating world is what psychologist Abraham Maslow called "self-actualization." He constructed a hierarchy of values whose lowest layer consisted of biological needs such as food, drink, and rest, while at the top of the pyramid were intangibles like understanding, the sublime, and realizing one's potential. He thought counselors could help people meet these "metaneeds" by asking questions like "What do you enjoy doing?" "What are you good at?" "What kinds of people do you like being around?" "Where do you find a sense of wonder or awe?" Indeed analyzing "peak experiences" can help to reveal one's mission in life, should we follow through with decisions based on what we've discovered. If we go against our best interests, however, we risk turning into spiritual dwarfs, mere remnants of a genuine human being. When our whole being is engaged, we come to perceive others, as Spinoza describes it, "under the aspect of eternity."[39] So Paul pushed the Corinthians to discern and develop their spiritual gifts, aspiring for the higher ones, so that the body of Christ could fully perform its umpteen functions (1 Cor. 12:4–31).

Baudelaire called his experiments with hashish and opium "false paradises"; he eventually forsook these, but by then it may have been too late.[40] To me the floating world illustrates how useless are our attempts to escape from our deepest selves by salving fears, sorrows, and pain with feel-good bromides. Francis Thompson immortalized his flight from God in "The Hound of Heaven":

> I fled Him, down the nights and down the days;
>   I fled Him, down the arches of the years;
> I fled Him, down the labyrinthine ways
>   Of my own mind; and in the midst of tears
> I hid from Him, and under running laughter. . . .
> Adown Titanic glooms of chasmèd fears,

From those strong Feet that followed, followed after. . . .
      Deliberate speed, majestic instancy,
      They beat—and a Voice beat
      More instant than the Feet—
   "All things betray thee, who betrayest Me."[41]

Our attitude toward God may be at the root of some of our deepest maladies. Doctors, psychiatrists, social workers, teachers, even pastors, may not be able to help if we're in a state of denial. When we pursue pleasure with heedless abandon, as if there were no tomorrow, having little in the way of core values and no moral compass to guide us, still God is relentless in his quest. Ever behind the scenes, he is drawing humankind to himself, as George Herbert's "The Pulley" shows: "Let him be rich and wearie, that at least, / If goodnesse leade him not, yet wearinesse / May tosse him to my breast."[42] In those now familiar words of Augustine, "You had made us for yourself, and our heart is restless until it rests in you."[43] Then he prays earnestly, "Who will give me help, so that I may rest in you? Who will help me, so that you will come into my heart and inebriate it, to the end that I may forget my evils and embrace you, my one good? . . . Too narrow is the house of my soul for you to enter into it: let it be enlarged by you. It lies in ruins; build it up again."[44] Plato relates the story of those who are chained inside a cave and can only dumbly stare at shadows like those marionettes might cast upon a wall. If one person does manage to escape, when he returns to tell his companions the glorious news that he has seen a reality beyond these shadows, he is most likely to be laughed at, even put to death.[45] Such is still the fate of evangelists who preach to those in darkness, who are unable to fathom entire realms outside their own.

For centuries philosophers have recommended an exercise to lend more gravity to our lives, that is, contemplating our mortality. A common epitaph one comes across on old tombstones is *memento mori,* "remember, you must die." "You got to walk that lonesome valley," says the American folk tune. "You got to go there by yourself, / Ain't nobody here can go there for you."[46] Death is a lonely road and you travel it but once. So people postpone writing wills, make excuses for not attending funerals, don't enter cemeteries after dark, freeze the corpse of loved ones in suspended animation, and practice a hundred other subterfuges to avoid thinking about the inevitable. Indeed psychologist Carl Jung, after counseling hundreds of patients, judged that everyone past the age of forty was, to some extent, affected by the fear of his own approaching death.[47]

Popular in seventeenth-century Holland was a form of still-life painting known as "Vanitas," which displayed the transience or uncertainty of life. The artist would carefully depict and arrange everyday objects that symbolized our mortality—a skull, an hour glass, a candle—perhaps alongside an overturned cup or bowl.

Beside these might be a crown or a purse, connoting possessions soon to be lost. Then, to give it all a Christian touch, there might appear the elements of the Eucharist, a glass of wine and a loaf of bread, to hint at resurrection.[48] "What a small part of the infinite abyss of time has been divided off for each of us," muses Roman emperor Marcus Aurelius, "for very quickly it disappears into eternity." Again, "we shall very soon be only ashes or dry bones."[49] All of our destinies are like that aristocratic family's in Ludwig Uhland's poem, "The Luck of Edenhall"—tied to a tall drinking glass of crystal, given by a fairy, that without any warning can splinter into a thousand pieces.[50]

"Each day postman Death / Knocks on our door," Arabic poet Abu al-Ala al-Ma'arri asserts. "Although he does not speak, / He hands us a standing invitation."[51] One never knows when an accident will happen or whether an incurable disease might cut short an otherwise productive life. "Oh, what great palaces, how many fair houses and noble dwellings, once filled with attendants and nobles and ladies, were emptied," the narrator in Boccaccio's *The Decameron* said concerning those days when the bubonic plague struck fourteenth-century Florence. "How many gallant men and fair ladies and handsome youths, whom Galen, Hippocrates and Aesculapius themselves would have said were in perfect health, at noon dined with their relatives and friends, and at night supped with their ancestors in the next world!"[52]

So instead of letting our days be frittered away on trifles or being overwhelmed by sensory data, how much better to emulate Montaigne: "Now that I see my life limited in time, I want to extend it in weight. I want to arrest the speed of its flight by the speed of my grasp and by the vigor of my use to compensate for the haste of its flow. To the extent that the possession of life is short, I have to make it the more profound and full."[53] Still, careful planning can only go so far. "Who has ever been able to seize life aright?" German poet August Graf von Platen-Hallermünde wondered aloud. "Who has not had to waste half of it in dreams, in feverish activity, in conversation with fools, in pains of love, in empty squandering of time?"[54] Every mouth is stopped by the contrariness of life; suddenly an unexpected gust comes up, threatening to capsize the ship.

In Thornton Wilder's play *Our Town*, the recently deceased Emily Webb desires to go back and relive one day of her life. However, she soon finds the experience too heart-wrenching and is forced to break it off. As one of the dead explains, "Now you know! That's what it was to be alive. To move about in a cloud of ignorance; to go up and down trampling on the feelings of those . . . of those about you. To spend and waste time as though you had a million years. To be always at the mercy of one self-centered passion, or another. Now you know—that's the happy existence you wanted to go back to. Ignorance and blindness."[55]

Tolstoy, in the twelfth chapter of *A Confession,* compares life to a boat careening downstream in a fast-moving river. Around him were vessels, some large, some small. In a few the oars were flying; in others they had all but been abandoned. Eventually he hears the roar of the rapids. As he watches boats being smashed, he realizes he, too, soon will perish. "Then I came to my senses," he writes. "I remembered the oars and the way to the shore and began to pull against the current and head back upstream toward it. The shore was God, the stream was tradition, and the oars were the free will given to me to make it to shore where I would be joined with God."[56]

Christianity doesn't seek to squelch pleasure; rather, it calls for the deep-seated joy that is independent of circumstances, not owing to substances that alter the brain's chemistry. The psalmist rejoices, "But you have put into my heart a greater happiness than others had from grain and wine in plenty"(Ps. 4:7 REV). So instead of carousing with convivial friends during the good times, why not join the people of God during periods of prosperity *and* affliction? Here the elixir that suffuses our being isn't some artificial stimulant but the love shed abroad in our hearts by the indwelling Holy Spirit. Here you may discover your true calling, unravel your real self, and be opened up to a spiritual dimension you hardly knew existed. And there will be time, all the time you'll ever need, to probe the meaning of unfading truth and assay the beauty that will not wither. Then, like homing pigeons who return to God their source, we roost in nests created for us from before the foundation of the world.

It's been said that if you put a conch to your ear, you can faintly hear the waves of the far-off sea. I say, if you put a stethoscope to a human soul, you will register, albeit feebly, the heartbeat of God. Thomas Hardy, in a flashback in his poem "The Oxen," conveys this universal yearning for the supernatural:

> Yet, I feel,
> If someone said on Christmas Eve,
>   "Come; see the oxen kneel
> In the lonely barton by yonder coomb
>   Our childhood used to know,"
> I should go with him in the gloom,
>   Hoping it might be so.[57]

J. R. R. Tolkien, author of that touchstone fantasy *The Lord of the Rings,* spoke of our longing for "the Consolation of the Happy Ending," so prominent in fairy tales. He then commented concerning the archetype—the birth, life, death, and resurrection of Christ—that "there is no tale ever told that men would rather find was true." Our proper response, Tolkien felt, was the joy of the *Gloria,* since "Legend and History have met and fused."[58]

CHAPTER 13

Gluttony, the Strong Craving

It has been said that one of the human race's greatest boons is to be able to eat when we're *not* hungry and to drink when we're *not* thirsty. This is due to our ability to reflect on the pleasures of the palate and our eagerness to prolong them.[1] According to tradition, the ancient Greek hedonist Philoxenus wished his throat was as long as a crane's, so as to better savor each morsel as it went down, and that he actually wept because the felicities of eating could not be spread over his entire body.[2]

Scientifically, food refers to those substances that the body can assimilate, use for maintenance, change into energy, or make into new tissue to replace parts that are continuously being worn out by the rigors of daily living.[3] *Homo sapiens* has incisors for slicing fruit, molars for crushing seeds and nuts, as well as canines for ripping apart flesh.[4] Our taste buds are so concentrated that we can experience sweet at the tip of the tongue, bitter at the back, sour on the sides, and salty almost everywhere, but mainly up front.[5] However, just as we can't smell something until it begins to evaporate, we can't taste something until it dissolves, hence our need for saliva.[6]

But taste, like all of the senses, can be distorted. The Israelites in the wilderness had a "strong craving." They remembered the meat they used to eat in Egypt as well as the fish, cucumbers, melons, leeks, onions, and garlic (Num. 11:4–5). Craving is at the heart of the sin of gluttony, which manifests itself, for instance, in obesity, drunkenness, or drug addiction. "Therefore the Lord will give you meat, and you shall eat. You shall eat not only one day, or two days, or five days, or ten days, or twenty days, but for a whole month—until it comes out of your nostrils and becomes loathsome to you—because you have rejected the Lord who is among you" (Num. 11:18–20).

Edmund Spenser's pageant of the seven deadly sins in *The Faerie Queene* depicts gluttony this way:

> And by his [Idlenesse's] side rode loathsome Gluttony,
> Deforméd creature, on a filthie swyne,
> His belly was up-blowne with luxury,
> And eke with fatnesse swollen were his eyne,
> And like a Crane his necke was long and fyne,
> With which he swallowd up excessive feast,
> For want whereof poore people oft did pyne;
> And all the way, most like a brutish beast,
> He spued up his gorge, that all did him deteast.

> . . . Still as he rode, he somewhat still did eat,
> And in his hand did beare a bouzing can,
> Of which he supt so oft, that on his seat
> His dronken corse he scarse upholden can,
> In shape and life more like a monster, than a man.

> . . . Whose mind in meat and drinke was drownéd so,
> That from his friend he seldome knew his fo:
> Full of diseases was his carcas blew,
> And a dry dropsie through his flesh did flow:
> Which by misdiet daily greater grew:
> Such one was Gluttony, the second of that crew.[7]

In the fourteenth-century satire *Piers the Ploughman,* gluttony is personified as one who decides to go to confession but on the way is lured into a tavern, becomes intoxicated, sunk into a two-day hangover, and is absolved only after he admits to Repentance:[8] "And I have let myself go at supper, and sometimes dinner too, so badly that I have thrown it all up again before I have gone a mile, and wasted food that might have been saved for the hungry. On fast-days I have eaten the tastiest foods I could get, and drunk the best wines, and sometimes sat so long at my meals that I've slept and eaten both at the same time. And to get more drink and hear some gossip, I've had my dinner at the pub on fast-days too."[9]

As for myself, during the month of August, I can subsist on fresh sweet corn and watermelon. It's just the other eleven months I have to worry about. A college friend and I used to sit around in the dining hall pontificating on the issues of the day, when suddenly his hand would reach across the table into my plate. He would soon be apologizing, "Ken, that chocolate chip cookie just seduced me." I confess to a special fondness for potato chips. Companies design them too large to fit into your mouth in order for you to hear that wonderful crackling sound. The chip was actually invented in 1853 at Moon Lake Lodge in Saratoga Springs, New York, when a chef became so angry at a diner who demanded thinner and thinner French fries that he sliced them almost to the vanishing point and then fried them until they were varnish-brown. To his chagrin, the diner gorged himself on them, other guests started requesting samples, and eventually George Crum started his own restaurant specializing in potato chips.[10]

My other secret passion is ice cream (especially homemade). There are so many scrumptious flavors to choose from—vanilla, chocolate chip, caramel, strawberry swirl, cherry nut. . . . You can take your cream-filled croissant, sugar donut, coconut macaroon, or slice of lemon meringue and put them back on their plates. I prefer dairy products scooped out of saucers, concurring with Wallace Stevens's whimsical line: "The only emperor is the emperor of ice-cream."[11]

Sensory experiences like these can conjure up a world of associations as in Proust's *Swann's Way*. When Marcel's aunt serves him tea and sweet cakes known as "madeleines," it's as if a light has thrown open the past. "I feel something start within me . . . palpitating in the depths of my being . . . the image, the visual memory . . . linked to that taste." "In that moment all the flowers in our garden and in M. Swann's park, and the water-lilies on the Vivonne and the good folk of the village and their little dwellings and the parish church and the whole of Combray and of its surroundings, taking their proper shapes and growing solid, sprang into being, town and gardens alike, from my cup of tea." It was Marcel's belief that smell and taste were ever poised to call forth hidden memories.[12] I know whenever I soak tough cookies in milk, I can't help thinking of my grandmother.

We need to be aware of our passions, since in certain circumstances they can turn addictive. "There are many things in the world I cannot understand," observes Kenkō, a fourteenth-century Buddhist priest. "I cannot imagine why people find it so enjoyable to press liquor on you the first thing, on every occasion, and force you to drink it. The drinker's face grimaces as if with unbearable distress, and he looks for a chance to get rid of the drink and escape unobserved, only to be stopped and senselessly forced to drink more." What follows is predictable enough: the familiar hangover. "The victim's head aches even the following day, and he lies abed, groaning, unable to eat, unable to recall what happened the day before. . . . He neglects important duties, both public and private, and the result is disaster."[13] Only by confronting such socially accepted behavior directly has Mothers Against Drunk Driving been able to make progress against the needless highway fatalities in our own day.

But what makes gluttony, or the strong craving, a sin? It's partly because the glutton is too enamored with the senses. It is the sign of a nature not finely tempered, remarks the Stoic philosopher Epictetus, "to give yourself up to things which relate to the body; to make, for instance, a great fuss about exercise, a great fuss about eating, a great fuss about drinking, a great fuss about walking, a great fuss about riding. All these things ought to be done merely by the way: the formation of the spirit and character must be our real concern."[14] As the apostle Paul recommended to Timothy, "Train yourself in godliness, for, while physical training is of some value, godliness is valuable in every way, holding promise for both the present life and the life to come" (1 Tim. 4:7–8).

People get so caught up in following bizarre diets, finding new health foods, or cooking exotic dishes. They are thrilled by the highs of binge drinking or enamored with the temporary release narcotics offer to mental anguish and physical pain. Yet over time these little indulgences can turn into preoccupations that absorb abnormal amounts of energy and time. One's life becomes a kind of subterfuge as it revolves around one's addiction and the host of codependents who support it. Like a member of a special armed forces unit, the addict concentrates on disguise. "I've known drunkards before," Lady Marchmain sternly warns Charles Ryder in Evelyn Waugh's *Brideshead Revisited*. "One of the most terrible things about them is their deceit. Love of truth is the first thing that goes."[15]

Eating or drinking then turns into a personal manifesto, with the glutton's world bounded by the distance from the fireplace to the table. Spanish baroque poet, Luis de Góngora, humorously expresses this philosophy: "Let others cope with governing / The kingdoms of the world, / While I let days be governed / By butter cakes and bread." He goes on then to list other favorites: rum and orangeade; sausage on the grill; chestnuts and acorns a'popping; snails and cockles. In the final stanza, alluding to those star-crossed lovers, Pyramus and Thisbe, who commit suicide by running themselves through with a sword,[16] Gongora, as glutton, mocks himself, seeing his Thisbe as a mulberry pie and the tooth, his "fatal sword."[17]

One recalls Rabelais's outrageous hero, Gargantua (named for his enormous throat), whose first words after being born were: "Give me a drink! a drink! a drink!" So, he was given a good stiff drink, and afterward, 17,913 cows were rounded up to provide him milk until he was twenty-two months of age. Whenever he cried, stamped his feet, or appeared out of sorts, some soothing liquid was placed between his lips, and instantly his good humor was restored. One of his maids claimed that "he was so accustomed to this treatment that at the very sound of pints and flagons, he would fall into an ecstasy, as though he were tasting the joys of paradise. . . . To amuse him every morning they would ring glasses with a knife in front of him, or flagons with their stoppers, or pints with their lids, at which sound, he would become very gay and leap for joy, and would rock himself back and forth in his cradle."[18] Stuffing the open mouth is a prominent theme in

Rabelais and allows his wit to be given full rein.[19] Indeed at times his characters seem more like inflatable balloons.

The sensualist has been called by Neilos the ascetic "a soul 'sitting on idols,'" referring to that incident in Genesis where Rachel hid her father's idols in her camel's saddle, and while sitting on them, was unable to rise to "higher things" (Gen. 31:34–35).[20] The glutton is held captive by oral fixations. "Every concern is tyrannical," warns theologian Paul Tillich, "and wants our whole heart and our whole mind and our whole strength. Every concern tries to become our ultimate concern, our god. The concern about our work often succeeds in becoming our god, as does the concern about another human being, or about pleasure." While these concerns have a legitimate place, requiring our "attention, devotion, passion," they should not become so all-encompassing as to demand "*infinite* attention, *unconditional* devotion, *ultimate* passion. They are important, often very important for you and for me and for the whole of mankind. But they are not *ultimately* important."[21] Remember how Jesus, in the fourth Gospel, invents those suggestive images of the "bread of life" and "living water" (John 6:35; 4:13–14, 7:37–38) to beckon his hearers beyond mundane hand-to-mouth preoccupations.

This does not mean pleasure is evil. Far from it! Each "day" of creation God called "good" (e.g., Gen. 1:12). The apostle Paul pronounced all foods to be "clean" (Rom. 14:20). The first "sign" Jesus performed in John's Gospel was turning water into wine during a wedding in Cana (John 2:9). "It is lawful when a man needs meat to choose the pleasanter," Christian moralist Jeremy Taylor writes, "even merely for their pleasures; . . . this is as lawful as the smell of a rose, or to lie in feathers, or change the posture of our body in bed for ease, or to hear music, or to walk in gardens rather than the highways; and God has given us leave to be delighted in those things."[22] All good things should be received with that simple grace attributed to Martin Luther: "Come, Lord Jesus, be our guest, / And may our meal by you be blest."[23] Even in the austere environs of the monastery, Benedict called for two types of cooked food at each meal (and a third, if fresh fruit or vegetables were in season), alongside the year-round staples of wine and bread. "In this way, the person who may not be able to eat one kind of food may partake of the other."[24]

In the culinary arts, timing or preservation techniques are critical. "Every substance has its peak of deliciousness," observes gastronome Brillat-Savarin, "some of them have already reached it before their full development, like capers, asparagus, young grey partridges, squab pigeons, and so on; others reach it at that precise moment when they are all that it is possible for them to be in perfection, like melons and almost all fruits, mutton, beef, venison, and red partridges; and finally still others at that point when they begin to decompose, like medlars, woodcock, and above all pheasant."[25]

Coloring, too, brightens up the festivities—whether green from parsley, amber from saffron, red from sandalwood, et cetera.[26] This is especially true for spirits, since, coming from the distillery, they are nearly clear. In England "Old Gold" sherries, port as black as night, deep amber hocks, and brown brandy were once popular, then rosé wines, tawny ports, paper-white hocks, and pale sherries and brandies became the vogue.[27] Too, let's not forget the spices. I add pepper or salt to nearly every main course I eat. Can you imagine a Chinese dish without soy sauce, an Indian without curry powder, a Mexican without hot peppers? Spices give everything that touches the tongue a zest and tang. Texture and smell, too, have prominent roles to play in dining. In what proportion the ingredients should be mixed, how long they should be cooked and at what temperature, and which condiments are to be added are essential to good recipes that can be passed on for generations.

Eating has always been a social occasion. "The pleasure of dining with one's friends is so great that nothing has ever given me more delight than their unexpected arrival," fourteenth-century Italian poet Petrarch pointed out, "nor have I ever willingly sat down to table without a companion."[28] I, too, enjoy meeting others for lunch or having them over for a meal while pleasant conversation flows. And how many business deals each day are clinched over a dessert?

The glutton knows this only too well. Unable to moderate his pleasures, he often has developed superior "social" skills, which make him seem somehow more acceptable and his sin that much harder to root out. He is considered "a harmless figure of fun, a cowardly lion of lovable proportions, a sinner who, although fallen from grace himself, nevertheless saves others by his insistence on bacchanalia and feast."[29] While the glutton's playful facade may make for marvelous comic relief, in the long run it masks profound, unresolved tensions.

Shakespeare's supreme comic creation is "that huge bombard of sack, that stuffed cloakbag of guts, that roasted Manningtree ox with the pudding in his belly,"[30] none other than Sir John Falstaff of *Henry IV* fame. Obese, witty, bawdy, lying, thieving, and boastful, he is a drinking companion for young Prince Hal.[31] But by Part 2 of the history, the relationship has become quite strained. After the prince assumes the responsibility of being king, he realizes he must put away childish things and, for the good of England, banish that unregenerate old knight, "the tutor and feeder of my riots."[32] Literary critic Samuel Johnson once remarked of Falstaff, "No man is more dangerous than he that, with a will to corrupt, hath the power to please."[33] So, my advice: Choose your friends with care.

In the end gluttony can enslave, for the glutton attributes magical properties to the substance he abuses. When he's down, it lifts him up; when he's nervous, it soothes him; when he's confused, it clears his mind. Concerning the alcoholic, the Book of Proverbs speaks, instead, of snakebite, hallucination, and nausea:[34]

> Do not look at wine when it is red,
>   when it sparkles in the cup
>   and goes down smoothly.
> At the last it bites like a serpent,
>   and stings like an adder.
> Your eyes will see strange things,
>   and your mind utter perverse things.
> You will be like one who lies down in the midst of the sea,
>   like one who lies on the top of a mast.
> "They struck me," you will say, "but I was not hurt;
>   they beat me, but I did not feel it.
> When shall I awake?
>   I will seek another drink." (23:31–35)

Like a groggy boxer who has been knocked to the mat, the alcoholic feels victorious simply because he can stand up and go back again for more punishment.[35] The drunkard, as Jeremy Taylor notes, "calls off the watchmen from their towers."[36] His conscience slumbers, inhibitions are released; thus, alcoholism is often intertwined with acts of violence and crime.[37]

In 1 Corinthians 6:12, Paul enunciates one of the great principles of the Christian life. He starts out, "All things are lawful for me." Here is that call to liberty so pervasive in his epistles. Read the Book of Galatians. Paul simply will not allow Gentile converts to be brought back under the yoke of Jewish ceremonial law and succumb to the now unnecessary rite of circumcision. He bitterly disputes Peter, calling him a hypocrite to his face for caving in to pressure groups from Jerusalem. Read Martin Luther's "Freedom of a Christian," where he defends that key doctrine of the Reformation, justification by faith. "A Christian is a perfectly free lord of all, subject to none,"[38] he boldly writes Pope Leo X.

Then Paul continues, "but not all things are beneficial." I may be free to eat and drink as I please, but does my behavior enhance spiritual growth? Are my actions worthwhile endeavors? Do they build me up or tear me down? And how will they serve the good of my neighbor? Luther, too, continues on rather paradoxically, that "a Christian is a perfectly dutiful servant of all, subject to all."[39] Paul repeats, "All things are lawful to me," yet qualifies it by adding, "but I will not be dominated by anything." I won't be enslaved by wine or desserts or cocaine, or any besetting encumbrance in all creation. You Corinthians like to boast of your freedom, but don't use it as a pretext for harming yourself or others.

Do any of you have a "strong craving"? Are you struggling with gluttony or have you fallen victim to addiction of any kind? Aquinas argued that the virtue which could overcome gluttony was temperance or abstinence. It's that Aristotelian mean, located somewhere between the twin errors of excess and deficiency, in a not always easy-to-define center.[40] All our habits are the result of previous decisions, whether conscious or unconscious, that are now second nature, hence difficult to dislodge. But there's still hope, because our souls lie transparent before him who created us. "When a man is convinced that, wherever he is, he always stands in the presence of God," counseled eighteenth-century Jewish ethicist Moses Luzzatto, "he is spontaneously imbued with fear lest he do anything wrong, and so detract from the exalted glory of God."[41] Instead of displaying a morbid fascination with sin, God is that utterly patient parent, anxious to tap into our better angels.

The Book of James says, "Resist the devil, and he will flee from you" (4:7). One of the best ways to break an old habit, according to psychologist William James, is to replace it with a new one, what behaviorist John Watson calls "stimulus substitution."[42] For example, do you like to devour a slice of cake before you go to bed? Why not substitute a favorite fruit such as an apple or peach? Do you like to hang around the bar after work? Maybe you could join a club or a sports team to fill that vacuum.

Start off that new habit with a bang. Place yourself in situations that reinforce your decision. Tell others what you're doing, to take advantage of their support. And, if at all possible, don't cheat. When you're winding up yarn, one lapse can unravel an incredible amount of string. Keep the momentum going with a little extra oomph beyond the minimum.[43] "Refrain tonight," advised Hamlet, "And that shall lend a kind of easiness / To the next abstinence; the next more easy; / For use almost can change the stamp of nature."[44] And should you fall, don't throw in the towel. Sincerely confess and pick yourself up again (cf. 1 John 1:8–10).

First, though, we must admit that we have a problem and that we need help, and then seek out friends or professionals. "I seemed every night to descend, not metaphorically, but literally to descend, into chasms and sunless abysses, depths below depths, from which it seemed hopeless that I could ever reascend," reports Thomas De Quincey, owning up to his opium addiction. "Opium had long ceased to found its empire on spells of pleasure; it was solely by the tortures connected with the attempt to abjure it, that it kept its hold. . . . However, a crisis arrived for the author's life. . . . I saw that I must die if I continued the opium: I determined, therefore, if that should be required, to die in throwing it off. . . . My first task" was "to reduce" the habit "to forty, to thirty, and, as fast as I could, to twelve grains. I triumphed: but think not, reader, that therefore my sufferings were ended. . . . Think of me as of one, even when four months had passed, still agitated, writhing, throbbing, palpitating, shattered." In a burst of optimism, he adds, "My case is at least a proof that opium, after a seventeen years' use, and an eight years' abuse of its powers, may still be renounced."[45] Or, at least, it could be better controlled.

"I held it truth . . . ," Alfred, Lord Tennyson replied to the fatalists of his day, "that men may rise on stepping-stones / Of their dead selves to higher things."[46] You may not be as hooked as De Quincey was, yet nevertheless be in dire straits. To delay is only to let the habit become more ingrained. "You cannot run away from a weakness"; charged Robert Louis Stevenson, "you must some time fight it out or perish; and if that be so, why not now, and where you stand?"[47] No doubt you have a few faithful friends or relatives, maybe a father or mother, brother or sister, or perhaps a spouse, who may sometimes seem far away, but probably cares more deeply than you can imagine. Here's the community of faith, which is committed to your welfare. And, of course, there's God, the most unobtrusive, and yet the most powerful, force in the universe. And he loves you intensely, and I guarantee he won't ever let go, even if everyone else does.

Excuses won't do. Think of those horrifying pictures of opium dens or crack houses, whose inhabitants are lethargic, leaden-eyed, lost in a kind of mental fog, and to all appearances, more zombies than genuine human beings. It's that "numb, despairing feeling," which heroin addict William S. Burroughs called "being buried alive."[48] "The drunken Rip Van Winkle, in Jefferson's play," psychologist William James writes, "excuses himself for every fresh dereliction by saying, 'I won't count this time!' Well! he may not count it, and a kind Heaven may not count it; but it is being counted none the less. Down among his nerve-cells and fibres the molecules are counting it, registering and storing it up to be used against him when the next temptation comes."[49]

Hopefully one day you'll make an entry in your journal like that of the brilliant English diarist Samuel Pepys, who penned on Sunday, January 26, 1662: "To church in the morning. But thanks be to God, since my leaving drinking of wine, I do find myself much better and do mind my business better, and do spend less money, and less time lost in idle company."[50] Yes, that strong craving of whatever kind can be surmounted, though it won't be easy, and deliverance may not be permanent. Habits are due to definite pathways formed in the nervous system, yet if they're not reinforced, they tend to fade.[51] So, I say, thanks be to God for each minor victory in our life of faith. May such victories occur ever more regularly and last unto everlasting life. "I have deceived myself, dear Christ," prayed early church father Gregory of Nazianzus, "I confess it; I have fallen from the heights to the depths. O lift me up again, for well I know delusion came because I wanted it."[52]

CHAPTER 14

The Faster and Various Imitators

Someone once asked the ancient Cynic philosopher Diogenes, what was the proper hour for dining? He replied, "If you are rich, whenever you please; if poor, whenever you can."[1] One's wealth certainly has much to do with one's eating habits. I'd like to make a case, however, for a largely forgotten spiritual discipline in this smorgasbord culture of self-indulgence, namely, that of fasting. Moses, when he received the law on Mount Sinai, fasted for forty days and forty nights (Exod. 34:28); Elijah did the same upon fleeing from Jezebel after the prophets of Baal had been slaughtered (1 Kings 19:8); and Jesus, at the outset of his ministry, fasted for a similar length of time, when the devil tempted him in the wilderness (Matt. 4:1–2).

In that early church manual, *The Didache,* fasting is recommended for candidates about to be baptized, and for all Christians twice a week.[2] But instead of Thursdays and Mondays, the days it was believed that Moses went up the mountain and then came down,[3] Christians, instead, were to observe Wednesdays and Fridays. Furthermore, on the Day of Atonement (Yom Kippur), all Israelites were obliged to "afflict themselves" or fast (Lev. 16:31–34) while the high priest offered sacrifices in the holy of holies on behalf of the sins of the entire nation; Christians, likewise, felt compelled to acts of self-renunciation and austerity on Good Friday, when Jesus, as the sacrificial lamb, was crucified for the transgressions of the whole world. In the words of the Gospels, when "the bridegroom has been taken away," then the disciples will fast (Luke 5:35).

Lent gradually evolved from the day or two before Easter to a full week, then to three weeks, and finally, commencing with Ash Wednesday, it lasted for forty days, modeled after Jesus' time in the desert.[4] Eventually regulations were established concerning what hour the fast should end, which foods were to be permitted, and who could legitimately be exempted from its rigors (e.g., according to Thomas Aquinas: children, the elderly, pilgrims, workers, and beggars).[5] By the thirteenth and fourteenth centuries, a Christian could loosely be defined as someone who received communion once a year, had his or her children baptized, paid tithes, and fasted on Fridays and during Lent.[6] In the modern era, however, Western Christianity has tended to frown upon feats of asceticism, choosing rather to highlight the goodness of creation and partaking of God's bounty. Yet Eastern Christianity still maintains its intense schedule of four annual fasts (Lent, post-Pentecost, the Assumption, and Advent) as well as the regular fast days of Wednesdays and Fridays. During Lent, not only is meat forbidden, but fish, animal products (e.g., butter, eggs, milk, cheese), and wine, as one's diet is restricted to vegetables, fruits, grains, honey, et cetera.[7]

I've come to believe that fasting is still a key ingredient in the spiritual life, provided it isn't carried to extremes. It is a foremost manifestation of self-control, or *sōphrosunē*, the virtue Aristotle so admired in his *Ethics*.[8] The fifth-century monk John Cassian went so far as to call fasting the first step in the pursuit of perfection, referring to it metaphorically as the departure from Egypt, after which the Israelites would do battle with the seven Canaanite nations, allegorized as sins. To cease fasting was symbolically to give up the fight and to return to Egypt.[9] In Paul's letter to the Corinthians, he compares the Christian life to an athletic competition, in which the contestants are continuously training in order to win the prize; so Paul "buffets" his body to bring it under strict control, lest after preaching to others, he, himself, should be disqualified (1 Cor. 9:24–27). The term he uses, *hypōpiazō*, can mean "to strike under the eye" or "to beat black and blue."[10] So Paul isn't referring to light, half-hearted measures. In fact Orthodox thinker Kallistos Ware claims that self-denial, which leads to self-mastery, is a necessary component in everything from sports to politics, scholarly research to prayer.[11]

Fasting demonstrates how far the world's values are from those of the kingdom of God. "God sells righteousness at a very low price to those who wish to buy it," desert father Epiphanius declared, "a little piece of bread, a cloak of no value, a cup of cold water, a mite."[12] Via seemingly insignificant items, God molds his chosen vessels into cups of honor. Japanese fiction writer Kawabata Yasunari tells how a woman taking care of an invalid husband chanced upon the idea of giving him a small hand mirror to view the vegetable garden. In it he saw "the sky, clouds, snow, distant mountains, and nearby woods. He had seen the moon. He had seen wild flowers, and birds of passage had made their way through the mirror. Men walked down the road in the mirror and children played in the garden. Kyoko was amazed at the richness of the world in the mirror. A mirror which had until then been regarded only as a toilet article, a hand mirror which had served only to show the back of one's neck, had created for the invalid a new life."[13] "The turning points of lives are not the great moments," eminent biographer William Woodward learned. "The real crises are often concealed in occurrences so trivial in appearance that they pass unobserved."[14]

So while fasting may begin with food, hopefully it doesn't end there. Benedict says in his rule, "the life of a monk ought to be a continuous Lent."[15] In some cultures a fast is enjoined as a prerequisite to an important rite of passage such as marriage or admission into a tribe, to induce dreams or visions from the spirit realm.[16] Norwegian theologian Ole Hallesby defines fasting as "a voluntary abstinence" for a short or long period so as to "loosen" one's "ties" to the material world; it means attending to what's "needful," concentrating on higher concerns, instead of being overwhelmed by the incidental. For a time, Hallesby asserts, we may need to renounce normal activities, which, in themselves, are "both permissible and profitable," such as meeting with friends or getting all the rest we would like. Thus fasting turns into an all-embracing spiritual concept.[17] Today monks still cultivate what are called "desert days," dedicated to prayer and silence, to take an inventory of their souls.[18] That renunciation may involve more than food can be seen in Paul's advice to the Corinthians (1 Cor. 7:5), where married couples are permitted to abstain from sexual relations (albeit by mutual consent), for brief spans, in order to pray.

Calvin, in the fourth book of his *Institutes,* argues for a prudent middle way. He sees three main objectives in fasting: (1) to weaken and subdue the flesh; (2) to better prepare ourselves for prayer and meditation; and (3) to demonstrate our self-abasement before God, when we want to confess.[19] He explains that fasting can entail a sacrifice of time (e.g., a day or some other regular period); an amount of food (e.g., a smaller than usual quantity or normal portions taken less frequently); as well as the kind of food (e.g., common fare vs. special delicacies).[20] Medieval Orthodox mystic Symeon the New Theologian sums up a good deal of Christian thinking when he says, "Fasting, aided by vigil, penetrates and softens hardness of heart."[21]

Judah Halevi, that great medieval Jewish poet and thinker, depicts the ideal Yom Kippur faster: "His soul frees itself from the whisperings of the imagination, wrath, and lust, and neither in thought or deed gives them any attention. Although his soul is unable to atone for sinful thoughts—the result of songs, tales, et cetera, heard in youth, and which cling to memory—it cleanses itself from real sins, confesses repentance for the former, and undertakes to allow them no more to escape his tongue, much less to put them into practice, as it is written: 'I am purposed that my mouth shall not transgress' (Ps. 17:3). The fast of this day is such as

brings one near to the angels, because it is spent in humility and contrition, standing, kneeling, praising, and singing. . . . The fast of a pious man is such that eye,
ear, and tongue share in it, that he regards nothing except that which brings him
near to God. This also refers to his innermost faculties, such as mind and imagination. To this he adds pious works."[22]

"To this he adds pious works" refers to the positive aspect of fasting, which is
above and beyond self-renunciation. Already Isaiah 58:3–10 couples fasting with
acts of justice and goodness. For fasting helps one to identify with the oppressed,
the downcast, or the destitute. In the second century, *The Shepherd of Hermas*
urged Christians to be content with bread and water during their fasts. They
should then calculate how much money they had saved on their food and give that
much to "a widow or an orphan or someone in need."[23] In one of his sermons, Augustine went so far as to argue that unless one made some gesture of this sort, fasting simply became another form of greed.[24] Contemporary world hunger
organizations have, at times, adopted similar strategies, asking members to fast
once a week (or once a month) and then donate the amount that was saved to
feeding the hungry. The fast may even constitute a rudimentary meal similar to
what someone from the Third World might eat in order to graphically illustrate
the poor's plight (although a lunch consisting of grass soup, which Solzhenitsyn
said was typical in the gulag,[25] might seem overly melodramatic).

G. K. Chesterton once drew a comparison between a cross and a circle, which I
think illustrates how true versus false fasting works. "The circle is perfect and infinite in its nature; but it is fixed for ever in its size; it can never be larger or smaller.
But the cross, though it has at its heart a collision and a contradiction, can extend
its four arms for ever without altering its shape. Because it has a paradox in its center it can grow without changing. The circle returns upon itself and is bound."[26]
False fasting is more concerned with self-purification and appearances, while true
fasting spurs greater involvement and outreach.

Among the circle-fasters are those dour-faced hypocrites whom Jesus denounced in the Gospels for parading their piety and fasting in public so as to be
flattered and to receive accolades from others. He concluded, "They have their
reward," hence, they have little to look forward to in the next life (Matt.
6:16–18 KJV). It's as though they were in some fasting contest, in which one tried
to outdo the other by how haggard or worn-out he looked. "I ate only a pome-
granate!" one might exclaim. "Well, I ate only a fig," another could chime in. "I
never touched wine for a week." "I subsisted merely on fruit juices." And so on
ad infinitum. "Thou fastest much in men's sight in order to be lean and pale, to
seem ghostly [that is, spiritual]," one medieval moralist surmised. "Thou art an
hypocrite."[27]

Such behavior is calculated to make one appear "good," rather than to truly seek God's favor. These contests remind me in some ways of Kafka's short story "A Hunger Artist." A young man performs fasts in public; spectators buy tickets to watch him waste away, while cynics speculate on how his behind-the-scenes nourishment goes undetected. Children gape at his protruding ribs or reach out to touch those bony arms. His manager stops the fasts at forty days, thinking that about the maximum length that would hold the public's attention. Later, the hunger artist joins a circus, where he is finally given the chance to fast for as long and hard as he wants. Each day his frame grows more concave, his legs more and more shaky, his head seems to wobble about his shoulders. Almost forgotten, he is discovered by an overseer, lying in the straw of his cage. Before expiring, the hunger artist confides that he had always wanted people to admire his fasting, but that they shouldn't. When asked why, he explained, "Because I couldn't find the food I liked. If I had found it, believe me, I should have made no fuss and stuffed myself like you or anyone else."[28] How sad.

The hunger artist, in turn, has marked similarities to that fifth-century spiritual acrobat Simeon Stylites. Stylites were ascetics who lived on top of pillars, which had huts or platforms to protect them from the wind. There they stood, day in and day out, as visual emblems to the faithful, or as skilled orators who could exhort the crowds gathered below.[29] Simeon, perhaps the most famous, lived for thirty-six years on top of one pillar, which was raised, over time, to a height of sixty feet. People would flock in to watch him fast. At the end of his first above-ground Lent, he was found lying unconscious on the floor of his cell. But he built up his stamina until he was able to remain conscious for all forty days; then, tying himself up for support, he learned to fast while standing. Such triumphs won for him an immense following. Emperors and bishops sought out his advice; other believers were eager to emulate his bizarre lifestyle.[30] To us moderns he seems more a powerful reminder of how difficult the prolonged fast is, and how, if it were attempted, it should be done only in stages.

Another impersonator of the faster is the anorexic. Anorexia, coupled with its frequent attendant bulimia (binge eating and self-induced vomiting), is particularly prominent in young women.[31] In 1686 physician Richard Morton described a twenty-year-old woman who had symptoms going back two years. He writes that she "fell into a total Suppression of her Monthly Courses from a multitude of Cares and Passions of her Mind. . . . From which time her Appetite began to abate, and her Digestion to be bad; her Flesh also began to be flaccid and loose, and her looks pale. . . . I do not remember that I did ever in all my Practice see one, that was conversant with the Living so much wasted with the greatest degree of a Consumption (like a Skeleton only clad with Skin), yet there was no Fever, but on the contrary a Coldness of the whole Body."[32] She turned down every medication he prescribed and three months later fainted and died.

Explanations for anorexia vary. Perhaps it is a passive form of refusal to an overbearing parent who offers little place for disagreement, or it may stem from some biochemical disposition toward depression. It can also be related to cultural stereotypes of thinness, or what's currently considered "sexy" or "submissive," since it's often manifest among those approaching puberty, who alternately fear or loathe their bodies.[33] Eating disorders can also be seen among mystics, who seek a kinship with Christ's suffering or the world's hurt, particularly during eras when patient endurance of disease or injury is considered "saintly."[34]

Such a fraudulent ideal reaches its acme in those who subsist solely on the host. One was the medieval peasant Alpaïs of Cudot. The Virgin Mary appeared to her: "[B]ecause, dear sister, you bore long starvation in humility and patience, in hunger and thirst, without any murmuring, I grant you now to be fattened with an angelic and spiritual food. And as long as you are in this little body, corporeal food and drink will not be necessary for the sustaining of your body." It was reported that "two or three times a week she was accustomed to accept some morsel. And she would roll it around for a time in her mouth . . . and then spit it back whole."[35] Her hagiographer focused on how much Alpaïs loved the Eucharist and the ensuing visions and spiritual teachings, while contemporary chroniclers were usually more fascinated by how little she ate, her inability to excrete, and the emptiness of her intestines.[36] Other female mystics ate, and afterward vomited, until they damaged their throats and digestive systems,[37] perhaps in imitation of the odd eating habits of the much-admired Catherine of Siena.[38] Fasting, as I'm defining it, however, is voluntary and capable of rational control, not primarily due to subliminal forces. Thus eating disorders of any kind are excluded.

Kallistos Ware draws a sharp distinction between what he calls "natural" and "unnatural" asceticism: "Natural asceticism reduces material life to the utmost simplicity, restricting our physical needs to a minimum, but not maiming the body or otherwise deliberately causing it to suffer. Unnatural asceticism, on the other hand, seeks out special forms of mortification that torment the body and gratuitously inflict pain upon it. Thus it is a form of natural asceticism to wear cheap and plain clothing, whereas it is unnatural to wear fetters with iron spikes piercing the flesh. It is a form of natural asceticism to sleep on the ground, whereas it is unnatural to sleep on a bed of nails. It is a form of natural asceticism to live in a hut or a cave, instead of a well-appointed house, whereas it is unnatural to chain oneself to a rock or to stand permanently on a pillar."[39]

True, natural fasting may be expressed as public penitence or take the form of social protest. In the Old Testament, fasts took place during times of national calamity (2 Chron. 20:3) or when mourning important figures (2 Sam. 1:12). Calvin recommended that pastors urge church members to fast during times of famine, pestilence, or war.[40] In medieval Ireland there arose a legal procedure known as "fasting to destrain," in which a creditor could fast to gain repayment of a debt, or one could fast against some adversary in order to obtain restitution.[41] The first modern mass political protest to resort to fasting was in 1774, when the colonies of Massachusetts and Virginia thus expressed their dissatisfaction with the governing policies of mother England.[42]

The modern activist who most promoted the "hunger strike" was Gandhi. He fasted seventeen times "to the death." Such a large number of sympathizers refused to light a candle or a lantern during the evenings of his fasts, that entire cities went dark.[43] His reliance on fasting might have partly been due to his mother, who had added personal fasts to an already strenuous Hindu calendar.[44] The acute vulnerability of Gandhi's frail body made each fast seem precarious, and the way the multitudes revered him as "mahatma" meant authorities had to pay close attention to his demands. Perhaps his finest hour was in the workers' strike against the Ahmedebad textile mills in 1918, when owners and workers wrangled for several weeks before he put his own body on the line on behalf of a 35 percent pay increase; within three days the owners had capitulated. Gandhi was to adopt this same technique over and over again during his campaign of passive resistance against British rule and on behalf of the untouchables. The "hunger strike" proved to be an ambiguous weapon, though, since it focused attention on the faster himself and sometimes downplayed the complex issues, which could have used a good public airing. The practice, however, did unify his disparate followers.

Of what is fasting comprised? It may mean skipping a meal and using the money saved for charitable purposes. It can mean setting aside time to think through a major decision, asking for specific leading from the Holy Spirit, as when the apostolic church sent out Paul and Barnabas to be missionaries to the Gentiles (Acts 13:2). It can be a weekly or monthly regimen to consecrate or renew one's inner being. Fasting may be either strict, consisting of the so-called "dry diet" of bread, salt, and water during daylight hours (sometimes with an odd vegetable or fruit thrown in),[45] or take some less strenuous form, such as refraining from a favorite food or animal product in order to eat lower down in the food chain (cf. Dan. 10:3). Certainly any prolonged fast should be undertaken only with a doctor's supervision, but all who claim that light fasts will sap one's strength or destroy healthy tissue are misguided. Benedictine monk Adalbert de Vogüé has pointed out that the custom of the British breakfast started gaining widespread support only in the nineteenth century, and that our modern concept of three healthy meals a day is really a historical aberration, since for centuries people ate one or two meals at most.[46] I know I've gone without breakfast for a number of decades without any noticeable physical deterioration.

Wole Soyinka, the 1986 Nobel Prize winner in literature, outlined his own experiments with fasting, based on his imprisonment in the Nigerian civil war (1967–69). One day, feeling resolute, he armed himself with "the power of veto" and proceeded "to thump the gavel." After several days of fasting, food's appeal dramatically decreased. He came to think of his body as nearly weightless; in his imagination, he compared it to an onion, with flesh peeling off layer after layer. He even started to feel he was superhuman, needing neither food nor drink, and soon could live without air. Visions and hallucinations followed. On the tenth day of the fast, he wrote, "I anoint my flesh / Thought is hallowed in the lean. / . . . Let the dark / Withdraw." By the twelfth day, he was approaching the null set: "I need nothing. I feel nothing. I desire nothing."[47] This sequence indicates just how dangerous the prolonged fast can be.

So fast, but not that intensely. Nor should one fast in order to obtain peer approval, fast without performing charitable deeds, nor attribute an eating disorder to piety. Fasting is merely a physical means to a spiritual objective. Thus Cassian advised the monks to stop their fast whenever a guest came, since hospitality was more important than self-renunciation. The guest's appearance he called the return of Christ as the bridegroom, when celebration and joy were in order, not mourning.[48] So if friends occasionally want to take you out to lunch during your fast, don't summarily give them the cold shoulder.

The soberness of Lent recalls the dual nature of Advent, a season designed both to announce the approaching birth of the Savior and his return as the coming judge at the great assize, with all its attendant terrors. Advent "was a season of mourning," notes George Foot Moore, "the Gloria in Excelsis was omitted in the Mass; the organ was silent; the pictures in the churches were covered; the altar cloths and the stoles of the priests were violet, the color of mourning. . . . [M]arriages were not solemnized."[49] Similarly on Good Friday, the altar is bare—with no candles, with no cloth coverings, and even without a cross; for the bridegroom has been taken away.[50] At such a time, it is appropriate that the disciple should fast, not like some hunger artist or dour-faced hypocrite, but as one who genuinely longs for and seeks after God's face. Such a ritual act gives us a small taste of deprivation. For a little while we experience the pangs of hunger, the gnawing emptiness, the lightheadedness, the sense of insecurity that millions around the globe know each and every day.[51] We are brought face-to-face with the harshness of life, for we are now on the *Via dolorosa,* heading toward Golgotha, where Jesus was crucified. Late medieval piety enshrined Jesus' passion in the form of fourteen stations of the cross, where pilgrims could stop and pray at representations of the events in his last days.[52]

A saint, G. K. Chesterton believed, is one who lives upside down so others can see the world aright.[53] "If a man saw the world upside down, with all the trees and towers hanging head downwards as in a pool, one effect would be to emphasise the idea of *dependence*. There is a Latin and literal connection; for the very word dependence only means hanging. It would make vivid the Scriptural text which says that God has hung the world upon nothing. If St. Francis had seen, in one of his strange dreams, the town of Assisi upside down, it need not have differed in a single detail from itself except in being entirely the other way round. But the point is this: that whereas to the normal eye the large masonry of its walls or the massive foundations of its watchtowers and its high citadel would make it seem safer and more permanent, the moment it was turned over the very same weight would make it seem more helpless and more in peril. . . . Instead of being merely proud of his strong city because it could not be moved, he would be thankful to God Almighty that it had not been dropped; he would be thankful to God for not dropping the whole cosmos like a vast crystal to be shattered into falling stars."[54]

Fasting, too, can have a revisioning effect. After abstaining from food, or sex, or companionship, or play, or whatever, one comes back to embrace the goodness of creation with renewed vigor. Similarly, after imposing limits on ourselves for a season, we can experience once more the glorious liberty that is ours in Christ. Fasting makes it crystal clear how our lives have become clogged with debris that should periodically be swept away. Sin hinders and prevents us from becoming fully human; but, if the Son should set you free, as the Gospel of John says, you will be free indeed (8:34–36). "The aim of fasting," Muslim mystic al-Ghazālī decided, "is to oppose your appetites and to double your capacity for works of piety."[55] Therefore let us pray in the manner of the fifth-century Gelasian Sacramentary: "We beseech you, O Lord, that as our bodies grow weaker for lack of food during the season of fasting, so our souls may grow stronger. May we learn to fight more valiantly against evil, and strive more earnestly for righteousness. Thus, through abstaining from the fruits of the earth, may we bear more abundantly the fruits of your spirit."[56] Amen.

CHAPTER 15

Sloth: Don't Lose Heart

T. S. Eliot in "The Love Song of J. Alfred Prufrock" paints a vivid portrait of the enervated individual who shies away from responsibilities, measuring his life out "with coffee spoons. / . . . Deferential, glad to be use, / Politic, cautious, / . . . but a bit obtuse. / . . . in short, I was afraid."[1] This is the type of Christian the author of Hebrews simply cannot stomach (e.g., Heb. 5:11–6:8; 10:19–39). The recipients of this epistle, or homily, have become sluggish, dull in understanding, unwilling to move forward in their faith. For by now they ought to be mature enough to be teachers, yet he finds himself again explaining to them elementary doctrines. They should be gulping down solid food and asking for seconds, but instead he must offer them milk as if they were still infants. Later in the book we discover that they suffer from what the author metaphorically calls "drooping hands" and "weak knees" (12:12). Their compassion and endurance, which had proved so exemplary during earlier suffering and hardship, had shriveled up, so the writer must warn of dire consequences if they persist in their present course. "My soul," says God in Hebrews 10:38, "takes no pleasure in any one who shrinks back."

The problem of sloth, or backsliding, is a common one in church history. The desert fathers spoke of the *daemon meridianus,* or "demon of the noontide," which struck down these solitary warriors in the heat of the midday, sapping their strength, bowing them down with despair.[2] The demon, according to fourth-century writer Evagrius Ponticus, "makes it seem that the sun barely moves, if at all, and that the day is fifty hours long," and "instills in the heart of the monk a hatred for the place, a hatred for his very life itself, a hatred for manual labor." It "leads him to reflect that charity has departed from among the brethren, that there is no one to give encouragement"; in short, it "leaves no leaf unturned to induce the monk to forsake his cell and drop out of the fight."[3]

In medieval iconography, sloth appears as a man riding on, or leaning against, a donkey.[4] In a decorative tabletop, Hieronymous Bosch places the eye of God in the axis, while all about the edges are a kaleidoscope of images depicting human sinfulness. There we see the slothful taking a nap, rather than saying their prayers.[5] In Dante's *Purgatorio,* on the level where the slothful are doing penance, he hears no prayers or hymns, for all are forced to do double shifts, working night and day to make up for lost opportunities on earth.[6]

In modern literature, apathy is that key element in Herman Melville's short story "Bartleby the Scrivener," where a copyist hired by a Wall Street firm keeps cutting back on his job description until he finally abandons work altogether. When Bartleby refuses to vacate the premises, the firm decides to move instead. The new landlord has him hauled off to prison for vagrancy, where he proceeds to starve himself to death. He once remarked, "I like to be stationary"; he was famous for his "dead-wall reveries"; and his stock response to almost any request for meaningful activity was "I would prefer not to."[7]

One of the most lethargic characters in all fiction is Ivan Goncharov's Oblomov, who has a terrible time making decisions, since for him "every disturbance was settled with a sigh, then dissolved into apathy or drowsiness."[8] He recalls the de Goncourt brothers' derogatory description of the writer Théophile Gautier as having "the lassitude of a hippopotamus with intermittent flashes of understanding."[9] Here Oblomov converses with a former colleague: "Tell me, what's new at the office?" "Oh, all sorts of things. We no longer end our letters with 'your humble servant,' but with 'accept our assurances'; we're no longer required to present records in duplicate; they're giving us three new departments and two officials for special commissions. Our committee has been closed. . . . Many changes."[10] Living off income from his estate, Oblomov lies in bed until afternoon and greets guests while still in his robe; and when a woman does come along who actually might lift him out of his torpor, he, of course, procrastinates too long in asking for her hand. Instead he marries his landlady/housekeeper, who pampers him as though she were his mother, before he dies prematurely from a stroke brought about by his sedentary lifestyle.[11]

The lazy, however, never seem to lack for good excuses. A midrash on Proverbs 26:13–14 mocks one who will not go out to study the Torah with his teacher. "When a sluggard is told, 'Your teacher is in the city nearby; go and learn Torah from him,' he replies, 'But I fear the lion in the way.' . . . When he is told, 'Your teacher is within your township; bestir yourself and go to him,' he replies, 'I fear that the lion may be in the streets.' . . . When he is told, 'Behold, your teacher is in his house,' he replies, 'If I go to his house, I am certain to find the door bolted.' Then he is told, 'But it is open.' . . . At that point, when he is at a loss to reply, he says, 'Whether the door is open or bolted, I want to sleep just a little longer.'"[12] To such flagrant procrastination, that American go-getter Benjamin Franklin might cry out, "O lazybones! Dost thou think that God would have given thee arms and legs, if he had not designed that thou should'st use them?"[13]

Anthropologists have discerned a "giving-up syndrome" not only among individuals but for entire cultures, especially during times of great social upheaval, as following an epidemic or the conquest by a foreign power. In a famous study of Pacific Islanders done early in the twentieth century, W. H. R. Rivers stressed how European powers introduced into Oceania diseases like measles, dysentery, and tuberculosis, which physically incapacitated the people. Family ties were weakened when adults had to seek employment on plantations far from home, as age-old tribal livelihoods no longer were economically viable. Many islands saw an alarming rise in cases of ennui, depression, and early death. Mortality rates shot up, birth rates sank, as people would say, "Why should we bring children into the world to work for the white man?" Yet it became apparent to researchers that some societies were actually thriving—especially those who had sought to resist Western encroachment, albeit with modest success, or those who wholeheartedly embraced Christianity, finding in this religion a vital new worldview.[14] The lesson seems to be that while victims have every right to be dismayed over their unjust lot, and should protest it vigorously, when they choose to do something, rather than moping about, caving in to the inevitable, their lives can again take on meaning.

"Nothing is so insufferable to man as to be completely at rest, without passions, without business, without diversion, without study," the seventeenth-century Christian apologist Pascal believed. Man "then feels his nothingness, his forlornness, his insufficiency, his dependence, his weakness, his emptiness. There will immediately arise from the depth of his heart weariness, gloom, sadness, fretfulness, vexation, despair."[15]

Carried to a logical extreme, "giving-up" can lead to a doctrine of nihilism, where nothing exists, or, if something does exist, we can't comprehend it, and in the end it doesn't matter. The theater of the absurd is especially good at conveying situations of this kind. For instance, in Ionesco's *The Chairs,* the professional orator, who is to deliver the message, turns out to be a deaf-mute. He can only utter guttural noises and write two coherent words on the blackboard, "Angelfood" and "Adieu."[16] In Sartre's novel *Nausea,* Roquentin, walking in a provincial park, is overcome by disgust at the meaninglessness of life.[17] Upon looking at the bloated roots of a chestnut tree, he decides, "Every existing thing is born without reason, prolongs itself out of weakness and dies by chance."[18] Such fatalism, though, is not new; in ancient Rome a common epitaph for gladiators and slaves read: "I was not. I was. I shall not be. I do not care."[19] Nihilism assumes we're Sisyphean characters who keep rolling that huge rock up the hill, only to have it roll back down again. ". . . Half my life spent attaching my heart / to this and that," seventeenth-century Persian lyricist Abu Talib Kalim claimed, "the rest, detaching it again."[20] The narrator in Brecht's poem "To Posterity" depicts his indifference: "I ate my food between massacres. / The shadow of murder lay upon my sleep. / And when I loved, I loved with indifference." Thus, he frittered away the time allotted him on earth.[21]

Virtue, on the other hand, entails time and passion. The ancient Greek poet Hesiod thought evil easy and her path smooth. "But Good is harder, for the gods have placed / In front of her much sweat; the road is steep / And long and rocky at the first."[22] The problem with sloth, or apathy, is that it seems to be a law of life that we're either growing or regressing—we cannot simply stand still. I know in my own field of publishing, since I haven't kept up with the newest computer technologies, my value to a potential employer has decreased significantly. I, who love the old and cling to the past, should learn to welcome the future, heeding Aurelius's maxim: "For all things are by nature intended to change, to be altered and destroyed, in order that other things in their turn may come to be."[23]

This same reasoning applies to our spiritual life. "One must occasionally make new efforts," the Pascals wrote their sister, "to acquire . . . newness of spirit, since one can preserve a former grace only by acquiring a new one; otherwise one loses what he thinks he retains; like those who wishing to wall in the light, manage only to shut in the darkness."[24] That's why church members go on retreat, attend conventions, bring in special speakers, or send young people to camp—to rejuvenate the ancient flame. We may want an effortless life, but that's just not going to happen. Gulliver, in his journeys, encountered a mathematician who thought that learning could be induced by means of a simple lozenge. "The proposition and demonstration were fairly written on a thin wafer, with ink composed of a cephalic tincture. This the student was to swallow upon a fasting stomach, and for three days following eat nothing but bread and water. As the wafer digested, the tincture mounted to his brain, bearing the proposition along with it."[25] The results, however, were mixed. Think of the hoopla surrounding sleep learning in our own day!

Some blame their own mediocre performance on their degenerate times—a silver or bronze age, or even one of iron.[26] If only there were exceptional leaders to emulate, they reason, great deeds could still be performed. But to urge people to sit still until another farsighted emperor such as Yao or Shun comes along, grumbled the Chinese realist Han Fei Tzu, "is like telling a man who is drowning in Middle China to wait till an expert swimmer arrives from Yüeh."[27] The feeble light we have should shine forth, regardless of our era's deficiencies. "Shall a man go and hang himself because he belongs to the race of pygmies, and not be the biggest pygmy that he can?" Thoreau asks.[28]

Our hammocklike existence must be shook up, that widening yawn stifled. American fiction writer Flannery O'Connor drew on the tradition of the grotesque to convey her vision of Christian truth. "To the hard of hearing you shout," she explained, "and for the almost blind you draw large and startling figures."[29] By depicting society's outcasts—the deformed, freaks, Baptist healers—she held up a critical mirror to contemporary society. "I am very well aware that for a majority of my readers," she writes, "baptism is a meaningless rite, and so in my novel I have to see that this baptism carries enough awe and mystery to jar the reader into some kind of emotional recognition of its significance." The devices she prefers are distortion, exaggeration, and shock.[30] Her approach is not unlike the farfetched conceits of the seventeenth-century metaphysicals who, to achieve their effect, violently yoked together the most heterogeneous ideas.[31]

If sloth has been defined as a "hatred of all spiritual things which entail effort" and "fainteheartedness in matters of difficulty,"[32] we need, in addition to courage, a fresh set of priorities. It is not enough to be busy, Thoreau believed; so are the ants. The question is: What are we busy about? "Think, also, of the ladies of the land weaving toilet cushions against the last day," he complained, "not to betray too green an interest in their fates! As if you could kill time without injuring eternity."[33] "We spin fabrics out of air and run after many tricks," thought eighteenth-century German poet Matthias Claudius, "and only get farther away from the goal."[34]

It is one of sloth's "favorite tricks," observes Dorothy Sayers, "to dissemble itself under cover of a whiffling activity of body."[35] We become fanatics of the inessential—playing cards, cleaning house, or putting in overtime—with the result, as Doctor Heatherlegh indicates in Kipling's "The Phantom Rickshaw," that "more men are killed by overwork than the importance of this world justifies."[36] Such diversions are not intrinsically easier than introspection or works of charity, for these pastimes also require practice for proficiency. But we would rather run from our fears than face them, content with superficial self-awareness rather than confronting the demons that trouble our souls. So we evade Jesus' open-ended demands with delaying tactics like "How can I inherit eternal life?" or "Who is my neighbor?"

That visitor from Asteroid B-612, the little prince, saw through our pretenses: "I know a planet where there is a certain red-faced gentleman. He has never smelled a flower. He has never looked at a star. He has never loved any one. He has never done anything in his life but add up figures. And all day he says over and over, just like you: 'I am busy with matters of consequence!' And that makes him swell up with pride. But he is not a man—he is a mushroom!"[37] It's not that the slothful are inactive, but the tasks they do perform seem so second-rate.

We today are more likely to know the full details of some catastrophe in the news than whether our next-door neighbor is seriously ill. In *Piers the Ploughman,* sloth blurts out, "I know plenty of ballads about Robin Hood and Randolph Earl of Chester, but I don't know a verse about our Lord or our Lady. . . . Nor have I ever once visited the sick or the prisoners chained in the dungeons. For I enjoy a bawdy joke, or a riotous day at the village wake, or a juicy bit of scandal about some neighbor, more than all Matthew, Mark, Luke, and John ever penned."[38]

The apostle Paul considered spiritual neglect so repugnant that he compared it to death (Eph. 5:14). How does such a tragedy occur? C. S. Lewis believed, "If you examined a hundred people who had lost their faith in Christianity, I wonder how many of them would turn out to have been reasoned out of it by honest argument? Do not most people simply drift away?" What then is Lewis's remedy? Daily prayers, religious reading, and church attendance. Why? "We have to be continually reminded of what we believe."[39] Worship, as the 1637 Scotch *Book of Common Prayer* says, is meant "to stir up the dull mind of man to the remembrance of his duty to God."[40]

By such means we ponder our obligations, consider the import of familiar commandments. "The nature of water is soft, that of stone is hard," mused desert father Abba Poemen, "but if a bottle is hung above the stone, allowing the water to fall drop by drop, it wears away the stone. So it is with the word of God; it is soft and our heart is hard, but the man who hears the word of God often, opens his heart to the fear of God."[41] The Christian most often associated with reading in Western iconography, Jerome, counseled Eustochium (who later succeeded her mother as head of a convent in Bethlehem), "Read often, learn all you can. Let sleep overcome you, the roll still in your hands; when your head falls, let it be on the sacred page."[42] In numerous works of art, Jerome himself is represented as seated in his study, poring over an open book, with pen and inkhorn nearby.[43]

Cotton Mather urged his fellow Puritans to be as ingenious and creative in religion as they were in their business endeavors.[44] He asked them to pity hurting neighbors, then let their pity "flame out" in prayer, visit and comfort them, standing ready, if need be, to give advice or assistance. Then, quoting the Greek church father Gregory of Nazianzus, he adds, "If you have nothing else to bestow upon the miserable, bestow a tear or two upon their miseries."[45]

To overcome sloth, we must not only establish new priorities, but find our own peculiar center of gravity. Schedule your day to do the hardest work when you're most alert, and the lightest when you tend to be drowsy. Then whatever form of spirituality you choose, be open to God's leading. As that old gospel hymn puts it, "Here am I, O Lord, send me. If the Master wants somebody to carry his holy word: Here am I, O Lord, send me."[46] Indeed, seventeenth-century Mexican poet Sor Juana called hope "the green spell-binder of human existence." "Those who wear green spectacles"[47] will recognize God as the unknown factor in every equation, who is able to change the outcome without a moment's notice. Being incalculable, he continuously redefines the parameters of surprise.

Practice the spiritual disciplines, whether inward, say, in the form of meditation; outward, in the form of service; or corporate, in the form of worship. "I cannot contentedly frame a Prayer for my selfe in particular," seventeenth-century English physician Thomas Browne relates, "without a catalogue of my friends, nor request a happinesse wherein my sociable disposition doth not desire the fellowship of my neighbour. I never heare the Toll of a passing Bell, though in my mirth [and at a Taverne] without my prayers and best wishes for the departing spirit; I cannot goe to cure the body of my Patient, but I forget my profession, and call unto God for his soule; . . . there are surely many happy that never saw me, and enjoy the blessing of mine unknowne devotions."[48] The spiritual disciplines draw us out from self to family, friends, the community, and the world at large.

One key to achieving a sense of balance, suggests comparative religion scholar Huston Smith, is the pattern of withdrawal and return, which is basic to human creativity. According to tradition, Buddha withdrew from the world for six years, then returned for forty-five. Likewise, during the year, he engaged in nine months of activity, followed by a three-month retreat with his monks during the rainy season. His daily habits were much the same. Although spending long hours in public, three times a day he withdrew to meditate and return to the sacred source.[49] The Judaeo-Christian concept of Sabbath has a quite similar function.

Over time our hearts are changed little by little. Paul applies the imagery from Exodus, where Moses' face shone after being with God on Mount Sinai, to the sanctification of individual believers. With faces unveiled, we now behold God as in a mirror and are transformed "from one degree of glory to another" (2 Cor. 3:18). In Eastern Orthodoxy, Christ's transfiguration is one of the twelve great feasts of the church year. It is that moment when his divine glory was especially manifest, when the uncreated light of the Godhead shone visibly through the garments of his flesh, just as at the resurrection, when the pressure from his divine life burst open the tomb. According to Theophan the Recluse, "Behind the veil of Christ's flesh, Christians behold the Triune God."[50] Thus icon apprentices are instructed first to paint the transfiguration, for it is only after their eyes have been illumined by Christ that they can perceive true reality.[51] Why, I daresay, if your local sanctuary could be bathed with spiritual, not physical, light, all would be awestruck at the inbreaking of God's presence in those around them. You would see glimmerings of glory, inklings of resurrection. The room would be like a summer meadow at dusk, aglow with twinkling fireflies. "Aspire to be changed!" Rilke cries, "Oh, rejoice at the flame."[52]

We can create beauty through either the work of our hands or the work of our minds. Some of the most exciting experiments with light are those stained glass windows in medieval cathedrals, which were formed by mixing certain minerals into the glass during its molten state, then using lead strips to outline figures and separate colors so as to prevent blurring at a distance.[53] Functioning almost like prisms, the panes set off a rainbow of colors in the dark, vaulted interior, reaching their acme in the awe-inspiring rose window. Here the three elements of the sublime cherished by scholastics converge: *integritas* (wholeness), *consonantia* (harmony), and *claritas* (radiance). To be truly sublime, it was felt, an object must be seen in its entirety, be marked by a kind of balance where one part plays against another, and, lastly, must shine.[54] The "three conditions of beauty," as enunciated by Thomas Aquinas, are "first, integrity or completeness, for broken things are ugly; second, due proportion and harmony; third, brightness and color."[55]

Abbot Suger, who oversaw the reconstruction of St. Denis, perhaps the first wholly "Gothic" structure, thought the house of God should be a repository of all that's beautiful;[56] in it he was lifted "from this inferior to that higher world in an anagogical manner."[57] The windows, no longer mere openings, became translucent surfaces to be adorned with sacred paintings;[58] as colors danced in the streaming sunlight, worshipers could sense the transcendent breaking in. (Interestingly, that leader of modern functional architecture, Walter Gropius, also had a penchant for glass, which he admired for "its sparkling insubstantiality, and the way it seems to float between wall and wall imponderably as the air," adding a special "note of gaiety."[59]) Though Gothic structures had their detractors, for their oversumptuousness and inordinate expense[60] (criticisms that should definitely be taken into account), when Christian communities do decide to build, it is imperative that they go forward with a strong aesthetic sense. "The Protestant principle that only God can speak of God," opined theologian Roger Hazelton, "needs to be complemented and corrected by the Catholic principle that now God has spoken, everything may speak of him."[61]

Occasionally God's gifts are so exceptional that they utterly transform the recipient.[62] Historian Venerable Bede tells the story of an illiterate herdsman living in seventh-century Britain who suddenly received the gift of song and composed the "Hymn of Creation," the first Christian poem in English. Whatever he learned about the faith, Caedmon would incorporate into his poetry, so, because of him, many came to despise the world and aspire to heavenly things.[63] "Thou takest the pen—and the lines dance," Dag Hammarskjöld ejaculates. "Thou takest the flute—and the notes shimmer. Thou takest the brush—and the colors sing. So all things have meaning and beauty in that space beyond time where Thou art. How, then, can I hold back anything from Thee?"[64]

Paul roused the Colossians to "teach and admonish one another in all wisdom;

and with gratitude in your hearts sing psalms, hymns, and spiritual songs to God" (3:16). For centuries monks have chanted the Psalms at their designated hours to keep God always in their hearts and minds, but it was Luther who nurtured the rise of congregational singing. During the middle ages, the liturgy was primarily sung by the choir and celebrant while laypeople joined in on a few vernacular responses.[65] This all changed in 1524 with the release of the *Wittenberg Gesangbuch,* which Luther and his collaborators continued to revise. They freely paraphrased Latin hymns (as well as some of the Psalms) into German, keeping each language's distinct stress patterns in mind.[66] (Too, they adapted the simple, singable melodies of the day, including children's tunes, folk songs, and carols.[67]) This choral tradition reached its climax in the cantatas, passions, and oratorios of Johann Sebastian Bach.[68] "My heart bubbles up and overflows in response to music," exclaimed Luther,[69] and thanks to him, today all manner of congregations are singing. I know that hymns have been an especially effective catalyst for compunction in my own Christian life.

A great name in Western music is classical composer Franz Joseph Haydn, who was also a devout Catholic. His music seemed to mature as he grew older, so much so that a number of his finest pieces were completed after the age of sixty. Looking back, he wrote, "God Almighty . . . gave me especially in music so much facility, that already in my sixth year I could sing with confidence some few masses in the choir, as well as play a little on the violin and clavier."[70] He composed important masses (e.g., *Paukenmesse, Lord Nelson Mass*), made significant contributions to the string quartet, and for his instrumental innovations, is sometimes referred to as "the father of the symphony." *The Creation* oratorio, based on Milton's *Paradise Lost,* has frequently been ranked alongside Handel's *Messiah.* He was a great friend of Mozart's and was generous in acknowledging his debt to others. Cheerful, yet profound, he lived by a simple code: "Be good and industrious, and serve God continually."[71] He opened his scores with *"In Nomine Domini"* ("In God's Name") and ended them with *"Laus Deo"* ("Praise Be to God"). Here was one genius who knew whence his inspiration sprang.[72]

Like Haydn, we should, for the most part, be marathon runners, not sprinters. I know one of the greatest boosts to my own faith is to meet and observe elderly men and women who have weathered all the world, the flesh, and the devil could hurl at them and are still buoyant witnesses for Christ. A Christian is to be a confessor like Polycarp, that second-century bishop of Smyrna, who when questioned by the Roman authorities refused to swear by the genius of Caesar. When the magistrate demanded, "Swear the oath, and I will release you; revile Christ"; Polycarp responded, "For eighty-six years I have been his servant, and he has done me no wrong. How can I blaspheme my King who saved me?"[73] Shortly afterward, an executioner stabbed him to death. Such martyrs were remembered annually at their tombs not for their deaths but for their heavenly birthdays[74] (February 21 or 22 in the case of Polycarp).[75] Historian Edward Gibbon comments, "The sober discretion of the present age will more readily censure than admire, but can more easily admire than imitate, the fervour of the first Christians, who, according to the lively expression of Sulpicius Severus, desired martyrdom with more eagerness than his own contemporaries solicited a bishopric."[76]

Early Irish Christians sought to broaden the concept of "martyrdom" by referring to three different colors: "red," for one who actually forfeits his life; "white," for one who "separates for the sake of God from everything he loves" due to exile or wandering as a pilgrim; and "green," for one who "separates from his desires, or suffers toil in penance and repentance" in a life of denial, though neither leaves home or gives up his life for the faith.[77] As Christ does call us to die, I wonder, which type of martyrdom will we choose? Paul Fleming, born the son of a village pastor in Saxony in 1609, expands on Paul's overriding conviction that "it is no longer I who live, but it is Christ who lives in me" (Gal. 2:20) in his poem "Devotion": "I live; yet 'tis not I. He lives in me. / . . . My life to him was death, his death my life, / Now give I him again what once he gave. / Through the death of me he lives."[78]

Paul, in Romans 6:3–8, makes baptism a powerful symbol of Christ's own death and resurrection. Augustine, referring to this imagery, proclaims, "This is the meaning of the great sacrament of baptism, that all who attain to this grace should die to sin, as he is said to have died to sin, because he died in the flesh, which is the likeness of sin; and rising from the font regenerate, as he arose alive from the grave, should begin a new life in the spirit, whatever may be the age of the body."[79] Cyril, bishop of Jerusalem in the fourth century, put it like this: "For you go down into the water bearing your sins, but the invocation of grace, placing a seal upon your soul, makes you proof against the dragon's maw. Though dead in sin when you went down, you will come up vivified. . . . [S]o you, also, after entering and being as it were buried in the water, as he was in the rock, are raised up again to walk in newness of life."[80] Twentieth-century architects Angelo Mangiarotti and Bruno Morassuti even sought to incorporate this motif into their design of the Church at Baranzate in Milan, where worshipers first descend into the baptistry, then afterward, ascend into the sanctuary.[81]

So, I say, let us shake off our sloth, and as Horace advises, "*carpe diem*," "seize the day."[82] Recall your baptismal vows, and the hand of God heretofore in your life, and run your race with perseverance. God still has much in store for you. That eighteenth-century wonder John Wesley, who preached tirelessly for decades and traveled perhaps several thousand miles a year by horseback, composed a short rule of conduct for the early Methodists: "Do all the good you can, / By all the means you can, / In all the ways you can, / In all the places you can, / At all the times you can, / To all the people you can, / As long as ever you can";[83] and even wrote a covenant ceremony that is still used by his followers (and those of other denominations) to dedicate their lives to be more zealous for God.[84] Otherwise, if we don't put our lives on target, we risk coming to the end of our days haunted by these lines from poet John Greenleaf Whittier:

> Of all sad words of tongue or pen,
> The saddest are these: "It might have been!"[85]

Let's recite from that Franciscan prayer first printed in France in 1913: "Grant that I may seek not so much to be consoled, as to console; to be understood, as to understand; to be loved, as to love. For it is by giving that we receive; it is by losing that we find; it is by forgiving that we are forgiven; and it is by dying that we rise again to eternal life, in Jesus Christ our Lord. Amen."[86]

CHAPTER 16

The Despondent

Believers are not immune from bouts of depression or melancholy. Jeremiah had a bitter message to deliver to his generation, so he was persecuted, imprisoned in an empty cistern (Jer. 38:6), and at times was suicidal (Jer. 20:14–18). In the Book of Lamentations (usually attributed to him) are heartrending images of desolation: God "has made my teeth grind on gravel, and made me cower in ashes; my soul is bereft of peace; I have forgotten what happiness is; so I say, 'Gone is my glory, and all that I had hoped for from the Lord'" (Lam. 3:16–18). Job, in the midst of his calamities, moans, "Why did I not die at birth, come forth from the womb and expire?" "Or why was I not buried like a stillborn child, like an infant that never sees the light?" (3:11, 16). Elijah, coming off his victory over the prophets of Baal, so feared Jezebel's wrath, that he asked God to take his life, thinking he was the only true Hebrew left. And what was God's response? "I have kept for myself seven thousand who have not bowed the knee to Baal" (Rom. 11:3–4; 1 Kings 19:4, 14, 18).

Then there's the eighteenth-century evangelical poet William Cowper, who collaborated with John Newton on the *Olney Hymns,* becoming known for such marvelous pieces as "God Moves in a Mysterious Way" and "Oh! for a Closer Walk with God." After he made several attempts at suicide (via an overdose of the drug laudanum; by nearly hurling himself from London Bridge; and seeking to hang himself in his room), he came to believe that he was damned.[1] He bares his soul in his memoirs: "While I traversed the apartment in the most horrible dismay of soul, expecting every moment that the earth would open her mouth and swallow me, my conscience scaring me, the avenger of blood pursuing me, and the city of refuge out of reach and out of sight, a strange and horrible darkness fell upon me. If it were possible that a heavy blow could light on the brain without touching the skull, such was the sensation I felt. I clapped my hand to my forehead and cried aloud through the pain it gave me. At every stroke, my thoughts and expressions became more wild and incoherent; all that remained clear was the sense of sin and the expectation of punishment."[2] Then, in his last terrifying poem, "The Castaway," he identifies with one who is lost at sea:

> No voice divine the storm allay'd,
>   No light propitious shone;
> When, snatch'd from all effectual aid,
>   We perish'd, each alone;
> But I beneath a rougher sea,
> And whelm'd in deeper gulphs than he.[3]

"O the mind, mind has mountains," cautioned poet Gerard Manley Hopkins, "cliffs of fall / Frightful, sheer, no-man-fathomed. Hold them cheap / May who ne'er hung there."[4] Terror also seized mystics like John of the Cross, who spoke of a "dark night of the soul" when he felt far from God's presence. Towards the end of her short life, nineteenth-century nun Thérèse of Lisieux imagined that she had been born in a country covered with a thick fog, and complained of "a wall which reaches right up to the heavens," so that her joy in God had disappeared.[5] In the Gospels, Jesus, too, sweat drops as of blood while praying in Gethsemane (Luke 22:44), and on the cross, quoted those forlorn lines from Psalm 22, "My God, my God, why have you forsaken me?" (Mark 15:34).

This feeling of dejection is exquisitely evoked in one of Baudelaire's versions of "Spleen." He speaks of a "low, heavy sky" that "weighs like a lid on the groaning mind." The entire landscape appears like a "humid dungeon" with incessant rain forming the bars of the cell. Funeral processions run through his brain. "Hope, vanquished, weeps; and atrocious, despotic Anguish on my bowed skull plants her black flag."[6] We feel as though our luck has run out and nothing can go right. "If I sold lamps and candles," medieval Hebrew poet Abraham ibn Ezra complained, "The sun would shine all night. / . . . Were selling shrouds my business, / No man would ever die!"[7]

Those tormented by insufferable misery, Robert Burton says, think of harming themselves. "In the day-time they are affrighted still by some terrible object, and torn in pieces with suspicion, fear, sorrow, discontents, cares, shame, anguish, et cetera, as so many wild horses, that they cannot be quiet an hour. . . . They murmur many times against the world, friends, allies, all mankind, even against God himself in the bitterness of their passion. . . . They seek at last, finding no comfort, no remedy in this wretched life, to be eased of all by death."[8]

In John Bunyan's *The Pilgrim's Progress*, Hopeful and Christian are taken captive by the Giant Despair, who locks them in a dark dungeon in Doubting-Castle.

After giving them neither bread nor water, the Giant proceeds to beat them, then recommends they commit suicide. "For why," he asks, "should you choose life, seeing it is attended with so much bitterness?" Christian tentatively agrees, "The grave is more easy for me than this dungeon." Hopeful, argues, though, that such a course would be wrong; besides, circumstances might change. "Who knows, but that God that made the world may cause that Giant Despair may die; or that, at some time or other he may forget to lock us in; or but he may in short time have another of his fits before us, and may lose the use of his limbs?" All of us at times feel overwhelmed by misfortune, unable to see a way out. Hopeful, though, reminds his companion of those hardships they have already endured and exhorts him to perseverance. Christian eventually remembers that he carries a key called "promise" (signifying God's character and faithfulness), which will unlock any door, and soon this allows them to escape.[9] Since Bunyan himself was intermittently in prison for nearly twelve years for preaching as a dissenter, the incident may have an autobiographical ring.

But what causes melancholy and how can it be alleviated? Freud, in his influential essay "Mourning and Melancholia," posited that inverted anger and unresolved grief lay at the heart of depression. "The distinguishing mental features of melancholia," Freud asserted, "are a profoundly painful dejection, abrogation of interest in the outside world, loss of the capacity to love, inhibition of all activity, and a lowering of the self-regarding feelings to a degree that finds utterance in self-reproaches and self-revilings, and culminates in a delusional expectation of punishment."[10] Too, "sometimes melancholy arises for no apparent cause," the monk John Cassian reported in the fifth century.[11] Indeed modern medicine indicates that chemical imbalances and genetic disorders can contribute to, even generate, feelings of depression.

Melancholy has been compared to the activity of moths or worms. "It's gnawing dejection," Cassian observes, "that eats away the priestly temple of the soul. Holes bore into my vestment or garment."[12] Despondency sucks the lifeblood of its victim, due to feelings of isolation, boredom, lack of purpose, and an inability to visualize the future. Those who are idle seem particularly susceptible. Thus the parson in Chaucer's *Canterbury Tales* chides, "An idle man is like a place without walls; the devil may enter on every side and shoot at him with temptations while he's unprotected."[13] I know that when I have no pressing responsibilities I'm most likely to wallow in either self-pity or self-loathing.

But what are some time-honored remedies for dejection? Psalm after psalm indicate that interior dialogue or the worship experience itself can profoundly transform one's moods. "Why are you cast down, O my soul, and why are you disquieted within me?" asks the author of Psalm 42, who then adds: "Hope in

God; for I shall again praise him, my help and my God" (v. 5). Twelfth-century Cistercian abbot Aelred of Rievaulx describes his practice: "Just as day declines to evening, so often after some little pleasure my heart declines into depression. Everything seems dull, every action feels like a burden. If anyone speaks, I scarcely listen. If anyone knocks, I scarcely hear. My heart is as hard as flint. Then I go out into the field to meditate, to read the holy Scriptures, and I write down my deepest thoughts in a letter to you. And suddenly your grace, dear Jesus, shatters the darkness with daylight, lifts the burden, relieves the tension. Soon tears follow sighs, and heavenly joy floods over me with tears."[14]

Music can be another way to lift our spirits. David used to play the lyre whenever King Saul was beset with overwhelming cares (1 Sam. 16:23). Martin Luther advised a friend, "When melancholy threatens to get the upper hand, say: 'Arise! I must play a song unto the Lord on my regal [a portable organ], for the Scriptures teach us that it pleases him to hear a joyful song and the music of stringed instruments.' Then begin striking the keys and singing in accompaniment, as David and Elisha did, until your sad thoughts vanish."[15] Singing, whistling, dancing, rhythmical movement of any sort can help dislodge our torpor. The nineteenth-century Hasidic rabbi Nahman of Bratslav noticed that when a melancholy person joined in the mystic dance, his sadness would lift. So Nahman came to teach that one who is melancholy should persuade himself to dance, for it is "an achievement to struggle and pursue that sadness, bringing it into the joy."[16] Then, pleasantly surprised by the turn of events, we can marvel with poet George Herbert, "Who would have thought my shrivel'd heart / Could have recover'd greennesse?"[17]

Humor, too, has a salutary effect. "A cheerful heart is a good medicine," Proverbs 17:22 declares, "but a downcast spirit dries up the bones." The world has a fault line running straight through it, which reveals countless anomalies, injustices, crimes, and utter folly.[18] Humor, though, has a subtle way of creeping up on our consciousness, when the defenses are lowered, and calling us back to our senses. "Satan fell by the force of gravity," G. K. Chesterton wryly commented, whereas "Angels can fly because they can take themselves lightly."[19] That's a lesson every melancholic needs to learn. Evelyn Waugh, the British satirist, knew periods of despair as a youth. In his autobiography, he recounts an incident where he swam out to sea, intending never to return. But comic incongruity even saved him here, for when he was attacked by a school of jellyfish, in order to escape the pain, he plied his way back to shore.[20]

Solitude is a particularly fertile breeding ground for melancholy. So it's important to mingle in public, visit friends, go to a play, attend a concert. Some of the best informal counseling I know is done at social gatherings among friends, relatives, and those who know us best. A listening ear can help sort out seemingly intractable difficulties, as when someone tells of an experience similar to our own or passes on a friendly word of advice. I can't begin to count the number of times when such a heartfelt sharing of information has been beneficial in my own life. Then approach that problem step-by-step, and so build up confidence, instead of trying to tackle it all at once and feeling inadequate. Kind, honest gestures count too. Mark Twain once quipped that he could live two weeks on a good compliment.[21]

What a difference attitude makes. Comparative religion scholar Wilfred Cantwell Smith defined the Hindu term for faith, *sraddha,* as "to set one's heart on." Its opposite is apathy, lack of commitment, or skepticism.[22] When the Roman satirist Lucian took a fictional voyage to the Isle of the Blest, he discovered "the people of the Academy wanted to come but were still holding off and arguing; the one point they couldn't come to any conclusion about was whether an island such as this existed. Besides," he continued, "I imagine they were afraid to stand judgment before Rhadamanthus; after all, they were the ones who denied all standards of judgment. Rumor had it that a big group of them" did start out, "but, being dawdlers and lacking the courage of conviction, fell behind and turned back at the halfway point."[23] At some point we must decide that one path is more promising than another, then pursue it. As Hebrews declares, "Without faith it is impossible to please God, for whoever would approach him must believe that he exists and that he rewards those who seek him" (11:6).

Near the end of Kazantzakis's novel, Zorba admonishes his overly cautious writer-friend: "You're on a long piece of string, boss; you come and go, and think you're free, but you never cut the string in two," and unless you do, your life will always have the flavor of "weak camomile tea."[24] This calls to mind Jesus' parables of abandonment, such as the merchant who finds "one pearl of great value," and sells all that he has in order to purchase it (Matt. 13:45–46). The French mathematician and Christian apologist Pascal proposed a common-sense argument for believing in God called "the wager." Finite creatures, he reasoned, cannot formulate accurate conceptions of the infinite, so the odds concerning God are really infinity or nothing. Why not then believe, since the rewards are enticing—salvation, eternal life, victory over noxious sins? Such gains far outweigh any conceivable losses. In decision theory, it's stated that if one choice is at least as good as its competitors under all circumstances, and actually exceeds them in some, that should be the dominant strategy or strongest option.[25] "A coin is being spun which will come down heads or tails." Pascal asks, "How will you wager?" [26]

The classic Christian reply came from Anselm of Canterbury in the eleventh century: "I do not seek to understand so that I may believe; but I believe so that I may understand. For I believe this also, that 'unless I believe, I shall not understand'" (cf. Isa. 7:9).[27] Poet Robert Bridges once asked his friend Gerard Manley

Hopkins for help in believing. Instead of some long, philosophical discourse, Hopkins simply wrote back: "Give alms." It may be that one concrete act, requiring a small measure of sacrifice on our part, can affect us more deeply than attending a whole series of lectures by some world-renowned theologian.[28] The heart must be touched, in addition to the head.

Innumerable consequences flow from such a decision. "For faith is not the clinging to a shrine but an endless pilgrimage of the heart," Jewish philosopher Abraham Heschel explains. "Audacious longing, burning songs, daring thoughts, an impulse overwhelming the heart, usurping the mind—these are all a drive towards serving Him who rings our hearts like a bell. . . . To rely on our faith would be idol-worship. We have only the right to rely on God. Faith is not an insurance, but a constant effort, constant listening to the eternal voice."[29]

A cobbler reproaches God for the death of his son in Tolstoy's tale "Where Love Is, God Is." A pilgrim who comes in, however, assures him that he is depressed because he is overly concerned about his own happiness, so urges him to buy a New Testament and read through the Gospels. Reading these texts transforms the cobbler. One night he has a vision in which Christ calls out, "Martin, Martin! Look out into the street tomorrow, for I shall come." That following day, half working and half peering out the window, the cobbler notices an elderly man trying to clean the snow off his window, so invites him in for tea and conversation. Next he observes an ill-clad mother desperately trying to shield her baby from the cold, and proceeds to give her bread and soup, a coat, and some money. Finally, seeing an apple-seller scold a boy for theft, Martin rushes out to separate them, coaxing the lad to confess and ask her forgiveness. That night, as he reads Matthew 25:42–45, concerning the hungry, the thirsty, the naked, the sick, the stranger, and those in prison, Christ confirms that it was he who appeared in those three earlier incidents.[30] Tolstoy seems to be asking, what would happen if we, even for a single day, put this teaching into practice, and expected to see Christ in those we met?

By faith, too, we learn to be grateful, no matter how dire the circumstances. Robinson Crusoe, shipwrecked on an apparently deserted island, roused his heart to thanksgiving by drawing up a list that had two columns. Evil: "I am cast upon a horrible desolate island, void of all hope of recovery." Good: "But I am alive, and not drowned, as all my ship's company was." Evil: "I am singled out and separated, as it were, from all the world to be miserable." Good: "But I am singled out, too, from all the ship's crew to be spared from death; and He that miraculously saved me from death can deliver me from this condition." Evil: "I have no soul to speak to, or relieve me." Good: "But God wonderfully sent the ship in near enough to the shore that I have gotten out so many necessary things as will either supply my wants, or enable me to supply myself even as long as I live."[31]

As the philosopher Nietzsche once said, "He who has a *why* to live for can bear with almost any *how*."[32] Interred for three years in Nazi concentration camps, Viktor Frankl came to the conclusion that this bleak world could only be surmounted if one had something to look forward to, and using this insight, pioneered a form of psychology known as logotherapy. "It is a peculiarity of man," he declared, "that he can only live by looking to the future—*sub specie aeternitatis*."[33]

The Christian view of history is a linear one, not cyclical, with an alpha point of creation and an omega point of millennium, divided by a once-and-for-all incarnation. History is not an "eternal hourglass," which is "turned upside down again and again," as Nietzsche supposed, where "every pain and every joy and every thought and sigh and everything unutterably small or great in your life will have to return to you, all in the same succession and sequence."[34] That view was dismissed in Hebrews 9:28, when the author used the Greek word *hapax* to stress how unique the incarnation was. It doesn't need to be repeated over and over again as the high priest's annual sacrifices were in the holy of holies, but is effective for all time.[35] In the impassioned words of Augustine: "Plato sat in the city of Athens and in the school called Academy teaching his pupils, so also through countless ages of the past at intervals which, however great are nevertheless certain, both the same Plato and the same city and the same school and the same pupils have been repeated, as they are destined to be repeated through countless ages of the future. God forbid, I say, that we should swallow such nonsense! Christ died, once and for all, for our sins."[36]

Theologians say eschatology, or the last things, has a retroactive capacity to modify the present. The future is so vital, vivid, that it spills over into our now. Consider the role-playing children do; once they settle on a goal or an occupation (say, enrolling in college or becoming a nurse), all their plans must be reshuffled.[37] In much the same way the starry imaginations of nineteenth-century science fiction writers like Jules Verne and H. G. Wells spurred the modern invention of the submarine, the tank, the airplane, and the spaceship.[38] As Christians we are a heaven-bound people, who look forward to that city with foundations, whose architect and builder is God (Heb. 11:10). So, being eager to live with God, we do all we can to be welcomed into his presence.

The despondent focus too morosely on sin and human fallibility, worship too stern a god. Robert Burton, in that seventeenth-century miscellany of counsel, *The Anatomy of Melancholy*, derides those preachers and theologians who weigh down the soul with harsh judgment and condemnation: These "aggravate sin, thunder out God's judgments . . . intempestively rail at and pronounce them damned . . . for giving so much to sports and honest recreations, making every small fault and thing indifferent an irremissible offence, they so rent, tear and wound men's consciences, that they are almost mad, and at their wits' end."[39]

The traditionalist's view of God as an overbearing father should be complemented with the image of God as a caring mother, since being sexless, he/she is the ideal parent. "As a mother comforts her child," God declares through the prophet Isaiah, "so will I comfort you" (Isa. 66:13). "This fair lovely word 'mother,'" Julian of Norwich expounds,"is so sweet and so kind in itself that it cannot truly be said of anyone or to anyone except of him and to him who is the true Mother of life and of all things. To the property of motherhood belong nature, love, wisdom, and knowledge, and this is God."[40] Images of Mary in Roman Catholicism and Eastern Orthodoxy have tried to do much the same. One recalls the "Mater Dolorosa" in medieval Catholic paintings and sculptures, who, due to her sympathy for humanity, seeks to soften God's heart,[41] or the Virgin of Vladimir, that much-admired Russian Orthodox icon representing God's tenderness, where the Christchild bends his neck ever so affectionately towards his beloved mother.[42]

"Where sin increased, grace abounded all the more," Paul told the church at Rome (Rom. 5:20). Is there such a thing as an unpardonable sin? Let's recount some of the vices of those well-known old covenant heroes—Abraham pawned his wife off as his sister to Pharaoh; David committed adultery and had Bathsheba's husband knocked off; Moses flew off the handle when the Israelites grumbled once too often in the wilderness. Yet all these are commended for their faith and identified as friends of God. Origen believed that even the turncoat Judas, who betrayed the Son of Man, could have been forgiven if it hadn't been for the terrible melancholy that led him to hang himself.[43]

The one unpardonable sin I know is giving up on God. Herman Melville describes the young sailor Billy Budd, who, though willing to listen to the stories about Jesus, never truly appropriates the message for himself. Salvation was to Budd, "like a gift placed in the palm of an out-reached hand upon which the fingers do not close."[44] Or there's that distressing entry the eminent biographer Gamaliel Bradford made in his journal at the age of fifty-seven: "I do not dare to read the New Testament for fear of its awakening a storm of anxiety and self-reproach and doubt and dread of having taken the wrong path, of having been traitor to the plain and simple God. Not that I do not know perfectly well that no reading would make me believe any more. But, oh, what agonies of fret and worry it would give me; for I should be able neither to believe nor to disbelieve nor to let it alone."[45]

One's destiny is not set in stone. In his last dying words, one bandit on the cross pleaded, "Jesus, remember me when you come into your kingdom," and was enheartened when the Savior replied, "Truly I tell you, today you will be with me in Paradise" (Luke 23:42–43). "Even late in life," discerns psychologist William James, "some thaw, some release may take place, some bolt be shot back in the barrenest breast, and the man's hard heart may soften and break into religious feeling. Such cases more than any others suggest the idea that sudden conversion is by miracle. So long as they exist, we must not imagine ourselves to deal with irretrievably fixed classes."[46]

As Christians who are focused on the future, we learn to defer gratification, and so increase our steadfastness. Hebrews says that Jesus "endured the cross" "for the sake of the joy that was set before him" (12:2). As Robert the Bruce (who lived from 1274–1329) was lying in bed after being defeated in battle, according to legend, he noticed a spider trying to swing from one ceiling beam to another. Six consecutive times the spider failed. Robert reflected that he, too, had been defeated in six consecutive battles, yet if that spider succeeded on the seventh try, he, too, would rise and fight again. The spider did make that leap, and not long afterward Scotland gained its independence from England under Robert I.[47] The Wizard of Menlo Park, Thomas Edison, defined invention as ninety parts perspiration and ten parts inspiration. He tested literally thousands of materials before finding one filament that would light up his electric bulb. "Genius? Nothing!" he declared, "Sticking to it is the genius!"[48]

Few of us will ever achieve real fame. Instead, more likely, we'll labor unnoticed, unappreciated in some forgotten cranny in God's vineyard, unsure whether our seed will ever bear fruit or even whether we've made the right choices, at times despondent and forlorn over the celestial silence. Surely no dove will perch on our shoulder, nor will the heavens open and God's voice verify our decisions. But that doesn't mean we should give up or grow weary (cf. Gal 6:9). As Christians our boughs should always be green for we live in joyous anticipation.

In C. S. Lewis's *The Lion, the Witch, and the Wardrobe*, it dawns on the characters that the Christlike figure of Aslan the lion is on the move when everywhere spring starts to make its presence known by means of chirping birds, running water, blooming crocuses; for the white witch's frigid grip has been loosened.[49] A seventy-two-year-old African American woman, who joined the civil rights boycott of segregated buses in Montgomery, Alabama in 1955, had no choice but to walk wherever she wanted to go. Yet when someone inquired how she was feeling, she replied with a note of triumph: "My feet is tired, but my soul is rested."[50] The melancholic has nothing to look forward to, feels as if his life has virtually ended, but a Christian should imitate that disciple of Bernard of Clairvaux, David of Himmerod, who, as his biographer put it, had "a face shining with joy; he had the face of one going toward Jerusalem."[51] As one anonymous medieval pilgrim exuberantly sings:

> Hiersualem, my happy home,
>> When shall I come to thee?
> When shall my sorrows have an end
>> Thy joys when shall I see?[52]

CHAPTER 17

St. Satan, Pray for Me

"When I go to bed," relates Martin Luther, "the Devil is always waiting for me. When he begins to plague me, I give him this answer: 'Devil, I must sleep. That's God's command. 'Work by day. Sleep by night.' So go away.' If that doesn't work and he brings out a catalog of sins, I say, 'Yes, old fellow, I know all about it. And I know some more you have overlooked. Here are an extra few. Put them down.' If he still won't quit and presses me hard and accuses me as a sinner, I scorn him and say, 'St. Satan, pray for me.'"[1]

The sixth chapter of Ephesians depicts Christians as soldiers in pitched battle. Our enemy, however, is not the latest despot intent on world empire, nor is he mortal in the sense that we can blow him away with some newfangled technological wonder. In fact the enemies' ranks are invisible, yet the havoc they wreak is apparent everywhere, whether it be broken families, lives destroyed by addictions, bigots bloated by prejudice, warring factions, partisans who will justify their cause by any means, slanderers, adulterers, idolaters, and any who are inflamed by passion for power or pleasure. According to verse 12, "Our struggle is not against enemies of blood and flesh, but against the rulers, against the authorities, against the cosmic powers of this present darkness, against the spiritual forces of evil in the heavenly places" (Eph. 6:12).

I'm referring, of course, to Satan and his cohorts. We have been in conflict with him since our conversion or baptism, and probably well before. To renounce his influence has always been paramount in salvation. A document dating back to the early third century known as *The Apostolic Tradition* describes baptismal rites then in practice: "And a deacon takes the oil of exorcism and stands on the priest's left; and another deacon takes the oil of thanksgiving and stands on the priest's right. And when the priest takes each one of those who are to receive baptism, he shall bid him renounce, saying 'I renounce you, Satan, and all your service and all your works.' And when each has renounced all this, he shall anoint him with the oil of exorcism, saying to him: 'Let every spirit depart far from you.'"[2] Seventeen centuries later, renunciation of evil is still central to baptism across denominational lines. Thus do we follow in the footsteps of Jesus, who, after being baptized by John, was tempted by the devil in the wilderness; so Jesus' life and ministry are cast as a "yes" to God and a "no" to evil.[3] In much the same way, during the second week of Ignatius's *Spiritual Exercises,* the believer is enjoined to meditate upon and choose between two contrasting lifestyles: Christ and the way of humility or Lucifer and the way of self-seeking.[4]

Our oldest creeds contain few explicit references to Satan. He has rather become shrouded in legend and absurd speculations. To give you a flavor for some of these odd beliefs, I'm going to conduct a fictional interview with this wily character. However, for the sake of argument, let's assume that the devil is, for the most part, telling the truth, something that is quite difficult for him to do.

Question: Today we are interviewing that archfiend, Mr. Beelzebul. Sir, what is your real name?

Answer: Satan, Leviathan, the Evil One, the Prince of Darkness, Mephistopheles, Lucifer, Apollyon, the Accuser, the Father of Lies, the Old Serpent, but most people just call me the devil. I suppose the name I especially loathe is Belial, "the Worthless One," because it implies all my activities will eventually come to nothing.

Q: And what is your occupation?

A: (quoting from an ancient Jewish magical incantation): "I destroy kings. I ally myself with foreign tyrants. And my own demons I set on to men, in order that the latter may believe in them and be lost. And the chosen servants of God, priests and faithful men, I excite unto desires for wicked sins, and evil heresies, and lawless deeds; and they obey me, and I bear them on to destruction. And I inspire men with envy, and murder, and for wars and sodomy, and other evil things. And I will destroy the world."[5]

Sometimes, too, I'm identified with mythological beasts, as when a twelfth-century Latin bestiary compares me to a dragon: "He is often borne into the air from his den, and the air around him blazes, for the Devil in raising himself from the lower regions translates himself into an angel of light and misleads the foolish with false hopes of glory and worldly bliss. He is said to have a crest or crown because he is the King of Pride, and his strength is not in his teeth but in his tail because he beguiles those whom he draws to him by deceit, their strength being destroyed. He lies hidden round the paths on which they saunter, because their way to heaven is encumbered by the knots of their sins, and he strangles them to death."[6]

The First Epistle of John points out three of my prime strategies: "the desire of the flesh, the desire of the eyes, the pride in riches" (2:16). In the thirteenth-century Islamic work, *The Book of Marzuban* by Al-Warawini, the chief demon holds a meeting on what to do about a certain pious man who is leading many into following God. Here's the advice that was eventually followed: "by satanic whispering and magical cunning . . . lay the foundations of worldliness in his breast, so that he may become occupied and infatuated with the trivialities of this abode of illusion. Place before his eyes a glittering picture of the gaily frescoed walls of the house of pleasures and delights, and let the honeyed droplets of lust so trickle from the branches of anticipation that he will fail to see the serpent of destiny waiting open-jawed at his feet."[7]

Q: By some accounts you were originally an angelic prosecutor in God's heavenly court (e.g., Job 1-2). What caused your "fall"?

A: Umm, that's a difficult question. Some say that I was an angel named Satanel, but lost my divine element (*el*) when I led a rebellion against God and was ousted from heaven.[8] Justin Martyr and Tertullian, following 1 Enoch, felt that I and my legions were offspring of the "sons of Gods" and beautiful women, so mysteriously referred to in Genesis 6:1-4.

Others believe that pride was my chief vice, pointing to human prototypes in such passages as Ezekiel 28 and Isaiah 14. Duns Scotus and the Franciscans claim I desired to be equal with God and loved myself too immoderately. Others, like Albert the Great and Thomas Aquinas, believe I wanted to attain natural beatitude through my own powers.[9] I'd rather not talk about it further since it's a rather sore point.

Q: I've heard varying accounts of the number of your associates. Who are some of your chief aides?

A: Once again Scripture is almost silent on the question, but popular fancy runs rampant. Lilith tempts men through sexual dreams and haunts desolate places in the company of such unclean birds as the kite, pelican, and owl. Resheph hovers like a vulture and is responsible for plagues and natural pestilence. Azazel inhabits the remote stretches of the desert and can snatch away any who trespass on his domain. "Terror in the Night" seeks to ruin matrimonial bliss, so escorts of a bridegroom will shoot arrows in the air or fire shots to ward him off. And the mighty "Seven" smite humankind with consumption, fever, inflammation, fiery heat, drought, blight, and mildew.[10] When one religion replaces another, the losing gods are frequently recast as evil spirits.[11]

Although my associates are normally invisible, if one sifts through ashes on a doorstep, demonic footprints resembling those of a rooster can sometimes be seen in the morning. My fiends also love to congregate in abandoned houses, marshes, and lavatories and like to attack invalids and engaged young couples.[12] To defend themselves, the superstitious have resorted to such good-luck charms as animals' teeth, pierced shells, and lunar crescents. A few ancient Hebrews even wore representations of pagan gods for protection: metal serpents, gold flies, and lapis lazuli hippopotamuses. Weren't such objects found on the bodies of Jewish soldiers during the wars of the Maccabees?[13]

Q: Your tactics seem rather sophisticated. I thought you were just the figment of someone's overwrought imagination.

A: It's true that in recent years there has been much debate, both inside and outside of the church, concerning my existence. You need to decide, "How can a good God permit evil?" If the righteous suffer, there must be a reason. Unlike Gnosticism, Christianity and Judaism believe that matter itself is neutral and doesn't cause people to sin. In the words of the psalmist, "The earth is the Lord's and all that is in it" (Ps. 24:1). Nor does either religion teach, like the Manicheans, that the battle between good and evil, God and myself, is eternal, for in the end God will triumph.

How much good and how much evil is in the universe is hotly debated. G. K. Chesterton once compared the universe to a sheet of paper on which pessimists saw a black background containing one or two nearly accidental specks of star dust; while optimists (such as Christian Scientists) saw against a gleaming white, a few dark smudges difficult to expunge. Dualists, on the other hand, saw life as a chessboard with equal measures of good and evil, "white squares on a black board" or "black squares on a white board." Chesterton himself opted for a view much like Thomas Aquinas's, where "every existence, as such, is good" and evil is freely acknowledged, though perceived as "an enormous exception," something like an invasion or a rebellion.[14]

The early church fathers had a quaint way of depicting God's victory. They claimed that I was a tyrant who tortured everyone who fell into my hands. Then along came Jesus, looking like any other human being. Deceived by his appearance, I put him to death. But I couldn't hold him because he had never sinned and I had no rightful claim over him. The devil, according to John Chrysostom, "smote the first man, because he found him guilty of sin; for it was through sin that death entered in." Then Jesus exclaims, "he did not find any sin in me; wherefore then did he fall on me and give me up to the power of death?"[15] I find the notion that God is stronger than I am open to debate, but the battle of Armageddon should decide that issue once and for all.

Q: What about those medieval sculptures and wood carvings where, if you'll pardon the expression, you look as ugly as sin?

A: Well . . . ! (calming himself). Once people thought I resembled a hairy goat;

other times I was portrayed as a man with two horns, a tail, and a cleft foot. A few people think I resemble those perfectly awful Halloween masks. "In our childhood," Reginald Scot wrote in 1584, "our mothers maids have so terrified us with an ouglie divell having hornes on his head, fier in his mouth, and a taile in his breech, eies like a bason, fanges like a dog, clawes like a beare, a skin like a Niger, and a voice roring like a lion" that "we start and are afraid when we heare one crie Bough."[16] I was likened in folklore to a "swarthy Ethiopian,"[17] who went about spouting magic spells. A few actually thought I could grant anyone's request as long as they sold their soul to me (you know: the Faust legend), or that in inclement weather, when thunder roared, the winds howled, and the lightning flashed, I was on the prowl.[18] Of course, all of this is apocryphal and quite far-fetched.

I prefer to consider myself an angel of light rather than some dark, murky figure of the night. Indeed that fourth-century desert ascetic, St. Antony, compared demons to actors, who "play parts as if they were on stage, changing their forms and striking fear . . . by the illusion of the hordes and their shapes."[19] Thomas Mann gives this shape-shifting full literary play in *Doktor Faustus,* when Mephistopheles urges composer Adrian Leverkühn to sell his capacity for love in return for twenty-four years of intense creativity. To do so, Mephistopheles takes up, in turn, the forms of confidence man, theologian, physician, procurer, businessman, and criminal, all created out of material from Adrian's own mind.[20]

I have also been blamed, with some justification, for witchcraft, astrology, magic, the evil eye, clairvoyance, and a host of despicable deeds. Martin Luther called me "God's ape," believing I was a mere imitator of the Almighty.[21] In the middle ages, some thought I had created an imitation Eucharist, where I ritually sacrificed animals and violated virgins. Instead of bread and wine, my followers ate turnips and blood mixed with wine. In paintings of the witches' Sabbath, I'm frequently shown with a second face on my rear end that my followers must kiss to show their subservience.[22] Such vulgar human imaginings are making my stomach queasy; I'm afraid I simply must say, "Adieu" (end of interview).

The devil is quite the character. Yet those who don't believe in him often find radical evil difficult to explain. What do you say before such enormous atrocities as Auschwitz? How do you account for sadism, where people actually enjoy giving pain?[23] Or what fuels such blanket prejudices as racism or anti-Semitism or ethnic cleansing of any kind? Our minds are stopped before this wanton conniving and the willingness to destroy on such a large scale. "As for the devil," that fourth-century champion of orthodoxy, Bishop Athanasius once said, "since he does not possess the truth, he comes with hatchets and axes."[24]

In Dostoyevsky's masterpiece, *The Brothers Karamazov,* Ivan rattles off a number of horrid deeds, mostly drawn from the newspapers of his day: A nobleman orders his hounds to tear a peasant boy to pieces in front of his mother; a man whips his struggling horse "on its gentle eyes"; parents lock their daughter in a freezing privy all night long, while she knocks on the walls pleading for mercy; a soldier entertains a baby with a shiny pistol before he blows its brains out. Explains Ivan, "I took only children to make my case clearer." "It's just the defencelessness of these little ones that tempts the torturers, the angelic trustfulness of the child, who has nowhere to go and no one to run to for protection."[25] Later the wily shape-shifter in a vision reveals: "I am Satan, and I consider nothing human alien to me," playing upon a line from Terence's play *The Self-Tormentor.*[26]

Calvin likens the human will to a horse ridden either by God or the devil. "If God sits astride it, then as a moderate and skilled rider, he guides it properly, spurs it if it is too slow, checks it if it is too swift, restrains it if it is too rough or too wild, subdues it if it balks, and leads it into the right path. But if the devil saddles it, he violently drives it far from the trail like a foolish and wanton rider, forces it into ditches, tumbles it over cliffs, and goads it into obstinacy and fierceness."[27] A wanton recklessness may, indeed, tip the devil's hand, but saints, too, have been known to push the limits of what's permitted.

Monstrous acts can be committed by people who give no outward indication of a diabolical nature. Political theorist Hannah Arendt commented on this "banality of evil" after studying the personality of Adolf Eichmann at the Nuremberg trials following World War II. Eichmann did not appear some bigger-than-life figure who immediately generated fear in those around him, but appeared rather ordinary, like someone you might sit next to in a restaurant and hardly know he was there. Yet it was Eichmann who had headed up the Gestapo's Jewish section, promoted the use of gas chambers for mass extermination in the concentration camps, and oversaw the murder of millions of Jews.[28]

In ending his interview so abruptly, the devil does make an important point. While there is surely a force for evil in the world, a number of the powers and feats we attribute to it (him) are suspect. A case in point is the infamous Salem witch trials in Puritan New England. They began when several young girls were discovered playing at fortune-telling with a crystal ball. To avoid punishment, the girls claimed they were tormented by witches. The town's new minister, Samuel Parris, didn't help matters when, during one of his sermons, he announced that witches were everywhere, even in "this very church."

Ultimately, 150 were imprisoned, of whom 50 confessed to "having signed the Devil's book," and 20 were put to death. A large number of those accused were single, middle-aged women or came from families opposed to Parris's ministry. Only after the governor looked into the matter and forbad the use of spectral testimony (that is, where a witness claimed a spirit or specter had appeared to pinpoint the witch), did the number of cases start to dwindle. Twenty years later, Massachusetts Bay Colony annulled all of the convictions and paid reparations to the survivors.[29]

Unfortunately some do start believing in phantasms: Cult leaders with a checkered past are suddenly perceived as messengers from God; patent elixirs or therapies make unsubstantiated claims for regenerating or prolonging life; voices purport to come from spirits, who turn out to have been fabricated. In Ivan's parable, the Grand Inquisitor observes, "Man seeks not so much God as miracles. And since man cannot bear to be left without miracles, he will go and create new miracles for himself, his own miracles this time, and will bow down to the miracles of quacks, or women's magic, though he be rebellious, heretical, and godless a hundred times over."[30] Such people, according to Lichtenberg, "think it nothing out of the ordinary if someone tells them six angels walked down the street today."[31]

Thus, the First Epistle of John counsels, "Beloved, do not believe every spirit, but test the spirits to see whether they are from God" (1 John 4:1). In the fifth century, John Cassian admonished his fellow monks to become like skilled changers of currency, who could evaluate whether their coins were truly gold or merely gleaming brass; whether the stamped images were rulers or usurpers; and if each piece weighed exactly the amount it should.[32] Such skills, though, took years to be perfected.

One recurring theme in Scripture I would like to focus on, however, is Satan's role as an accuser. The desert fathers spoke of Satanic assaults that "stirred up memories." These memories might include their former life in the world; doubts concerning families or loved ones who had been left behind; recollections of words or actions that had wounded others; worries that a lifetime of Christian struggle had resulted in one apparent defeat after another.[33] Prone to depression, eighteenth-century evangelical poet William Cowper complains, "The accuser of the brethren was ever busy with me night and day, bringing to my recollection in dreams the commission of long-forgotten sins and charging upon my conscience things of an indifferent nature as atrocious crimes."[34]

This type of assault can be seen in John Bunyan's *The Pilgrim's Progress,* where Apollyon accuses Christian of being untrue and proceeds to recount episodes from his journey to prove it. Christian asks, "Wherein, O Apollyon, have I been unfaithful to him (Christ)? Apollyon: Thou didst faint at first setting out, when thou wast almost choked in the Gulf of Despond. Thou didst attempt wrong ways to be rid of thy burden, whereas thou shouldest have stayed till thy Prince had taken it off. Thou didst sinfully sleep, and lose thy choice thing: thou wast also almost persuaded to go back at the sight of the lions; and when thou talkest of thy journey, and of what thou hast heard and seen, thou art inwardly desirous of vainglory in all thou sayest or doest."

How should one respond to Apollyon's attack? I like Christian's approach. "All this is true, and much more, which thou hast left out; but the Prince whom I serve and honour is merciful and ready to forgive: but besides, these infirmities possessed me in thy country, for there I sucked them in, and I have groaned under them, been sorry for them, and have obtained pardon of my Prince."[35]

It seems that there are two equal and opposite errors when it comes to the devil; the presumptuous soul underestimates his power while those with low self-esteem are too easily threatened by his bluster. But the devil "can do nothing without permission from our Lord Jesus," insists English mystic Walter Hilton, "not so much as enter into a pig, as the Gospel attests; much less, then, can he injure any man."[36] Indeed our strong man has come and he has defeated the wiles of the evil one. As Jesus cries out in Milton's *Paradise Regain'd*, "Be frustrate, all ye strategems of Hell, / And devilish machinations, come to nought."[37] Luther both warned and encouraged fellow believers in his great hymn:

> For still our ancient foe
> Doth seek to work us woe—
> His craft and pow'r are great,
> And, armed with cruel hate,
> On earth is not his equal. . . .
> The prince of darkness grim—
> We tremble not for him;
> His rage we can endure,
> For lo! his doom is sure.[38]

Modern theologians have compared Christ's resurrection to the Allied landing at Normandy during World War II. While major battles still loom before us, the war's turning point has taken place, and we are now on the downside toward victory. As the prophet Elisha shouts, "There are more on our side than on theirs" (2 Kings 6:16 NJB). When the King of Aram had surrounded the city of Dothan with a mighty army, Elisha's attendant grew alarmed. Then the prophet prayed and the Lord "opened the servant's eyes, and he saw the mountain covered in fiery horses and chariots" (2 Kings 6:17 NJB).

But to do battle, we need to put on the whole armor of God described in the Book of Ephesians—fastening the belt of truth around our waist, attaching the breastplate of righteousness, strapping on shoes ready to proclaim the gospel of peace. We should, too, take up the shield of faith, put on the helmet of salvation, and wield the sword of the Spirit (which is the word of God), staying alert and praying at all times. Since we are fighting a spiritual battle, we must rely on spiritual weapons. Commentators have compared this passage to a speech some ancient military commander might give to his troops before an upcoming engagement. The dangers of the enemy are clearly set forth; the troops are exhorted to stand firm and be alert before multipronged assaults; but they are assured of triumph due to superior strength, resources, and equipment.[39] When poet William Blake protested against the "dark Satanic mills" of the early industrial revolution that blackened the landscape around him, he resolved,[40] "I will not cease from Mental Fight, / Nor shall my Sword sleep in my hand, / Till we have built Jerusalem / In England's green and pleasant land."[41]

"Warfare goes on constantly," said the twelfth-century Byzantine reformer Symeon the New Theologian, "and the soldiers of Christ must at all times be armed with their weapons. Neither by night nor by day nor for a single instant is this warfare interrupted, but even when we eat or drink or do anything else (cf. 1 Cor. 10:31) we find ourselves in the thick of battle. It is incorporeal enemies that we face; they are constantly facing us even though we do not see them. They are watching us closely to see whether they can find some member of ours unprotected so that they may be able to stab it with their weapons and slay us. . . . On all men there lies the inescapable necessity of joining in this conflict. No one may escape the alternatives of either winning and staying alive or being overcome and dying."[42]

As a consequence, it's critical to evaluate our own strengths and weaknesses. In his seminal treatment of ethics, Aristotle advised, "We must notice the errors into which we ourselves are liable to fall (because we all have different natural tendencies—we shall find out what ours are from the pleasure and pain that they give us), and we must drag ourselves in the contrary direction; . . . just like somebody straightening a warped piece of wood."[43] Is lust for the opposite sex your hang-up or do you have a hair-trigger temper or are you inordinately anxious that your bank account be doubled? Beware, lest the arrows of the devil pierce your Achilles' heel. Ponder: what can be done to counteract your natural proclivities?

In ancient Ireland a *lorica* was a spiritual coat or breastplate which charmed away danger and secured a place in heaven for those who wore it always. The most famous literary *lorica* that has come down to us is the breastplate attributed to St. Patrick, which has been made into a hymn. It begins, "I bind unto myself to-day / The strong name of the Trinity"; then the second stanza continues, "I bind this day to me for ever / By power of faith, Christ's incarnation"; but probably best-known is the eighth stanza:

> Christ be with me, Christ within me,
>   Christ behind me, Christ before me,
> Christ beside me, Christ to win me,
>   Christ to comfort and restore me.

Christ beneath me, Christ above me,
   Christ in quiet, Christ in danger,
Christ in hearts of all that love me,
   Christ in mouth of friend and stranger.[44]

When that time of trouble comes, and believe me, it will, here is where I would turn. Memorize that hymn, sing it, hum it. It's more potent than any good-luck charm because it binds you to the one who rose from the tomb and broke Satan's spell forever. The devil's nature consists of lies and deception. He stands like some circus barker before a barren desert, proclaiming it to be the way to paradise.[45] But we know better, for we know it leads only to ruin and destruction. "O foolish pleasure," Faust once moaned, "into what a weary labyrinth hast thou brought me, blinding mine eyes in the clearest day?"[46]

In one of the visions of twelfth-century abbess Hildegard of Bingen, a warrior, brandishing a sword, encourages her, "O mighty God! Who can resist or oppose you? The ancient serpent, the devilish dragon, cannot. Hence, with your help, I, too, choose to resist him so that no one may prevail over me or throw me down, be he strong or weak, prince or outcast, noble or baseborn, rich or poor. . . . Because of you, O mighty God, no one can dash me in pieces. Through you I arise to overthrow the devil."[47]

CHAPTER 18

Flaming Love

Lord, it is my chief complaint,
That my love is weak and faint;
Yet I love thee and adore,
Oh for grace to love thee more!
—William Cowper[1]

How does one live a virtuous life without some concrete example? "We need to set our affections on some good man and keep him constantly before our eyes," contends the ancient Stoic philosopher Seneca, "so that we may live as if he were watching us and do everything as if he saw what we were doing." It should be a person who improves us not only when we're in his presence, but also, when he's simply in our thoughts. Our misdeeds would be "greatly diminished" if we sensed such a witness always standing near. "Choose someone," insists Seneca, "whose way of life as well as words, and whose very face as mirroring the character that lies behind it, have won your approval." This person will be the standard we measure ourselves up against, like a wooden ruler. Seneca then proceeds to commend those Roman dignitaries Cato and Laelius.[2]

But I think there's one who commands our respect even more. Nineteenth-century Irish historian W. E. H. Lecky wrote, "It was reserved for Christianity to present to the world an ideal character, which through all the changes of eighteen centuries has inspired the hearts of men with an impassioned love; has shown itself capable of acting on all ages, nations, temperaments, and conditions; has been not only the highest pattern of virtue but the strongest incentive to its practice; and has exercised so deep an influence that it may be truly said that the simple record of three short years of active life has done more to regenerate and to soften mankind than all the disquisitions of philosophers, and all the exhortations of moralists."[3] The short, unhappy life of Jesus of Nazareth in an obscure Roman province two thousand years ago has dramatically changed the course of history. More scores of music, more paintings and sculptures, more lines of poetry have been dedicated to his memory than anyone else the world has ever seen. Missionaries have toiled on every continent, so Christianity is less confined by geography than any competing religion.

As light bends in a prism and spreads into a rainbow of delightful hues, so Jesus has been depicted in multifarious images; every era and personality type seize on different aspects to admire. Jaroslav Pelikan's *Jesus through the Centuries* discusses, for instance, rabbi Jeshua bar-Joseph, the apologist's light to the Gentiles, Constantinian King of Kings, Byzantine icon of the invisible God, medieval bleeding Savior, Franciscan comforter-friend, mystical bridegroom, Renaissance universal man, Anabaptist Prince of Peace, the rationalist's teacher of common sense, romantic poet of the spirit, and the revolutionary's economic and social liberator.[4] While all these images contain elements of heavenly light, some are also intermingled with darker, heretical elements.

How far-reaching has been Jesus' influence! Napoleon, who conquered much of Europe in the early nineteenth century, admitted, "Alexander, Caesar, Charlemagne and myself founded empires. But upon what did we rest the creation of our genius? Upon force. Jesus Christ alone founded his upon love and at this hour, millions would die for him. I die before my time, and my body will become food for worms. Such is the fate of him who has been called the great Napoleon. What an abyss between my deep misery and the eternal kingdom of Christ, which is proclaimed, loved, and adored, and is extending over the whole earth."[5] Eleven days before his death that Teutonic polymath Goethe confided to Eckermann, "The grandeur and the moral culture of Christianity, as it shines in resplendent brightness from the Gospels, will never be surpassed!"[6]

Let's look more carefully at the love which so distinguished Jesus. Paul outlined its most salient characteristics in chapter thirteen of his letter to the Corinthians. Nineteenth-century Scottish evangelist Henry Drummond wrote a moving meditation on these verses called *The Greatest Thing in the World*, charting nine distinct elements:

Patience . . .	"Love suffereth long."
Kindness . . .	"And is kind."
Generosity . . .	"Love envieth not."

Humility . . .	"Love vaunteth not itself, is not puffed up."
Courtesy . . .	"Doth not behave itself unseemly."
Unselfishness . . .	"Seeketh not her own."
Good Temper . . .	"Is not easily provoked."
Guilelessness . . .	"Thinketh no evil."
Sincerity . . .	"Rejoiceth not in iniquity, but rejoiceth in the truth."[7]

When it comes to love, I'd like to refute several common misconceptions. One is that you should love all people equally. This is an impossibility. How can you spend the same amount of time with everyone? Jesus, on one of his missions, sent out seventy followers (Luke 10:1); twelve were known as his closest associates (Luke 6:13); finally, in the inner circle were three: Peter, James, and John (Luke 9:28); while a coterie of women cared for many of the group's needs (Luke 8:1–3). Jesus, also, had close friends like Lazarus, Mary, and Martha (John 11). Theologians call this the "scandal of particularity."[8] Indeed from all the peoples in the ancient world, God chose only one with which to make his covenant—Israel. Out of the nine planets in the solar system, he apparently created only one with intelligent life that he could have communion with. Since God reveals himself in time and space, there will, of necessity, be certain high points in the history of salvation.

Mystics have sometimes likened love to the steps of a ladder. First you reach one plateau, say, where you give up self; then gradually you learn to love a friend or a neighbor; with another leap you might even show kindness to an enemy; ultimately you unite in ecstasy with God. As helpful as these mental constructs may be, they don't wash in the test tube of experience. At least I rarely find myself living on one plateau for very long. One hour we might be doing a wonderful kindness for a child, and the very next we're screaming at our spouse about something of little consequence. Think how soon after Peter confessed Jesus to be the Messiah he was reprimanded by Christ for being a tool of Satan (Matt. 16:15–19, 23). The ladder conception of love attaches too much importance to self-scrutiny and inner purity (perhaps even masks a measure of self-deception), when it would be better to concentrate on the acts and deeds that are the fruit of love.

In a Nativity sermon, Luther admonished his audience, "There are many of you in this congregation who think to yourselves: 'If only I had been there! How quick I would have been to help the Baby! I would have washed his linen. How happy I would have been to go with the shepherds to see the Lord lying in the manger!' Yes, you would! You say that because you know how great Christ is, but if you had been there at that time you would have done no better than the people of Bethlehem. Childish and silly thoughts are these! Why don't you do it now? You have Christ in your neighbor. You ought to serve him, for what you do to your neighbor in need you do to the Lord Christ himself."[9] Too often we deceive ourselves; indeed modern psychology has made it painfully obvious that even our best intentions are a mixture of both altruism and egotism.[10] I feel more comfortable with the honesty of a Mark Twain, who, during a stay in Italy, wrote, "I know it is my duty to 'pray for them that despitefully use me'; and therefore, hard as it is, I shall still try to pray for these fumigating, maccaroni-stuffing organ-grinders."[11] When we try to love those who irritate us, it's never easy.

Christian love is sacrificial. We must learn to stretch ourselves. "Ah, but a man's reach should exceed his grasp," the painter Andrea del Sarto claims in a Robert Browning dramatic monologue, "Or what's a heaven for?"[12] Jesus bids, "If any want to become my followers, let them deny themselves and take up their cross and follow me" (Matt. 16:24). Far too many positive thinkers confuse feeling good about themselves with doing the will of God. Jesus' life was not pleasant; he wasn't popular, successful, or wealthy. The cross connotes the place of death, where we learn to say "no" to natural inclinations, "no" to legitimate self-interests, "no" to anything that hurts a faithful witness. The cross speaks of hardship and pain. In a German passional, God says to Francis of Assisi, "Take the bitter thing for the sweet, and spurn thyself that thou mayest acknowledge me."[13] "If we obey God," Father Mapple exhorted his flock in *Moby Dick*, "we must disobey ourselves; and it is in this disobeying ourselves, wherein the hardness of obeying God consists."[14] Jacopone da Todi, the thirteenth-century Italian Franciscan, cries out: "Why do you wound me, Lord, with your cruel charity? / . . . My heart trembles, and my soul cracks and breaks, / Why do you cast me into the furnace of suffering? / Like wax melting under heat, I feel I am melting unto death."[15]

However, there is an incredible chasm between sacrificial love and fanaticism. Terrorists only too gladly give up their lives in an explosion which they hope will kill hundreds of others. Cult followers, like those in Jonestown in Guyana or Heaven's Gate in California, die in what to many outsiders appear as futile mass suicides. Sacrifice, in and of itself, is not enough, as Paul makes clear, "If I hand over my body" to be burned (e.g., if I'm a martyr for whatever cause), "but do not have love, I gain nothing" (1 Cor. 13:3). God wants people who will love him with all their hearts, their souls, and their minds, not blind automatons who will do whatever their all-too-human leader tells them.

Sacrifice must be complemented by service. There's a story of the desert fathers in which "a brother asked a certain old man saying, 'There will be two brothers, and one of them is quiet in his cell, and prolongs his fast for six days, and lays much travail on himself: but the other tends the sick. Whose work is the more acceptable to God?' And the old man answered, 'If that brother who carries his fast for six days were to hang himself up by the nostrils, he could not equal the other, who does service to the sick.'"[16]

It is the love of Christ that impels missionaries to take the gospel to remote nations and tribes. "Much of the Western theory and practice of translation," notes linguist George Steiner, "stems immediately from the need to disseminate the Gospels, to speak holy writ in other tongues."[17] Such was Jerome's desire with the Vulgate, Cyril's use of the Slavonic, Luther's work in German, Tyndale's in English, and the goal of countless others since. In the preface to his critical edition of the Greek New Testament, Eramus desires (in Royce's rendition) that "the gospell and Paules epistles . . . were translated in to the tonges of all men." If the Bible were in the vernacular, it was hoped that "the plowman wold singe a texte of the scripture at his plowbeme / And that the wever at his lowme / with this wold drive away the tediousness of tyme . . . the wayfaringe man with this pastyme / wold expelle the werynes of his iorney."[18]

In the late eighteenth century, Baptist William Carey, arriving in Bengal, India, established a pattern of Bible translation and printing, evangelism and church planting, and education and medical relief that has since become normative in a variety of circles. One of his most astonishing personal achievements was the supervision and editing of translations of the Bible into thirty-six languages.[19] His approach harks back to Eastern Orthodox predecessors who put the Scriptures into Coptic, Syrian, Old Latin, Ethiopian, Georgian, Armenian, Gothic, and Old Slavonic.[20] It was Christian missionaries, after all, who formed the first alphabet and created a written language for a number of the predominately oral cultures around the globe.[21]

Christians desire that the gospel take root in every culture. As Samuel Johnson once admitted to his biographer, James Boswell, "You are to a certain degree hurt by knowing that even one man does not believe."[21a] Paul told the Corinthians, "To those under the law I became as one under the law . . . so that I might win those under the law. . . . To the weak I became weak, so that I might win the weak. I have become all things to all people, that I might by all means save some" (1 Cor. 9:20–22). This doesn't mean that Paul is acting like "Chameleon Man" in Woody Allen's *Zelig,* eager to blend in with whatever group he's with; instead Paul is stressing flexibility, sensitivity, and empathy.[22]

One notable illustration of this inculturation is the Jesuit Matteo Ricci's labors in China from 1583–1610. He adopted the manner and dress of a Chinese scholar, translated books from Chinese into Latin, and became the official astronomer and mathematician to the emperor.[23] As the Chinese language didn't have an exact word for "God," he used *T'ien Chu,* "Lord of Heaven." "Those that adore Heaven instead of the Lord of Heaven," he wrote in an early catechism "are like a man who, desiring to pay the emperor homage, prostrates himself before the imperial palace at Peking and venerates its beauty." While he attracted only a small number of adherents, they were key to the future development of Christianity in China.[24] A few of Ricci's accommodations to culture, however, such as allowing believers to practice Confucian rites of ancestor "worship," were to embroil the Catholic missionary movement in controversy for decades. According to Vatican II, though, we can legitimately "borrow from the customs, traditions, wisdom, teaching, arts, and sciences" of any people, taking advantage of "everything which could be used to praise the glory of the Creator, manifest the grace of the savior, or contribute to the right ordering of Christian life."[25]

"In everything do to others as you would have them do to you" (Matt. 7:12), the Golden Rule states. Thus to become involved requires an act of the imagination, a putting oneself in the other fellow's shoes. "People would instantly care for others as well as themselves," John Ruskin, the nineteenth-century art critic, suggests, "if only they could imagine others as well as themselves. Let a child fall into the river before the roughest man's eyes; he will usually do what he can to get it out, even at some risk to himself; and all the town will triumph in the saving of one little life. Let the same man be shown that hundreds of children are dying of fever for want of some sanitary measure which will cost him trouble to urge, and he will make no effort; and probably all the town would resist if he did."[26]

"I usually found that my interest in any given side of a question of justice was aroused by some concrete case," Theodore Roosevelt, a leader in the American progressive movement, noted. "It was the examination I made into the miseries attendant upon the manufacture of cigars in tenement-houses that first opened my eyes to the need of legislation on such subjects. . . . The need for a workmen's compensation act was driven home to me by my knowing a brakeman who had lost his legs in an accident, and whose family was thereby at once reduced from self-respecting comfort to conditions that at one time became very dreadful."[27] We are most likely to be awakened to the needs of others by our own suffering or by the pain of those close to us. It was Walter Rauschenbusch's eleven-year ministry (1886–97) at a German Baptist congregation near New York City's notorious Hell's Kitchen that led him to so forcefully formulate the social gospel; in that blighted district an endless procession of men "out of work, out of clothes, out of shoes, and out of hope" wore away at the sensitive young pastor's heart.[28]

In addition to sacrificially serving others, love should be creative. The psalmist exhorts Israel to "sing to the Lord a new song" (Ps. 149:1). There's a widely referred-to experiment done some years ago using a tachistoscope, a device that flashes visual images on the screen for brief periods of time. Researchers deliberately changed the colors in a pack of ordinary playing cards, inserting occasional anomalies, e.g., a *red* ace of spades or a *black* four of hearts. However, only a fraction of the viewers caught on to the deception; many reported simply seeing a six of hearts instead of a red six of spades. Only after experimenters mentioned that although hearts are usually red, this does not mean they will always be red, did the subjects begin to perceive what was happening.[29]

So it is with most of us—our preconceptions, our tired set of assumptions, need to be jolted if we're ever to truly become aware of the kingdom of heaven. Jesus, through his stories and parables with their myriad twists and turns and unforeseen elements of surprise, forces us to come to terms with our own limitations. If only we had that childlike openness, so we could, in the words of one of Lewis Carroll's characters, believe in six impossibilities before breakfast.[30] A father discovered his four-year-old son sitting in front of a row of chairs playing "train." Reaching out to hug the boy, he was told, "Don't kiss the engine, Daddy, or the carriages won't think it's real."[31] The founder of the Salvation Army, William Booth, displayed creative love when he asked, "What use is it providing an ambulance at the bottom of the cliff, if you do not build a fence at the top?"[32] He established an organization that has ministered to the urban down-and-out for over 120 years.

In 1964 a horrifying story caught the media's attention. It was the case of Kitty Genovese, a young woman who, returning late one night to her New York City apartment, was attacked and beaten for half an hour before dying. From their windows thirty-eight people had witnessed the event, but none had called the police.[33] It was a time of national soul-searching in which commentators asked, "How could this have happened?" In one of the most important studies to come from this incident (and others like it), entitled *The Unresponsive Bystander,* researchers Latané and Darley pointed out that at least three things must take place before someone actually intervenes in an emergency.

First, the onlooker must *notice* that something is happening. We must tear ourselves away from our private thoughts long enough to see an unusual event. Second, the onlooker must *decide* it as an emergency. (I'm afraid this is where I would most likely fail.) Sometimes it turns out to be not just another family quarrel; instead something has gone terribly wrong, yet we are afraid to step out of the crowd and appear the fool. Third, one must *take personal responsibility* and act, rather than wait for someone else to assume the lead.[34]

What causes people to become involved? Studies indicate that we're more likely to intervene if we know the hurt person, have special skills that might be of use (e.g., medical training), or if the victim somehow seems like ourselves.[35] The Princeton sociologist Robert Wuthnow identified an additional factor. He found that those who knew the Good Samaritan story (Luke 10:25–37) and could relate it to their own experience or that of someone they knew, were nearly twice as likely to perform charitable deeds or to be active as volunteers in their community as those who didn't.[36] It is on this subconscious (hard-to-measure) level that the Bible, the church, and Christianity profoundly shape people's beliefs, values, and behavior.

As William Langland tells it, the Good Samaritan, when he happened upon a man fallen among thieves, "jumped down from his horse and, leading it by the bridle, went up and looked at his wounds. He felt his pulse, and found that unless he could be brought round quickly he might never stir again. So he rushed for his two bottles, opened them hastily, and washed the man's wounds with wine and oil, then anointed him and bandaged up his head. And laying him across his lap he mounted his horse and carried him to an outlying hamlet. . . . Here he lodged him at an inn, and called out to the inn-keeper, 'Take this man and look after him until I return. . . . Here is some money to buy ointment for his wounds.' Then he gave him twopence more for the man's keep, adding, 'If he spends anything over and above this, I will make it right with you when I come back.'"[37]

In van Gogh's painting "The Good Samaritan," one sees how difficult it is for the Samaritan to lift the wounded man upon his horse and how entirely dependent the victim is on outside help.[38] Our life should be an ongoing crescendo of good works. "I was eyes to the blind," Job pointed out, "and feet to the lame. I was a father to the needy, and I championed the cause of the stranger. I broke the fangs of the unrighteous, and made them drop their prey from their teeth" (Job 29:15–17). Thomas à Kempis, in *The Imitation of Christ,* asserts that the magnitude of the action isn't so important as the intention: "The outward deed without charity is little to be praised, but whatever is done from charity, even if it be ever so little and worthless in the sight of the world, is very profitable before God, who judges all things according to the intent of the doer, not according to the greatness or worthiness of the deed."[39]

Such active concern is far from minimalist ethics, which enumerate all the evil things one hasn't done or simply equates duty with some gentlemanly code of etiquette. In the eighteenth century, Lord Chesterfield wrote a series of letters to his son, which came to enshrine the aristocratic ideal of worldly advancement, where style prevailed over substance: "You had better return a dropped fan genteelly, than give a thousand pounds awkwardly; and you had better refuse a favour gracefully, than grant it clumsily. Manner is all in everything; it is by manner only that you can please, and consequently rise."[40] Jesus' parables aren't designed to woo polite society but to rouse reconfiguration. Since we expect to see Christ in heaven, Augustine said in one of his sermons, let us now recognize him lying in the street.[41]

Those who say theology doesn't matter are talking utter nonsense. How we view God, the world, and other forms of life colors everything we say or do.

"There is hardly any human action, however particular it may be," nineteenth-century French social philosopher Alexis de Tocqueville laid down, "that does not originate in some very general idea men have conceived of the Deity, of his relation to mankind, of the nature of their own souls, and of their duties to their fellow creatures. Nor can anything prevent these ideas from being the common spring from which all the rest emanates."[42] Beliefs affect us on micro- and macrolevels.

Some of the most brutal atrocities ever carried out on this planet were due to people unable to see others as created in the image of God (Gen. 1:27). In a debate on the Talmud, Rabbi Akiva announced that "Love your neighbor as yourself" (Lev. 19:18) was "the most basic rule of Scripture." But his colleague, Ben Azai, averred that "This is the book of the generations of Adam" (Gen. 5:1–2) was even more basic. He was reminding the great romantic that love, of itself, cannot be the basis for ethics, since we also need to treat the other as a *tselem elohim* (image of God),[43] if justice is ever to be nurtured. In the sixteenth century, after Spain had conquered much of the new world, a council was held in which the issue of the treatment of Indians was raised. Upon being informed that there were natives who thought the Ave Maria was something to eat, Cardinal Loaysa declared that they were incapable of learning the holy faith ("no more than parrots"), hence could be enslaved at will.[44] But Bernadino de Minaya, Bartholomé de Las Casas, and others took the matter up further, until in 1537 Pope Paul III ruled quite the opposite.[45]

In Dostoyevsky's *Crime and Punishment,* a young law student murders a pawnbroker (and her stepsister) with an axe. No one sees him strike the blow; nevertheless, he feels profoundly guilty. He consoles himself by reflecting that the woman was an old hag, one of a despised race, and plied a disreputable trade. He tells a kindly prostitute, "I only killed a louse, Sonya, a useless, vile, pernicious louse." Horrified, she screams, "A human being a louse!" He then owns up, "Of course I know she wasn't a louse."[46] Deep down, in our heart of hearts, there is a nagging suspicion that those who are of another race, religion, or ethnic group are not so very different from ourselves.

During the 1960s, missionary Don Richardson was preaching to a tribe of cannibals in Irian Jaya. When he told the story of Jesus, the Sawis whistled with delight, *not* at Jesus' resurrection but at Judas's treachery![47] The Sawis took particular pride in their ability to do in an opponent through treachery. They even had a special phrase for it, *"tuwi asonai man,"* or "to fatten up a man with friendship for unsuspected slaughter."[48] Praying for a key to reach these people, Richardson one day witnessed the "peace child" ceremony. While two tribes were engaged in war, one man tearfully grabbed his son and offered it as a symbol of peace. Moral: "If a man would actually give his own son to the enemies, that man could be trusted."[49] By using this analogy, Richardson was able to convey the gospel in terms the Sawis could understand, and some did come to believe.

In truth God has so loved the world that he did send his only son (John 3:16); the incarnation speaks volumes about the nature of God. God is not some abstract principle, disdainful of matter; rather he revels in the concrete. Like G. K. Chesterton he is excited by "the startling wetness of water . . . the steeliness of steel, the unutterable muddiness of mud."[50] Athanasius, the fourth-century champion against Arianism, writes, "You know what happens when a portrait that has been painted on a panel becomes obliterated through external stains. The artist does not throw away the panel, but the subject of the portrait has to come and sit for it again, and then the likeness is re-drawn on the same material. Even so was it with the all-holy Son of God. He, the image of the Father, came and dwelt in our midst, in order that he might renew mankind made after himself, and seek out his lost sheep."[51] God took on human nature in order to restore us to the pristine state. As Catherine of Siena put it, "His divinity is kneaded into the clay of your humanity like one bread."[52]

One thinks of Catherine of Genoa, who, after undergoing a conversion in 1473, took up for nearly twenty years the care of the sick and dying poor at the Pammatone hospital, even going to live on the premises. At first she was involved in menial tasks, but ended up director from 1490–96, staying at her post during the bubonic plague when many of the townspeople died and she herself became gravely ill. Though at times prone to mystical and ascetic extremes, she felt the Spirit wanted her "to work with human misery" as if she "were kneading bread, and even, if need be, to taste it a bit." This "bread," for Catherine, no doubt, referred to Christ's own torn flesh, which she partook of daily: "Take, eat; this is my body" (Matt. 26:26).[53]

This is the opposite pole from Nietzsche's contention that the weak should be allowed to perish. In his sneering at the "slave morality" of Christianity, he railed against those qualities "which serve to ease existence for those who suffer . . . pity, the complaisant and obliging hand, the warm heart, patience, industry, humility, and friendliness."[54] Yet these character traits, which Nietzsche so despised, are among the ones Jesus counts as the highest virtues.

Another outstanding instance of sacrificial, creative service is the life of Joseph de Veuster, otherwise known as Father Damien. The son of a Belgian farmer, he joined the Society of the Sacred Heart of Jesus and Mary and became a missionary to the Pacific Islands in 1863. Ordained in Honolulu, he volunteered nine years later to take charge of a settlement of lepers which the Hawaiian government had deported to the remote Kalawao Peninsula of Molokai Island.[55] Upon arriving at his charge, he found little running water, and wasted lepers living in vermin-infested huts, who were not being given proper medical care. The little food that was brought in was fought over by these disfigured stumps of human beings. The dead were literally thrown into a shallow ditch. Soon afterward he forbad the distillation of alcohol. To restore order, he sometimes had to act like a policeman with a billy club, protecting the weak and innocent.

Every morning he led a bucket brigade to bring water down from nearby mountain springs, before a flume was eventually completed. He taught the lepers how to plant crops in the fertile soil. He burned down the disease-ridden, decrepit huts and built new ones in their place. He laid out a cemetery for burials. In his spare time he constructed window frames, doors, and small furniture to distribute as presents.[56] Indeed, using the hammer, saw, and spade, he transformed this living hell into a semblance of community. Due to his preaching, the sacraments, and his practical everyday example, many lepers embraced Christianity. Then one day he discovered he, too, had contracted leprosy; now his use of the first person plural, "we lepers," was no longer poetic license.[57] He lived for another four years. Gradually his story reached the outside world, attracting an influx of money, volunteers, and assistance to this much-neglected area.[58]

But he was far from being perfect. He was not a good administrator and resigned from that position shortly after it was given him. He could be domineering as well as indiscreet. He had a narrow, though intense, faith; at times he was a bigot. His superiors had to rebuke him, sometimes rather bluntly. He never enjoyed being in the public eye. He retained throughout his life a number of the coarse habits of his upbringing. Yet he was honest and extraordinarily generous, with a good sense of humor and a remarkable steadfastness of mission. Of his life Robert Louis Stevenson remarked, "The least tender should be moved to tears; the most incredulous to prayer."[59] Almost single-handedly he had ministered to the physical and spiritual needs of some six hundred lepers for sixteen years—an incredible feat—plus, he had inspired others to follow in his footsteps so that the work would not be lost.

Whenever we despair at how little we can do with our lives, we should remember Father Damien. His gifts and talents were not that earthshaking. But he took what he had and gave it to God, and that made all the difference. And what about "smiting on an anvil, sawing a beam, whitewashing a wall, driving horses, sweeping, scouring"? "To lift up the hands in prayer gives God glory," nineteenth-century poet Gerard Manley Hopkins maintained, "but a man with a dungfork in his hand, a woman with a sloppail, give him glory too. He is so great that all things give him glory if you mean they should. So then, my brethren, live."[60] Even something as simple as passing on to a child or an apprentice how to make clothes, how to fish, or how to read has myriad ramifications. "It is a low benefit to give me something," Emerson felt; "it is a high benefit to enable me to do somewhat of myself."[61]

What can you offer the Lord? Perhaps you can dedicate a child to the Lord's work (if they are so inclined), as Elkanah and Hannah did with Samuel (1 Samuel 1) or the elderly Zechariah and Elizabeth (Luke 1:5–24) did with John the Baptist. In Rudolf's life of Leoba, who lived in the eighth century, we read how the barren Aebba, wife of Dynno, had a dream "in which she saw herself bearing in her bosom a church bell, which on being drawn out with her hand rang merrily. When she woke up she called her old nurse to her and told her what she had dreamed. The nurse said to her: 'We shall yet see a daughter from your womb and it is your duty to consecrate her straightway to God.'" The newborn, nicknamed Leoba, did become a nun, renowned for her learning and holiness, and eventually was called by Boniface to help with his missionary endeavors in Germany.[62]

In the Book of Exodus, to help with the construction of the tabernacle, God called metalworkers, woodcarvers, craftsmen in stone, embroiderers, weavers, in short, everyone to whom he had "given skill" and "whose heart was stirred," till Moses had to restrain the people from coming (Exod. 35:30–36:7). These were voluntary, freewill offerings in profusion. The main thrust of Jesus' well-known parable of the talents seems to be: take advantage of your opportunities; in economic lingo, "be busy buying and selling" (Matt. 25:14–30). Interestingly the Greek word used, *talanton*, refers to a large sum of money, equivalent to years of hard work,[63] but, because of the parable's influence on the English language, has now come to mean all one's potential.[64] "Thou that has giv'n so much to me," acknowledges country parson George Herbert, "Give one thing more, a gratefull heart."[65] So, I ask again, what can *you* do for the Lord? In one of the most influential New World treatises on philanthropy, Puritan divine Cotton Mather compared a good deed to "a stone falling on a pool. . . . One circle (and service) will produce another, until they extend, who can tell, how far?"[66]

Let's make the prayer of the seventeenth-century Russian Orthodox bishop, Dimitrii of Rostov, our own: "Come, flame of divine love, and burn up the thorns of my sins, kindling my heart with the flame of your love. Come, my king, sit upon the throne of my heart and reign there. For you alone are my king and my lord."[67] Amen.

Acknowledgments

I want to offer special thanks to my wife, Barbara. Her numerous editorial corrections and recommendations were always well thought out, even if not always duly heeded. Her slow, persistent hand as a writing teacher has, over the years, immensely improved my style. She also helped me to locate difficult sources and suggested a few quotations of her own.

Frank Oveis and his team of copyeditors and proofreaders made many worthwhile changes. He has been particularly patient in explaining and guiding me through *The Chicago Manual of Style*. That he and Ulla Schnell and others at Continuum were willing to take a chance on a relatively unknown author is something that I will continue to be grateful for.

I particularly want to praise four previous works: Solomon Schimmel's *Seven Deadly Sins,* Stanford Lyman's *Seven Deadly Sins: Society and Evil,* Henry Fairlee's *The Seven Deadly Sins Today,* and Cornelius Plantinga's *Not the Way It's Supposed to Be: A Breviary of Sin.* These set me thinking in new directions and referred me to a host of primary materials for further exploration. A fifth, in a class by itself, *A Dictionary of Biblical Tradition in English Literature,* edited by David Lyle Jeffrey, is an inexhaustible treasure. Throughout I have tried to acknowledge a portion of my debt to these authors in the footnotes. Also, two books I read some years ago that were filled with marvelous quotations, *The Parables of Peanuts* by Robert Short and *The Mark of Cain* by Stuart Babbage, led me to set up my own literary filing system.

Also, I'd like to honor those little-recognized translators who labor so hard to make world literature accessible to English speakers. Without their efforts, those of us who are not polyglots would have only a dim awareness of other cultures. All quotations from Scripture are taken from the NRSV, unless otherwise noted. Too, I want to express my gratitude to Grinnell College for opening its library to the public, enabling me to peruse a number of the works inside these pages.

Four of these chapters appeared in embryonic form as articles: "Guilt Unraveled" in *Currents in Theology and Mission* (August, 1978); "From Romance to Commitment" in *Cresset* (September, 1979); "The Faultfinder" in *Quaker Life* (1981); "Satan: 'The Father of Lies'" in *New Media Bible Times* (Luke 3; 1979). For the last piece, I'd like to thank The Genesis Project for allowing me permission to reprint the fictional interview with Satan in chapter 17.

Finally, reader, I have been formed by all whom I have met, so should you know me, don't be surpised to find bits of yourself within these covers.

Notes

Introduction

1. Joseph Goering, "Pastoralia: The Popular Literature of the Care of Souls," *Medieval Latin: An Introduction and Bibliographical Guide,* ed. F. A. C. Mantello and A. G. Rigg (Catholic University of America Press, 1996), pp. 673–74.

2. Chapter 6, H. V. S. Eck, *Sin* (Longmans, Green, and Co., 1907), pp. 120–21. Cf. chapter 2, Janice Brown, *The Seven Deadly Sins in the Work of Dorothy L. Sayers* (Kent State University Press, 1998).

3. Archbishop Thoresby, *The Lay Folks' Catechism,* ed. Thomas Frederick Simmons and Henry Edward Nolloth (Kegan Paul, Trench, Trubner & Co., 1901), pp. xii and 87 ff.

4. A full history of how the seven deadly sins evolved, including earlier formulations, can be found in Morton W. Bloomfield, *The Seven Deadly Sins* (Michigan State University Press, 1967). See especially chapters 2 and 3. Evagrius, Cassian, and Gregory I are key figures in the Christian tradition.

5. Eck, *Sin,* pp. 121–22.

6. "The Aleph," Jorge Luis Borges, *A Personal Anthology,* ed. Anthony Kerrigan (Grove, 1967), p. 154.

6a. Part 4, Hugh White, tr., *Ancrene Wisse* (Penguin, 1993), pp. 93–96.

7. Chapter 10, Alasdair MacIntyre, *After Virtue,* 2nd ed. (University of Notre Dame Press, 1984), p. 121.

8. Chapter 7, Nathan A. Scott Jr., *The Broken Center* (Yale University Press, 1967) pp. 224–25.

9. R. C. Amore, "Dhammapada," *Abingdon Dictionary of Living Religions,* ed. Keith Crim (Abingdon, 1981), p. 217.

10. "Perirrhanterium," section I, *Herbert,* ed. Dudley Fitts (Dell, 1966), p. 27.

11. "No. 1129," *The Complete Poems of Emily Dickinson,* ed. Thomas H. Johnson (Little, Brown & Company, 1960), pp. 506–7.

12. *The Point of View,* A: 1, "The Esthetic Writing," *The Essential Kierkegaard,* ed. Howard V. Hong and Edna H. Hong (Princeton University Press, 2000), p. 459.

13. Act 2, scene 2, lines 600–617, William Shakespeare, *The Tragedy of Hamlet,* ed. Edward Hubler (New American Library, 1963), p. 90.

14. "Introduction," Paul L. Maier, tr., *Eusebius: The Church History* (Kregel, 1999), pp. 16–17.

15. "Introduction," Robin Gill, *A Textbook of Christian Ethics,* 2nd ed. (T. & T. Clark, 1995), p. 3.

16. "Epilogue," C. S. Lewis, *An Experiment in Criticism* (Cambridge University Press, 1992), p. 140.

17. Herman Melville, "Hawthorne and His Mosses," *The Theory of the American Novel,* ed. George Perkins (Holt, Rinehart and Winston, 1970), p. 80.

18. "Proverb as Literary Form," Leland Ryken, James C. Wilhoit, and Tremper Longman III, eds., *Dictionary of Biblical Imagery* (InterVarsity, 1998), p. 679.

19. John Gross, ed., *The Oxford Book of Aphorisms* (Oxford University Press, 1983), pp. vii–viii.

20. "Conclusion," Edward Rehatsek, tr., *The Gulistan or Rose Garden of Sa'di,* ed. W. G. Archer (George Allen & Unwin, 1964), p. 265.

21. Ambrose Bierce, *The Devil's Dictionary* (Dover, 1958), p. 31.

22. Quoted in chapter 6, David Lyle Jeffrey, *People of the Book* (Eerdmans, 1996), pp. 170–71.

23. "Of the Education of Children," book 1, chapter 26, Donald M. Frame, tr., *The Complete Essays of Montaigne* (Stanford University Press, 1979), p. 107.

24. "Montaigne, Michel Eyquem de," *The Reader's Companion to World Literature,* ed. Lillian Herlands Hornstein (New American Library, 1956), pp. 303–4.

25. Frame, tr., *Complete Essays of Montaigne,* p. 108.

26. Ibid., p. 111.

27. Quoted in Jeffrey, *People of the Book,* p. 170.

28. "Poem 34: Proverbs and Song-Verse, IV," Alan S. Trueblood, tr., *Antonio Machado: Selected Poems* (Harvard University Press, 1982), p. 143.

29. "Uses of Great Men" (the introductory chapter to Emerson's *Representative Men*), *Great Essays,* ed. Houston Peterson (Washington Square, 1965), p. 176.

30. "The Medieval West," Michael Counsell, comp., *2000 Years of Prayer* (Morehouse, 1999), pp. 97–108. Cf. "The Origin or Authorship of Each Collect" by Ian Curteis in *A Prayer for All Seasons: The Collects of the Book of Common Prayer* (Lutterworth, 1999), pp. 18–21.

31. Introduction, John Henry Cardinal Newman, *An Essay on the Development of Christian Doctrine,* 6th ed. (University of Notre Dame Press, 1989), p. 30.

32. Chapter 1, section 1, ibid., pp. 38–39.

33. Cf. the paradigm shifts in Hans Küng, *Christianity,* tr. John Bowden (Continuum, 1996).

34. "The Epilogue: A Short Story of Antichrist," *A Solovyov Anthology,* arr. S. L. Frank, tr. Natalie Duddington (Charles Scribner's, 1950), pp. 239–41.

35. *On Learned Ignorance,* book 1, chapter 3, Nicholas of Cusa, *Selected Spiritual Writings,* tr. H. Lawrence Bond (Paulist, 1997), p. 91.

36. Chapter 6, Samuel Hugh Moffett, *A History of Christianity in Asia,* vol. 1, 2nd rev. ed. (Orbis, 1998), pp. 445–51.

37. Thomas McInerney, tr., section 28, "Dogmatic Constitution on the Church," chapter 7, *Vatican Council II,* vol. 1, revised, ed. Austin Flannery (Costello, 1998), pp. 407–13.

38. "*Ecclesia,*" Richard A. Muller, *Dictionary of Latin and Greek Theological Terms* (Baker, 1985), p. 99.

39. "The Collects: Traditional; Holy Days," *The Book of Common Prayer* (Seabury, 1979), p. 194.

40. Michael Witczak, "All Saints, Feast of," *The New Dictionary of Sacramental Worship,* ed. Peter E. Fink (Liturgical, 1990), p. 41.

41. "All Saints' Day," "All Souls' Day," Philip H. Pfatteicher, *A Dictionary of Liturgical Terms* (Trinity Press International, 1991), p. 4.

42. Quoted in chapter 12, Timothy Ware, *The Orthodox Church*, rev. ed. (Penguin, 1993), pp. 255–56. Cf. "The Practical and Theological Chapters" (the third chapter), Symeon the New Theologian, *The Practical and Theological Chapters* and *The Three Theological Discourses*, tr. Paul McGuckin (Cistercian, 1982), pp. 72–73.

43. Appendix C: "Rating the Popes," Richard P. McBrien, *Lives of the Popes* (HarperCollins, 2000), pp. 430–38. See individual entries as well.

44. Chapter 3, Alister McGrath, *The Journey* (Doubleday, 1999), pp. 33–35.

45. "Apology II," section 13, *The Early Christian Fathers*, ed. Henry Betterson (Oxford University Press, 1976), p. 63.

46. Chapter 5, section 2, John Calvin, *Institutes of the Christian Religion*, vol. 1, ed. John T. McNeill, tr. Ford Lewis Battles (Westminster, 1960), pp. 53–54.

47. Section 1, T. S. Eliot, *After Strange Gods* (Harcourt, Brace and Company, 1934), pp. 30–31.

48. Section 4, T. S. Eliot, *Four Quartets* (Harcourt, Brace & World, 1971), p. 19.

49. "Milton I," T. S. Eliot, *Selected Prose*, ed. John Hayward (Penguin, 1958), p. 125.

50. "The Poetry of the Theater," Maurice Charney, *How to Read Shakespeare* (McGraw-Hill, 1971), p. 55.

51. "Introduction," Ernest F. Kevan, *The Grace of Law* (Baker, 1983), p. 32.

52. "Koan, the Word" and "Satori," Ernest Wood, *Zen Dictionary* (Penguin, 1977), pp. 56–57, 91.

53. Quoted in Peter Brown, "A New Augustine," *The New York Review of Books* (24 June 1999), p. 48.

Chapter 1: Everyman's Dilemma

1. *Following the Equator*, "Pudd'nhead Wilson's New Calendar," *The Portable Mark Twain*, ed. Bernard DeVoto (Penguin, 1977), p. 564.

2. Paul Leicester Ford, ed., *The New-England Primer* (Teachers College at Columbia University, 1962), p. 30 illustrated.

3. "Thoughts in Exile," Kenneth Rexroth, tr., *One Hundred Poems from the Chinese* (New Directions, 1971), p. 81.

4. Quoted in Isaiah Berlin, *The Crooked Timber of Humanity*, ed. Henry Hardy (Vintage, 1992), pp. vii and xi.

5. Chapter 10, David Riggs, *Ben Jonson: A Life* (Harvard University Press, 1989), pp. 205–7. Impresa depicted.

6. "Sin," chapter 86, *The Great Ideas*, vol. 2, ed. Mortimer Adler (Encyclopedia Britannica, 1952), pp. 755–56. Cf. Augustine, *The Confessions*, book 2, chap. 4 ff.

7. Chapter 10, Charles Norris Cochrane, *Christianity and Classical Culture* (Oxford University Press, 1968), pp. 386–87.

8. Chapter 1, Reinhold Niebuhr, *The Nature and Destiny of Man*, vol. 1 (Charles Scribner's Sons, 1964), p. 16.

9. *Heart of Darkness*, section 3, *The Portable Conrad*, ed. Morton Dauwen Zabel (Penguin, 1977), p. 573.

10. Hans Christian Andersen, *Andersen's Fairy Tales*, tr. Mrs. E. V. Lucas and Mrs. H. B. Paull (Grosset & Dunlap, 1945), pp. 108–10. Cf. chapter 5, Vigen Guroian, *Tending the Heart of Virtue* (Oxford University Press, 1998), pp. 112–39.

11. "Sinne (II)," *Herbert*, ed. Dudley Fitts (Dell, 1966), p. 73.

12. Chapter 7, Rudolf Otto, *The Idea of the Holy*, tr. John W. Harvey (Oxford University Press, 1976), p. 41.

13. A. C. Cawley, ed., *Everyman and Medieval Miracle Plays* (Dutton, 1959), p. 20–21.

14. "Man, The Fall of," Peter and Linda Murray, *The Oxford Companion to Christian Art and Architecture* (Oxford University Press, 1996), pp. 298–99.

15. Chapter 6, Berard Marthaler, *The Creed,* rev. ed. (Twenty-Third Publications, 1993), p. 107. Cf. attributed to Ambrose, "Easter Eve," *The Penguin Book of Latin Verse,* ed. Frederick Brittain (Penguin, 1962), pp. 93–94.

16. Chapter 5, Martin Luther, *Lectures on Romans,* tr. Wilhelm Pauck (Westminster, 1961), pp. 159–60.

17. Chapter 1, A. A. Milne, *Winnie-the-Pooh* (Dell, 1980), p. 4.

18. "Themistocles," Plutarch, *The Lives of the Noble Grecians and Romans,* tr. John Dryden, rev. Arthur Hugh Clough (Modern Library, n.d.), p. 144.

19. Seventeenth lecture, Sigmund Freud, *A General Introduction to Psychoanalysis,* tr. Joan Riviere (Pocket, 1969), p. 269.

20. Chapter 1, Roy F. Baumeister, *Evil: Inside Human Violence and Cruelty* (Freeman, 1997), p. 8.

21. Part 3, chapter 2, George Foot Moore, *Judaism in the First Three Centuries of the Christian Era,* vol. 1 (Shocken, 1974), p. 470.

22. "The Flying Stars," *As I Was Saying: A Chesterton Reader,* ed. Robert Knille (Eerdmans, 1985), pp. 199–200.

23. Chapter 6, Adrienne von Speyr, *Confession: The Encounter with Christ in Penance,* tr. A. V. Littledale (Herder and Herder, 1964), p. 107.

24. Chapter 7, Helen de Borchgrave, *A Journey into Christian Art* (Fortress, 2000), pp. 108–11.

25. Chapter 16, *Einstein on Peace,* ed. Otto Nathan and Heinz Norden (Simon & Schuster, 1960), p. 556.

26. "White moon, white," *Anthology of Korean Literature,* ed. Peter H. Lee (University of Hawaii, 1992), p. 93.

27. "Notes from Underground," part 1, section 7, Fyodor Dostoyevsky, *Three Short Novels,* tr. Constance Garnett (Dell, 1973), p. 41.

28. Andersen, *Andersen's Fairy Tales,* pp. 113–14.

29. Chapter 9, Paul Radin, *The World of Primitive Man* (Dutton, 1971), p. 256.

30. "Vacillation," W. B. Yeats, *The Collected Poems of W. B. Yeats* (Macmillan, 1979), p. 246.

31. "Of Vanity," book 3, chapter 9, Donald M. Frame, tr., *The Complete Essays of Montaigne* (Stanford University Press, 1979), p. 757.

32. *Boswell's London Journal, 1762–1763,* ed. Frederick A. Pottle (McGraw-Hill, 1950), pp. 53–54.

33. "Sermon preached at the funeral of William Cokayne (Dec. 12, 1626)," *The Complete Poetry and Selected Prose of John Donne,* ed. Charles M. Coffin (Modern Library, 1952), p. 525.

34. "*Simul iustus et peccator,*" J. C. O'Neill, *The Westminster Dictionary of Christian Theology,* ed. Alan Richardson and John Bowden (Westminster, 1983), p. 538.

35. Chapter 4, Luther, *Lectures on Romans,* pp. 124–27.

36. "Of Repentance," book 3, chapter 2, Frame, tr., *Complete Essays of Montaigne,* p. 617.

37. Chapter 7, C. S. Lewis, *The Voyage of the "Dawn Treader,"* (Macmillan, 1952), pp. 88–90. Cf. chapter 1, Wesley A. Kort, *C. S. Lewis Then and Now* (Oxford University Press, 2001), p. 27.

38. Book 3, chapter 17, Alfred Edersheim, *The Life and Times of Jesus the Messiah,* vol. 1 (Eerdmans, 1969), p. 511.

39. Act 3, Scene 3, lines 51–56, 70–71, 97–98, William Shakespeare, *The Tragedy of Hamlet,* ed. Edward Hubler (New American Library, 1963), pp. 114–15.

40. Charles S. Singleton, tr., commentary on *The Divine Comedy: Purgatorio* (Princeton University Press, 1982), pp. 61–62.

41. Chapter 5, Jakob Rosenberg, Seymour Slive, E. H. ter Kuile, *Dutch Art and Architecture 1600–1800,* 3rd ed. (Penguin, 1977), p. 138. Cf. part 3, Henri J. M. Nouwen, *The Return of the Prodigal Son* (Doubleday, 1992), pp. 83 ff.

42. "Luke 10, 12, 15," Hidde Hoekstra, *Rembrandt and the Bible,* tr. Royal Smeets Offset (Magna Books, 1990), pp. 334–39.

43. Chapter 3, Kallistos Ware, *The Inner Kingdom* (SVS Press, 2000), p. 46. Cf. chapter 5, Igumen Chariton of Valamo, comp., *The Art of Prayer,* tr. E. Kadloubovsky and E. M. Palmer (Faber & Faber, 1978), p. 182.

44. "The Capital of the World," Ernest Hemingway, *The Short Stories* (Charles Scribner's Sons, 1966), p. 38.

45. "A Temple of the Holy Ghost," Flannery O'Connor, *The Complete Stories* (Farrar, Straus and Giroux, 1980), pp. 236–38.

46. "A Hymn to God the Father," *The Metaphysical Poets,* revised, ed. Helen Gardner (Penguin, 1970), pp. 90–91.

Chapter 2: Guilt Unraveled

1. Scene 9, Archibald MacLeish, *J. B.* (Houghton Mifflin, 1986), p. 121.

2. Examples are taken from Monroe Peaston, chapter 7, *Personal Living* (Harper & Row, 1972) p. 61.

3. Chapter 7, Edward V. Stein, *Guilt Theory and Therapy* (Westminster, 1968), p. 189.

4. Chapter 8, Paul Tournier, *Guilt and Grace,* tr. Arthur W. Heathcote (Harper & Brothers, 1962), p. 75.

5. Chapter 7, Sigmund Freud, *Civilization and Its Discontents,* tr. James Strachey (Norton, 1961), p. 74.

6. Tournier, *Guilt and Grace,* p. 67.

7. Chapter 17, "The Obstructed Will," William James, *Psychology: The Briefer Course,* ed. Gordon Allport (University of Notre Dame Press, 1985), pp. 308–9.

8. *Metamorphoses,* book 7, line 19, quoted in *The Anchor Book of Latin Quotations,* comp. Norman Guterman (Anchor, 1990), pp. 226–27.

9. Quoted in *The Climate of Faith in Modern Literature,* ed. Nathan A. Scott Jr. (Seabury, 1964), p. 77.

10. Book 5, chapter 10, Augustine, *The City of God,* abridged, ed. Vernon J. Bourke, tr. Gerald C. Walsh, Demetrius B. Zema, Grace Monahan, and Daniel J. Honan (Image, 1958), p. 109.

11. No. 418, Blaise Pascal, *Pensées and the Provincial Letters,* tr. W. F. Trotter (Modern Library, 1941), p. 132.

12. "Henry Jekyll's Full Statement of the Case," *The Strange Case of Dr. Jekyll and Mr. Hyde and Other Stories by Robert Louis Stevenson,* ed. Robert Hawkins (Dell, 1966), p. 70.

13. "Of the Inconsistency of Our Actions," book 2, chapter 1, Donald M. Frame, tr., *The Complete Essays of Montaigne* (Stanford University Press, 1979), p. 242.

14. Albert Camus, *The Fall,* tr. Justin O'Brien (Vintage, 1956), p. 108.

15. Chapter 3, Paul Ricoeur, *The Symbolism of Evil,* tr. Emerson Buchanan (Beacon, 1969), p. 146.

16. Chapter 7, Nathaniel Hawthorne, *The Scarlet Letter,* ed. Sculley Bradley (Norton, 1962), p. 78.

17. Act 5, scene 1, William Shakespeare, *The Tragedy of Macbeth,* ed. Sylvan Barnet (New American Library, 1963), p. 116.

18. Act 5, Scene 3, ibid., p. 121.

19. Chapter 16, G. Rattray Taylor, *Sex in History* (Harper & Row, 1973), pp. 304–5.

20. Chapter 5, Tournier, *Guilt and Grace,* p. 45.

21. Chapter 4, James A. Knight, *Conscience and Guilt* (Appleton-Century-Crofts, 1969), p. 87.

22. A. J. Franklyn Dulley, "Guilt," *Baker's Dictionary of Christian Ethics,* ed. Carl F. H. Henry (Canon, 1973) p. 280.

23. Chapter 32, Martin Luther, *Lectures on Genesis: Chapters 31–37,* ed. Jaroslav Pelikan, (Concordia, 1970), p. 133.

24. Book 12, section 18, *The Trinity,* ed. John E. Rotelle, tr. Edmund Hill (New City Press, 1991), p. 332. Cf. James F. Forrest "*Delectatio Morosa,*" *A Dictionary of Biblical Tradition in English Literature,* ed. David Lyle Jeffrey (Eerdmans, 1992), p. 193.

25. Chapter 1, Tournier, *Guilt and Grace,* p. 14.

26. Chapter 4, ibid., p. 33.

27. Quoted in chapter 5, Ilza Veith, *Hysteria: The History of a Disease* (University of Chicago Press, 1970), p. 78.

28. Preface, Benedict de Spinoza, *A Theologico-Political Treatise,* tr. R. H. M. Elwes (Dover, 1951), p. 3.

29. Chapter 1, John G. McKenzie, *Guilt: Its Meaning and Significance* (Abingdon, 1962), p. 23.

30. "Wernher von Braun," Tom Lehrer, *That Was the Year That Was* (Reprise, recorded in July 1965).

31. Chapter 6, Tournier, *Guilt and Grace,* pp. 58–59.

32. "Meditation XVII," John Donne, *Devotions upon Emergent Occasions* (University of Michigan Press, 1978), p. 109.

33. "Sermons," *Handbook of Preaching Resources from English Literature,* ed. James Douglas Robertson (Macmillan, 1962), p. 149.

34. Donne, *Devotions upon Emergent Occasions,* p. 108.

35. Third lecture, Sigmund Freud, *A General Introduction to Psychoanalysis,* tr. Joan Riviere (Pocket, 1969), p. 56.

36. Quoted in chapter 19, Tournier, *Guilt and Grace,* p. 169.

37. "Of Vanity," book 3, chapter 9, Donald M. Frame, tr., *The Complete Essays of Montaigne,* p. 743.

38. "Shooting an Elephant," *An Age Like This: 1920–1940,* ed. Sonia Orwell and Ian Angus (Harcourt Brace Jovanovich, 1968), p. 239.

39. Chapter 6, Erving Goffman, *The Presentation of Self in Everyday Life* (Anchor, 1959), p. 237.

40. "Self-love," # 978, Blaise Pascal, *Pensées,* revised, tr. A. J. Krailsheimer (Penguin, 1995), p. 326.

41. Part 4: Soul and Body, section 2, Milan Kundera, *The Unbearable Lightness of Being,* tr. Michael Henry Heim (Harper & Row, 1985), p. 133.

42. Chapter 3, Goffman, *Presentation of Self,* p. 128. Cf. Prologue, Jeffrey Rosen, *The Unwanted Gaze* (Random House, 2000), pp. 11–12.

43. Stein, *Guilt Theory and Therapy,* p. 165.

44. Book 7, Flavius Arrianus Xenophon, *The Campaigns of Alexander the Great,* tr. Aubrey de Selincourt (Penguin, 1971), p. 396.

45. "Maxim 1060," John Bartlett, *Familiar Quotations,* 14th ed., revised and enlarged, ed. Emily Morison Beck (Little, Brown and Company, 1968), p. 127.

46. Chapter 6, McKenzie, *Guilt: Its Meaning and Significance,* p. 167.

47. "Mary at the Cross," *The Penguin Book of Greek Verse,* ed. Constantine A. Trypanis (Penguin, 1979), pp. 406, 409. Cf. "On the Lament of the Mother of God," Romanos the Melodist, *Kontakia: On the Life of Christ,* tr. Ephrem Lash (HarperCollins, 1995), pp. 143–50.

48. Book 1, chapter 2, Søren Kierkegaard, *Concluding Unscientific Postscript,* tr. David F. Swenson and Walter Lowrie (Princeton University Press, 1971), p. 49.

49. Lecture 9, William James, *The Varieties of Religious Experience* (New American Library, 1958), p. 172.

50. Handwritten note by Samuel Coleridge in a copy of *The Pilgrim's Progress, Table Talk II,* ed. Carl Woodring, recorded by Henry Nelson Coleridge (Princeton University Press, 1990), p. 102.

51. Part 1, John Bunyan, *The Pilgrim's Progress,* ed. Roger Sharrock (Penguin, 1987), p. 82.

52. "Confession and Thanksgiving to Christ, Son of God, the Savior of the World," *A Treasury of Russian Spirituality,* vol. 2, ed. George P. Fedotov (Nordland, 1975), pp. 216, 223, 221, 223.

53. Section 4, "The Memorial," Pascal, *Pensées,* p. 285.

54. Quoted in chapter 6, Max Brod, *Franz Kafka: A Biography,* 2nd, enlarged, ed. (Schocken, 1960), p. 173.

55. "1956," Dag Hammarskjöld, *Markings,* tr. Leif Sjöberg and W. H. Auden (Ballantine, 1993), p. 105.

56. "Confessions of an Enquiring Spirit," quoted in chapter 8, David Lyle Jeffrey, *People of the Book* (Eerdmans, 1996), p. 304.

57. Book 9, chapter 6, John K. Ryan, tr., *The Confessions of St. Augustine* (Doubleday, 1960), p. 214.

58. Part 8, section 8, Leo Tolstoy, *Anna Karenin,* revised, tr. Rosemary Edmonds (Penguin, 1978), p. 821.

59. *The First Apology,* section 14, Leslie William Barnard, tr., *St. Justin Martyr: The First and Second Apologies* (Paulist, 1997), pp. 31–32.

60. John A. McGuckin, tr., *At the Lighting of the Lamps* (Morehouse, 1995), p. 35.

Chapter 3: Pride: The Way up Is Down

1. "Christ," *What Luther Says,* comp. Edwald M. Plass (Concordia, 1991), p. 206.

2. Chapter 2, Solomon Schimmel, *The Seven Deadly Sins* (Free Press, 1992), p. 36.

3. *Paradise Lost,* book 1, lines 249–55, 258–63, *The Complete Poetry of John Milton,* revised, ed. John T. Shawcross (Doubleday, 1971), p. 257.

4. Chapter 14, A. B. Bruce, *The Training of the Twelve* (Kregel, 1980), p. 204.

5. Section 13, Roland N. Stromberg, ed., *Realism, Naturalism, and Symbolism* (Walker, 1968), p. 135.

6. "VIII: On Rules for Conduct in Life," maxim 17, Edward Rehatsek, tr., *The Gulistan or Rose Garden of Sa'di,* ed. W. G. Archer (George Allen & Unwin, 1964), p. 243.

7. "The Secret Life of Walter Mitty," James Thurber, *The Thurber Carnival* (Harper & Row, 1945), pp. 47–51.

8. Quoted in "Of Vainglory," *Francis Bacon: A Selection of His Works,* ed. Sidney Warhaft (Odyssey, 1965), p. 180.

9. "Pride," James Hall, *Dictionary of Subjects and Symbols in Art,* revised (Harper & Row, 1979), p. 253.

10. "Tusculan Disputations," 1:15, quoted in *Francis Bacon: A Selection of His Works,* ed. Warhaft, p. 181.

11. Chapter 1, Napoleon A. Chagnon, *Studying the Yanomanö* (Holt, Rinehart and Winston, 1974), p. 3.

12. Book 2, introduction, Vitruvius, *The Ten Books on Architecture,* tr. Morris Hicky Morgan (Dover, 1960), p. 35.

13. Louis de Rouvroy, Duc de Saint-Simon, "Memoirs," *Ideas and Institutions in European History: 800–1715,* ed. Thomas C. Mendenhall, Basil D. Henning, and A. S. Foord (Holt, Rinehart and Winston, 1966), pp. 302–3.

14. *Travels into Several Remote Nations of the World . . . by Lemuel Gulliver,* part 1, chapter 3, *The Portable Swift,* ed. Carl Van Doren (Viking, 1963), p. 239.

15. Chapter 3, Theodore Caplow and Reece J. McGee, *The Academic Marketplace* (Anchor, 1965), p. 37.

16. Desiderius Erasmus, *Praise of Folly,* tr. Betty Radice (Penguin, 1993), p. 83.

17. "The Seven Steps of the Ladder of Spiritual Love," chapter 4, *Readings in Christian Thought,* ed. Hugh T. Kerr (Abingdon, 1966), p. 131.

18. J. R. Beck, "Pride," *Baker Encyclopedia of Psychology,* ed. David G. Benner (Baker, 1985), p. 869.

19. "Clementine Homilies," 2: 22, *Gnosticism,* ed. Robert M. Grant (AMS Press, 1978), p. 26.

20. "The Book Concerning the Philosophers," *The Portable Renaissance Reader,* ed. James Bruce Ross and Mary Martin McLaughlin (Viking, 1972), p. 553.

21. Part 1, Walter C. Langer, *The Mind of Adolf Hitler* (New American Library, 1973), p. 37.

22. G. C. Argan, *Renaissance Painting* (Dell, 1968), p. 185. (This is volume 3 of *20,000 Years of World Painting,* ed. Hans L. C. Jaffe, tr. Robert Allen.) Cf. Tiziana Frati, *Bruegel: Every Painting,* tr. Jane Carroll (Rizzoli, 1980), pp. 9, 78–79, 82–85.

23. Chapter 54, Samuel Butler, *The Way of All Flesh* (New American Library, 1960), pp. 223–24.

24. Chapter 4, Stanford M. Lyman, *The Seven Deadly Sins: Society and Evil,* revised and expanded (General Hall, 1989), p. 167. Cf. *The Diary of Michael Wigglesworth, 1653–1657,* ed. Edmund S. Morgan (Harper & Row, 1965), p. 105.

25. Scene 7, *Drama in the Modern World,* ed. Samuel A. Weiss (D. C. Heath, 1964), p. 446.

26. C. R. Ridley, "Self-Esteem," *Dictionary of Pastoral Care and Counseling,* ed. Rodney J. Hunter (Abingdon, 1990), pp. 1131–32.

27. Rosemary Goring, *Larousse Dictionary of Literary Characters* (Larousse, 1994), p. 339.

28. Chapter 8, James S. Pickering, *1001 Questions Answered about Astronomy* (Grosset & Dunlap, 1958), p. 140.

29. Robert John Russell, "Cosmology," *A New Handbook of Christian Theology,* ed. Donald W. Musser and Joseph L. Price (Abingdon, 1992), p. 101. (No doubt these figures will need to be adjusted based on the most recent astronomical findings.)

30. "Isabella's Religious Experience," Sojourner Truth, *Narrative of Sojourner Truth* (Dover, 1997), pp. 35–36.

31. Chapter 18, Henry David Thoreau, *Walden; or, Life in the Woods* (New American Library, 1960), p. 218.

32. "Of Presumption," Book 2, essay 17, Donald M. Frame, tr., *Montaigne's Essays and Selected Writings* (St. Martin's Press, 1963), pp. 261–63.

33. Chapter 17, Louis Trenchard More, *Isaac Newton: A Biography* (Scribners, 1934), p. 664.

34. "The Wasteland," Section 5, lines 360–63, T. S. Eliot, *The Complete Poems and Plays* (Harcourt Brace Jovanovich, 1980), pp. 48, 54.

35. Epilogue, Roland Huntford, *Shackleton* (Atheneum, 1986), pp. 695–97.

36. "Humility," chapter 2, section 4, Jeremy Taylor, *The Rule and Exercises of Holy Living* (Longmans, Green & Co., 1941), pp. 76–77.

37. "Maundy Thursday," R. F. Buxton, *The New Westminster Dictionary of Liturgy and Worship,* ed. J. G. Davies (Westminster, 1986), p. 367.

38. Chapter 8, James F. White, *Introduction to Christian Worship,* revised (Abingdon, 1990), p. 224.

39. Section 8, quoted in Laurence Binyon, *The Spirit of Man in Asian Art* (Dover, 1965), p. 73.

40. Chapter 3, Huston Smith, *The World's Religions,* revised (HarperCollins, 1991), p. 124.

41. Section 1: 133–34, *Buddhism,* ed. Charles H. Hamilton (Bobbs-Merrill, 1952), p. 108.

42. *Philosophical Fragments* in *The Parables of Kierkegaard,* ed. Thomas C. Oden (Princeton University Press, 1989), pp. 40–45.

43. "The Blessed Virgin Mary," Jacopone da Todi, *The Lauds,* tr. Serge and Elizabeth Hughes (Paulist, 1982), pp. 70–71.

44. Chapter 2, Pegram Johnson III and Edna M. Troiano, eds., *The Roads from Bethlehem* (Westminster/John Knox, 1993), p. 84.

45. "That It Is the Highest Wisdom to Be Thought Mad for Love of Christ," *The Penguin Book of Italian Verse,* ed. George R. Kay (Penguin, 1958), p. 17. Cf. Jacopone da Todi, *The Lauds,* p. 241.

46. "How We Are to Love Christ Freely As He Loved Us," Jacopone da Todi, *The Lauds,* pp. 243–44.

47. "O, like a tiny cradle," *O Holy Night! Masterworks of Christmas Poetry,* ed. Johann M. Moser (Sophia Institute, 1995), p. 95.

48. Rolland Hein, ed., *The Heart of George MacDonald* (Harold Shaw, 1994), pp. 193, 196, 197, 203.

49. "The Heirs of Heaven and Earth," *Life Essential: The Hope of the Gospel,* ed. Rolland Hein (Harold Shaw, 1974), p. 44.

50. Chapter 12, George P. Fedotov, *The Russian Religious Mind (II): The Middle Ages* (Nordland, 1975), pp. 316–20.

51. "The Russian Spirit," Sergei Hackel, *The Story of Christian Spirituality,* ed. Gordon Mursell (Fortress, 2001), p. 159.

52. Chapter 10, Kallistos Ware, *The Inner Kingdom* (SVS Press, 2000), p. 153.

53. Chapter 21, Giles Fletcher, *Of the Russe Commonwealth,* facsimile of 1591 ed. with variants, ed. Richard Pipes and John V. A. Fine Jr. (Harvard University Press, 1966), p. 90.

54. "The Teacher," Russell Freedman, *Out of Darkness: The Story of Louis Braille* (Clarion, 1997), p. 61.

55. "Braille," Donald Wing Hathaway, *The World Book Encyclopedia,* vol. 2 (Field Enterprises Educational Corporation, 1960), p. 458.

56. Much of Braille's story is adapted from "In the Land of the Blind," A. J. Dunning, *Extremes: Reflections on Human Behavior,* tr. Johan Theron (Harcourt Brace Jovanovich, 1992), pp. 180–90.

57. Verse 5, Samuel J. Stone, "The Church's One Foundation," *The United Methodist Hymnal* (United Methodist Publishing House, 1990), no. 545.

Chapter 4: The Faultfinder

1. "A Prayer to Go to Paradise with the Donkeys," Richard Wilbur, tr., *Poems from France,* comp. William Jay Smith (Crowell, 1972), pp. 149–51.

2. Chapter 14, Robert Lauer, *Science Object Lessons,* no. 2 (Zondervan, 1970), p. 57.

3. Ibid., p. 60.

4. Saki, *Incredible Tales,* ed. Richard Corbin and Ned E. Hoopes (Dell, 1974), pp. 174–78.

5. Chapter 1, M. Luckiesh, *Visual Illusions* (Dover, 1965) pp. 1–2.

6. Chapter 6, Barry Lopez, *Arctic Dreams* (Bantam, 1987), p. 213.

7. Chapter 13, Luckiesh, *Visual Illusions,* pp. 199–200.

8. "Perspective," Edward Lucie-Smith, *Thames and Hudson Dictionary of Art Terms* (Thames and Hudson, 1990), p. 145.

9. Chapter 21, E. H. Gombrich, *The Story of Art,* 12th ed. (Phaidon, 1972), pp. 347–49.

10. Chapter 3, Colin Blakemore, *Mechanics of the Mind* (Cambridge University Press, 1978), p. 75.

11. *De docta ignorantia,* 2, chapter 12, quoted in Alexandre Koyre, *From the Closed World to the Infinite Universe* (John Hopkins University Press, 1979), p. 17.

12. "The Hoax," John Berendt, *Decker's Patterns of Exposition 15,* ed. Randall Decker and Robert A. Schwegler (Longman, 1998), p. 358.

13. Chapter 13, David Wallechinsky and Irving Wallace, *The People's Almanac* (Doubleday, 1975), pp. 701–2, and chapter 28, *The People's Almanac #2* (Bantam, 1978), pp. 1243–44.

14. "The Critic," act 1, scene 1, lines 295–97, *Sheridan's Plays,* ed. Cecil Price (Oxford University Press, 1975), p. 347.

15. *Journals,* 4 November 1858, *The Norton Book of Nature Writing,* ed. Robert Finch and John Elder (Norton, 1990), p. 197.

16. Quoted in chapter 14, C. S. Lewis, *Surprised by Joy* (Fount, 1977), p. 170.

17. Volume 2, chapter 17, Jane Austen, *Pride and Prejudice,* ed. Donald J. Gray (Norton, 1966), p. 155.

18. Part 2, chapter 64, Spiros Zodhiates, *The Behavior of Belief* (Eerdmans, 1966), p. 321.

19. Quoted in Henry Kamen, *The Spanish Inquisition* (New American Library, 1968), p. 22. Cf. "The Jew, a Misfortune for the People," Bertolt Brecht, *Selected Poems,* tr. H. R. Hays (Grove, 1959), pp. 126–27.

20. Chapter 5, section 5, J. N. D. Kelly, *Golden Mouth: The Story of John Chrysostom* (Cornell University Press, 1995), pp. 62–66.

21. Quoted in chapter 21, James Carroll, *Constantine's Sword: The Church and the Jews* (Houghton Mifflin, 2001), p. 213.

22. Chapter 6, Maureen Fiedler and Linda Rabben, eds., *Rome Has Spoken . . .* (Crossroad, 1998), pp. 69, 71.

23. Chapter 36, Carroll, *Constantine's Sword,* pp. 375–76.

24. Chapter 22, Roland H. Bainton, *Here I Stand: A Life of Martin Luther* (New American Library, 1950), p. 297.

25. Chapter 33, "Concerning the Jews and their Lies," *The Jew in the Medieval World, A Source Book: 315–1791,* ed. Jacob R. Marcus (Atheneum, 1978), pp. 163–69.

26. Chapter 3, Donald E. Gowan, *Reclaiming the Old Testament for the Christian Pulpit* (T. & T. Clark, 1994), p. 67.

27. As opposed to being a Calvinist.

28. "The Question, 'What Is an Arminian?' Answered," *The Works of John Wesley,* Vol. 10 (Zondervan, 1958), p. 358.

29. W. H. Auden and Louis Kronenberger, comps., *The Viking Book of Aphorisms* (Penguin, 1981), p. 81.

30. Part 4, "To Mistrust and Persecute Catholics," Jim Hill and Rand Cheadle, *The Bible Tells Me So* (Anchor, 1996), p. 84. Cf. *The New-England Primer,* ed. Paul Leicester Ford (Teachers College at Columbia University, 1962), p. 50.

31. Zodhiates, *Behavior of Belief,* p. 320.

32. Ibid., p. 323.

33. "1348," *Knighton's Chronicle 1337–1396,* ed. G. H. Martin (Oxford University Press, 1995), pp. 94–97.

34. Chapter 12, Edmund Gosse, *Father and Son* (Norton, 1963), p. 221.

35. Chapter 8, Ruth Benedict, *Patterns of Culture* (Houghton Mifflin, 1959), pp. 277–78.

36. Chapter 2, John Stuart Mill, *On Liberty,* ed. David Spitz (Norton, 1975), p. 44.

37. Victoria Cross, a bronze Maltese cross, which is Britain's highest military award for conspicuous valor.

38. Book 3, chapter 4, C. S. Lewis, *Mere Christianity* (Macmillan, 1968), p. 85.

39. Chapter 18, Henry David Thoreau, *Walden; or, Life in the Woods* (New American Library, 1960), p. 216.

40. S. A. Hanford, tr., *Fables of Aesop* (Penguin, 1977), p. 5.

41. "Letter to Ermolao Barbaro," 3 June 1485, Arturo B. Fallico and Herman Shapiro, trs., *Renaissance Philosophy,* vol. 1 (Modern Library, 1967), p. 111.

42. "Democritus Junior to the Reader," Robert Burton, *The Anatomy of Melancholy,* ed. Holbrook Jackson (Vintage, 1977), p. 26.

43. Chapter 27, Gordon W. Allport, *The Nature of Prejudice,* abridged (Anchor, 1958), p. 408.

44. Chapter 4, section 4, *Selections from the Notebooks of Leonardo da Vinci,* ed. Irma A. Richter (Oxford University Press, 1977), p. 221.

45. Chapter 3, Moses Hayyim Luzzatto, *The Path of the Upright,* tr. Mordecai M. Kaplan (Jason Aronson, 1995), p. 23.

46. "To a Louse," stanza 8, *The Poems and Songs of Robert Burns* (P. F. Collier & Son, 1909), p. 199.

47. "Of Friendship," *Francis Bacon: A Selection of His Works,* ed. Sidney Warhaft (Odyssey Press, 1965), p. 117.

48. Book 3, chapter 39, Aelred of Rievaulx, *The Mirror of Charity,* tr. Elizabeth Connor, (Cistercian, 1990), pp. 298–99.

49. "Celtic Spirituality," Diarmuid O'Laoghaire, *The Study of Spirituality,* ed. Cheslyn Jones, Geoffrey Wainwright, and Edward Yarnold (Oxford University Press, 1986), p. 222.

50. "Of Books," Jean de La Bruyère, *Characters,* tr. Jean Stewart (Penguin, 1970), p. 28.

51. Appendix 3, Frederick Treves, "The Elephant Man," Michael Howell and Peter Ford, *The True History of the Elephant Man* (Penguin, 1981), pp. 191–92. Daily hospital baths made Merrick's stench all but disappear.

52. "Of Practice," book 2, chapter 6, Donald M. Frame, tr., *The Complete Essays of Montaigne* (Stanford University Press, 1979), p. 270.

53. Appendix 6, Carr Gomm's letter to *The Times,* 16 April 1890, Ashley Montagu, *The Elephant Man,* 2nd ed. (Dutton, 1979), pp. 118–19.

54. Chapter 3, ibid., pp. 66–67.

55. Howell and Ford, *True History of the Elephant Man,* p. 210.

56. Flannery O'Connor, *The Complete Stories* (Farrar, Straus and Giroux, 1980), pp. 502, 508–9. Cf. James F. Forrest, "Deformity," *A Dictionary of Biblical Tradition in English Literature,* ed. David Lyle Jeffrey (Eerdmans, 1992), pp. 191–93.

57. "The Southwell Litany" pamphlet (Forward Movement Publications, n.d.).

Chapter 5: Envy, the Secret Sin

1. Book 5, William Langland, *Piers the Ploughman,* tr. J. F. Goodridge (Penguin, 1974), pp. 63–64.

2. Chapter 16, Robert Graves and Raphael Patai, *Hebrew Myths: The Book of Genesis* (McGraw-Hill, 1964), p. 91.

3. "Cain and Abel" (N. town cycle), *Everyman and Medieval Miracle Plays,* ed. A. C. Cawley (Dutton, 1959), p. 30.

4. Chapter 38, John Steinbeck, *East of Eden* (Bantam, 1979), p. 509.

5. Iona and Peter Opie, *The Classic Fairy Tales* (Oxford, 1992), pp. 123–27.

6. Quoted in "The Parson's Tale," lines 483–84, Geoffrey Chaucer, *The Canterbury Tales,* tr. Ronald L. Ecker and Eugene J. Crook (Hodge & Braddock, 1993), p. 536. Cf. Augustine, *Confessions,* book 10, section 39.

7. *Rhetoric,* book 2, chapter 10, *The Complete Works of Aristotle,* vol. 2, ed. Jonathan Barnes (Princeton University Press, 1991), p. 2211.

8. Part 1, following line 183, Bernard Mandeville, *The Fable of the Bees,* ed. Irwin Primer (Capricorn, 1962), p. 95.

9. Chapter 9, Cornelius Plantinga Jr., *Not the Way It's Supposed to Be* (Eerdmans, 1995), p. 167.

10. "The Laurel," *The Penguin Book of Greek Verse,* ed. Constantine A. Trypanis (Penguin, 1979), p. 523.

11. "Of Envy," *Francis Bacon: A Selection of His Works,* ed. Sidney Warhaft (Odyssey, 1965), p. 66.

12. No. 29, William Shakespeare, *The Sonnets,* ed. William Burto (New American Library, 1964), p. 69.

13. Chapters 1, 2, 5, Helmut Schoek, *Envy: A Theory of Social Behavior,* tr. Michael Glenny and Betty Ross (Harcourt, Brace & World, 1970), pp. 6, 18, 49. In such cultures even lightning strikes are attributed to malicious intent.

14. Chapter 8, Miguel de Cervantes Saavedra, *The Adventures of Don Quixote,* tr. J. M. Cohen (Penguin, 1970), pp. 65, 69.

15. "Envy or *Invidia,*" Henry Fairlee, *The Seven Deadly Sins Today* (University of Notre Dame Press, 1995), p. 66.

16. Mandeville, *Fable of the Bees,* p. 96.

17. "Foreword," Arthur E. R. Boak, Procopius, *Secret History* (University of Michigan Press, 1976), pp. viii–xiv. Cf. chapters 9, 12.

18. "Religio Medici," part 2, section 3, *The Prose of Sir Thomas Browne,* ed. Norman Endicott (Norton, 1972), p. 72. A "basilisco" is a type of cannon.

19. *The Ethics,* part 3, proposition 2 note, Benedict de Spinoza, *On the Improvement of the Understanding, The Ethics, Correspondence,* tr. R. H. M. Elwes (Dover, 1955), p. 133.

20. "Satires" 1: 3, *The Complete Works of Horace,* ed. Casper J. Kraemer Jr. (Modern Library, 1936), p. 14.

21. "No. 183," Tuesday, 17 December 1751, Samuel Johnson, *Rasselas, Poems, and Selected Prose,* 3rd ed., enlarged, ed. Bertrand H. Bronson (Rinehart, 1971), p. 137.

22. "I: The Manner of Kings," story 15, Edward Rehatsek, tr., *The Gulistan or Rose Garden of Sa'di,* ed. W. G. Archer (George Allen & Unwin, 1964), p. 91.

23. "Of the Covetous Man and of the Envious Man," Eugene Mason, tr., *Aucassin and Nicolette and Other Medieval Romances and Legends* (Dutton, 1958), pp. 139–41.

24. Chapter 5, Stanford M. Lyman, *The Seven Deadly Sins: Society and Evil,* revised and expanded (General Hall, 1989), p. 195.

25. "Ancient Documentation and Testimony of the Holy Fathers Concerning Images," John of Damascus, *On the Divine Images,* tr. David Anderson (SVS Press, 1980), p. 39. Cf. chapter 2, Anton C. Vrame, *The Educating Icon* (Holy Cross Orthodox Press, 1999), pp. 48–52.

26. "Sailing to Byzantium," stanza 3, W. B. Yeats, *The Collected Poems of W. B. Yeats* (Macmillan, 1979), p. 191.

27. "Celtic Spirituality," Diarmuid O'Laoghaire, *The Study of Spirituality,* ed. Cheslyn Jones, Geoffrey Wainwright, and Edward Yarnold (Oxford University Press, 1986), p. 221.

28. John Fawcett, "Blest Be the Tie that Binds," verse 3, Kenneth W. Osbeck, *101 Hymn Stories* (Kregel, 1984), p. 45.

29. Fairlee, *Seven Deadly Sins Today,* p. 68. Cf. canto 13, lines 70–72.

30. "No. 19," La Rochefoucauld, *Maxims,* tr. Leonard Tancock (Penguin, 1981), p. 39.

31. "19 October 1769," James Boswell, *The Life of Samuel Johnson,* abr. Bergen Evans (Modern Library, 1965), pp. 163–64.

32. Johnson Oatman Jr., "Count Your Blessings," verse 1, Osbeck, *101 Hymn Stories,* p. 54.

33. Chapter 3, Solomon Schimmel, *The Seven Deadly Sins* (Free Press, 1992), p. 70.

34. Shakespeare, *The Sonnets,* p. 69.

35. Act 1, scene 2, Peter Schaffer, *Amadeus* (New American Library, 1984), p. 12.

36. "Envy," James Stalker, *The Seven Deadly Sins and the Seven Cardinal Virtues* (NavPress, 1998), p. 53.

37. "On Free Will," *The Portable Renaissance Reader,* ed. James Bruce Ross and Mary Martin McLaughlin (Viking, 1972), p. 693. Cf. section 8, Desiderius Erasmus, "A Diatribe or Sermon Concerning Free Will," Ernst F. Winter, tr. and ed., *Erasmus-Luther: Discourse on Free Will* (Ungar, 1974), p. 94.

38. Henry Drummond, *The Greatest Thing in the World* (Guideposts Associates, n.d.) p. 19.

39. "Thoughts for Life's Journey," quoted in chapter 16, Spiros Zodhiates, *To Love Is to Live* (Eerdmans, 1967), p. 81.

40. Chapter 33, *Manon of the Springs,* Marcel Pagnol, *Jean de Florette and Manon of the Springs,* tr. W. E. van Heyningen (North Point, 1995), pp. 439–40. I have made a few minor changes in the translation to make it read more smoothly.

Chapter 6: The Overzealous Egalitarian, or Leveler

1. Chapter 3, Lewis Carroll, *Alice's Adventures in Wonderland* and *Through the Looking-Glass* (New American Library, 1962), p. 33.

2. Book 2, chapter 1, section 2, John Locke, *An Essay Concerning Human Understanding,* vol. 1, collated and annotated by Alexander Campbell Fraser (Dover, 1959), p. 121.

3. "Some Thoughts Concerning Education," section 2, *Three Thousand Years of Educational Wisdom,* 2nd ed., enlarged, ed. Robert Ulich (Harvard University Press, 1979), p. 356.

4. Letter to John Taylor of Carolina, 15 April 1814, *The Portable Conservative Reader,* ed. Russell Kirk (Penguin, 1982), pp. 67–68.

5. Chapter 5, Stanford M. Lyman, *The Seven Deadly Sins: Society and Evil,* revised and expanded (General Hall, 1989), p. 187.

6. Book 1, part 2, chapter 10, Alexis de Tocqueville, *Democracy in America,* vol. 2, ed. Phillips Bradley (Vintage, 1945), p. 42.

7. Laurie F. Maffly-Kipp, "Utopianism," Edward L. Queen II, Stephen R. Prothero, and Gardiner H. Shattuck Jr., *The Encyclopedia of American Religious History,* vol. 2 (Facts on File, 1996) pp. 693–95.

8. "Marginal Notes to the Programme of the German Workers' Party," *The Portable Karl Marx,* ed. Eugene Kamenka (Penguin, 1986), p. 541.

9. "Collectivization," *The Harper Dictionary of Modern Thought,* revised, ed. Alan Bullock and Stephen Trombley (Harper & Row, 1988), p. 142.

10. "Great Leap Forward," ibid., p. 367.

11. Book 2, "Their Occupations," Thomas More, *Utopia,* tr. and ed. Robert M. Adams (Norton, 1975), p. 40.

12. Chapter 10, George Orwell, *Animal Farm* (New American Library, 1946), p. 123.

13. "No. 55," Alexander Hamilton, John Jay, and James Madison, *The Federalist* (Modern Library, 1937), p. 365.

14. Chapter 3, Glenn Tinder, *The Political Meaning of Christianity* (Louisiana State University Press, 1989), p. 113.

15. "5 April 1887," John Emerich Edward Dalberg Acton, *Essays on Freedom and Power,* ed. Gertrude Himmelfarb (Meridian, 1959), p. 335.

16. Cf. Reinhold Niebuhr, *The Irony of American History* (Charles Scribner's Sons, 1952).

17. Chapter 1, Max L. Stackhouse, *Creeds, Society, and Human Rights* (Eerdmans, 1984), p. 4.

18. "Collectivization," *Harper Dictionary of Modern Thought,* ed. Bullock and Trombley, p. 142.

19. "General Introduction," Owen Chadwick, ed., *Western Asceticism* (Westminster, 1958), p. 28.

20. Book 4, Count de Montalembert, *The Monks of the West,* vol. 1 (Patrick Donahoe, 1872), p. 343.

21. Gardiner H. Shattuck Jr., "Perfectionism," Queen II, Prothero, and Shattuck Jr., *Encyclopedia of American Religious History,* vol. 2, pp. 505–6.

22. Quoted in chapter 3, Steven Ozment, *The Age of Reform 1250–1550* (Yale University Press, 1980), p. 93. Cf. chapter 10, Malcolm Lambert, *Medieval Heresy,* 2nd ed. (Barnes & Noble, 1998), pp. 185–88.

23. Quoted in chapter 4, R. A. Markus, *The End of Ancient Christianity* (Cambridge University Press, 1998), p. 54. Cf. Augustine, *Confessions,* book 10, chapter 33.

24. Part 8, section 11, Leo Tolstoy, *Anna Karenin,* revised, tr. Rosemary Edmonds (Penguin, 1978), p. 829.

25. Part 8, section 19, ibid., p. 853.

26. Laurie F. Maffly-Kipp, "John Humphrey Noyes," Queen II, Prothero, and Shattuck Jr., *Encyclopedia of American Religious History,* vol. 2, pp. 475–77.

27. Chapter 1, Tinder, *Political Meaning of Christianity*, p. 37.

28. "Napoleon," A. J. P. Taylor, *From Napoleon to Lenin: Historical Essays* (Harper & Row, 1966), p. 2.

29. Part 4, section 3: B, Paul Tillich, *Systematic Theology*, vol. 3 (University of Chicago Press, 1976), p. 245.

30. "Reformation," Jaroslav Pelikan, *The Melody of Theology* (Harvard University Press, 1988), p. 198.

31. Chapters 7, 13, F. E. Peters, *Jerusalem* (Princeton University Press, 1985), pp. 258–68, 571–72.

32. Chapter 4, William J. La Due, *The Chair of Saint Peter* (Orbis, 1999), pp. 74–75.

33. Desiderius Eramus, *Praise of Folly*, tr. Betty Radice (Penguin, 1993), pp. 63–66. Cf. Virgil, *Aeneid*, 6: 625–27.

34. "An Enquiry Concerning Human Understanding," section 10, part 2, David Hume, *On Religion*, ed. Richard Wollheim (Meridian, 1967), p. 213.

35. Chapter 8, *Reinhold Niebuhr*, ed. Larry Rasmussen (Fortress, 1991), p. 259.

36. *A Large Number*, "Utopia," Wislawa Szymborska, *View with a Grain of Sand*, tr. Stanislaw Baranczak and Clare Cavanagh (Harcourt Brace & Company, 1995), pp. 127–28.

37. Chapter 1, Maureen Fielder and Linda Rabben, eds., *Rome Has Spoken . . .* (Crossroad, 1998), pp. 11–21.

38. Chapter 7, Dorothy Sayers, *Creed or Chaos?* (Sophia Institute, 1995), p. 104.

39. Quoted in chapter 3, Edward Shepherd Creasy, *Decisive Battles of the World*, revised (Colonial Press, 1899), p. 58.

40. Erasmus, *Praise of Folly*, pp. 67–68.

41. "Envy or *Invidia*," Henry Fairlie, *Seven Deadly Sins Today*, p. 63.

42. Quoted in chapter 2, Helmut Schoek, *Envy: A Theory of Social Behaviour*, tr. Michael Glenny and Betty Ross (Harcourt, Brace & World, 1970), p. 20.

43. "The Faerie Queene," part 1:4, stanzas 30–32, *Edmund Spenser's Poetry*, ed. Hugh MacLean (Norton, 1968), pp. 46–47.

44. "Homily 11: Concerning Envy," Saint Basil, *Ascetical Works*, tr. M. Monica Wagner (Catholic University of America, 1962), pp. 470–71. Cf. chapter 3, Solomon Schimmel, *The Seven Deadly Sins* (Free Press, 1992), p. 74.

45. Chapter 10, Annie Dillard, *Pilgrim at Tinker Creek* (HarperCollins, 1988), pp. 175–76.

46. Book 4, part 9, Arthur Waley, tr., *The Analects of Confucius* (Vintage, 1938), pp. 103–4.

47. Part 4, Hugh White, tr., *Ancrene Wisse* (Penguin, 1993), p. 89.

48. Chapter 3, Wayne A. Meeks, *The First Urban Christians* (Yale University Press, 1983), pp. 74 ff.

49. Chapter 12, Timothy Ware, *The Orthodox Church*, revised (Penguin, 1993), pp. 242–43.

50. Chapter 6, Kallistos Ware, *The Orthodox Way*, revised (SVS Press, 1995), p. 125. Cf. "Homily 15," Pseudo-Macarius, *The Fifty Spiritual Homilies and The Great Letter*, tr. George A. Maloney (Paulist, 1992), p. 112.

51. Meeks, *First Urban Christians*, p. 90.

52. Chapter 11, Ware, *The Orthodox Church*, p. 216.

53. Chapter 3, Gibson Winter, *The Suburban Captivity of the Churches* (Macmillan, 1966), p. 87.

54. Chapter 6, Robert N. Bellah, Richard Madsen, William M. Sullivan, Ann Swidler, and Steven M. Tipton, *Habits of the Heart*, updated (University of California Press, 1996), p. 153.

55. Chapter 2, Tinder, *Political Meaning of Christianity*, p. 87.

56. Chapter 2, Robert Wuthnow, *Christianity in the 21st Century* (Oxford University Press, 1995), p. 32.

57. "Religion Booknotes," Lawrence S. Cunningham, *Commonweal* (8 September 2000), p. 41.

58. Chapter 3, Gustavo Gutiérrez, *We Drink from Our Own Wells*, tr. Matthew J. O'Connell (Orbis, 1984), p. 53

59. Ibid., p. 37.

60. "Teresa of Calcutta, Mother," "*Taizé*," and "*L'Arche*," Richard P. McBrien, gen. ed., *The HarperCollins Encyclopedia of Catholicism* (HarperCollins, 1995), pp. 1246, 1240, 749.

61. "Habitat for Humanity International," David Walls, *The Activist's Almanac* (Fireside, 1993), pp. 293–97.

62. Geffrey B. Kelly and F. Burton Nelson, eds., *A Testament to Freedom: The Essential Writings of Dietrich Bonhoeffer* (HarperCollins, 1990), p. 340.

63. "Life Together," chapter 1, ibid., p. 344.

64. Chapter 4, Martin Luther, *Lectures on Romans*, tr. Wilhelm Pauck (Westminster, 1961), p. 130.

65. Horton Davies, ed., *The Communion of Saints* (Eerdmans, 1990), p. 60.

Chapter 7: An Antidote to Anger

1. Cf. book 1, Homer, *The Iliad*, tr. W. H. D. Rouse (New American Library, 1938), pp. 11–21.

2. Chapter 41, Herman Melville, *Moby Dick*, ed. Harrison Hayford and Hershel Parker (Norton, 1967), p. 160.

3. "Medea," Pierre Grimal, *The Penguin Dictionary of Classical Mythology*, ed. Stephen Kershaw, tr. A. R. Maxwell-Hyslop (Penguin, 1991), pp. 259–60. Cf. Euripides' "Medea."

4. "On Anger," book 2, section 36, Lucius Annaeus Seneca, *Moral Essays*, vol. 1, tr. John W. Basore (Harvard University Press, 1998), pp. 249–51. Cf. chapter 4, Solomon Schimmel, *The Seven Deadly Sins* (Free Press, 1992), p. 97.

5. Chapter 14, Ivan Morris, tr. and ed., *The Pillow Book of Sei Shōnagon* (Penguin, 1981), pp. 44–47.

6. Chapter 6, Ted Peters, *Sin: Radical Evil in Soul and Society* (Eerdmans, 1994), p. 183.

7. Book 5, William Langland, *Piers the Ploughman*, tr. J. F. Goodridge (Penguin, 1974), p. 66.

8. "Legends," chapter 4, Robert Louis Stevenson, *Edinburgh: Picturesque Notes* (Macmillan, 1889), pp. 69–70.

9. "Songs of Experience," *William Blake*, ed. Michael Mason (Oxford University Press, 1988), p. 276.

10. Chapter 1, Carol Tavris, *Anger: The Misunderstood Emotion*, revised (Touchstone, 1989) pp. 27–47.

11. "Letter to Herodotus," section 9, Epicurus, *Letters, Principal Doctrines, and Vatican Sayings*, tr. Russel M. Geer (Bobbs-Merrill, 1964), p. 31.

12. Chapter 8, Kosuke Koyama, *Water Buffalo Theology*, revised (Orbis, 1999), p. 68. Cf. Lactantius, *The Minor Works*, tr. Mary Francis McDonald (Catholic University of America, 1965), pp. 59–116.

13. *Nicomachean Ethics*, book 7, section 6, *The Complete Works of Aristotle*, vol. 2, ed. Jonathan Barnes (Princeton University Press, 1991), p. 1815.

14. "Anger," James Stalker, *The Seven Deadly Sins and the Seven Cardinal Virtues* (NavPress, 1998), p. 71.

15. "On Restraining Anger," Arthur Richard Shilleto, tr., *Plutarch's Morals* (George Bell and Sons, 1888), p. 273.

16. "Epistles," 1: 2, *The Complete Works of Horace* with a literal translation (David McKay, 1952), pp. 370–71.

17. "Erinyes," Grimal, *Penguin Dictionary of Classical Mythology*, pp. 142–43.

18. Plutarch, *Roman Apophthegms: Caesar Augustus*, John Bartlett, *The Shorter Bartlett's Familiar Quotations*, ed. Christopher Morley (Pocket, 1965), p. 295.

19. Book 3, section 9, Seneca, *Moral Essays*, vol. 1, p. 277.

20. Chapter 12, Robert Bolton, *People Skills* (Touchstone, 1986), p. 211.

21. "Anger," Roy B. Zuck, *The Speaker's Quote Book* (Kregel, 1997), p. 14.

22. Chapter 5, Mary Margaret Funk, *Thoughts Matter* (Continuum, 1998), p. 78.

23. Book 3, section 11, Seneca, *Moral Essays*, vol. 1, p. 283.

24. Chapter 5, James Davison Hunter, *Culture Wars* (Basic, 1991), pp. 138–41.

25. "26 January 1895," *Pages from the Goncourt Journal*, ed. Robert Baldick (Penguin, 1984), pp. 398–99.

26. Desiderius Erasmus, *Praise of Folly*, tr. Betty Radice (Penguin, 1993), p. 7.

27. "13 July 1943," Anne Frank, *The Diary of a Young Girl*, ed. Otto H. Frank and Mirjam Pressler, tr. Susan Massotty (Doubleday, 1995), p. 113.

28. "29 July 1943," ibid., p. 120.

29. Section 45, Donald Keene, tr., *Essays in Idleness: The Tsurezuregusa of Kenkō* (Columbia University Press, 1967), p. 40.

30. "Of Anger," *Francis Bacon: A Selection of His Works*, ed. Sidney Warhaft (Odyssey, 1965), p. 188.

31. Part 1: "Developmental Phases of Marriage," Paul Plattner, *Conflict and Understanding in Marriage*, tr. John R. Bodo (John Knox, 1970), p. 61.

32. Book 1, Homer, *The Iliad*, p. 15.

33. *Travels into Several Remote Nations of the World . . . by Lemuel Gulliver*, part 1, chapter 4, *The Portable Swift*, ed. Carl Van Doren (Viking, 1963), p. 246.

34. G. Stanley Hall, "A Study of Anger," *American Journal of Psychology*, 10, 1899, p. 565. Quoted in chapter 3, Tavris, *Anger: The Misunderstood Emotion*, pp. 71–72.

35. "Selflessness," Wendy Beckett, *A Child's Book of Prayer in Art* (Dorling Kindersley, 1995), pp. 28–29.

36. W. H. Auden and Louis Kronenberger, comps., *Viking Book of Aphorisms* (Penguin, 1981), p. 18.

37. Book 8, Marcus Aurelius Antoninus, *The Meditations*, tr. G. M. A. Grube (Bobbs-Merrill, 1975), p. 74.

38. "Part 5: 2," Gilbert Highet, *The Anatomy of Satire* (Princeton University Press, 1972), p. 236.

39. Chapter 1, Roger Greenacre and Jeremy Haselock, *The Sacrament of Easter* (Eerdmans, 1995), p. 11. Cf. chapter 9, Joseph Martos, *Doors to the Sacred*, revised (Liguori, 2001) pp. 278–91.

40. Chapter 5, Stephen Williams and Gerard Friell, *Theodosius: The Empire at Bay* (Yale University Press, 1994), pp. 67–70.

41. "Reflections," *The Poetry and Prose of Heinrich Heine*, ed. Frederic Ewen (Citadel, 1959), p. 488.

42. "On the Pleasure of Hating," William Hazlitt, *Selected Writings*, ed. Ronald Blythe (Penguin, 1970), p. 405.

43. "I: The Manner of Kings," story 21, Edward Rehatsek, tr., *The Gulistan or Rose Garden of Sa'di*, ed. W. G. Archer (George Allen & Unwin, 1964), pp. 97–98.

44. Canto 16: 16–21, Dante Alighieri, *The Divine Comedy: Purgatorio*, tr. Charles S. Singleton (Princeton University Press, 1982), pp. 167–69 and p. 343 in commentary.

45. Stanza 5, *The Metaphysical Poets*, ed. Helen Gardner (Penguin, 1970), p. 34.

46. Chapter 10, Roland H. Bainton, *Here I Stand: A Life of Martin Luther* (New American Library, 1950), p. 144.

47. Author's note, Aleksandr I. Solzhenitsyn, *The Gulag Archipelago 1918–1956*, abr. Edward E. Ericson Jr. (Perennial, 2002), p. xxiii.

48. Book 1, chapter 16, John Bartlett, *Familiar Quotations*, 14th ed., revised and enlarged, ed. Emily Morison Beck (Little, Brown and Company, 1968), p. 170.

49. "Mutual Forbearance," *The Poetical Works of William Cowper,* 4th ed., ed. H. S. Mitford (Oxford University Press, 1934), p. 316.

50. Leo Tolstoy, *Walk in the Light and Twenty-Three Tales,* tr. Louise and Aylmer Maude (Plough, 1998), pp. 69–77.

51. "Christian Morals," part 1, section 15, *The Prose of Sir Thomas Browne,* ed. Norman Endicott (Norton, 1972), p. 376.

52. "1960," Dag Hammarskjöld, *Markings,* tr. Leif Sjöberg and W. H. Auden (Ballantine, 1993), p. 173.

53. William Roper, "The Life of Sir Thomas More," *Two Early Tudor Lives,* ed. Richard S. Sylvester and Davis P. Harding (Yale University Press, 1975), pp. 197, 250. Cf. Miroslav Volf, "A Politician for All Seasons," *Christian Century* (13 December 2000), p. 1306.

54. Chapter 3, Alan Paton, *Instrument of Thy Peace,* revised (Ballantine, 1989), p. 12.

Chapter 8: Violence Begets More Violence

1. Quoted in Dun J. Li, *The Ageless Chinese: A History,* 2nd ed. (Charles Scribner's Sons, 1971), p. 250.

2. "Cellini, Benvenuto," J. R. Hale, ed., *A Concise Encyclopedia of the Italian Renaissance* (Oxford University Press, 1981), p. 77.

3. Benvenuto Cellini, *Autobiography,* tr. George Bull (Penguin, 1980), p. 76.

4. Book 1, section 17, Baldesar Castiglione, *The Book of the Courtier,* tr. Charles S. Singleton (Anchor, 1959), pp. 32–33.

5. Collage of lines taken from "The Sentry," *"Dulce Et Decorum Est,"* "The Show," "Strange Meeting," "Anthem for Doomed Youth," *The Penguin Book of First World War Poetry,* 2nd ed., ed. John Silkin (Penguin, 1981), pp. 180–202.

6. Chapter 4, section 4, Edmund Burke, *Reflections on the Revolution in France,* ed. Thomas H. D. Mahoney (Bobbs-Merrill, 1955), p. 66.

7. "Introduction," Louis I. Bredvold and Ralph G. Ross, eds., *The Philosophy of Edmund Burke: A Selection* (University of Michigan Press, 1977), p. 6.

8. Ibid., p. 5.

9. Chapter 10, section 1, Burke, *Reflections on the Revolution in France,* p. 162.

10. Chapter 9, Richard Abanes, *American Militias* (InterVarsity, 1996), pp. 98–109.

11. "Introduction," ibid., p. 1.

12. Chapter 5, ibid., p. 50.

13. Chapter 13, Mark Arnold-Forster, *The World at War* (New American Library, 1974), pp. 272–73.

14. Walter Van Tilburg Clark, *The Ox-Bow Incident* (New American Library, 1960).

15. Section 18, Lewis A. Coser, ed., *Sociology through Literature,* 2nd ed. (Prentice-Hall, 1972), p. 430.

16. "The Crowd," Elias Canetti, *Crowds and Power,* tr. Carol Stewart (Penguin, 1973), pp. 18–21.

17. Book 1, chapter 2, Gustave Le Bon, *The Crowd* (Viking, 1969), p. 41.

18. Robert K. Merton, "Introduction," ibid., p. x.

19. "Michael Kohlhaas," *German Romantic Novellas,* ed. Frank G. Ryder and Robert M. Browning (Continuum, 1985), p. 39.

20. Chapter 1, Aldous Huxley, *Ends and Means* (Harper & Brothers, 1937), p. 10.

21. Vol. 1, chapter 15, Edward Gibbon, *The History of the Decline and Fall of the Roman Empire,* vol. 1, ed. David Womersley (Penguin, 1995), p. 446.

22. "Why Another Crusade?" *The World's Famous Orations,* vol. 7, ed. William Jennings Bryan (Funk and Wagnalls, 1906), p. 21.

23. Book 1, chapter 27, Fulcher of Chartres, *A History of the Expedition to Jerusalem, 1095–1127,* ed. Harold S. Fink, tr. Frances Rita Ryan (Norton, 1973), p. 122.

24. Quoted in chapter 5, Thomas A. Idinopulos, *Jerusalem Blessed, Jerusalem Cursed* (Ivan Dee, 1991), pp. 167–68.

25. "The Faerie Queene," Part 1:4, stanzas 33–34, *Edmund Spenser's Poetry,* ed. Hugh MacLean (Norton, 1968), p. 47.

26. *In Front of Your Nose: 1945–1950,* ed. Sonia Orwell and Ian Angus (Harcourt Brace Jovanovich, 1968), p. 136.

27. Ibid., p. 137.

28. Conclusion, Tia M. Kolbaba, *The Byzantine Lists: Errors of the Latins* (University of Illinois Press, 2000), pp. 163–71.

29. Canto 16, lines 109–10, Dante Alighieri, *The Divine Comedy: Purgatorio,* tr. Charles S. Singleton (Princeton University Press, 1982), p. 175.

30. *Summa Theologica,* 2, question 11, article 3, *Basic Documents in Medieval History,* ed. Norton Downs (Van Nostrand, 1959), p. 116.

31. Chapter 8, Stuart Babbage, *The Mark of Cain* (Eerdmans, 1966), p. 126.

32. Quoted in chapter 5, John Emerich Edward Dalberg Acton, *Essays on Freedom and Power* (Meridian, 1959), p. 123.

33. *Epistolae,* quoted in chapter 4, Roland H. Bainton, *The Travail of Religious Liberty* (Harper & Brothers, 1958), p. 114.

34. Lectures 14 and 15, William James, *The Varieties of Religious Experience* (New American Library, 1958), p. 264.

35. Part 3, canto 3, lines 547–48, Samuel Butler, *Hudibras,* ed. John Wilders (Oxford University Press, 1967), p. 293.

36. E. H. Palmer, tr., "The Parrot of Bagdad," *The Rubáiyát of Omar Khayyám and Other Persian Poems,* ed. A. J. Arberry (J. M. Dent & Sons, 1954), p. 122.

37. Edwin Muir, *Selected Poems,* ed. T. S. Eliot (Faber & Faber, 1965), p. 80.

38. Quoted in chapter 1, Carol Tavris, *Anger: The Misunderstood Emotion,* revised (Touchstone, 1989), p. 28.

39. "The Prince," chapter 14, *The Portable Machiavelli,* tr. and ed. Peter Bondanella and Mark Musa (Penguin, 1979), p. 124.

40. Quoting from a combination of Chuang Tzu and Leih Tzu, part 1, Arthur Waley, *Three Ways of Thought in Ancient China* (Anchor, 1956), p. 11. Cf. chapter 2, Burton Watson, tr., *The Complete Works of Chuang Tzu* (Columbia University Press, 1968), p. 41.

41. Chapter 5, Martin Luther King Jr., *Why We Can't Wait* (New American Library, 1964), p. 78.

42. Ibid., pp. 83–4.

43. "Sertorius," Plutarch, *The Lives of the Noble Grecians and Romans,* tr. John Dryden, rev. Arthur Hugh Clough (Modern Library, n.d.), p. 688.

44. "Speech on Moving His Resolutions for Conciliation with the Colonies," 22 March 1775, *Edmund Burke: Selected Writings and Speeches,* ed. Peter J. Stanlis (Anchor, 1963), p. 181.

45. "Patience, Patience," quoted in "Rilke, Part II," Gabriel Marcel, *Homo Viator,* tr. Emma Craufurd (Harper & Row, 1965), p. 264. Cf. "Palm," *An Anthology of French Poetry from Nerval to Valery,* revised, ed. Angel Flores (Anchor, 1958), pp. 284, 442.

46. Chapter 2, section 10, Jean-Pierre de Caussade, *Abandonment to Divine Providence,* tr. John Beevers (Doubleday, 1975), p. 50.

47. Chapter 2, section 11, ibid., p. 54.

48. "1956," Dag Hammarskjöld, *Markings,* tr. Leif Sjoberg and W. H. Auden (Ballantine, 1993), p. 121.

49. *Treatise on Unity* in *Modern Islamic Literature from 1800 to the Present,* ed. James Kritzeck (New American Library, 1970), p. 66.

50. *The Literary Works of Abraham Lincoln,* ed. David D. Anderson (Charles E. Merrill Publishing, 1970), p. 269.

Chapter 9: Avarice, the Gleaming Deception

1. Walter Jerrold, ed., *The Complete Poetical Works of Thomas Hood* (Oxford University Press, 1911), p. 600.

2. Stave 1, Charles Dickens, *A Christmas Carol* (Airmont, 1963), pp. 9, 20, 13, 17.

3. Ibid., p. 10.

4. Honoré de Balzac, *Eugénie Grandet,* tr. Marion Ayton Crawford (Penguin, 1971), p. 51.

5. Chapter 1, F. Scott Fitzgerald, *The Great Gatsby* (Charles Scribner's Sons, 1953), p. 5.

6. Chapter 14, Matthew Josephson, *The Robber Barons* (Harcourt, Brace & World, 1962), pp. 332–41.

7. Chapter 15, J. P. Sullivan, tr., *Petronius: The Satyricon and Seneca: The Apocolocyntosis* (Penguin, 1981), pp. 48–55.

8. "How Much Land Does a Man Need?" Leo Tolstoy, *The Raid and Other Stories,* tr. Louise and Aylmer Maude (Oxford University Press, 1982), pp. 213–27.

9. *Travels into Several Remote Nations of the World . . . by Lemuel Gulliver,* part 4, chapter 12, *The Portable Swift,* ed. Carl Van Doren (Viking, 1963), p. 526.

10. Chapter 16, D. K. Fieldhouse, *The Colonial Empires* (Dell, 1971), p. 373.

11. A. E. Taylor, tr., *Laws,* book 5, *The Collected Dialogues of Plato,* ed. Edith Hamilton and Huntington Cairns (Princeton University Press, 1989), p. 1327.

12. Ambrose Bierce, *The Devil's Dictionary* (Dover, 1958), p. 53.

13. Book 1, chapter 10, part 2, Adam Smith, *The Wealth of Nations* (Penguin, 1980), p. 232.

14. Part 4, Christopher Tunnard and Henry Hope Reed, *American Skyline* (New American Library, 1956), pp. 95–96.

15. Part 2, chapter 1, Gontran de Poncins, *Kabloona* (Time-Life, 1980), p. 106.

16. Cf. Eric Schlosser, *Fast Food Nation* (Houghton Mifflin, 2001).

17. "Of Vanity," book 3, chapter 9, Donald M. Frame, tr., *The Complete Essays of Montaigne* (Stanford University Press, 1979), p. 758.

18. Sections 5, 33, 34, *The Social Teachings of the Church,* ed. Anne Freemantle (New American Library, 1963), pp. 23, 44, 46.

19. Chapter 4, section 42, Gaius Suetonius Tranquillus, *The Twelve Caesars,* revised, tr. Robert Graves, rev. Michael Grant (Penguin, 1987), p. 175.

20. "El Dorado," Alberto Manguel and Gianni Guadalupi, *The Dictionary of Imaginary Places,* expanded (Harcourt Brace Jovanovich, 1987), p. 108.

21. Part 3, section 1, Robert Burton, *The Anatomy of Melancholy,* ed. Holbrook Jackson (Vintage, 1977), p. 19.

22. Chapter 6, *The Broken Spears: The Aztec Account of the Conquest of Mexico,* ed. Miguel Leon-Portilla (Beacon, 1962), pp. 51–52.

23. Chapter 7, Helen de Borchgrave, *A Journey into Christian Art* (Fortress, 2000), pp. 131–32.

24. Chapter 4, Roland H. Bainton, *Here I Stand: A Life of Martin Luther* (New American Library, 1950), pp. 58–60.

25. "Moral Thoughts and Reflections," *Halifax: Complete Works,* ed. J. P. Kenyon (Penguin, 1969), p. 226.

26. Part 1, Joseph Gallagher, *To Hell and Back with Dante* (Triumph, 1996), pp. 44–45.

27. John T. Noonan Jr., "Bribery," *Westminster Dictionary of Christian Ethics,* ed. James F. Childress and John Macquarrie (Westminster, 1986), p. 66.

28. "The Spectator," no. 239 (4 December 1711), Joseph Addison and Richard Steele, *Selec-*

tions from the Tatler and the Spectator, 2nd ed., ed. Robert J. Allen (Holt, Rinehart and Winston, 1970), p. 345.

29. Section 2, Athanasius, *The Life of Antony and The Letter to Marcellinus,* tr. Robert C. Gregg (Paulist, 1980), p. 31.

30. Chapter 4, Omer Englebert, *Saint Francis of Assisi: A Biography,* 2nd ed., revised and augmented, tr. Eve Marie Cooper (Servant, 1979), p. 43.

31. "The Testament," *Francis of Assisi: The Saint,* ed. Regis Armstrong, J. A. Wayne Hellman, and William J. Short (New City Press, 1999), p. 125.

32. "The Later Rule," ibid., p. 103.

33. Chapter 2, Henry David Thoreau, *Walden; or, Life in the Woods* (New American Library, 1960), p. 66.

34. "Letter to Menoeceus," Epicurus, *Letters, Principal Doctrines, and Vatican Sayings,* tr. Russel M. Geer (Bobbs-Merrill, 1964), p. 56.

35. "Wealth," *The Complete Essays and Other Writings of Ralph Waldo Emerson,* ed. Brooks Atkinson (Modern Library, 1940), p. 703.

36. Chapter 12, Charles Dickens, *David Copperfield* (Modern Library, 1950), p. 185.

37. Moses Hadas, ed., *The Complete Plays of Aristophanes* (Bantam, 1971), pp. 120–22.

38. Atkinson, ed., *Complete Essays and Other Writings of Ralph Waldo Emerson,* p. 710.

39. Chapter 8, Dom Helder Camara, *Revolution through Peace,* tr. Amparo McLean (Harper & Row, 1971), pp. 142–43.

40. Robert Baldick, tr. and ed., *Pages from the Goncourt Journal* (Penguin, 1984), p. 136.

41. Book 2, chapter 3, Victor Hugo, *Les Misérables,* tr. Lee Fahnestock and Norman MacAfee (New American Library, 1987), p. 76.

42. Book 2, chapter 12, ibid., p. 105.

43. "Generosity," Donald De Marco, *The Heart of Virtue* (Ignatius, 1996), pp. 77–79.

44. "Miscellanea Hibernica," section 5, Kuno Meyer, *University of Illinois Studies in Language and Literature,* 2:4, (November 1916) pp. 24–25.

45. Section 10, "Babette's Feast," Isak Dinesen, *Anecdotes of Destiny and Ehrengard* (Vintage, 1993), p. 51.

46. Isobel Murray, ed., *Oscar Wilde* (Oxford University Press, 1989), pp. 28–35.

47. Book 2, Thomas More, *Utopia,* tr. Robert M. Adams (Norton, 1975), p. 58.

48. Quoted in chapter 5, David Batson, *The Treasure Chest of the Early Christians* (Eerdmans, 2001), p. 64. Cf. Tertullian, *Apology,* chapter 39.

49. Ibid., p. 68.

50. "The Parson's Tale," Geoffrey Chaucer, *The Canterbury Tales,* tr. Ronald L. Ecker and Eugene J. Crook (Hodge & Braddock, 1993), p. 551. Cf. book 1, chapter 10, Augustine, *The City of God,* tr. Henry Bettenson (Penguin, 1984), pp. 17–20.

51. "Man the Reformer," *The Portable Emerson,* ed. Mark Van Doren (Viking, 1965), p. 76.

52. Letter 127, F. A. Wright, tr., *Selected Letters of St. Jerome* (Heinemann, 1933), p. 445.

Chapter 10: The Workaholic

1. *Technics and Civilization,* "The Monastery and the Clock," *Of Men and Machines,* ed. Arthur O. Lewis Jr. (Dutton, 1963), p. 61.

2. *Travels into Several Remote Nations of the World . . . by Lemuel Gulliver,* part 1, chapter 2, *The Portable Swift,* ed. Carl Van Doren (Viking, 1963), p. 230.

3. *Society and Solitude,* "Works and Days," *Of Men and Machines,* ed. Lewis Jr., p. 68.

4. Chapter 8, Gerald Mast, *The Comic Mind,* 2nd ed. (University of Chicago Press, 1979), pp. 110–12.

5. Chapter 4, E. F. Schumacher, *Small Is Beautiful* (Harper & Row, 1975), pp. 54–55.

6. Chapter 7, section 5: 5, Thomas Aquinas, *Summa Theologiae: A Concise Translation,* ed. Timothy McDermott (Christian Classics, 1989), p. 181.

7. Chapter 48, *RB 1980: The Rule of St. Benedict,* ed. Timothy Fry (Liturgical, 1981), p. 249.

8. M. Dodds, tr., *The City of God,* book 19, chapter 19, *Basic Writings of Saint Augustine,* vol. 2, ed. Whitney J. Oates (Baker, 1980), p. 495.

9. *B. Ber.* 43b, *The Book of Legends,* ed. Hayim Nahman Bialik and Yehoshua Hana Ravnitzky, tr. William G. Braude (Schocken, 1992), p. 608.

10. Book 3, section 55, Origen, *Contra Celsum,* tr. Henry Chadwick (Cambridge University Press, 1980), p. 165.

11. Carl Sandburg, *Harvest Poems: 1910–1960* (Harcourt, Brace & World, 1960), p. 35.

12. *B. Kid.* 29a, Bialik and Ravnitzky, eds., *Book of Legends,* p. 608.

13. Chapter 5, William Langland, *Piers the Ploughman,* tr. J. F. Goodridge (Penguin, 1974), p. 67.

14. Canto 30, lines 58 ff., Dante Alighieri, *The Divine Comedy: Inferno,* tr. Charles S. Singleton (Princeton University Press, 1980), pp. 555–56 commentary.

15. Chapter 3, "The Journal of John Woolman," *Quaker Spirituality: Selected Writings,* ed. Douglas V. Steere (Paulist, 1984), pp. 176–77.

16. Schumacher, *Small Is Beautiful,* p. 58.

17. Chapter 2, Søren Kierkegaard, *Christian Discourses, Etc.,* tr. Walter Lowrie (Princeton University Press, 1971), p. 27.

18. "Materialism," David W. Bercot, ed., *A Dictionary of Early Christian Beliefs* (Hendrickson, 1998), p. 441.

19. Untitled poem, *The New Oxford Book of English Verse: 1250–1950,* ed. Helen Gardner (Oxford University Press, 1972), p. 507.

20. Chapter 8, Lewis Carroll, *Alice's Adventures in Wonderland* and *Through the Looking-Glass* (New American Library, 1962), p. 206.

21. Commentators argue about whether the Greek word *skepasmata* includes shelter. Cf. J. N. D. Kelly, *The Pastoral Epistles* (Hendrickson, 1960), p. 137.

22. Chapter 55, *RB 1980: Rule of St. Benedict,* ed. Timothy Fry, pp. 263–65.

23. "Economic Possibilities for Our Grandchildren," John Maynard Keynes, *Essays in Persuasion* (Norton, 1963), p. 365.

24. "Mencius," Arthur Waley, *Three Ways of Thought in Ancient China* (Anchor, 1956), p. 123. Cf. part 3, section 25, "Moderation in Funerals," Burton Watson, tr., *Mo Tzu: Basic Writings* (Columbia University Press, 1963), p. 67.

25. Chapter 5, Juliet B. Schor, *The Overworked American* (Basic, 1991), p. 110.

26. Part 5, chapter 1, section 4, Adam Smith, *The Theory of Moral Sentiments,* ed. D. D. Raphael and A. L. MacFie (Oxford University Press, 1976), p. 195.

27. Chapter 3, Leigh Eric Schmidt, *Consumer Rites: The Buying and Selling of American Holidays* (Princeton University Press, 1997), pp. 123, 130, 134, 152, 156.

28. Chapter 7, Stanford M. Lyman, *The Seven Deadly Sins: Society and Evil,* revised and expanded (General Hall, 1989), p. 236.

29. Schmidt, *Consumer Rites,* pp. 126–27.

30. Thomas of Celano, "The Life of Saint Francis," book 1, chapter 30, *Francis of Assisi: The Saint,* ed. Regis J. Armstrong, J. A. Wayne Hellman, and William J. Short (New City, 1999), pp. 254–56.

31. Dietrich Bonhoeffer, *The Mystery of Holy Night,* ed. Manfred Weber, tr. Peter Heinegg (Crossroad, 1996), p. 2. Cf. "28 Nov. 1943," Dietrich Bonhoeffer, *Letters and Papers from Prison,* enlarged, ed. Eberhard Bethge (Macmillan, 1974), p. 152.

32. Ibid., p. 17.

33. Quoted in Lyman, *Seven Deadly Sins,* p. 235.

34. Quoted in chapter 5, Max Weber, *The Protestant Ethic and the Spirit of Capitalism,* tr. Talcott Parsons (Charles Scribner's Sons, 1958), p. 175.

35. Chapter 7, J. N. D. Kelly, *Golden Mouth: The Story of John Chrysostom* (Cornell University Press, 1995), p. 98.

36. Part 2, chapter 3, Francois Vandenbroucke, "The Franciscan Spring," Jean LeClercq, Francois Vandenbroucke, and Louis Bouyer, *The Spirituality of the Middle Ages,* tr. Benedictines of Holme Eden Abbey in Carlisle (Seabury, 1968), p. 296.

37. "The Tulipomania," Charles Mackay, *Extraordinary Popular Delusions and the Madness of Crowds* (Three Rivers, 1980), pp. 92–101.

38. Lyman, *Seven Deadly Sins,* p. 249. Cf. chapter 1, Lewis A. Coser, *Greedy Institutions* (Free Press, 1974), pp. 4–6.

39. "On Lying in Bed," *The Idler's Companion,* ed. Tom Hodgkinson and Matthew DeAbaitua (Ecco, 1997), p. 58.

40. "'Tis the Gift to Be Simple," *Hymnbook 1982* (Church Hymnal Corporation, 1985), no. 554.

41. Chapter 2, Alexander Findlay, *A Hundred Years of Chemistry,* 3rd ed., rev. Trevor I. Williams (Methuen, 1965), pp. 39–40.

42. Chapter 3, Evelyn Underhill, *Mysticism* (New American Library, 1955), p. 50.

43. "The Garden," *Marvell,* ed. Joseph H. Summers (Dell, 1961), p. 102.

43a. Chapter 2, Richard J. Foster, *Celebration of Discipline,* rev. ed. (Harper & Row, 1988), p. 27.

44. "Preface to Lyrical Ballads," William Wordsworth, *The Prelude, Selected Poems and Sonnets,* revised and enlarged, ed. Carlos Baker (Holt, Rinehart and Winston, 1954), p. 25.

45. "Daffodils," *New Oxford Book of English Verse: 1250–1950,* ed. Gardner, p. 506.

46. Chapter 4, James A. Nash, *Loving Nature* (Abingdon, 1991), p. 112. Cf. lecture 19, William Temple, *Nature, Man and God* (Macmillan, 1940), pp. 493–95.

47. Section 16, "Religio Medici," *The Prose of Sir Thomas Browne,* ed. Norman Endicott (Norton, 1972), p. 21.

48. Quoted in chapter 8, Kelly James Clark, *When Faith Is Not Enough* (Eerdmans, 1997), p. 133.

49. Thomas Mann, *Death in Venice and Seven Other Stories,* tr. H. T. Lowe-Porter (Vintage, 1936), pp. 9–12.

50. Quoted in chapter 1, Josef Pieper, *Leisure: The Basis of Culture,* tr. Alexander Dru (New American Library, 1963), p. 20.

51. "Spiritual Maxims," Brother Lawrence of the Resurrection, *Writings and Conversations on the Practice of the Presence of God,* tr. Salvatore Sciurba (ICS Publications, 1994), p. 43.

52. "Letter 2," ibid., p. 54.

53. "Letter 1," ibid., p. 49.

54. "Spiritual Maxims," ibid., p. 35.

55. "Second Conversation," ibid., p. 93.

56. "Fourth Conversation," ibid., p. 97.

57. Book 5, no. 308, Angelus Silesius, *The Cherubinic Wanderer,* tr. Maria Shrady (Paulist, 1986), p. 122.

58. "Our Lady's Tumbler," Eugene Mason, tr., *Aucassin and Nicolette and Other Medieval Romances and Legends* (Dutton, 1958), pp. 59–73.

59. "Prayer of the Teats," Alexander Carmichael, *Carmina Gadelica: Hymns and Incantations,* ed. C. J. Moore (Lindisfarne, 1992), pp. 344–45.

60. "Reaping Blessing," ibid., p. 98.

61. Quoted in chapter 1, S. I. Hayakawa, *Language in Thought and Action,* 3rd ed. (Harcourt Brace Jovanovich, 1972), p. 8.

62. Chapter 5, G. K. Chesterton, *Saint Francis of Assisi* (Image, 1990), p. 75.

63. Quoted in chapter 12, Charles Norris Cochrane, *Christianity and Classical Culture* (Oxford University Press, 1968), p. 504.

64. Chapter 6, C. S. Lewis, *The Four Loves* (Harcourt Brace Jovanovich, 1960), p. 180.

65. Chapter 6, "Of Worldly Goods," Jean de La Bruyère, *Characters*, tr. Jean Stewart (Penguin, 1970), p. 102.

Chapter 11: Lust: From Attraction to Commitment

1. *The Forsythe Saga*, quoted in chapter 5, Stuart Babbage, *Sex and Sanity* (Westminster, 1965), p. 48.

2. "The New Morality," *Time* (21 November 1977), p. E12.

3. Mary Stewart Van Leeuwen, "Deconstructing the Culture of Divorce," *Christian Century* (30 July–6 August 1997), pp. 690–91.

4. Chapter 21, Judith S. Wallerstein, Julia M. Lewis, and Sandra Blakeslee, *The Unexpected Legacy of Divorce* (Hyperion, 2000), pp. 289–93.

5. Chapter 5, Solomon Schimmel, *The Seven Deadly Sins* (Free Press, 1992), pp. 111–12.

6. "Introduction," Wallerstein, Lewis, and Blakeslee, *Unexpected Legacy of Divorce*, pp. xxiii–xxiv.

7. Book 4, no. 79, Angelus Silesius, *The Cherubinic Wanderer*, tr. Maria Shrady (Paulist, 1986), p. 92.

8. Chapter 5, C. S. Lewis, *The Four Loves* (Harcourt Brace Jovanovich, 1960), p. 143.

9. Sections 45–47, Athanasius, *The Life of Antony and the Letter of Marcellinus*, tr. Robert C. Gregg (Paulist, 1980), pp. 65–67.

10. "To Eustochium," A.D. 384, *Letters from Saints to Sinners*, ed. John Cumming (Crossroad, 1996), p. 68.

11. Chapter 2, William Graham Cole, *Sex in Christianity and Psychoanalysis* (Oxford University Press, 1966), p. 62. Cf. Augustine, *City of God*, book 15, chapter 26.

12. Chapter 12, Maureen Fielder and Linda Rabben, eds., *Rome Has Spoken . . .* (Crossroad, 1998), pp. 138–39.

13. Luther felt celibacy was still the most desirable state, but recognized it to be a rare gift that could not be forced. Cf. chapter 5, Erik H. Erikson, *Young Man Luther* (Norton, 1962), p. 162.

14. Cf. opening statements, "The Celebration and Blessing of a Marriage," *The Book of Common Prayer*.

15. "Tetrachordon," *The Works of John Milton*, vol. 4, ed. Chilton Latham Powell (Columbia University Press, 1931), p. 83.

16. "Ein Fichtenbaum steht einsam," *The Penguin Book of German Verse*, revised, ed. Leonard Forster (Penguin, 1959), p. 328.

17. N. K. Gottwald, "Song of Songs," *The Interpreter's Dictionary of the Bible*, vol. 4, ed. George Buttrick (Abingdon, 1962), p. 425.

18. Chapter 2, Thorleif Boman, *Hebrew Thought Compared with Greek*, tr. Jules L. Moreau (Norton, 1970), p. 82.

19. "Elegy 19," John Donne, *The Complete English Poems*, ed. A. J. Smith (Penguin, 1986), pp. 124–26.

20. Chapter 8, section 5, Max Lerner, *America as a Civilization* (Simon & Schuster, 1957), p. 590.

21. Book 6, section 3, Denis de Rougemont, *Love in the Western World*, revised and augmented, tr. Montgomery Belgion (Harper & Row, 1974), p. 282.

22. Book 2, chapter 8, Andreas Capellanus, *The Art of Courtly Love*, tr. John Jay Parry (Norton, 1969), p. 186.

23. Part 1, section 9, Gustave Flaubert, *Madame Bovary*, tr. Paul de Man (Norton, 1965), p. 48.

24. Part 1, section 7, ibid., p. 29.

25. Chapter 4, Robert N. Bellah, Richard Madsen, William M. Sullivan, Ann Swidler, and Steven M. Tipton, *Habits of the Heart*, updated (University of California Press, 1996), p. 98.

26. Francois Truffaut, *The Story of Adele H.,* ed. Helen C. Scott (Grove, 1976), p. 152.

27. Ibid., pp. 183–84.

28. "Catullus, Gaius Valerius," *The Reader's Companion to World Literature,* ed. Lillian Herlands Hornstein (New American Library, 1956), p. 81.

29. No. 70, Carl Sesar, tr., *Selected Poems of Catullus* (Mason & Lipscomb, 1974).

30. Anonymous, "Mass of Love," *Translations from Hispanic Poets.* tr. Anna Pursche (Hispanic Society of America, 1938), pp. 27–28.

31. Chapter 16, "The Blushful Mystery," H. L. Mencken, *Prejudices: First Series* (Knopf, 1921), p. 200.

32. No. 130, William Shakespeare, *The Sonnets,* ed. William Burto (New American Library, 1964), p. 170.

33. Chapter 26, William James, *The Principles of Psychology,* vol. 2 (Dover, 1950), pp. 564–66. Cf. chapter 10, Rollo May, *Love and Will* (Dell, 1974), p. 269.

34. Chapter 9, Stuart Babbage, *The Mark of Cain* (Eerdmans, 1966), p. 144.

35. Chapter 1, May, *Love and Will,* p. 29.

36. Chapter 11, Linda J. Waite and Maggie Gallagher, *The Case for Marriage* (Broadway, 2000), pp. 150–60.

37. Key passages are put in chronological order in chapter 7, *The Oxford Book of Marriage,* ed. Helge Rubinstein (Oxford University Press, 1990), pp. 216–24, quotations from pp. 219, 223.

38. Betty Radice, tr., *The Letters of Abelard and Heloise* (Penguin, 1974), p. 65.

39. "8 July 1892," *Pages from the Goncourt Journal,* tr. and ed. Robert Baldick (Penguin, 1984), p. 377.

40. Book 6, chapter 19, John Cassian, *The Monastic Institutes,* tr. Jerome Bertram (Saint Austin, 1999), p. 104.

41. Radice, tr., *Letters of Abelard and Heloise,* p. 67.

42. *The Ethics,* chapter 3, *Medieval Philosophy,* ed. Herman Shapiro (Modern Library, 1964), p. 148.

43. Loc. cit.

44. Chapter 6, R. E. O. White, *Christian Ethics* (John Knox, 1981), p. 121.

45. *The Ethics,* chapter 13, *Medieval Philosophy,* ed. Shapiro, p. 164.

46. Book 1, 1723–1728, Jean-Jacques Rousseau, *The Confessions,* tr. J. M. Cohen (Penguin, 1973), p. 44.

47. "Apology for Raymond Sebond," book 2, chapter 12, Donald M. Frame, tr., *Montaigne's Essays and Selected Writings* (St. Martin's, 1963), p. 245.

48. Quoted in chapter 5, Rubinstein, ed., *Oxford Book of Marriage,* pp. 148–49.

49. Quoted in chapter 3, Roland H. Bainton, *What Christianity Says about Sex, Love, and Marriage* (Association, 1957), pp. 68–69.

50. Chapter 6, Oscar E. Feucht, ed., *Sex and the Church* (Concordia, 1961), p. 81.

51. Chapter 6, G. S. Kirk and J. E. Raven, *The Presocratic Philosophers* (Cambridge University Press, 1977), pp. 196–97. Cf. Plato, *Cratylus,* 402a.

52. Quoted in part 1, "The Developmental Phases of Marriage," Paul Plattner, *Conflict and Understanding in Marriage,* tr. John R. Bodo (John Knox, 1970), p. 57.

53. Mark Searle and Kenneth W. Stevenson, eds., *Documents of the Marriage Liturgy* (Pueblo, 1992), p. 166.

54. Ibid., p. 215.

55. Quoted in chapter 6, Theodor Bovet, *A Handbook to Marriage* (Doubleday, 1969), p. 124.

56. Chapter 4, Waite and Gallagher, *The Case for Marriage,* pp. 55–57, 62–64.

57. Act 2, Scene 1, Joseph Stein, *Fiddler on the Roof* (Pocket, 1965), pp. 127–28.

58. Part 7, section 15, Leo Tolstoy, *Anna Karenin,* revised, tr. Rosemary Edmonds (Penguin, 1978), p. 749.

59. "Lust or *Luxuria,*" Henry Fairlie, *The Seven Deadly Sins Today* (University of Notre Dame Press, 1995), p. 181.

60. Canto 25, verse 121, Dante Alighieri, *The Divine Comedy: Purgatorio,* tr. Charles S. Singleton (Princeton University Press, 1982), p. 621 commentary.

Chapter 12: The Hedonist or Aesthete

1. Quoted in chapter 1, Howard Hibbett, *The Floating World in Japanese Fiction* (Tuttle, 1978), p. 11.

2. "The Story of Seijuro in Himeji," chapter 3, Ihara Saikaku, *Five Women Who Loved Love,* tr. William Theodore de Bary (Tuttle, 1982), pp. 56–57.

3. Quoted in chapter 6, Joan Stanley-Baker, *Japanese Art* (Thames and Hudson, 1984), p. 186.

4. Chapter 2, Hibbett, *Floating World in Japanese Fiction,* p. 32.

5. Ibid., p. 11.

6. Helen Gardner, ed., *The New Oxford Book of English Verse: 1250–1950* (Oxford University Press, 1972), p. 305.

7. "Aristippus," Diogenes Laërtius, *Lives of the Philosophers,* tr. A. Robert Caponigri (Gateway, 1969), p. 169.

8. Ibid., p. 176.

9. Ibid., pp. 172, 174.

10. Ibid., p. 177.

11. "Don Juan: Haidée," canto 2, stanza 178, *Selected Poetry and Prose of Byron,* ed. W. H. Auden (New American Library, 1966), p. 272.

12. Chapter 8, Alfred C. Kinsey, Wardell B. Pomeroy, and Clyde E. Martin, *Sexual Behavior in the Human Male* (Saunders, 1948), p. 263.

13. Part 1, Joseph Gallagher, *To Hell and Back with Dante* (Triumph, 1996), p. 15. Cf. Dante, *Inferno,* canto 5, line 43.

14. Chapter 3, Aldous Huxley, *Brave New World* (Bantam, 1962), p. 30.

15. Ibid., p. 26.

16. Lewy Olfson, ed., *Plot Outlines of 100 Famous Novels: The Second Hundred* (Dolphin, 1966), p. 135.

17. Huxley, *Brave New World,* p. 23.

18. Ibid., p. 37.

19. Chapter 14, ibid., pp. 134–41.

20. Ibid., p. 35.

21. Part 2, "The Pleasures of Opium," 1821 ed., Thomas De Quincey, *Confessions of an English Opium Eater,* ed. Alethea Hayter (Penguin, 1975), p. 72.

22. Chapters 2, 3, Philip Yancey, *Where Is God When It Hurts?* revised and updated (HarperCollins, 1996), pp. 18–26.

23. Chapter 13, Anthony Smith, *The Body,* revised (Penguin, 1986), pp. 158–59. Cf. Donald Caton, *What a Blessing She Had Chloroform: The Medical and Social Response to the Pain of Childbirth from 1800 to the Present* (Yale University Press, 1999).

24. Lecture 2, I. P. Pavlov, *Conditioned Reflexes,* tr. G. V. Anrep (Dover, 1960), pp. 29–30.

25. "On the Suffering of the World," Arthur Schopenhauer, *Essays and Aphorisms,* tr. R.J. Hollingdale (Penguin, 1981), p. 43.

26. *F. D. R.: Personal Letters 1905–1928,* ed. Elliott Roosevelt in *Franklin Delano Roosevelt,* ed. Gerald D. Nash (Prentice Hall, 1967), p. 85.

27. John P. Bradley, Leo F. Daniels, and Thomas C. Jones, comps., *The International Dictionary of Thoughts* (J. G. Ferguson Publishing, 1975), p. 18.

28. Letter to Eberhard Bethge (16 July 1944), Dietrich Bonhoeffer, *Letters and Papers from Prison,* enlarged, ed. Eberhard Bethge (Macmillan, 1974), p. 361.

29. *"Theologia crucis,"* Richard A. Muller, *Dictionary of Latin and Greek Theological Terms* (Baker, 1985), p. 300.

30. Book 8, chapter 7, John K. Ryan, tr., *The Confessions of St. Augustine* (Image, 1960), p. 194.

31. "Don Giovanni," Ernest Newman, *Great Operas,* vol. 2 (Vintage, 1958), p. 133.

32. Book 8, chapter 5, Ryan, *Confessions of St. Augustine,* p. 190.

33. Ibid., p. 188.

34. Chapter 10, John C. Burham, *Bad Habits* (New York University Press, 1993), pp. 267–72.

35. Chapter 1, F. Max Müller, tr., *Buddhism,* ed. Clarence H. Hamilton (Bobbs-Merrill, 1952), p. 65.

36. A. J. Dunning, *Extremes,* tr. Johan Theron (Harcourt Brace Jovanovich, 1992), pp. 196–97.

37. Chapters 4, 3, 23, David Riesman, *Individualism Reconsidered* (Free Press, 1965), pp. 69, 46, 379.

38. Chapter 5, Catherine Drinker Bowen, *The Lion and the Throne* (Atlantic Monthly, 1957), p. 55.

39. Chapter 3, A. H. Maslow, *The Farther Reaches of Human Nature* (Viking, 1973), pp. 41–53.

40. Dunning, *Extremes,* p. 198.

41. Arthur J. Carr, ed., *Victorian Poetry* (Holt, Rinehart and Winston, 1959), p. 340.

42. Dudley Fitts, ed., *Herbert* (Dell, 1966), p. 150.

43. Book 1, chapter 1, Ryan, *Confessions of St. Augustine,* p. 43.

44. Book 1, chapter 5, ibid., pp. 45–46.

45. Paul Shorey, tr., *Republic,* book 7, *The Collected Dialogues of Plato,* ed. Edith Hamilton and Huntington Cairns (Princeton University Press, 1989), pp. 747–49.

46. "Lonesome Valley," *Folk Song U.S.A.,* ed. Alan Lomax (New American Library, 1966), pp. 444–45.

47. Chapter 8, Huston Smith, *The World's Religions,* revised and updated (HarperCollins, 1991), p. 333.

48. "Still life," James Hall, *Dictionary of Subjects and Symbols in Art,* revised (Harper & Row, 1979), p. 291.

49. Book 12, section 32; book 5, section 33, Marcus Aurelius Antoninus, *The Meditations,* tr. G. M. A. Grube (Bobbs-Merrill, 1975), pp. 128–29, 47.

50. Leonard Forster, ed., *The Penguin Book of German Verse,* revised (Penguin, 1959), pp. 308–11.

51. "Needles have stitched a death shroud with our life thread," G. B. H. Wightman and A. Y. al-Udhari, trs., *Birds through a Ceiling of Alabaster* (Penguin, 1975), p. 114.

52. "The First Day," Giovanni Boccaccio, *The Decameron,* tr. Richard Aldington (Dell, 1974), p. 36.

53. Quoted in chapter 10, Jacques Choron, *Death and Western Thought* (Collier, 1975), p. 101.

54. "Wer wusste je das Leben recht zu fassen," *Penguin Book of German Verse,* ed. Forster, p. 320.

55. Act 3, Thornton Wilder, *Three Plays* (Bantam, 1965), p. 63.

56. Amy Mandelker and Elizabeth Powers, eds., *Pilgrim Souls* (Simon & Schuster, 1999), p. 64.

57. "The Oxen," *Selected Shorter Poems of Thomas Hardy,* ed. John Wain (Macmillan, 1972), p. 77.

58. "On Fairy-stories," epilogue, J. R. R. Tolkien, *The Tolkien Reader* (Ballantine, 1966) pp. 68–73.

Chapter 13: Gluttony, the Strong Craving

1. Meditation 21, section 102, Jean Anthelme Brillat-Savarin, *The Physiology of Taste*, tr. M. F. K. Fisher (North Point, 1986), p. 241.

2. "The House of Feasting, or, the Epicure's Measures," part 2, Jeremy Taylor, *The Sermons* (Robert Carter & Brothers, 1850), p. 122.

3. "Food," Diagram Group, *Man's Body* (Bantam, 1979), section G05.

4. "Taste," Diane Ackerman, *A Natural History of the Senses* (Random House, 1990), pp. 133–34.

5. Ibid., pp. 138–39.

6. Ibid., p. 140.

7. Book 1, canto 4, stanzas 21–23, *Edmund Spenser's Poetry*, ed. Hugh Maclean (Norton, 1968), pp. 44–45.

8. Chapter 6, Stanford M. Lyman, *The Seven Deadly Sins: Society and Evil*, revised and expanded (General Hall, 1989), p. 214.

9. Book 5, William Langland, *Piers the Ploughman*, tr. J. F. Goodridge (Penguin, 1974), p. 72.

10. Ackerman, *Natural History of the Senses*, pp. 142–43.

11. "The Emperor of Ice-Cream," Wallace Stevens, *The Collected Poems of Wallace Stevens* (Vintage, 1982), p. 64.

12. "Overture," Marcel Proust, *Swann's Way*, tr. C. K. Scott Moncrieff (Vintage, 1970), pp. 34–36.

13. Section 175, Donald Keene, tr., *Essays in Idleness: The Tsurezuregusa of Kenkō* (Columbia University Press, 1967), p. 150.

14. Quoted in chapter 1, "Sweetness and Light," Matthew Arnold, *Culture and Anarchy*, ed. J. Dover Wilson (Cambridge University Press, 1969), p. 53. Cf. Epictetus, *The Encheiridion, or Manual*, section 41.

15. Chapter 5, Evelyn Waugh, *Brideshead Revisited* (Little, Brown and Company, 1973), p. 143.

16. Book 4, Ovid, *Metamorphoses*, tr. Mary M. Innes (Penguin, 1964), pp. 95–98.

17. William M. Davis, tr., "Roistering I'll Chaff . . . ," *An Anthology of Spanish Poetry*, ed. Angel Flores (Anchor, 1961), pp. 89–90.

18. "Gargantua," book 1, *The Portable Rabelais*, tr. and ed. Samuel Putnam (Viking, 1968), pp. 69–72.

19. Chapter 4, Mikhail Bakhtin, *Rabelais and His World*, tr. Hélène Iswolsky (Indiana University Press, 1984), p. 279.

20. Nikodimos of the Holy Mountain and Makarios of Corinth, comps., *The Philokalia*, vol. 1, trs. G. E. H. Palmer, Philip Sherrard, and Kallistos Ware (Faber and Faber, 1983), p. 237.

21. Chapter 20, Paul Tillich, *The New Being* (Charles Scribner's Sons, 1955), pp. 157–58, 153.

22. Taylor, *The Sermons*, p. 122. Cf. chapter 6, Solomon Schimmel, *The Seven Deadly Sins* (Free Press, 1992), p. 144.

23. Tony Castle, ed., *The New Book of Christian Prayers* (Crossroad, 1986), p. 129.

24. Chapter 39, *RB 1980: The Rule of St. Benedict*, ed. Timothy Fry (Liturgical, 1981), p. 239.

25. "Varieties," section 12, Brillat-Savarin, *Physiology of Taste*, p. 374.

26. "Peacocks, Parsley, Princely Pie," Madeleine Pelner Cosman, *Fabulous Feasts: Medieval Cookery and Ceremony* (Braziller, 1976), pp. 39–40.

27. "Colour," André L. Simon, *A Dictionary of Wines, Spirits, and Liqueurs* (Citadel, 1963), p. 62.

28. "Letter to Posterity," *The Portable Medieval Reader*, ed. James Bruce Ross and Mary Martin McLaughlin (Viking, 1961), p. 391.

29. Lyman, *The Seven Deadly Sins*, p. 231.

30. Act 2, scene 4, lines 450–53, William Shakespeare, *The History of Henry IV (Part 1),* ed. Maynard Mack (New American Library, 1965), p. 92.

31. "Falstaff," Michael Rheta Martin and Richard C. Harrier, *The Concise Encyclopedic Guide to Shakespeare* (Discus, 1975), p. 118.

32. Act 5, scene 5, line 63, William Shakespeare, *The Second Part of Henry IV,* ed. Norman N. Holland (New American Library, 1965), p. 166.

33. *Notes on Shakespeare,* Samuel Johnson, *Selected Writings,* ed. Patrick Cruttwell (Penguin, 1968), p. 293.

34. Richard J. Clifford, *Proverbs,* OTL (Westminster/John Knox, 1999), pp. 213–14.

35. Roland E. Murphy, *Proverbs,* WBC (Thomas Nelson, 1998), p. 177.

36. Chapter 2, section 2, Jeremy Taylor, *The Rule and Exercises of Holy Living* (Longmans, Green & Co., 1941), p. 57.

37. Chapter 3, Roy F. Baumeister, *Evil: Inside Human Violence and Cruelty* (W. H. Freeman, 1997), p. 83.

38. "The Freedom of a Christian," Martin Luther, *Three Treatises,* tr. W. A. Lambert, rev. Harold J. Grimm (Fortress, 1970), p. 277.

39. Loc. cit.

40. T. E. Jessop, "Mean, Doctrine of the," *The Westminster Dictionary of Christian Ethics,* ed. James F. Childress and John Macquarrie (Westminster, 1986), p. 373.

41. Chapter 25, Moses Hayyim Luzzatto, *The Path of the Upright,* tr. Mordecai M. Kaplan (Aronson, 1995), p. 219.

42. Chapter 2, John B. Watson, *Behaviorism* (Norton, 1970), p. 28.

43. Chapter 4, William James, *The Principles of Psychology,* vol. 1 (Dover, 1950), pp. 122–27.

44. Act 3, scene 4, lines 166–69, William Shakespeare, *The Tragedy of Hamlet,* ed. Edward Hubler (New American Library, 1963), p. 122.

45. Part 2, "The Pains of Opium," 1821 ed., Thomas De Quincey, *Confessions of an English Opium Eater,* ed. Alethea Hayter (Penguin, 1975), pp. 103, 114–15.

46. "In Memoriam A. H. H.," section 1, *Alfred, Lord Tennyson: Selected Poetry,* ed. Herbert Marshall McLuhan (Holt, Rinehart and Winston, 1961), pp. 119–20.

47. *The Amateur Emigrant,* part 1, "Steerage Types," Robert Louis Stevenson, *From Scotland to Silverado,* ed. James D. Hart (Harvard University Press, 1966), p. 34.

48. Quoted in Craig Lambert, "Deep Cravings," *Harvard Magazine* (March–April 2000), p. 66.

49. James, *Principles of Psychology,* vol. 1, p. 127.

50. Richard Le Gallienne, ed., *The Diary of Samuel Pepys* (Modern Library, n.d.), p. 60.

51. Graeme M. Griffin, "Habit," *Westminster Dictionary of Christian Ethics,* ed. Childress and Macquarrie, p. 258.

52. No. 254, *Early Christian Prayers,* ed. A. Hamman, tr. Walter Mitchell (Regnery, 1961), p. 166.

Chapter 14: The Faster and Various Imitators

1. "Diogenes" (paraphrased), Diogenes Laertius, *Lives of the Philosophers,* tr. A. Robert Caponigri (Regnery, 1969), p. 138.

2. Sections 7 and 8, James A. Kleist, tr., *The Didache* (Paulist, 1948), p. 19.

3. Book 3, chapter 28, Alfred Edersheim, *The Life and Times of Jesus the Messiah,* vol. 1 (Eerdmans, 1969), p. 662.

4. Chapter 2, Adalbert de Vogüé, *To Love Fasting,* tr. Jean Baptist Hasbrouck (St. Bede's Publications, 1989), p. 27.

5. Chapter 2, Caroline Walker Bynum, *Holy Feast and Holy Fast* (University of California Press, 1988), p. 41.

6. Ibid., p. 40.

7. Chapter 15, Timothy Ware, *The Orthodox Church,* revised (Penguin, 1993), pp. 300–1.

8. Book 1, section 13, Aristotle, *The Nicomachean Ethics,* tr. J. A. K. Thompson, rev. Hugh Tredennick (Penguin, 1976), p. 94.

9. Fifth conference, section 18, Boniface Ramsey, tr., *John Cassian: The Conferences* (Paulist, 1997), p. 198–99.

10. Cleon L. Rogers Jr. and Cleon Rogers III, *The New Linguistic and Exegetical Key to the Greek New Testament* (Zondervan, 1998), p. 370.

11. Kallistos Ware, "The Way of the Ascetics: Negative or Affirmative?" *Asceticism,* ed. Vincent L. Wimbush and Richard Valantasis (Oxford University Press, 1995), p. 3.

12. "Epiphanius," Benedicta Ward, tr., *The Sayings of the Desert Fathers,* revised (Cistercian, 1984), p. 59.

13. "The Moon on the Water," *The World of Japanese Fiction,* ed. Yoshinobu Hakutani and Arthur O. Lewis (Dutton, 1973), p. 284.

14. Chapter 3, William E. Woodward, *George Washington* (Boni and Liveright, 1926), p. 33.

15. Chapter 49, *RB: 1980, The Rule of St. Benedict,* ed. Timothy Fry (Liturgical, 1981), p. 253.

16. O. H., "Fasting," *Encyclopedia Britannica,* vol. 9 (William Benton, 1960), p. 108.

17. Book 5, O. Hallesby, *Prayer,* tr. Clarence J. Carlsen (Augsburg, 1994), p. 114.

18. Chapter 2, Mary Margaret Funk, *Thoughts Matter* (Continuum, 1998), p. 34.

19. Book 4, chapter 12, section 15, John Calvin, *Institutes of the Christian Religion,* vol. 2, ed. John T. McNeill, tr. Ford Lewis Battles (Westminster, 1960), p. 1242.

20. Section 18, ibid., p. 1244.

21. Section 11, Symeon the New Theologian, *The Discourses,* tr. C. J. deCatanzaro (Paulist, 1980), p. 168.

22. Part 3, Judah Halevi, *The Kuzari,* tr. Hartwig Hirschfeld (Schocken, 1974), pp. 140–41.

23. "The Parables," section 56:7, J. B. Lightfoot and J. R. Harmer, trs., *The Apostolic Fathers,* 2nd ed., rev. Michael W. Holmes (Baker, 1992), p. 433.

24. Joan M. Nuth, "Fasting," *The New Dictionary of Catholic Spirituality,* ed. Michael Downey (Liturgical, 1993), p. 391. Cf. sermon 208, "On the Beginning of Lent," Augustine, *Sermons* III/6, ed. John E. Rotelle, tr. Edmund Hill (New City, 1993), p. 113.

25. "Taste," Diane Ackerman, *A Natural History of the Senses* (Random House, 1990), p. 135.

26. Chapter 2, G. K. Chesterton, *Orthodoxy* (Ignatius, 1995), p. 33.

27. "Jacob's Well," quoted in William Ian Miller, "Gluttony," *Wicked Pleasures,* ed. Robert C. Solomon (Rowman & Littlefield, 1999), p. 41. Cf. part 1, Arthur Brandeis, ed., *Jacob's Well* (Kegan, Paul, Trench, Trübner & Co., 1900), p. 143.

28. Franz Kafka, *The Complete Stories,* ed. Nahum N. Glatzer (Schocken, 1978), p. 277.

29. Peter Toon, "Stylite," "Simeon the Stylite," *New International Dictionary of the Christian Church,* 2nd ed., ed. J. D. Douglas (Zondervan, 1978), p. 937.

30. De Vogüé, *To Love Fasting,* p. 33.

31. Chapter 1, Rudolph M. Bell, *Holy Anorexia* (University of Chicago Press, 1987), pp. 2–3.

32. Ibid., pp. 3–4.

33. Chapter 6, Bynum, *Holy Feast and Holy Fast,* p. 197.

34. Ibid., p. 199.

35. Chapter 3, ibid., p. 73.

36. Ibid., p. 84.

37. Ibid., p. 203.

38. Ibid., p. 84.

39. Kallistos Ware, "The Way of the Ascetics," *Asceticism,* ed. Wimbush and Valantasis, p. 9.

40. Section 17, Calvin, *Institutes of Christian Religion,* p. 1243.

41. Bynum, *Holy Feast and Holy Fast,* p. 192.

42. Loc. cit.

43. Part 3, section 4, Erik H. Erikson, *Gandhi's Truth* (Norton, 1969), p. 351.

44. Bynum, *Holy Feast and Holy Fast*, p. 192. Cf. chapter 1, Mohandas K. Gandhi, *An Autobiography*, tr. Mahadev Desai (Beacon, 1972), pp. 4–5.

45. Chapter 2, Bynum, *Holy Feast and Holy Fast*, p. 38.

46. Chapter 4, de Vogüé, *To Love Fasting*, pp. 85–87. Cf. chapter 5, Morris Bishop, *The Middle Ages* (Houghton Mifflin, 2001), p. 161.

47. Wole Soyinka, "Why Do I Fast?" *The Art of the Personal Essay*, ed. Phillip Lopate (Anchor, 1994), pp. 454–57.

48. "Cassian," Ward, *Sayings of the Desert Fathers*, p. 113.

49. Part 4, section 4, George Foot Moore, *Judaism in the First Centuries of the Christian Era*, vol. 2 (Schocken, 1975), p. 65.

50. "Easter," J. C. J. Metford, *The Christian Year* (Crossroad, 1991), pp. 63–64. The cross also can slowly be unveiled as during the veneration ceremony.

51. Mark Buchanan, "Go Fast and Live," *Christian Century* (28 February 2001), p. 19.

52. "Stations of the Cross," Richard P. McBrien, gen. ed., *The HarperCollins Encyclopedia of Catholicism* (HarperCollins, 1995), p. 1222.

53. Chapter 2, David W. Fagerberg, *The Size of Chesterton's Catholicism* (University of Notre Dame Press, 1998), p. 42.

54. Chapter 5, G. K. Chesterton, *Saint Francis of Assisi* (Image, 1990), pp. 74–75.

55. "The Beginning of Guidance," part 1, W. Montgomery Watt, tr., *The Faith and Practice of al-Ghazālī* (George Allen and Unwin, 1963), p. 130.

56. Robert van de Weyer, ed., *The HarperCollins Book of Prayers* (HarperCollins, 1993), p. 166.

Chapter 15: Sloth: Don't Lose Heart

1. T. S. Eliot, *The Complete Poems and Plays 1909–1950* (Harcourt Brace Jovanovich, 1980), pp. 5, 7, 6.

2. Book 10, John Cassian, *The Monastic Institutes*, tr. Jerome Bertram (Saint Austin, 1999), pp. 145. ff.

3. Chapter 12, Evagrius Ponticus, *The Praktikos and Chapters on Prayer*, tr. John Eudes Bamberger (Cistercian, 1981), pp. 18–19.

4. "Sloth," James Hall, *Dictionary of Subjects and Symbols in Art*, revised (Harper & Row, 1979), p. 285.

5. Solomon Schimmel, *The Seven Deadly Sins* (Free Press, 1992), black-and-white insert near p. 155.

6. Part 2, Joseph Gallagher, *To Hell and Back with Dante* (Triumph, 1996), p. 96.

7. James K. Bowen and Richard VanDerBeets, eds., *American Short Fiction* (Bobbs-Merrill, 1970), pp. 89, 78, 71, 79.

8. Part 1, Ivan Goncharov, *Oblomov*, tr. Ann Dunnigan (New American Library, 1963), p. 22.

9. "3 January 1857," *Pages from the Goncourt Journal*, tr. and ed. Robert Baldick (Penguin, 1984), p. 23.

10. Part 2, Goncharov, *Oblomov*, pp. 39–40.

11. "Oblomov," Abraham H. Lass and Brooks Wright, eds., *A Student's Guide to 50 European Novels* (Washington Square, 1967), pp. 122–23.

12. *Deut. R.* 8:6; *Yalkut, Prov.*, 961, *The Book of Legends*, ed. Hayim Nahman Bialik and Yehoshua Hana Ravnitzky, tr. William G. Braude (Schocken, 1992), p. 429.

13. "Poor Richard's Almanack," *The Benjamin Franklin Sampler*, ed. Nathan G. Goodman (Fawcett, 1956), p. 110.

14. W. H. R. Rivers, "On the Psychological 'Giving-Up' Syndrome as a Factor in the Depopu-

lation of Aboriginal Peoples," *Frontiers of Anthropology,* ed. Ashley Montagu (Capricorn, 1974), pp. 390–409. Cf. chapter 1, Stanford M. Lyman, *The Seven Deadly Sins: Society and Evil,* revised and expanded (General Hall, 1989), pp. 38–39.

15. No. 131, Blaise Pascal, *Pensées and Provincial Letters,* tr. W. F. Trotter (Modern Library, 1941), p. 47.

16. Eugène Ionesco, *Four Plays,* tr. Donald M. Allen (Grove, 1978), pp. 159–60.

17. Chapter 10, William Barrett, *Irrational Man* (Anchor, 1990), p. 254.

18. "Wednesday, 6:00 p.m.," Jean-Paul Sartre, *Nausea,* tr. Lloyd Alexander (New Directions, 1964), p. 180.

19. Quoted in chapter 13, A. D. Nock, *Conversion* (Oxford University Press, 1969), p. 246.

20. Omar S. Pound, tr., ". . . Half my life spent attaching my heart," *Poetry of Asia,* ed. Keith Bosley (Weatherhill, 1979), p. 220.

21. Bertolt Brecht, *Selected Poems,* tr. H. R. Hays (Grove, 1959), p. 175.

22. "Works and Days," lines 289–91, Dorothea Wender, tr. *Hesiod and Theognis* (Penguin, 1977), pp. 67–68.

23. Book 12, section 21, Marcus Aurelius Antoninus, *The Meditations,* tr. G. M. A. Grube (Bobbs-Merrill, 1975), p. 82.

24. Letter to Mme. Périer, 5 November 1648, quoted in introduction, Georges Poulet, *Studies in Human Time,* tr. Elliott Coleman (Harper & Brothers, 1959), pp. 17–18.

25. *Travels into Several Remote Nations of the World . . . by Lemuel Gulliver,* part 3, chapter 5, *The Portable Swift,* ed. Carl Van Doren (Viking, 1963), p. 404.

26. "Works and Days," lines 108–202, Wender, tr., *Hesiod and Theognis,* pp. 62–65.

27. "The Realists," Arthur Waley, *Three Ways of Thought in Ancient China* (Anchor, 1956), p. 160.

28. Chapter 18, Henry David Thoreau, *Walden; or, Life in the Woods* (New American Library, 1960), p. 216.

29. "The Fiction Writer and His Country," Flannery O'Connor, *Collected Works,* ed. Sally Fitzgerald (Library of America, 1988), p. 806.

30. "Novelist and Believer," *Religion and Modern Literature,* ed. G. B. Tennyson and Edward E. Erickson Jr. (Eerdmans, 1975), pp. 71–72.

31. Cf. Johnson's criticism of the metaphysicals in "The Life of Cowley," *Samuel Johnson: Selected Writings,* ed. Patrick Cruttwell (Penguin, 1968), pp. 404–5.

32. "Sloth or *Acedia,*" Henry Fairlie, *The Seven Deadly Sins Today* (University of Notre Dame Press, 1995), p. 123.

33. Chapter 1, Thoreau, *Walden,* p. 10.

34. "Evening Hymn," *The Penguin Book of German Verse,* revised, ed. Leonard Forster (Penguin, 1959), p. 174.

35. "The Other Six Deadly Sins," Dorothy L. Sayers, *Creed or Chaos?* (Sophia Institute, 1974), p. 109.

36. Edward Parone, ed., *Kipling* (Dell, 1960), p. 12.

37. Antoine de Saint Exupéry, *The Little Prince,* tr. Katherine Woods (Harcourt Brace Jovanovich, 1971), p. 29.

38. Book 5, William Langland, *Piers the Ploughman,* tr. J. F. Goodridge (Penguin, 1974), p. 73.

39. "Christian Behaviour," chapter 11, C. S. Lewis, *Mere Christianity* (Macmillan, 1978), p. 124.

40. Quoted in chapter 15, Evelyn Underhill, *Worship* (Nisbet & Co., 1943), p. 318.

41. "Poemen," Benedicta Ward, tr., *The Sayings of the Desert Fathers,* revised (Cistercian, 1984), pp. 192–93.

42. W. H. Freemantle, tr., Letter 22, "To Eustochium, on the preservation of virginity," section 17, *Nicene and Post-Nicene Fathers,* ed. Henry Wace and Philip Schaff (Christian Literature Company, 1893), p. 28.

43. "Jerome," Hall, *Dictionary of Subjects and Symbols in Art*, pp. 168–69.

44. Schimmel, *The Seven Deadly Sins*, p. 212.

45. "Bonifacius," *The American Puritans*, ed. Perry Miller (Columbia University Press, 1962), pp. 217–18.

46. Georgia Peach and Her Gospel Singers, "Do Lord Send Me," *Jubilation! Great Gospel Performances*, vol. 1, *Black Gospel* (Rhino Records, 1992), recorded 17 October 1942.

47. "To Hope," *The Penguin Book of Spanish Verse*, revised, ed. J. M. Cohen (Penguin, 1965), p. 316.

48. "Religio Medici," part 2, section 6, *The Prose of Sir Thomas Browne*, ed. Norman J. Endicott (Norton, 1972), p. 76.

49. Chapter 3, Huston Smith, *The World's Religions*, revised (HarperCollins, 1991), p. 87.

50. Chapter 11, Timothy Ware, *The Orthodox Church*, revised (Penguin, 1993), pp. 225–26.

51. Chapter 6, Richard Harries, *Art and the Beauty of God* (Mowbray, 1993), p. 84.

52. "Sonnets to Orpheus," 2: 12, *Penguin Book of German Verse*, ed. Forster, p. 405.

53. Chapter 7, William Fleming, *Arts and Ideas*, revised (Holt, Rinehart and Winston, 1966), p. 272.

54. Chapter 3, Robert Barron, *Heaven in Stone and Glass* (Crossroad, 2000), p. 30.

55. Chapter 3, *St. Thomas Aquinas: Philosophical Texts*, ed. and tr. Thomas Gilby (Oxford University Press, 1962), p. 78. Cf. *Summa Theologica*, part 1, question 39, article 8, *Basic Writings of Saint Thomas Aquinas*, vol. 1, ed. Anton C. Pegis (Random House, 1945), p. 378.

56. Chapter 1, Umberto Eco, *Art and Beauty in the Middle Ages*, tr. Hugh Bredin (Yale University Press, 1986), p. 13.

57. "On What Was Done under His Administration," section 33, *A Documentary History of Art*, vol. 1, ed. Elizabeth Gilmore Holt (Anchor, 1957), p. 30.

58. Chapter 4, Otto von Simson, *The Gothic Cathedral*, 3rd ed., expanded (Princeton University Press, 1989), p. 122.

59. Walter Gropius, *The New Architecture and the Bauhaus*, tr. P. Morton Shand (M. I. T. Press, 1979), p. 29.

60. Section 1, "Twelfth-Century Critics of the New Architecture," *Gothic Art 1140–c.1450*, ed. Teresa G. Frisch (Prentice-Hall, 1971), pp. 30–33.

61. Chapter 2, Roger Hazelton, *A Theological Approach to Art* (Abingdon, 1967), p. 84.

62. Chapter 6, Paul Cavill, *Anglo-Saxon Christianity* (Fount, 1999), p. 107.

63. Book 4, chapter 24, Venerable Bede, *Ecclesiastical History of the English People*, revised, tr. Leo Sherley-Price (Penguin, 1990), p. 248.

64. "12/25/55," Dag Hammarskjöld, *Markings*, tr. Leif Sjöberg and W. H. Auden (Ballantine, 1993), p. 100.

65. Chapter 19, Roland H. Bainton, *Here I Stand: A Life of Martin Luther* (New American Library, 1950), pp. 269–70.

66. Chapter 10, Andrew Wilson-Dickson, *The Story of Christian Music* (Lion, 1992), p. 62.

67. Ibid., p. 63.

68. Chapter 13, Jaroslav Pelikan, *Jesus through the Centuries* (Yale University Press, 1985), p. 163.

69. Bainton, *Here I Stand*, p. 267.

70. "To Fräulein Leonore _____?" (6 July 1776), *Pleasures of Music*, ed. Jacques Barzun (Viking, 1961), p. 533.

71. "Franz Joseph Haydn," Philip G. Goulding, *Classical Music* (Fawcett Columbine, 1995), p. 160.

72. Chapter 23, Edwin John Stringham, *Listening to Music Creatively*, 2nd ed. (Prentice-Hall, 1959), p. 435.

73. "The Martyrdom of Polycarp," section 9, J. B. Lightfoot and J. R. Harmer, trs., *The Apostolic Fathers*, 2nd ed., rev. Michael W. Holmes (Baker, 1992), p. 235.

74. Chapter 2, William A. Clebsch, *Christianity in European History* (Oxford University Press, 1979), p. 48.

75. "The Martyrdom of Polycarp," sections 18, 21, Lightfoot and Harmer, trs., *Apostolic Fathers,* pp. 241–43.

76. Vol. 1, chapter 16, Edward Gibbon, *The History of the Decline and Fall of the Roman Empire,* vol. 1, ed. David Womersley (Penguin, 1995), p. 546.

77. Section 3, Esther de Waal, *Every Earthly Blessing* (Servant, 1991), pp. 107–8.

78. Frank J. Warnke, *European Metaphysical Poetry* (Yale University Press, 1974), p. 183.

79. Section 42, St. Augustine, *The Enchiridion,* ed. Henry Paolucci, tr. J. F. Shaw (Regnery, 1965), pp. 52–53.

80. *Catechesis* 3: 12, Leo P. McCauley and Anthony A. Stephenson, trs., *The Works of Saint Cyril of Jerusalem,* vol. 1 (Catholic University of America Press, 1969), pp. 115–16.

81. "Church at Baranzate," Robert Maguire and Keith Murray, *Modern Churches of the World* (Dutton, 1965), pp. 13, 98–101.

82. C. O. Sylvester Mawson, *Dictionary of Foreign Terms,* rev. Charles Berlitz (Barnes & Noble, 1979), p. 66. Cf. Horace, Ode 11, "To Leuconöe," line 7.

83. John Bartlett, *Familiar Quotations,* 14th ed., revised and enlarged, ed. Emily Morison Beck (Little, Brown and Company, 1968), p. 421.

84. "Covenant Service," John and Charles Wesley, *Selected Prayers, Hymns, Journal Notes, Sermons, Letters and Treatises,* ed. Frank Whaling (Paulist, 1981), pp. 134–45; 381–87.

85. "Maud Muller," stanza 53, *The New Pocket Anthology of American Verse,* ed. Oscar Williams (Washington Square, 1965), p. 593.

86. "The Prayer of St. Francis," in "The Mendicant Orders or Friars," *2000 Years of Prayer,* comp. Michael Counsell (Morehouse, 1999), p 143.

Chapter 16: The Despondent

1. "William Cowper," David Lyle Jeffrey, ed., *English Spirituality in the Age of Wesley* (Eerdmans, 1994), p. 458.

2. William Cowper, "Memoir of the Early Life of William Cowper," ibid., p. 462.

3. Geoffrey Tillotson, Paul Fussell Jr., and Marshall Waingrow, eds., *Eighteenth-Century English Literature* (Harcourt, Brace and World, 1969), p. 1328.

4. "No Worst," *Gerard Manley Hopkins,* ed. Catherine Phillips (Oxford University Press, 1991), p. 167.

5. Chapter 10, Thérèse of Lisieux, *Story of a Soul,* tr. John Clark (ICS Publications, 1976), pp. 211–14.

6. Elaine Marks, ed., *French Poetry from Baudelaire to the Present* (Dell, 1965), pp. 56–57.

7. "Out of Luck," S. Solis-Cohen, tr., *Poetry of Asia,* ed. Keith Bosley (Weatherhill, 1979), p. 295.

8. Part 1, section 4, Robert Burton, *The Anatomy of Melancholy,* ed. Holbrook Jackson (Vintage, 1977), pp. 431–32. Cf. chapter 1, Kay Redfield Jamison, *Night Falls Fast* (Vintage, 2000), p. 25.

9. Part 1, John Bunyan, *The Pilgrim's Progress,* ed. Roger Sharrock (Penguin, 1987), pp. 163–68.

10. "Mourning and Melancholia," *A General Selection from the Works of Sigmund Freud,* ed. John Rickman (Anchor, 1957), p. 125.

11. Book 9, section 4, John Cassian, *The Monastic Institutes,* tr. Jerome Bertram (Saint Austin, 1999), p. 140.

12. Quoted in chapter 6, Mary Margaret Funk, *Thoughts Matter* (Continuum, 1998), pp. 85–86. Cf. Cassian, *The Monastic Institutes,* book 9, sections 2–3.

13. "The Parson's Tale," lines 713–14, Geoffrey Chaucer, *The Canterbury Tales,* tr. Ronald L. Ecker and Eugene J. Crook (Hodge & Braddock, Publishers, 1993), p. 549.

14. Robert Van de Weyer, ed., *The HarperCollins Book of Prayers* (HarperCollins, 1993), p. 21.

15. Martin Luther, "Assurance in Anxiety," *Jesus, Remember Me,* ed. Barbara Owen (Augsburg, 1998), p. 60.

16. Quoted in chapter 6, Annie Dillard, *For the Time Being* (Knopf, 1999), p. 144.

17. "The Flower," *Herbert,* ed. Dudley Fitts (Dell, 1966), p. 155.

18. "Third Essay: The Mythos of Winter," Northrop Frye, *Anatomy of Criticism* (Princeton University Press, 1957), p. 226.

19. Chapter 7, G. K. Chesterton, *Orthodoxy* (Ignatius, 1995), pp. 127–28.

20. Chapter 9, Evelyn Waugh, *A Little Learning* (Methuen, 1983), pp. 229–30.

21. "Letter to Gertrude Natkin," (2 March 1906), *The Quotable Mark Twain,* ed. R. Kent Rasmussen (Contemporary Books, 1997), p. 61.

22. Chapter 4, Wilfred Cantwell Smith, *Faith and Belief* (Princeton University Press, 1979), pp. 61–62.

23. Part 2, section 18, *A True Story,* Lionel Casson, tr., *Selected Satires of Lucian* (Norton, 1968), pp. 40–41.

24. Chapter 26, Nikos Kazantzakis, *Zorba the Greek,* tr. Carl Wildman (Faber and Faber, 1961), pp. 303–4.

25. "Pascal's Wager," "Dominance," Simon Blackburn, *The Oxford Dictionary of Philosophy* (Oxford University Press, 1996), pp. 278–79, 109.

26. Section 2, series 2, Blaise Pascal, *Pensées,* tr. A. J. Krailsheimer (Penguin, 1995), p. 122.

27. Chapter 1, M. J. Charlesworth, tr., *St. Anselm's* Proslogion (University of Notre Dame Press, 1979), p. 115.

28. Letter (19 January 1879), *A Hopkins Reader,* revised and enlarged, ed. John Pick (Image, 1966), p. 362.

29. Chapter 17, Abraham Joshua Heschel, *Man Is Not Alone* (Farrar, Straus & Giroux, 1995), p. 174.

30. Leo Tolstoy, *Walk in the Light and Twenty-Three Tales,* tr. Louise and Aylmer Maude (Plough, 1998), pp. 189–201.

31. "First Days," Daniel Defoe, *Robinson Crusoe* (Bantam, 1981), p. 58.

32. Quoted in Viktor E. Frankl, *Man's Search for Meaning* (Pocket, 1963), p. 121.

33. Ibid., p. 115.

34. Book 4, section 341, Friedrich Nietzsche, *The Gay Science,* tr. Walter Kaufmann (Vintage, 1974), p. 273.

35. Horst Balz, *"Hapax," Exegetical Dictionary of the New Testament,* vol. 1, ed. Horst Balz and Gerhard Schneider (Eerdmans, 1990), p. 115.

36. Quoted in chapter 12, Charles Norris Cochrane, *Christianity and Classical Culture* (Oxford University Press, 1968), p. 484. Cf. Augustine, *The City of God,* book 12, chapter 14.

37. Benjamin Singer, "The Future-Focused Role Image," *Learning for Tomorrow,* ed. Alvin Toffler (Vintage, 1974), pp. 19–32.

38. Dennis Livingston, "Science Fiction as an Educational Tool," ibid., p. 240.

39. Part 3, section 4, Burton, *Anatomy of Melancholy,* p. 400.

40. Long text, chapter 60, Julian of Norwich, *Showings,* tr. Edmund Colledge and James Walsh (Paulist, 1978), pp. 298–99.

41. Chapter 9, Jaroslav Pelikan, *Mary through the Centuries* (Yale University Press, 1996), pp. 125–38.

42. "Icons of Loving-Kindness," Leonid Ouspensky and Vladimir Lossky, *The Meaning of Icons,* tr. G. E. H. Palmer and E. Kadloubovsky (SVS Press, 1989), pp. 92–97.

43. Faye Pauli Whitaker, "Despair," *A Dictionary of Biblical Tradition in English Literature,* ed. David Lyle Jeffrey (Eerdmans, 1992), p. 197.

44. Section 25, Herman Melville, *Billy Budd* (Scholastic, 1963), p. 124.

45. 8 September 1921, *The Journal of Gamaliel Bradford 1883–1932,* ed. Van Wyck Brooks (Houghton Mifflin, 1933), p. 274.

46. Lecture 9, William James, *The Varieties of Religious Experience* (New American Library, 1958), p. 168.

47. "Determination," Donald DeMarco, *The Heart of Virtue* (Ignatius, 1996), p. 60.

48. Chapter 3, Henry Petroski, *The Evolution of Useful Things* (Vintage, 1994), p. 49.

49. Chapter 11, C. S. Lewis, *The Lion, the Witch, and the Wardrobe* (Macmillan, 1953), pp. 95–98.

50. "Letter from Birmingham Jail," *A Testament of Hope: The Essential Writings and Speeches of Martin Luther King Jr.,* ed. James M. Washington (HarperCollins, 1991), p. 302.

51. Chapter 4, Jean Leclercq, *The Love of Learning and the Desire for God,* tr. Catharine Misrahi (Fordham University Press, 1974), p. 69.

52. Anonymous, "Hierusalem, My Happy Home," *The New Oxford Book of English Verse: 1250–1950,* ed. Helen Gardner (Oxford University Press, 1972), p. 163.

Chapter 17: St. Satan, Pray for Me

1. Chapter 21, Roland H. Bainton, *Here I Stand: A Life of Martin Luther* (New American Library, 1950), p. 284.

2. Chapter 7, James F. White, *Documents of Christian Worship* (Westminster/John Knox, 1992), p. 154. Cf. *The Apostolic Tradition,* section 21.

3. Werner Foerster, *"Satanas,"* *Theological Dictionary of the New Testament,* vol. 7, ed. Gerhard Friedrich (Eerdmans, 1971), p. 159.

4. "Second week, fourth day," Pierre Wolff, tr., *The Spiritual Exercises of Saint Ignatius* (Triumph, 1997), pp. 38–41.

5. "Magical Incantations," *The Origins of Christianity,* ed. Howard Clark Kee (Prentice-Hall, 1973), p. 88.

6. "Book 3: Reptiles and Fishes," *The Bestiary: A Book of Beasts,* ed. and tr. T. H. White (Capricorn, 1960), p. 167.

7. Reuben Levy, tr., *The Book of Marzuban* in *Anthology of Islamic Literature,* ed. James Kritzeck (New American Library, 1966), p. 214.

8. T. H. Gaster, "Satan," *The Interpreter's Dictionary of the Bible,* vol. 4, ed. George Buttrick (Abingdon, 1962), p. 225. Cf. 2 Enoch 29:4.

9. "Devil," F. L. Cross and E. A. Livingstone, eds., *The Oxford Dictionary of the Christian Church,* 2nd ed. (Oxford University Press, 1977), p. 397.

10. T. H. Gaster, "Demon, Demonology," *Interpreter's Dictionary of the Bible,* vol. 1, ed. Buttrick, pp. 817–24.

11. Chapter 2, Jeffrey Burton Russell, *The Prince of Darkness* (Cornell University Press, 1988), p. 8. Cf. Karel van der Toorn, Bob Becking, and Pieter W. van der Horst, eds., *Dictionary of Deities and Demons in the Bible,* 2nd extensively rev. ed. (Eerdmans/Brill), 1999.

12. Chapter 11, Henri Daniel-Rops, *Daily Life in the Time of Jesus,* tr. Patrick O'Brian (New American Library, 1964), p. 305.

13. Ibid., p. 306. Cf. 2 Maccabees 12:40.

14. Part 2, chapter 5, G. K. Chesterton, *The Everlasting Man* (Ignatius, 1993), pp. 244–45.

15. Chapter 3, Gustaf Aulén, *Christus Victor,* tr. A. G. Hebert (Macmillan, 1986), pp. 50–51.

16. Book 7, chapter 15, Reginald Scot, *The Discoverie of Witchcraft* (Dover, 1972), p. 86.

17. Chapter 14, Lucien Regnault, *The Day-to-Day Life of the Desert Fathers in Fourth-Century Egypt,* tr. Étienne Poirier Jr. (St. Bede's Publications, 1999), p. 187.

18. Chapter 15, Keith Thomas, *Religion and the Decline of Magic* (Charles Scribner's Sons, 1971), p. 472.

19. Section 28, Athanasius, *The Life of Antony and The Letter to Marcellinus,* tr. Robert C. Gregg (Paulist, 1980), p. 53.

20. Chapter 16, Russell, *Prince of Darkness,* p. 266.

21. "Of God's Works," section 67, Martin Luther, *Table Talk,* tr. William Hazlitt (Fount, 1995), p. 35.

22. "Devil," Hans Biedermann, *Dictionary of Symbolism,* tr. James Hulbert (Facts on File, 1992), p. 94.

23. Chapter 3, Roy F. Baumeister, *Evil: Inside Human Cruelty and Violence* (W. H. Freeman, 1997), p. 69.

24. Quoted in "Intolerance," Denis Diderot, *The Encyclopedia: Selections,* ed. and tr. Stephen J. Gendzier (Harper & Row, 1967), p. 155.

25. Book 5, chapter 4; book 11, chapter 9, Fyodor Dostoyevsky, *The Brothers Karamazov,* vols. 1 and 2, tr. David Magarshack (Penguin, 1970), pp. 285, 279–83; 751.

26. Chapter 15, Russell, *Prince of Darkness,* pp. 251–54. Line 77 in Terence's play: "I am a man: nothing human is alien to me."

27. Book 2, chapter 4, John Calvin, *Institutes of the Christian Religion,* vol. 1, ed. John T. McNeill, tr. Ford Lewis Battles (Westminster, 1960), p. 309.

28. Postscript, Hannah Arendt, *Eichmann in Jerusalem,* revised and enlarged (Penguin, 1980), pp. 287–88.

29. Edward L. Queen II, "Salem Witchcraft Trials," *The Encyclopedia of American Religious History,* vol. 2, ed. Edward L. Queen II, Stephen R. Prothero, and Gardiner H. Shattuck Jr. (Facts on File, 1996), pp. 581–82.

30. Book 5, chapter 5, Fyodor Dostoevsky, *The Brothers Karamazov,* tr. Richard Pevear and Larissa Volokhonsky (Vintage, 1991), pp. 255–56.

31. Notebook A: 1765–1770, George Christoph Lichtenberg, *Aphorisms,* tr. R. J. Hollingdale (Penguin, 1990), p. 22.

32. First Conference, 20:1, John Cassian, *The Conferences,* tr. Boniface Ramsey (Paulist, 1997), p. 59.

33. Chapter 4, Douglas Burton-Christie, *The Word in the Desert* (Oxford University Press, 1993), p. 125.

34. William Cowper, "Memoir of the Early Life of William Cowper," *English Spirituality in the Age of Wesley,* ed. David Lyle Jeffrey (Eerdmans, 1994), p. 463.

35. Part 1, John Bunyan, *The Pilgrim's Progress,* ed. Roger Sharrock (Penguin, 1987), pp. 104–5.

36. Chapter 45, Walter Hilton, *The Stairway of Perfection,* tr. M. L. Del Mastro (Image, 1979), p. 337.

37. Book 1, lines 180–81, *The Complete Poetry of John Milton,* revised, ed. John T. Shawcross (Anchor, 1971), p. 524.

38. Frederick H. Hedge, tr., "A Mighty Fortress Is Our God," Kenneth W. Osbeck, *101 Hymn Stories* (Kregel, 1984), p. 13.

39. Andrew T. Lincoln, *Ephesians* (Word, 1990), p. 433.

40. Chapter 2, Elizabeth Drew, *Poetry* (Dell, 1967), pp. 33–34.

41. "Jerusalem," *The New Oxford Book of English Verse 1250–1950,* ed. Helen Gardner (Oxford University Press, 1972), p. 486.

42. Book 3, section 9, Symeon the New Theologian, *The Discourses,* tr. C. J. de Catanzaro (Paulist, 1980), pp. 68–69.

43. Book 2, section 9, Aristotle, *Nicomachean Ethics,* tr. J. A. K. Thompson, rev. Hugh Tredennick (Penguin, 1976), p. 109.

44. Cecil Frances Alexander, tr., "I bind unto myself to-day," *The Book of Hymns,* ed. Ian Bradley (Overlook, 1989), pp. 183–87.

45. G. K. Berkouwer, "Satan and the Demons," *Basic Christian Doctrines,* ed. Carl F. H. Henry (Baker, 1973), p. 74.

46. Chapter 60, *The Historie of the Damnable Life and Deserved Death of Doctor John Faustus,* ed. and modernized by William Rose (University of Notre Dame Press, 1963), pp. 196–97.

47. Book 3, vision 9, section 3, Hildegard of Bingen, *Scivias,* tr. Columba Hart and Jane Bishop (Paulist, 1990), p. 453.

Chapter 18: Flaming Love

1. "Lovest Thou Me?" *A Book of Religious Verse,* ed. Helen Gardner (Oxford University Press, 1972), p. 227.

2. Letter 11, Lucius Annaeus Seneca, *Letters from a Stoic,* tr. Robin Campbell (Penguin, 1969), p. 56. Seneca attributes the basis for this advice to the philosophy of Epicurus.

3. Volume 2, chapter 4, W. E. H. Lecky, *History of European Morals from Augustus to Charlemagne* (George Braziller, 1955), pp. 8–9.

4. Jaroslav Pelikan, *Jesus through the Centuries* (Yale University Press, 1985).

5. Quoted in "Beyond Superstar," *Campus Life* (March 1972), p. 59. Cf. Frank S. Mead, ed., *The Encyclopedia of Religious Quotations* (Pillar Books, 1976), p. 88.

6. 11 March 1832, J. P. Eckermann, *Conversations with Goethe,* ed. Hans Kohn, tr. Gisela C. O'Brien (Ungar, 1964), p. 224.

7. Henry Drummond, *The Greatest Thing in the World* (Guideposts Associates, n.d.), p. 16.

8. Chapter 1, Thomas C. Oden, *The Living God* (Harper & Row, 1987), pp. 20–21.

9. "Nativity," *Martin Luther's Christmas Book,* ed. Roland H. Bainton (Augsburg, 1997), p. 31.

10. Elizabeth Dreyer, "Love," *The New Dictionary of Catholic Spirituality,* ed. Michael Downey (Liturgical, 1993), p. 621.

11. Chapter 20, Mark Twain, *The Innocents Abroad* (New American Library, 1966), p. 143.

12. "Andrea Del Sarto," lines 97–98, *Poems of Robert Browning,* ed. Donald Smalley (Houghton Mifflin, 1956), p. 216.

13. "St. Francis of Assisi in Dante's *Commedia,*" Erich Auerbach, *Scenes from the Drama of European Literature* (Peter Smith, 1973), p. 94.

14. Chapter 9, Herman Melville, *Moby Dick,* ed. Harrison Hayford and Hershel Parker (Norton, 1967), p. 45.

15. Robert van de Weyer, ed., *The HarperCollins Book of Prayers* (HarperCollins, 1993), p. 207. Cf. "The Lament of the Soul for the Intensity of Infused Charity," Jacopone da Todi, *The Lauds,* tr. Serge and Elizabeth Hughes (Paulist, 1982), p. 257.

16. Book 17, Helen Waddell, tr., *The Desert Fathers* (Vintage, 1998), p. 129.

17. Chapter 4, George Steiner, *After Babel* (Oxford University Press, 1977), p. 245.

18. Desiderius Erasmus's *Paraclesis,* lines 184–85, 192–96 (in translation): Douglas H. Parker, ed., William Royce's *An exhortation to the diligent studye of scripture and An exposition in to the seventh chaptre of the pistle to the Corinthians* (University of Toronto Press, 2000), p. 77.

19. A. Moran Derham, "William Carey," *The New International Dictionary of the Christian Church,* 2nd ed., ed. J. D. Douglas (Zondervan, 1978), p. 192.

20. Chapter 8, Friedrich Heer, *The Medieval World,* tr. Janet Sondheimer (New American Library, 1962), p. 200.

21. David Lyle Jeffrey, "The Gift of Literacy," *Christianity Today* (6 December 1999), p. 54.

21a. 3 April 1779, James Boswell, *The Life of Samuel Johnson,* abr. Bergen Evans (Modern Library, 1965), p. 424.

22. Quoting J. Christiaan Beker in chapter 4, David J. Bosch, *Transforming Mission* (Orbis, 1993), p. 136.

23. Chapter 15, Francis M. DuBose, ed., *Classics of Christian Missions* (Broadman, 1979), p. 167.

24. "Matthew Ricci," eds. of "Christian History," *131 Christians Everyone Should Know* (Broadman & Holman, 2000), pp. 240–41.

25. *Ad Gentes Divinitus,* section 22, *Documents of Vatican II,* ed. Austin P. Flannery (Eerdmans, 1975), p. 839.

26. Quoted in chapter 4, Robert Hunter, *Poverty,* ed. Peter d' A. Jones (Harper & Row, 1965), p. 177.

27. "How I Became a Progressive," *The Progressives,* ed. Carl Resek (Bobbs-Merrill, 1967), p. 334.

28. Chapter 47, Sydney E. Ahlstrom, *A Religious History of the American People* (Yale University Press, 1973), p. 801.

29. Chapter 1, Robert E. Ornstein, *The Psychology of Consciousness,* 2nd ed. (Harcourt Brace Jovanovich, 1977), p. 4.

30. *Through the Looking-Glass,* chapter 5, "Wool and Water," Lewis Carroll, *Alice's Adventures in Wonderland* and *Through the Looking-Glass* (New American Library, 1962), p. 174.

31. Chapter 1, Johan Huizinga, *Homo Ludens* (Beacon Press, 1955), p. 8.

32. Quoted in "Sitting on a Fence," *The War Cry* (18 January 1975), p. 2.

33. Chapter 1, Bibb Latané and John M. Darley, *The Unresponsive Bystander* (Appleton-Century Crofts, 1970), p. 1.

34. Chapter 4, ibid., pp. 31–33.

35. S. P. McNeel, "Helping Behavior," *Baker Encyclopedia of Psychology,* ed. David G. Benner (Baker, 1985), p. 505.

36. Chapter 6, Robert Wuthnow, *Acts of Compassion* (Princeton University Press, 1991), pp. 161–62.

37. Book 17, William Langland, *Piers the Ploughman,* tr. J. F. Goodridge (Penguin, 1974), p. 209.

38. Chapter 5, Kathleen Powers Erickson, *At Eternity's Gate: The Spiritual Vision of Vincent van Gogh* (Eerdmans, 1998), pp. 159–60 and plate 8.

39. Book 1, chapter 15, Thomas à Kempis, *The Imitation of Christ,* ed. Harold C. Gardiner, tr. Richard Whitford (Image, 1955), p. 48.

40. 18 March 1751, *Lord Chesterfield's Letters to His Son and Others* (Dutton, 1957), p. 222.

41. Sermon 25, section 8, Augustine, *Sermons,* vol. III/2, ed. John E. Rotelle, tr. Edmund Hill (New City Press, 1990), p. 86.

42. Book 1, part 2, chapter 5, Alexis de Tocqueville, *Democracy in America,* vol. 2, ed. Phillips Bradley (Vintage, 1945), p. 21.

43. *"Tselem Elohim,"* Arthur Green, *These Are the Words* (Jewish Lights, 1999), p. 183.

44. "King of the World," William Brandon, *The American Heritage Book of Indians* (Dell, 1968), p. 127.

45. Chapter 2, section 1, *A Documentary History of Religion in America to the Civil War,* 2nd ed., ed. Edwin S. Gaustad (Eerdmans, 1993), p. 64.

46. Part 5, chapter 4, Feodor Dostoevsky, *Crime and Punishment,* ed. George Gibian (Norton, 1975), p. 351.

47. Chapter 15, Don Richardson, *Peace Child* (Regal Books, 1975), pp. 203–4.

48. Ibid., p. 207.

49. Chapter 17, ibid., p. 242.

50. Quoted in chapter 2, David W. Fagerberg, *The Size of Chesterton's Catholicism* (University of Notre Dame Press, 1998), p. 23.

51. Section 14, Athanasius, *On the Incarnation,* tr. and ed. a Religious of C. S. M. V. (St. Vladimir's Orthodox Theological Seminary, 1953), pp. 41–42.

52. "The Bridge," Catherine of Siena, *The Dialogue,* tr. Suzanne Noffke (Paulist, 1980), p. 65.

53. "Saint Catherine of Genoa," Carol Lee Flinders, *Enduring Grace* (HarperCollins, 1993), p. 141. Cf. "Spiritual Dialogue, 130," Catherine of Genoa, *Purgation and Purgatory/The Spiritual Dialogue,* tr. Serge Hughes (Paulist, 1979), p. 130.

54. "What Is Noble," Friedrich Nietzsche, *Beyond Good and Evil* (Vintage, 1966), p. 207.

55. "Father Damien," *Encyclopedia Britannica,* vol. 7 (William Denton, 1960), p. 5.

56. Chapter 8, John Farrow, *Damien the Leper* (Image, 1999), p. 149.

57. "Bd. Damien of Molokai," Robert Ellsberg, *All Saints* (Crossroad, 1997), p. 170.

58. Chapter 10, Henri Daniel-Rops, *The Heroes of God* (Doubleday, 1965), pp. 161–74.

59. M. Lincoln Schuster, ed., *A Treasury of the World's Great Letters* (Simon & Schuster, 1968), pp. 410–17.

60. "Further notes on the Spiritual Exercises: The Principle or Foundation," *Gerard Manley Hopkins,* ed. Catherine Phillips (Oxford University Press, 1991), p. 292.

61. "An Address," 15 July 1838, *The Portable Emerson,* ed. Mark Van Doren (Viking, 1965), p. 56.

62. C. H. Talbot, tr., "Life of Saint Leoba," sections 6, 10, *Soldiers of Christ,* ed. Thomas F. X. Noble and Thomas Head (Pennsylvania State University Press, 1995), pp. 262, 265.

63. B. Schwank, *"Talanton,"* *Exegetical Dictionary of the New Testament,* vol. 3, ed. Horst Balz and Gerhard Schneider (Eerdmans, 1993), p. 332.

64. "Talent," T. F. Hoad, ed., *The Concise Oxford Dictionary of English Etymology* (Oxford University Press, 1992), p. 481.

65. "Gratefulnesse," *Herbert,* ed. Dudley Fitts (Dell, 1966), p. 124.

66. Chapter 1, section 9, Cotton Mather, *Bonifacius: An Essay upon the Good,* ed. David Levin (Harvard University Press, 1966), p. 33. Cf. chapter 1, Robert H. Bremner, *American Philanthropy* (University of Chicago Press, 1966), pp. 12–15.

67. Quoted in chapter 1, Kallistos Ware, *The Orthodox Way,* revised (SVS Press, 1995), p. 18.

Name and Title Index